DOUGHBOYS ON THE GREAT WAR

Doughboys on the Great War

How American Soldiers Viewed Their Military Service

EDWARD A. GUTIÉRREZ

 University Press of Kansas

Published by the University Press of Kansas (Lawrence, Kansas 66045), which was organized
by the Kansas Board of Regents and is operated and funded by Emporia State University,
Fort Hays State University, Kansas State University, Pittsburg State University, the University
of Kansas, and Wichita State University

Library of Congress Cataloging-in-Publication Data

Gutiérrez, Edward A.
Doughboys on the Great War : how American soldiers viewed their military service /
Edward A. Gutiérrez
pages cm. — (Modern war studies)
Includes bibliographical references and index.
ISBN 978-0-7006-1990-0
1. World War, 1914–1918—United States. 2. United States. Army—History—World War,
1914–1918. 3. Soldiers—United States—Attitudes. 4. United States. Army. American
Expeditionary Forces. 5. United States. Army—Military life—History—20th century—
Sources. 6. World War, 1914–1918—United States—Sources. I. Title. II. Title: How
American soldiers viewed their military service.
D570.2G88 2014
940.4'1273—dc23
2014014487

British Library Cataloguing-in-Publication Data is available.

Printed in the United States of America

10 9 8 7 6 5 4 3 2 1

The paper used in this publication is recycled and contains 30 percent postconsumer waste.
It is acid free and meets the minimum requirements of the American National Standard for
Permanence of Paper for Printed Library Materials z39.48-1992.

For my mother and Geoffrey Parker

Contents

Acknowledgments

The work for this book began in 2000. I have therefore incurred innumerable debts to many amiable scholars, archivists, and librarians. This project could not have been completed without the generous financial support of the Harry Frank Guggenheim Foundation. The foundation's directors and committee members enabled me to focus on completing the manuscript. In particular, I am extremely grateful to Josiah Bunting III, Andrew Roberts, Joel Wallman, Deirdre Hamill, and Karen Colvard. I was also fortunate to receive financial support from the United States Army Center of Military History, the Lynde and Harry Bradley Foundation, the George C. Marshall/Baruch Foundation, the Triangle Institute for Security Studies, the Mershon Center for International Security Studies, and the Ohio State University.

In 2010–2011, I had the honor of being a postdoctoral fellow with the Centre National de la Recherche Scientifique in Paris, France, and participated in a research project titled "Memory and Memorialization: Representing Trauma and War." During the fellowship, I benefited from the time and acumen of Edward Berenson, Denis Peschanski, Richard Rechtman, Katia Dauchot, Clarisse Berthezène, André Loez, Annette Becker, Laura Lee Downs, and Alice Braun.

As I traveled throughout the United States, a host of talented archivists, librarians, and staff spent considerable time locating materials for me and providing other assistance. In particular, I spent countless hours at several libraries, combing through documents, and I would like to thank the following individuals (and staffs) at these institutions: Bruce P. Stark, LeAnn Power, and Mark H. Jones of the Connecticut State Library; Roger Christman of the Library of Virginia; Steve Nielsen of the Minnesota Historical Society; Anthony G. Castro of the Utah State Archives; Michael E. Lynch and David A. Keough of the United States Army Military History Institute, Carlisle, Pennsylvania; and Mitchell A. Yockelson at the National Archives, College Park, Maryland. In addition, thank you to the numerous other professionals I corresponded with who helped me track down valuable materials around the country.

Eugene E. Leach, Jonathan Elukin, Jeffrey P. Bayliss, Johannes Evelein, Isabel Evelein, Thomas M. Truxes, Samuel D. Kassow, Kenneth J. Andrien, Allan R. Millett, Lisa S. Bevevino, John D. Plating, Brian D. Joseph, Jason W. Warren, Lawrence A. Tritle, Waldemar Heckel, Robert M. Citino, Michael S. Neiberg, David Silbey, John W. Hall, Jonathan F. Vance, and the Reverend Wilson D. Miscamble, C.S.C., all supported this project in varying capacities and provided me with extensive time and advice.

Edward G. Lengel, Steven Trout, and Jennifer D. Keene contributed vital revisions and pointed out my many errors. Lisa Wehrle and Linda J. Lotz tirelessly copyedited the manuscript and corrected many more mistakes. Any remaining flaws in this work are mine alone. I am also beholden to the editors and staff of the University Press of Kansas, especially editor in chief Michael Briggs, who patiently answered questions and offered assistance throughout the publication process.

I am extremely grateful for the continued support of John F. Guilmartin Jr., Peter R. Mansoor, and Leonard V. Smith, each of whom has provided invaluable insight and sage counsel for years. From the beginning, Borden W. Painter Jr. and Howard A. Mayer bestowed on me their stalwart guidance and unwavering encouragement. I owe the most thanks, however, to my adviser Geoffrey Parker, without whom this book would still be a dream rather than a reality, and to my mother, who has never doubted me and always supported my endeavors.

DOUGHBOYS ON THE GREAT WAR

Introduction: *"Sherman Was Right"*

On 27 February 2011, the last US World War I veteran, Corporal Frank W. Buckles, passed away at the age of 110. With his passing, the Great War moved from memory to history in the United States. Lost too was any opportunity to ask these veterans the question that drives this monograph: What motivated World War I doughboys, whether volunteer or conscript, to answer their country's call?[1]

Even if we could ask Buckles or other veterans this question, would their answers be the same ones given in their youth? Perhaps with confabulation, decades of reflection, tempered passions, and shifting sociocultural and political views, their opinions would have been different from their 1918 assessments. Would the true reasons they fought now elude them?

I mulled these questions as I traveled to Kansas City, Missouri, to the National World War I Museum at Liberty Memorial. And there, quite unexpectedly, I discovered an important clue. After my second day of research, I noticed an exhibit displaying artifacts recovered from the RMS *Titanic*. In the lower levels of historic Union Station, through which many Great War veterans had passed, were several large rooms of *Titanic* relics and displays. Before the last room was a large, darkened area, lit only by a faux starry sky and a few lights to illuminate the showcases containing small artifacts. Amidst the stars were printed quotations from contemporaries commenting on the *Titanic* disaster. I froze when I saw the name of Benjamin Guggenheim. What serendipity, I thought. My research was being supported by the Harry Frank Guggenheim Foundation, and there had been a famous Guggenheim aboard the *Titanic*—a fact that, I humbly admit, I had forgotten. Guggenheim's words, however, were what truly struck me: "We've dressed up in our best . . . and are prepared to go down like gentlemen."[2] Those words answered the question I had devoted more than a decade to understanding: Why did doughboys fight? Duty. For Guggenheim and most men of his generation, including the American soldiers of World War I, that reason was paramount.

Guggenheim's story encapsulates an age when honor mattered a great deal to a man. On board the doomed ship, as Guggenheim and his valet, Victor Giglio, dressed in their evening clothes and without their life belts, Guggenheim told *Titanic* steward James Etches, "If anything should happen to me, tell my wife in New York that I've done my best in doing my duty."[3] That night, the men in second class volunteered to remain on the ship, as did the eight-man orchestra. Only 8 percent of the men in second class survived, and the entire orchestra was lost. Belowdecks, in the engine and boiler rooms, the *Titanic*'s engineers and crew fought against the inevitable and delayed the ship's sinking, thus saving hundreds of lives while sacrificing their own. Some have tried to debunk the male heroism displayed on the *Titanic*, but the fact remains that only 20 percent of the male passengers survived, compared with 74 percent of the women and 50 percent of the children.[4] Male heroism was not universal—self-interest and cowardice existed then, as now—but the concepts of honor and duty played greater roles in 1912 society and occupied men's thoughts more often.

This book examines the psyche of the doughboys—men of Guggenheim's time. It focuses not on battles or military strategy but on American combatants' *conceptions* of battle—before, during, and after the conflict.[5] My writing follows the lead of Denis Winter, whose fascinating study of the war as seen through British soldiers' eyes begins with this observation by Ardant Du Picq: "The man is the first weapon of battle. Let us study the soldier for it is he who brings reality to it."[6] Toward this end, I concentrate on enlisted men's assessments of the actualities of war (although some officers' voices are heard), which, in his study of German soldiers in World War II, Stephen G. Fritz dubs "The View from Below."[7] *Doughboys on the Great War* is a sociocultural examination of how war transforms an individual, an approach Peter Englund aptly describes in his own work: "It is not . . . a book about what it *was* . . . but a book about what it was *like*."[8]

Digging for Answers

Few World War I scholars have delved deeply enough into doughboys' motivations, combat experiences, and Western Front reactions. In particular, historians have overlooked the importance of duty and the influence of the Civil War, which spurred most doughboys toward the trenches.[9] But how do we fully answer such a complex question as why men fought in World War I without interviewing any veterans? Although memoirs, diaries, letters, and after-action reports all have value, surveys or interviews that ask hundreds of soldiers the same questions produce unique data that can establish broader patterns of understanding and ascertain why men fought.

The majority of soldiers from the American Expeditionary Forces (AEF) returned home from Europe in 1919. Whereas only 67 percent of the AEF saw combat, all the returning veterans received the admiration of hundreds of thousands of citizens, who honored them with parades and festivals.[10] Many veterans received something else: a simple card or sheet of paper from their home states asking for basic data concerning their backgrounds and units. Four states—Utah, Minnesota, Connecticut, and Virginia—asked for more than basic information from their veterans. Veterans from Utah and Minnesota received a four-page questionnaire asking for additional information about their families, their time in the service, and the types of wounds or citations they received. Utah also provided a "Remarks" section at the end of the form. Connecticut and Virginia veterans received the most complex survey: a four-page questionnaire entitled the Military Service Record (MSR). Though similar to the questionnaires distributed in Utah and Minnesota, the MSR also contained a number of subjective questions on the last page, asking soldiers to describe their experiences and the war's impact on their characters.[11] Of the 12,947 Connecticut, 3,000 Utah, and 14,900 Virginia MSRs, 1,264 of the questionnaires were fully completed, the veterans answering every question in detail. For the last fourteen years, I have studied this information supplied by these AEF veterans as they returned home.

The last pages of the questionnaires filled out by Samuel B. Yaffo, a Russian Jewish soldier living in Hartford, Connecticut, and James P. Spencer, an African American Baptist from Charlotte, Virginia, are reproduced here. Their responses illustrate the value of this source. Both men participated in major engagements with the AEF; Yaffo lost his brother Max and several close friends in combat, and Spencer was wounded in the hand during a firefight. The questionnaire also asked each veteran to send in two photographs—one as a civilian and one taken while in service.

Unlike Yaffo and Spencer, many veterans refused to answer these questionnaires. Some found the form too tedious to fill out and the questions too intrusive, or they thought the government might be asking them to reenlist. However, the 27,847 respondents from Connecticut and Virginia who did fill out their questionnaires left a unique and previously unused source of primary evidence about the doughboy and his participation in the Great War.[12]

The importance of collecting information, especially subjective information, as close to an event as possible is illustrated by the case of author Maurice Genevoix, a French veteran of the Great War. He entered the conflict in 1914 at age twenty-four and served until he was wounded in 1915. On 10 September 1914, during the Battle of the Marne, Genevoix encountered some German soldiers, and he later described the event: "I came across three isolated Ger-

What was your attitude toward military service in general and toward your call in particular? *I have always favored and advocated military service for young men, and was ready when wanted. Did not wait to be drafted either*

What were the effects of camp experiences in the United States upon yourself — mental and physical? *Best of effects*

What were the effects upon yourself of your overseas experience, either in the army or navy or in camp in France or in England? *Upon arrival to England we were greeted by a representative of King George, fine Country. Did not get as good a treatment in France as expected*

If you took part in the fighting, what impressions were made upon you by this experience? *At first I could not get any thoughts in the frame to want to Kill them, after I saw my pals fall in agony from their shells, I did the rest.*

What has been the effect of all these experiences as contrasted with your state of mind before the war? *No bad effects at all only I lost a brother in this conflict and can't get over it, don't even Know where he is.*

Photographs — If possible enclose one taken before entering the service and one taken afterwards in uniform, both signed and dated.

Additional data *I have in my posession some German Revolvers as war trophies, and would be glad to loan them for exebition if wanted*

Signed at *Hartford Conn* (place) on *Nov 8* (date) 1 1 9

Samuel B. Yaffo (full name) *Sgt.* (rank) *Ord. Dep. U.S.A* (branch of service)

The information contained in this record, unless otherwise indicated, was obtained from the following persons or sources:

Page four of Samuel B. Yaffo's MSR, 8 November 1919. (Box 15, Military Service Questionnaires, 1920–1930, War Records Department, Record Group 12, State Archives, Connecticut State Library)

ADDITIONAL INFORMATION

What was your attitude toward military service in general and toward your call in particular?...........

I felt that it was my patriotic duty to serve my country at the most critical hour in the Nation's history, although my Race had not been given the proper rights

What were the effects of camp experiences in the United States upon yourself—mental and physical?

Made me mentally more alert to the political social problems of the day; made me physically stronger to perform that great task of meeting the enemy face to face

What were the effects upon yourself of your overseas experience?

Broke down some bodily strong qualities by hardships

What effect, if any, did your experience have on your religious belief?

That God suffered the Great War to come in order that Christianity might be disseminated; that Ethiopia might be shown to the world, etc.

If you took part in the fighting, what impressions were made upon you by this experience?

My experience at the front impressed me with the idea that blood seems to be the only atonement for man's sin; the price of all true sacrifices

What has been the effect of all these experiences as contrasted with your state of mind before the war?

That most wars are fought from a selfish viewpoint; fought from an economic viewpoint; that the Great War was fought over the Germany's desire to exploit Ethiopia and her rich countries instead of England and other countries

Photographs—If possible enclose one taken before entering the service and one taken afterwards in uniform, both signed and dated.

Additional data *Am now about to post-graduate from Va. Normal and Industrial Institute to serve my Race in my humble capacity, and to help the Old Dominion to still be great among the many states*

Signed at *Newand. N.C*   on *April 25,*   *1921*
   (place)   (date)

James Custon Spencer   *Pvt*   *Infantry*
(full name)   (rank)   (branch of service)

The information contained in this record, unless otherwise indicated, was obtained from the following persons or sources:

James Custon Spencer

Page four of James P. Spencer's MSR, 25 April 1921. (Box 3, War History Commission, series I: Individual Service Records [Questionnaires], 1919–1924, Library of Virginia)

Russian Samuel B. Yaffo of Hartford, Connecticut, in France, 1918. (Box 15, Connecticut State Library)

man soldiers, each running behind the other at the same pace. I fired a bullet from my revolver into the head or back of each of them. Each one collapsed, with the same strangled cry." Over the next six decades, Genevoix recalled this experience several times, and in each recollection, he changed the details. When Genevoix reflected on the incident in 1950, he called it a choice of "kill or be killed" and said it had "made an ineffaceable imprint on my memory."[13] In 1961, Genevoix retold the experience as an epic struggle, filled with romanticism and meticulous detail; he described the weather conditions, the German soldiers' uniforms, and their cries. This time, two Germans were set to engage him, rather than three running away single file. Genevoix recalled, "He was going to turn around, turn around. . . . Understanding this, I raised the weapon in my

James P. Spencer of Charlotte, Virginia, in France, 1918. (Box 3, Library of Virginia)

right hand and fired." Near the end of his life, in 1977, his recollection was filled with self-doubt, and he lamented, "I very much hope I did not kill them."[14]

It is clear that human memory is altered by and fades with the passage of time. Thus, memoirs written years after the Great War present a distorted view compared with the recorded memories and feelings of veterans in 1919, when their experiences were untainted by age or cultural norms. In the midst of war, soldiers were expected to shoot fleeing enemies, but as the years passed, enemies were no longer enemies. Genevoix's story changed perhaps because of shifting societal viewpoints or because he forgot the facts. Either way, all versions of his story could not be fully true. As William L. Langer wrote in 1965 regarding his own 1919 memoir, "I find its immediacy rather appealing. It has nothing of the sophisticated rationalization that invariably creeps into reminiscences recorded long after the event."[15]

Genevoix's opaque memories parallel those of the doughboys Richard Rubin interviewed for his book *The Last of the Doughboys*. Rubin tracked down around two dozen American veterans before they passed away, and he admits that "many of the veterans I interviewed—though not Mr. Moffitt—didn't recognize me the second time I visited . . . they had completely forgotten our first meeting."[16] But even Laurence Moffitt's story changed from one interview to the next: during the first, Moffitt stated he had never seen anyone killed, but during the second, he said he had seen a great deal of killing.[17] Immediacy is critical to obtaining the most accurate assessment of events.

The majority of men filled out their questionnaires in 1919, when their memories of the Western Front were still vivid. Most of the rest did so in 1920 or 1921, and the remainder did so in 1923, the year the last AEF soldiers returned from Germany. This makes the MSRs distinct from the World War I questionnaires distributed by the US Army Military History Institute (MHI) beginning in 1975. Based on previous models for earlier wars, the survey was created by Don Rickey Jr. and was sent to every known veteran still living. Each of these former soldiers and sailors, ranging in age from late seventies to early nineties, completed an eleven-page survey covering topics such as training camps, duty overseas, and combat experience. Most of the questionnaires were completed during the 1980s.

The MHI at Carlisle, Pennsylvania, holds approximately 5,800 responses from these veterans (fewer than 200 veterans fully completed their questionnaires), and in recent years, several historians have made excellent use of them, most notably in two well-researched studies: Gary Mead's *The Doughboys* (2000) and Jennifer D. Keene's *Doughboys, the Great War and the Remaking of America* (2001). In spite of the value of the MHI questionnaire, a weakness exists: the lapse of time. As Robert J. Clark acknowledged when asked to recall his combat service, "Time loose & impossible to tell you now at the age of 85 in November 1982."[18] How long do memories stay fresh and accurate? There is no specific age at which memory begins to fade, but a memory decrement over time is normal.[19] And because the MHI conducted the survey more than sixty years after the fact, only the youngest veterans could participate.

To compensate for the limitations of the MHI questionnaires, various historians have used diaries, memoirs, letters, interviews, and official armed services reports, but until now, only three have used the Connecticut and Virginia MSRs collected in 1919: Christopher M. Sterba, Chad L. Williams, and Jonathan H. Ebel. In his book *Good Americans*, Sterba uses only twenty-three Connecticut questionnaires—specifically, those filled out by New Haven Italians.[20] Williams's *Torchbearers of Democracy* is about African American soldiers and includes only forty-four Virginia questionnaires.[21] Like Williams, Ebel's *Faith in the Fight* uses only Virginia MSRs completed by African Americans and cites twenty-two of them.[22] Sterba, Williams, and Ebel make no connection to other states' questionnaires. Why have scholars not used these records? Perhaps the answer lies in the strange origin of the MSRs and in the war history commissions that distributed them to veterans.

Following the armistice, historians and veterans of the war began to write about the AEF's role in the conflict. The great majority of publications in 1919 and the 1920s consisted of unit histories and personal memoirs (e.g., Frank P. Sibley, *With the Yankee Division in France* [1919], and Hervey Allen, *Toward the Flame* [1925]). Not until Edward M. Coffman's *The War to End All Wars* (1968) did a historian study all aspects of America's role in the war, including the infantryman's experience. He relies on several interviews to detail the life of the common soldier, making it one of the first scholarly texts in decades to discuss the experiences of the AEF. Coffman also employs a variety of sources from the National Archives and state collections; his use of personal accounts enriches the narrative. The strength of his work stems from its wide scope and its discussion of individuals and divisions. This, however, also limits the book's intimacy: it touches on infantrymen's experiences but does not explore the intensity of the Western Front or the war's effect on them.

Recent studies such as Byron Farwell's *Over There* (1999), John S. D. Eisenhower's *Yanks* (2001), and Mark Ethan Grotelueschen's *The AEF Way of War* (2007) update Coffman's work with new research. Although Farwell uses memoirs, diaries, and letters to give the AEF infantrymen voices, his book, like those of Eisenhower and Grotelueschen, is a top-down study of American battlefield performance, generals, and the AEF's contribution to the Allied victory. Similar to Coffman's book in scope, Mead's *The Doughboys* covers the Western Front and the home front; it also makes great use of the MHI archives, as does Keene's *Doughboys, the Great War and the Remaking of America*. Mead's work touches on only who the soldiers were and how the war changed them mentally and physically. Keene focuses on the importance of the Bonus Bill and the veterans' struggle to obtain the money promised to them by the government. Stephen R. Ortiz also explores the Bonus Bill in *Beyond the Bonus March and GI Bill* (2010). These authors portray the experiences of the soldiers, but only to a certain degree.

The MSRs from 1919 asked the veterans difficult questions and pushed them to reflect on experiences that were still fresh in their minds. By examining the 1919 MSRs of Connecticut, Utah, and Virginia, this book focuses on these contemporary memories. Comparing veterans' responses from 1919 to those provided in 1975 would furnish further insight into the sociological and sociocultural aspects of military history: Did decades of reflection alter the opinions of veterans? If so, how? What patterns, if any, are seen? An in-depth examination of these questions is beyond the scope of this book, but they are important ones.

Faded Memories and Shaky Pens

Six decades later, the feelings of duty and pride of service remained, but two strong differences are evident when comparing the 1919 MSRs and the 1975 MHI questionnaires. The 5,800 MHI questionnaires contain bitter responses aimed at a different enemy. As the veterans' passions toward the Germans waned, their wrath found a new target. In 1975, many veterans expressed anger toward the US government; they felt cheated out of a future, which the GI Bill had provided for World War II veterans. This is especially apparent in part IV, questions 41 and 42, of the 1975 questionnaire: "If the Army sent you to school, please recount your experience there" and "What were your expectations of civilian life upon leaving service (post-war America, G-I benefits, educational and career opportunities)." Typical responses were, "G.I. benefits were in WWII!" and "WWI veterans did not have any benefits!" As Sergeant Aaron Coplin emphasized, "None—things were so different then—60–61 years ago— No modern convenience—we got 'nothing' then—or now."[23]

The second difference is the level of respect rather than disdain for the Germans. In 1919, the MSRs were filled with celebratory remarks about how the "Huns" could not contend with the military might of the United States. Decades later, the doughboys expressed deference for the superiority of the German soldier. Part III, question 34, of the 1975 questionnaire read: "Did you and your comrades consider the enemy good fighters? Better trained? Better equipped?" Sergeant Paul J. McMahon answered, "Yes Germans were best, even better than us."[24] Louis C. Ciccone believed that "they were the same as everyone else fighting for their country."[25] The old doughboys felt the Germans were "like Americans" and "human beings." These two sentiments represent the bulk of veterans' replies.

As mentioned earlier, not all the veterans filled out the MSRs completely. Many left the fourth page blank or only partially answered some of the questions. Yet for the Connecticut and Virginia questionnaires, the fourth page, entitled "Additional Information," is the most interesting and produces the richest material—the soldier's personal thoughts about the war. In rare cases, some Minnesota veterans provided valuable additional data, such as letters, and included the photographs requested by the MSRs; unfortunately, they did not share their impressions of the war (notably, their combat experiences) in the blank space provided, but seventy-two Utah veterans did. These pages reveal feelings, attitudes, and insights. Many men did not want to share their memories, especially of combat; numerous soldiers did not answer questions about the actions they had participated in. Almost 400 men gave a taut three-word answer: "Sherman was right" or "War is hell."[26] They were referring to Civil War general William Tecumseh Sherman's famous words from a speech he delivered at a veterans' reunion in Columbus, Ohio, on 11 August 1880: "There is many a boy here to-day who looks on war as all glory, but, boys, it is all hell. You can bear this warning voice to generations yet to come. I look upon war with horror, but if it has to come I am here."[27] In response to questions about their combat experiences, other veterans wrote, "Are you kidding," "Impossible to answer," or "Cannot explain."

The majority of men who gave such short answers had participated in a great deal of combat and usually suffered serious injuries from machine gun or small-arms fire, grenade fragmentation, artillery shrapnel, or poison gas. Others who engaged in heavy combat wrote more expansively, such as Private First Class Finlan D. Cuddy of New Haven, Connecticut: "I took part in the fighting in the Argonne forests its an experience I never will forget. I'll say war is worse the Hell."[28] "I did not realize what war really was. No one can know who hasn't been there. It is worse than hell and may this be the end of war," stressed Corporal Egbert B. Inman of Hartford.[29] Marine Corps private first class William W. Ward, a Chicago native, concluded, "Learned that Sherman told the truth, the whole truth, and nothing but the truth."[30] Private Bernard C. Paggett of Alexandria, Virginia, who worked as a brick mason both before and after the war, declared, "Sherman was right but mild in expression."[31] "Sherman knew what he was talking about" stated another Virginian, Captain Charles Johnston, who was wounded in the right leg during combat.[32]

Second Lieutenant Roy D. Hitchcock, who served with Machine Gun Company, 111th Infantry, and came from East Hampton, Connecticut, commented, "That war was much worse than the famous remark of General Sherman."[33] Private John B. Vaninetty of New Britain, Connecticut, admitted, "The impression was terrible to realize that what I was thinking theorically it was in facts as General Sherman described."[34] Marine Corps private Jerry M. Davis of Hartford remarked, "When I first went into action at Cheteau Thierry sector I did not seem to relize what war was untill 600 fell in action in my Bn it made me feel as Sherman expressed it, WAR IS HELL."[35] New Haven resident Private Jack F. Molloy, who served in the Medical Corps, concluded that combat "verified to me Gen Shermans opinion of war. It sure was Hell."[36] "Little change except to know now that war is H-ll instead of having to believe what Sherman said," stressed First Lieutenant Edgar H. Dowson of New Haven.[37]

These veterans' responses show that memories of the Civil War dwelled in the minds of the doughboys. The passing decades, however, had diminished the horrors of the 1860s, and the Western Front spawned a level of brutality that none of America's regular or enlisted soldiers anticipated. How did ordinary men cope with relentless artillery bombardment and lethal hand-to-hand combat, and how did the war alter their psyches? Their experience remains relevant today, since the cornerstone of America's strategy against terrorism is the infantryman. It is unlikely that this policy will change. In particular, we need to understand why individuals volunteer to go to war, and, if reality fails to match expectations (as it did for almost every doughboy), we need to ascertain the causes of these erroneous presumptions.

This work surveys men's reactions to every facet of the war: prewar emotion, life in the trenches, and reflective return. It examines the knowledge of the American soldier—not only of his time on the front but also his identity throughout the war. Coffman writes, "It is impossible to reproduce the state of mind of the men who waged war in 1917 and 1918."[38] This volume seeks to change that statement. Toward this end, the Connecticut, Minnesota, Utah, and Virginia questionnaires are unique. A search of America's archives and the secondary literature has found nothing comparable.

Nonetheless, this book cannot definitively address all aspects of the doughboys' mentality and motivation. All 1,390,000 of them who fought in France are now gone, and unlike Yaffo and Spencer, many of them failed to answer their questionnaires in their entirety. Many others died serving their country, and we will never know what they thought. As Primo Levi attests, the true voices of Auschwitz-Birkenau belonged to those who perished at the death camp. Those who survived and spoke, like Levi, were, by definition, atypical. Yet theirs are the only voices we can hear, and they deserve to be heard. Levi asserts, "Even if they had paper and pen, the drowned would not have testified because their death had begun before that of their body. Weeks and months before being snuffed out, they had already lost the ability to observe, to remember, to compare and express themselves. We speak in their stead, by proxy."[39] *Doughboys on the Great War* attempts to do the same for the AEF.

The Doughboys

Although this book includes some naval and aerial matters, as well as some of the women of the AEF (nurses and stenographers), it focuses on infantrymen on the Western Front. However, Americans also served in Italy and Russia. The American Military Mission to Italy, consisting of the 332nd Regiment (part of the 83rd Division), was sent to aid the Italians during the last year of the war. The AEF also served in northern Russia and Siberia from 15 August 1918 to 1 April 1920. Pressured by the Allies, President Woodrow Wilson agreed to send American troops there, provided they did not become involved in Russia's internal revolution. The American Expeditionary Force North Russia (AEFNR), often called the Polar Bear Expedition, was a force of 4,487 men, half of whom were conscripts from Michigan and Wisconsin. Despite US intentions, the AEFNR skirmished with units of the Bolshevik Sixth Red Army. Wilson also dispatched 5,100 soldiers to Siberia (AEF Siberia) to protect the Trans-Siberian

Railroad and important supplies. These two Russian expeditions claimed more than 500 Americans captured, wounded, or killed in action.[40]

Soldiers from Connecticut, Utah, and Virginia came from the 26th, 29th, 40th (originally 19th), and 91st Divisions. The first three were created from existing National Guard units; the 26th and 29th saw heavy combat, which included front-line sectors in Aisne, Champagne, Marne, Meuse-Argonne, Lorraine, and Saint-Mihiel. The 40th Division included Utahans and became the 6th Depot Division in France, which acted as a replacement unit for other divisions. The 76th and 80th Divisions included draftees from Connecticut and Virginia. The 76th also became a replacement unit—the 3rd Depot Division—and the 80th saw some action on several fronts: Meuse-Argonne, Picardy, and Saint-Mihiel. In total, these six divisions (excluding the 40th) sustained 6,033 men killed in action or died of wounds and 25,364 wounded.[41] In addition, each of these divisions spent eighty-five days in active sectors.[42]

Because the military was segregated, African Americans from Connecticut and Virginia who filled out MSRs, along with blacks from around the country, served only in the 92nd and 93rd Divisions. The latter served under the French and comprised just four infantry regiments, including the famous 369th. Men from the US Marine Corps also filled out MSRs. Marines who fought on the Western Front were from the 4th Marine Brigade, which represented part of the army's 2nd Division.[43]

This book follows the doughboy from his ethnic, religious, and cultural origins through his training in the States and abroad, his life on the front, and his readjustment to civilian life. Chapter 1, "The Great Adventure," discusses the similarity between the doughboys and their European brethren in 1914. American men longed to "do their bit" when the United States declared war on 6 April 1917, just as their European counterparts did three years earlier. Unaware of the power of modern industrialized warfare, these future soldiers—inexperienced, but with steady constitutions—wanted to repay the French for their help and sacrifice during the American Revolution. Enhanced by the Victorian milieu of boxing and football and by the legacy of the Civil War, the trenches of the Western Front offered American men a perfect chance to display their manhood.

Chapter 2, "Gimme da Gun," answers social and cultural questions. Who were these men? What factors shaped the AEF soldier? Each man's experience logically depended on his ethnic, religious, and educational background. Some men felt they had something to prove, and others hoped the war would facilitate their transformation from boys into men. Whether conscript or enlistee, they all felt it was their duty to fight.

Chapter 3, "Wooden Weapons," examines the men's military education in America. Whether this occurred at Camp Devens, Kearny, Lewis, Lee, or Upton or one of the other training camps around the country, the men had strong feelings—either respect or hatred—about their military training. Most men did not participate in live-fire exercises, and some trained with wooden replicas instead of real rifles and artillery pieces. Despite its inadequacy, this training gave the men a false sense of combat prowess (which many of them believed they possessed innately), and it proved fatal on the Western Front.

Chapter 4, "Across the Pond," discusses the veterans' experiences as they crossed the Atlantic and dealt with the threat of German U-boats and influenza. After that two-week journey, most received additional training in England or in quiet sectors of France. The majority of men benefited from this additional military training and enjoyed the opportunity to explore foreign cities. But this illusion of merriment would not last long.

Chapter 5, "The Supreme Test," analyzes the doughboys in combat. Finally, they faced their true trial—after all, they thought, the war was all about defeating the enemy by going over the top on the glorious Western Front. The trenches, mud, rats, constant shelling, and death shocked the doughboys. Where was the adventure? Once they experienced the true nature of war, most were disheartened; they disliked the front and deplored the killing. It was not what they expected.

Chapter 6, "Would Not Take Anything for It," discusses the war's effect on these men after the armistice. Knowing what they now knew, would the doughboys enlist with the same enthusiasm or be as patriotic in the future? Most veterans said they would think twice about signing up again or would wait for the government to draft them; a minority said they were ready to go a second round. Most doughboys returned to their old jobs in factories or on farms, but some could not due to physical injury or mental unrest. Though most of them now condemned war, the veterans were proud they had done their duty.

The conclusion, "If It Has to Come I Am Here," summarizes the American experience in the Great War. Doughboys did not enjoy combat, yet they valued their war experience. They voiced a "war is hell, but I'm glad I served" outlook. This may seem paradoxical, but it is not. If Civil War veterans had been given questionnaires in 1866, their responses likely would have paralleled those of the doughboys in 1919. Both fought for honor, manhood, comrades, and adventure, but especially for duty.

Although sociocultural conceptions of war changed after the First World War, the majority of veterans of later conflicts remained proud of their service as the years passed. The combat endured by marine corporal E. B. Sledge in the Pacific during World War II haunted him for years. Nonetheless, according to Sledge, "Until the millennium arrives and countries cease trying to enslave others, it will be necessary to accept one's responsibilities and to be willing to make sacrifices for one's country—as my comrades did. As the troops used to say, 'If the country is good enough to live in, it's good enough to fight for.' With privilege goes responsibility."[44] Vietnam War veteran Lieutenant Frederick Downs was glad he served, despite losing his left arm. Downs concluded, "I'm now sixty-one and have had a rich, full life with family, friends, job, church, travel, and much else. I often think back to that day in Vietnam when I stepped on the Bouncing Betty and my life changed forever. It has been a good life."[45] During his four tours in the Iraq War (2003–2011), Chief Petty Officer Chris Kyle, a navy SEAL, killed more than 150 Iraqi insurgents. A devout Christian, Kyle believed God would judge him and probably punish him for the men he had killed. Nonetheless, Kyle acknowledged, "I'm not the same guy I was when I first went to war. No one is. Before you're in combat, you have this innocence about you. Then, all of the sudden, you see this whole other side of life. I don't regret any of it. I'd do it again."[46] War affected each of these men in different ways: psychologically, physically, and spiritually. But what they all have in common is that they are glad they served—just like the doughboys.

Throughout history, men have marched into war despite the warnings of prior generations. Some sought honor. Others searched for adventure, glory, or manhood. But many served because of a sense of duty. Soldiers brushed off their fear and entered the fray. The doughboys were no different. The popular image of the doughboy is one of the Lost Generation—a misnomer coined by Gertrude Stein and then aggrandized by Ernest Hemingway and his literary contemporaries. It continues to misguide our understanding of the conflict. The war shocked them, but it did not shatter them. Duty- and honor-bound, the doughboys were young and eager to fight on the Western Front. Only when they returned home did they have a full understanding of the brutality of war. Even though the doughboys experienced the horrors of modern warfare, it ennobled them. They were honored to make the sacrifice.

I

The Great Adventure

      The war had been raging in Europe for almost three and a half years before the doughboys arrived in France—brave, eager, and naïve. Similar to most of their European brethren, American men had become intoxicated with excitement at their country's declaration of war.[1] The horrors of Verdun and the Somme did not deter these raw young recruits from what they thought would be a great adventure— a semester abroad, for some. The heroic legacy of warfare was already present in America and fostered a sense of exhilaration; the Civil War literature of the time, the short and victorious Spanish-American War, and the propaganda machine of the British and US governments augmented the Victorian image of romantic warfare.

The Common Bond

      During the years between the Civil War and the Great War, newspapers, churches, and schools emphasized nationalism and the importance of war. Americans lauded their generals and soldiers—to die in battle was glorious. The country viewed the Spanish-American War as an opportunity for patriotism and honor. Civil War veterans, especially those from the South, urged young men to demonstrate their bravery and display their heroism by joining the military. Veterans from both the North and the South told tales to the younger generation that extolled the rewards of serving one's country. While not declaring their love of war or killing, these men were proud to be Civil War veterans. James Marten notes, "Their service defined them, made them different, provided unique rewards and self-esteem beyond anything most Gilded Age Americans could muster."[2]

      During the 1880s, tributes to and the memorialization of the Civil War and its veterans increased. Memorial Day events (the first was held

1 May 1865 in Charleston, South Carolina, to honor dead Union prisoners of war), gatherings of veterans, monument construction, and the publication of books and magazines all commemorated the conflict. One of the most popular Gilded Age books was Ulysses S. Grant's *Personal Memoirs*. Americans had purchased 300,000 sets of these books four months before the first volume's delivery date.[3] Throughout the 1880s and 1890s, periodicals and novels helped revive interest in the war. *Century Magazine* printed the "Battles and Leaders of the Civil War" series between 1884 and 1887, which later influenced novelist Stephen Crane.

On 30 May 1888, during a Memorial Day address at Seven Pines National Cemetery in Sandston, Virginia, orator Theodore W. Bean stated, "The great fatherhood of our country . . . left a progeny North and South, whose loyalty to leaders, whose bravery in battle, whose industry and indurance, demonstrates the glory of our enheritance, and in the grand battles fought between ourselves, however unfortunate in some respects, reveals a manhood of the Republic, as now reunited, capable and willing to protect and defend the Union against the political powers of the earth."[4] In an 1890 address to veterans of the Army of Tennessee, General William Tecumseh Sherman compared Civil War soldiers to the knights of old: "There is nothing in life more beautiful than the soldier," he declared, and "a knight errant with steel casque, lance in hand, has always commanded the admiration of men and women."[5] Two years later, at a Memorial Day ceremony in Dubuque, Iowa, a speaker noted that Civil War veterans "remind us that with all the greed there is in this world, the holy leaven of manliness, true manliness may yet be found."[6] The admiration for Civil War (and Spanish-American War) veterans inspired young men to serve as doughboys. The romantic vision, in the words of James McPherson, stirred "the quest for adventure, for excitement, for the glory to be won by 'whipping' the enemy and returning home as heroes to an adoring populace."[7] These ideals impelled countless young men to follow their sense of duty and serve in the Civil War, the Spanish-American War, and the First World War.

As a captain in the 12th Connecticut Volunteers during the Civil War, John William De Forest participated in the capture of New Orleans, the Port Hudson campaign, and the Battle of Cedar Creek in Virginia. When asked whether he "liked the business" of war, De Forest stated, "I did not like it, except in some expansive moments when this or that stirring success filled me with excitement." Fighting, he continued, "is just tolerable; you can put up with it; but you can't honestly praise it . . . it is much like being in a rich cholera district in the height of the season." De Forest called on his own experience as a veteran to answer the question: why do men fight in war? He declared, "'Self-preservation is the first law of nature.' The man who does not dread to die or to be mutilated is a lunatic. The man who, dreading these things, still faces them for the sake of duty and honor is a hero."[8] Men who fought in the Great War were inspired by the courage of their Civil War ancestors. But under the stress of modern warfare, the doughboys' courage was tested. They discovered that courage meant overcoming fear and completing the task of a soldier.

On 4 July 1913 President Woodrow Wilson spoke at an event in Gettysburg, Pennsylvania, commemorating the semicentennial anniversary of the Civil War. In his oration, Wilson memorialized "the splendid valour, the manly devotion of the men" who had fought on the fields of Gettysburg and praised "the high recklessness of exalted devotion which does not count the cost . . . the blood and sacrifice of multitudes of unknown men lifted to a great stature in the view of all generations by knowing no limit to their manly willingness to serve."[9]

How many future doughboys heard or read Wilson's words and took them to heart when, a year later, the war in Europe began? The "splendid valour" and "manly willingness to serve" of the Civil War soldiers inspired thousands of young men to prove their own heroism on the battlefields of France. These words could pertain to the doughboys of 1917 as well as to their Civil War counterparts. Bell Irvin Wiley observes, "Yanks and Rebs were far more alike than not. For the common soldiers of both sides the qualities that stand out were: pride in themselves and their families; a strong sense of duty; courage; a capacity for suffering; a will and strength to endure; and, for most, a devotion to country and cause which exceeded that of the folk at home."[10]

The correspondence of Civil War soldiers from both sides of the Mason-Dixon Line attests to the characteristics Wiley defined. In August 1861 seventeen-year-old Day Elmore enlisted in the 36th Illinois Infantry. In spite of being wounded and taken prisoner, he reenlisted. In a letter to his father, Elmore explained his motivation: "I can not Express my self so I will only say that my whole soul is wrapt up in this our countrys caus I ought to be at school but I feel that I am only doeing my Duty to my self and you, Pa." Elmore died from wounds he received at Franklin, Tennessee, in 1864, three months before his twenty-first birthday.[11] When J. T. Terrell's mother suggested he acquire a substitute to replace him in the Confederate army, the soldier from Aberdeen, Mississippi, declared, "I can say I do not want any as I think it is the duty of every man to bear an equal part in this struggle." After serving for three years and spending time in a Union prison camp, Terrell reenlisted in 1864. He was killed by a sharpshooter while on watch outside Atlanta on 22 August 1864.[12] The deaths of Elmore, Terrell, and 752,000 other Civil War soldiers left an immeasurable imprint on Victorian America. As a result, the doughboy had a strong connection with Billy Yank and Johnny Reb. The American soldiers of 1861–1865 and 1917–1918 fought for the same reasons—above all, duty.

The literary works of Stephen Crane, Oliver Optic (pseudonym of William Taylor Adams), and others made a deep impression of the warrior ethos on the future doughboys. Alice Fahs concludes that the books left "an underlying consensus that the war had been—and should remain in memory—a white, masculinist experience in American life."[13] Crane's Civil War novel *The Red Badge of Courage* sparked young men's quest for combat the moment it first appeared in a serialized version in newspapers in 1894; it was published as a book a year later. The novel chronicles the war experiences of young soldier Henry Fleming and his path to manhood. Crane places readers in the midst of violence— connecting manhood and war. When Fleming engages in a skirmish with Confederate troops and fights with a fierceness he did not realize he possessed, his lieutenant, who "seemed drunk with fighting," called out to him, "'By heavens, if I had ten thousand wild cats like you I could tear th' stomach outa this war in less'n a week.'" Fleming's fellow soldiers "now looked upon him as a war devil."[14] War transforms Fleming, as described at the novel's conclusion: "He felt a quiet manhood, non-assertive but of sturdy and strong blood. He knew that he would no more quail before his guides wherever they should point. He had been to touch the great death, and found that, after all, it was but the great death. He was a man."[15]

Some critics argue that *The Red Badge of Courage* is an antiwar novel, a story saturated with irony and full of deception. This ironic interpretation became stylish in the 1960s and continues today.[16] To these critics, Henry Fleming is no more than a deluded, misguided young man lost in his own fantasies, simply a pawn in a symbolic battle.[17] As Michael C. C. Adams suggests, "The fact is that *The Red Badge* is about how boys achieve manhood by facing violence."[18]

Henry Fleming is a boy who, like Crane himself, dreamed of war. Crane grew up in the post–Civil War era; he met many veterans and listened to their stories, absorbing the details they imparted. As a young man, he read a series on the Civil War published by *Century Magazine* between 1884 and 1887, but he found that the articles lacked color and human feelings. He complained to his friend, Corwin Linson, "I wonder that some of these fellows don't tell how they felt in those scraps! They spout eternally of what they did but they are emotionless as rocks!"[19] His childhood dreams, his fascination with history, and the *Century Magazine* articles sparked Crane's interest in writing his own Civil War story, in which he chooses a specific field of combat and describes the scenes with stark realism. When D. Appleton & Company published *The Red Badge of Courage* in its complete form, it was well received. In a letter to John N. Hilliard in January 1896, Crane wrote about his "meager success" as an author and noted, "My chiefest desire was to write plainly and unmistakably, so that all men (and some women) might read and understand. That to my mind is good writing."[20] In another letter to Hilliard the following year, Crane expressed his pleasure at the positive reviews his novel had received in England (where he lived at the time): "The big reviews here praise it for just what I intended it to be, a psychological portrayal of fear. . . . I have never been in a battle, but I believe that I got my sense of the rage of conflict on the football field, or else fighting is a hereditary instinct, and I wrote intuitively; for the Cranes were a family of fighters in the old days, and in the Revolution every member did his duty."[21]

Although Crane never experienced combat, he did pursue adventure, serving as a war correspondent during the Greco-Turkish War in 1897 and the Spanish-American War in 1898. At Velestino, where the Turks assaulted the Greeks, fellow war correspondent John Bass asked, "Crane, what impresses you most in this affair?" The author answered, "Between the two great armies battling against each other the interesting thing is the mental attitude of the men."[22] In Cuba, while covering the Spanish-American War, Crane witnessed Colonel Theodore Roosevelt's victory at Kettle Hill and saw the Rough Riders, the Regulars, and the 1st and 10th Cavalries push the Spanish from San Juan Hill. As a group of journalists watched the action unfold, someone yelled, "By God, there go our boys up the hill!" Crane wrote of the scene, "There is many a good American who would give an arm to get the thrill of patriotic insanity that coursed through us when we heard that yell."[23]

In *The Red Badge of Courage*, as well as his other war stories, Crane explores the "mental attitude" of his characters. In Crane's short story "The Veteran," published in 1896, an older, gray Henry Fleming enters a burning barn numerous times to rescue the trapped horses and cows. In contrast, the other men, fumbling with water buckets, are as terror-stricken as the animals. Crane describes one such man: "The Swede had been running to and fro babbling," carrying an empty pail. Fleming saves the Swede by dragging him out of the barn. When the Swede remembers that two young colts are still trapped inside, Fleming braves the inferno and rushes back in to rescue the "poor little things." The roof collapses on Fleming, killing him, and as the smoke and flames rise to the sky, Crane concludes, "Perhaps the unutterable midnights of the universe will have no power to daunt the color of his soul."[24] As Marten states, "'The Veteran' showed that once a man came to grips with mortal peril in battle, the strength he drew from that special brand of terror and accomplishment would last the rest of his life."[25]

Biographer Linda H. Davis writes, "Stephen Crane was a product of his time; duty and honor were inseparable from his notion of masculinity."[26] To the future doughboys reading Crane's stories, duty and honor were paramount. They, like Fleming, sought manhood on the battlefield. The doughboys witnessed the realities of war, but like Fleming, they were gratified by their service. In the end, American veterans would feel that their wartime experiences made them better men.

Literary characters like Henry Fleming, along with the legacy of the Civil War, created a sense of duty and a vision of heroic warfare. Another hallmark of Victorian America was a keen interest in sports, especially boxing, football, and baseball. "Amateur games were especially important to those coming of age after the Civil War, for violent contests on athletic 'fields of battle' allowed young men to replicate the heroism of fathers who had sacrificed so much in their selfless commitment to saving the Union. Here the martial values of hardiness, courage, and endurance took their place beside the older Victorian ideals of piety and earnest hard work," explains Elliott J. Gorn.[27] This competitive drive also led men to form clubs and secret societies where they could express their manhood and brotherhood.[28]

Bolstered by the legacy of the Civil War and the Spanish-American War and by a growing interest in sports and private clubs, American men felt they had much to gain when the United States declared war, especially after listening to the lectures of the Four Minute Men (and women). These four-minute speakers, all volunteers, promoted the reasons for joining the war. George Creel led them into action as director of the Commission on Public Information, which President Wilson had established to encourage fervent patriotism and support for the war. In addition, the president passed the Espionage Act of 1917 and the Sedition Act of 1918. The latter stated that any antiwar actions, writings, or sentiments "shall be punished by a fine of not more than 10,000 dollars or imprisonment for not more than twenty years, or both."[29] Meanwhile, at movie theaters, churches, synagogues, and meeting halls of all types, the Four Minute Men injected their audiences with enthusiasm, nationalism, and an inescapable sense of duty. Many of the women who spoke read the following poem, "It's Duty Boy," to crowds across the country:

My boy must never bring disgrace to his immortal sires
At Valley Forge and Lexington they kindled freedom's fires,
John's father died at Gettysburg, mine fell at Chancellorsville;
While John himself was with the boys who charged up San Juan Hill.
And John, if he was living now, would surely say with me,
"No son of ours shall e'er disgrace our grand old family tree
By turning out a slacker when his country needs his aid."
It is not of such timber that America was made.
I'd rather you had died at birth or not been born at all,
Than know that I had raised a son who cannot hear the call
That freedom has sent round the world, its previous rights to save
This call is meant for you, my boy, and I would have you brave;
And though my heart is breaking, boy, I bid you do your part,

And show the world no son of mine is cursed with craven heart;
And if, perchance, you ne'er return, my later days to cheer,
And I have only memories of my brave boy, so dear,
I'd rather have it so, my boy, and know you bravely died
Than have a living coward sit supinely by my side.
To save the world from sin, my boy, God gave His only son
He's asking for My boy, today, and may His will be done.[30]

It was as if Creel had resurrected the mothers of ancient Sparta, who gave their sons the following instructions before departing for battle: "Come back with your shield—or on it."[31] Even before young men heard speeches like these, former president Theodore Roosevelt had exclaimed, "A mother who is not willing to raise her boy to be a soldier, is not fit for citizenship."[32] Many families urged their sons to enlist, but most young men did not need to be pushed too hard.

During the war, the enemy became an object of hatred among the citizenry. Crowd psychology took control of individuals' thinking, affecting even members of the clergy, whose sermons preaching hatred and violence seemed inconsistent with their religious calling. The clergy joined in depicting Kaiser Wilhelm II as Satan and in vilifying Germany. To the majority of American clergy, the Great War represented a holy war. Protestant preacher Billy Sunday declared, "If you turn hell upside down, you will find 'Made in Germany' stamped on the bottom." In April 1918 Sunday went even further, calling Germans a "bunch of pretzel-chewing, sauerkraut spawn of blood-thirsty Huns."[33] At the First Baptist Church of New London, the pastor, who became a chaplain during the war, preached to his congregation in uniform as he stood beside a machine gun and an American flag.

Inflamed by church and state, the doughboys were filled with patriotism. Regardless of color or creed, and despite varying reasons for becoming soldiers, men expressed enthusiasm for and pride in military service. Every doughboy, whether drafted or enlisted, felt it was his duty to fight.

Nineteen-year-old Garnett D. Claman was curious about the world outside his farm in Bristol, Virginia. When he entered the service on 28 July 1917, he hoped "to go to France that I might have the knowledge of travel, of association with different nationalities, and I wanted to know what war meant."[34] Henry A. Isleib of Marlborough, Connecticut, a farmer and lumberman, joined the infantry on 29 March 1918, "spurred on by my country's needs and my own patriotic thoughts."[35] Joseph J. O'Connell of Manchester, Connecticut, enlisted due to a sense of "patriotism and a desire for adventure."[36] James P. Spencer, an African American student at Virginia Normal and Industrial Institute, was thirty years old when he entered the infantry on 26 October 1917. Spencer had no misgivings about his military service and remarked, "I felt that it was my patriotic duty to serve my country at the most critical hour in the Nation's history, though my race had not been given the proper rights."[37]

Niels A. W. Johnson, a Manchester, Connecticut, resident who served with the 102nd Infantry, expressed the sentiments of many when he said that he had enlisted "to fight for the United States and Democracy."[38] Another Manchester man, Harold J. Dougan, served as a sergeant in the infantry and explained, "A man knowing that his country's honor was at stake, that he, a very small factor, was needed to do his little part, I went willingly."[39] Infantryman James O. McKarney, a farmer from Washington County, Virginia, commented, "I thought it was our duty to go and help win the war before I was drafted. I am glad to know that I was able to help win the war."[40]

"When I received my call, I thought it over, and considered it an honor as well as a great privilege to go and fight or die for my country," reflected Thomas M. Clary, an African American blacksmith and farmer from White Plains, Virginia.[41] "At the time I was called I was employed in the US Navy yard and was urged to claim exemption on same grounds, but my thoughts were that someone else would have to go if I did not. I was young and was willing to do my share," commented Paul T. Wysocki of Norfolk, Virginia.[42] Wysocki, the son of Polish immigrants, entered the Machine Gun Company of the 318th Infantry, 80th Division, on 22 September 1917, three months before his twenty-second birthday.

"Well I did not know anything about the military, I had as much patriotism as anybody. And I made sure that I got the first uniform on of boys that night," stated twenty-six-year-old Arthur F. Lundin, a sheet metal worker and farmer from Oxford, Connecticut.[43] William W. Parker, employed as a welder and sheriff in Norfolk, Virginia, enlisted in the infantry on 9 June 1917 at the age of twenty-four. Said Parker, "My attitude towards military service is of the highest that any man can have, and I felt it was necessary that I do my duty for I am an American and fight for her principles."[44]

"When men first began to be drafted I thought to myself that if others were to go, I might as well go along too, and when my call came I was ready for it," observed African American John S. Fields, a twenty-two-year-old teamster from Church Roads, Virginia.[45] Arthur A. Grove, a merchant from Luray, Virginia, and a member of the National Guard, reflected, "I believed then and I believe now that it is the duty of every man to serve his country in time of need. I was over the age for the first Draft but would not have felt right if I had not gone into the Army, especially as I had a good many year's service in the Virginia National Guard."[46]

The soldiers of the American Expeditionary Forces (AEF) shared President Wilson's conviction that "the world must be made safe for democracy."[47] "The man who was unwilling to fight for this country at such a critical period has no right to protection under its flag. I was ready and willing to go when called," remarked Emory P. Barrow of Alberta, Virginia.[48] Barrow, inducted on 10 May 1918, five days after his twenty-seventh birthday, had been a student before the war. "I think that if a country is good enough to live in its good enough to fight for," stated Theodore Elmore of Richmond, Virginia. At age sixteen, Elmore joined the Marine Corps on 30 June 1916 as a drummer and trumpeter in the infantry.[49] Edgar C. Outten, a twenty-six-year-old clerk and private secretary from Hampton, Virginia, remarked, "Military Service beneficial to all who serve. A Very essential part of our Gov't. A means by which we may learn the obligation and privilege of citizenship." Outten continued, "Belonged to National Guard when war was declared. Glad to be of service to my country."[50]

Young doughboys like these entered the military with preconceived notions of what war would be like; the heroic legacy of warfare made them impetuous, and they believed war was the path to manhood. The average AEF soldier did not know and did not care to know what the war was about or how it had started. The June 1914 assassination of Francis Ferdinand, heir to the throne of the Austro-Hungarian Empire, enveloped all of Europe in a massive conflict that would cause 10 million military deaths. After the Battle of the Marne in September 1914, which halted the German army's plan to crush France, both the Allied and German forces dug in, and a series of trenches formed from the North Sea down to the border of neutral Switzerland. While England, France, Germany, Austria-Hungary, Russia, and their allies engaged in brutal modern warfare, across the Atlantic, young men watched and waited to see whether the United States would enter the fray. To Americans, the events in Europe were a world away.

The Fall of Isolationism

The four years of World War I spawned some of the bloodiest combat the world has ever seen, resulting in an unequaled loss of human life. The conflicts at Verdun and the Somme in 1916 would become infamous; 19,240 British troops lost their lives on the first day of the Battle of the Somme.[51] Americans read about these disasters in newspapers, but most citizens still clung to isolationism—a long-standing tradition dating from President George Washington's warning in his Farewell Address (19 September 1796) to beware of foreign authority and perpetual alliances.[52] Washington admonished Americans "against the insidious wiles of foreign influence." He cautioned, "'Tis our true policy to steer clear of permanent Alliances, with any portion of the foreign world," and he counseled "against the mischiefs of foreign Intriegue."[53] President James Monroe strengthened Washington's original message when he issued the Monroe Doctrine on 2 December 1823, stating that the countries of Europe, especially Great Britain, should mind their business within the Western Hemisphere and vowing that the United States would refrain from involvement in European affairs. Monroe declared, "The American continents, by the free and independent condition which they have assumed and maintain, are henceforth not to be considered as subjects for future colonization by any European powers. . . . We should consider any attempt on their part to extend their system to any portion of this hemisphere as dangerous to our peace and safety."[54]

Throughout the nineteenth century, while the countries of Europe vied for global domination, the United States remained preoccupied with its own expansion. The venture into Cuba, Guam, the Philippines, and Puerto Rico beginning in 1898 marked the first major US attempt to expand its rule overseas. Up to this point, westward expansion in the continental United States had been the focus, but once the Indian Wars were over, the country sought a new enterprise. After the short four-month war against Spain, America began its own style of imperialism against former Spanish colonies, but it still distanced itself from European international affairs.

The United States held true to Washington's recommendation when President Woodrow Wilson was elected for a second term in 1916. During the campaign, Americans had praised Wilson's promise to keep the United States out of the war in Europe; this neutral stance helped him defeat Republican candidate Charles E. Hughes. Despite Americans' isolationist sentiments, Wilson had a sense of foreboding. Even though most Americans wanted no part of the conflict, many people had already taken sides, some for the Allies and some for the Central Powers. Many Americans, especially in the Northeast, were foreign-born and had strong family ties to Germany, Italy, France, or Britain. Table 1.1 shows Connecticut's diverse population during the war years.

As 1915 and 1916 passed, the United States crept closer to war: British propaganda, the sinking of the RMS *Lusitania*, the Zimmermann telegram, and Germany's resumption of unrestricted submarine warfare all drew America into the conflict. Gary Mead stresses that France and especially Britain waged a "propaganda campaign" in the United States well before 6 April 1917 to convince Americans to join them in war against Germany. The Allies made the most of stories of German atrocities to persuade Americans to enter the war.[55] Although American journalists were in France to cover the war and report objectively on events, the French did not permit them to travel near the front lines. Most of the information they received was from the British; in fact, most accounts of the war originated in Britain and were cabled to American newspapers. Moreover, the British could execute as a spy any journalist who attempted to cover the war from the German point of view. "The Great War," writes Jay M. Winter, "spawned the most spectacular advertising campaign to date. Its product was justification of war."[56]

The Allies and the Central Powers both employed propaganda to gain support from the civilian population and military personnel. Britain, France, and the United States all exploited allegations of enemy atrocities, but Britain had

Table 1.1. Distribution of Foreign-Born in Connecticut's Five Largest Cities, 1920

Country of Origin	Hartford Number	Hartford Percent	Bridgeport Number	Bridgeport Percent	New Haven Number	New Haven Percent	Waterbury Number	Waterbury Percent	New Britain Number	New Britain Percent
Austria	919	0.6	2,697	1.8	675	0.4	343	0.4	634	1.0
England	2,049	1.4	3,491	2.4	1,955	1.2	1,086	1.1	730	1.2
Germany	1,820	1.3	1,979	1.3	2,770	1.7	1,010	1.1	1,112	1.9
Hungary	272	0.1	6,230	4.3	421	0.2	131	0.1	109	0.2
Ireland	6,116	4.4	4,300	2.9	7,219	4.4	4,507	4.9	986	1.7
Italy	7,101	5.1	8,789	6.1	15,084	9.2	9,232	10.1	3,177	5.3
Lithuania	1,260	0.9	698	0.4	721	0.4	3,674	4.0	1,246	2.1
Poland	4,880	3.5	3,061	2.1	3,009	1.8	1,629	1.7	7,804	13.1
Russia	7,654	5.5	5,395	3.7	8,080	4.9	3,209	3.4	1,152	1.9
Sweden	2,315	1.6	1,783	1.2	1,266	0.7	556	0.6	2,102	3.5
Total foreign-born	40,667	29.4	46,414	32.3	45,686	28.1	29,899	32.6	21,230	35.8
Total population	138,036		143,555		162,537		91,715		59,316	

Source: Figures calculated from US Bureau of the Census, *Fourteenth Census of the United States: State Compendium, Connecticut* (Washington, DC: Bureau of the Census, 1924), 25.

the most effective and refined propaganda campaign. Yellow journalism infiltrated American homes and altered the perception of Germany.[57] Stories of the German soldiers' barbarity, especially toward women and children in occupied Belgium; the inoculation of prisoners with the tuberculosis bacterium; and other reports from Britain were permeated with distortions, exaggerations, and outright falsehoods. These accounts, accompanied by British pleas to join the war in support of the Allies, helped convince the American people and the US government to enter the war.

Germany's sinking of the British liner *Lusitania* on 7 May 1915 killed 1,198 people—128 of whom were Americans. From the Germans' point of view, the *Lusitania* was fair game, since it was a military reserve and carried some munitions. Furthermore, Germany had warned that traveling on such a vessel could be dangerous.[58] Nevertheless, Germany risked incurring the anger of the United States, and when it protested, Germany halted the strategy the following month.

The Zimmermann telegram, sent on 12 November 1916 by German Foreign Minister Alfred Zimmermann to Heinrich von Eckhardt, German ambassador to Mexico, alluded to a Mexican-German alliance designed to embroil the United States in a conflict with Mexico. Zimmermann proposed that if the United States declared war on Germany, Mexico should declare war on America. In exchange, Mexico would receive German financial aid and the return of Arizona, New Mexico, and Texas. Zimmermann also planned to encourage Japan to join the proposed German-Mexican alliance. British intelligence intercepted the telegram, and the US ambassador to Britain, Walter H. Page, forwarded it to President Wilson on 23 February 1917. Wilson authorized publication of the telegram on 1 March 1917, and its contents outraged Americans. The Zimmermann telegram aggravated tensions between the United States and Mexico, which had already been strained when Mexican revolutionary Pancho Villa and 500 men attacked Columbus, New Mexico, killing seventeen Americans, on 8 March 1916.[59]

The final and decisive political factor was Germany's resumption of unrestricted submarine warfare on 1 February 1917 in an attempt to strangle supply lines to Britain. President Wilson, who had won reelection just months earlier based on his firm commitment to American neutrality, went to Congress on the night of 2 April 1917 and asked for a declaration of war. In a voice that grew more passionate with each paragraph of his address, Wilson declared that there was no other course of action; the United States must enter the conflict and fight for democracy. He concluded, "To such a task we can dedicate our lives and our fortunes, everything that we are and everything that we have, with the pride of those who know that the day has come when America is privileged to spend her blood and her might for the principles that gave her birth and happiness and the peace which she has treasured. God helping her, she can do no other."[60] His words were met with thunderous applause. Later that evening, Wilson said to his secretary, Joseph P. Tumulty, "Think what it was they were applauding. My message today was a message of death for our young men. How strange it seems to applaud that."[61] Four days later, on 6 April 1917, America went to war.

An Ill-Equipped Ally

America was unprepared for war. A US Army expeditionary force, led by General John J. Pershing, had spent the past year engaged in the Punitive Expedition (March 1916–February 1917)—a humiliatingly unsuccessful attempt to hunt down the elusive Pancho Villa in northern Mexico. The Punitive Expedition devoured supplies, leaving insufficient materiel for the AEF. Pershing's troops had been trained in some modern tactics, such as trench warfare, but they soon forgot those lessons as they played cat and mouse with Villa across the vast terrain of Chihuahua, Mexico. More important, the army's attention was focused on Mexico rather than on preparations for possible intervention in Europe; homeland defense and open field battle remained the hallmarks of army doctrine.[62] The US Army's total strength was fewer than 200,000 men. The US Navy, though the third largest in the world behind Britain and Germany, consisted of many outdated battleships; it was ill prepared to face the German U-boat menace or, more important, to transport soldiers across the Atlantic. In the air, America was also far behind; the US Air Service (USAS) possessed only fifty-five trainer planes, almost all of which were outdated and not combat ready.[63] Although the Wright brothers had introduced the airplane to the world in 1903, as late as 1911, the US Signal Corps had only one plane and one pilot.[64] In addition, the military did not officially distinguish pilots until 1912, and from 1908 to 1913 the United States spent only $430,000 on aviation, compared with the $22 million spent by France and Germany.[65]

The National Defense Act of 1916 had cut the general staff of the army to the bare minimum; as a result, it appeared that the United States was incapable of coming to the aid of the Allies. Although Congress had established the Council of National Defense to prepare American industries for war, it actually worked against preparedness. The council, comprising engineers, academics, and industrialists, created advisory networks that operated in each state, but this type of state and national organization proved unwieldy. In addition, the Council of National Defense limited itself to compiling data and taking inventory of the resources necessary for wartime. The US Army was thus an inefficient operation with limited funds in 1916; Congress was not willing to provide the resources needed to ensure its growth, and in general, the populace did not support militarism.

Secretary of War Newton D. Baker favored the decentralization of government, as did the rest of Wilson's administration, and Baker disregarded the army officials who warned that the military lacked staff and supplies. This situation continued even after the United States declared war. Troops had no uniforms; weapons and supplies of every sort were scarce. Only when Congress questioned Baker in January 1918 did the Wilson administration react to the lack of military supplies. North Carolina senator Lee S. Overman sponsored the Overman Act, passed by Congress on 20 May 1918, which enabled Wilson to consolidate six agencies into one and gave him greater power to spend money for wartime purposes.

The Regular Army was small, the National Guard was limited in size, and both forces were sorely underequipped: they had no tanks, no gas masks, only 742 field pieces, a mere 43 heavy guns, and 2,000 antiquated machine guns.[66] Ammunition was also in short supply. As discussed later, during their training on Governor's Island and at other camps, some new soldiers drilled with wooden replicas instead of guns. General Johnson Hagood, chief of staff of the Services of Supply, lamented the War Department's lack of preparation: "The fourteen years, 1903 to 1917, during which the General staff had been in existence had not been spent in making plans for war, the purpose for which it was created, but in squabbling over the control of the routine peace-time administration and supply of the Regular Army and in attempts to place the blame for unpreparedness upon Congress." Hagood also charged that, from 1914 to 1917, the War Department had not anticipated the country's entry into the war and had failed to plan. "Hindsight is better than foresight," he commented, "and I, like all the rest, did not have the brains—or the genius—to see preparedness in its true light."[67]

After the war, many returning veterans also lamented the lack of preparation. A captain in the infantry, George W. Cheney of Manchester, Connecticut, stated, "My experience was that the American Army never did reach the point of being completely equipped and organized as had been contemplated in War Department plans. This goes to show that we were woefully unprepared in spite of repeated warnings, and the fact that we entered the war three years after it started. We should have a standing army of 500,000 and compulsory military training for one year for each boy reaching age 18."[68]

"I am a strong advocate of preparedness. If the U.S. Army had had the proper equipment and some trained officers our losses would have been less and the Army better managed," said infantry sergeant Marcel W. Rice of New Haven. "We should keep a large well-trained National Guard and fair-sized regular army. The volunteer is the better soldier. We should develop a strong air service so that in future wars our infantry will not suffer for lack of eyes."[69] When Second Lieutenant John M. Ross returned home to New Haven after the war, he expressed "a hope that our United States will never again be caught un-prepared and that our military program will be adequate for its full protection, both on land and on the sea."[70]

Yet in spite of its many deficiencies, the United States mobilized and pre-pared a large fighting force in a remarkably short time. The nation's strong in-dustrial foundation, along with its vast population, enabled the rapid creation of a formidable military force. The Fighting 69th Infantry Regiment of New York City had no lack of volunteers, in spite of its recruiting slogan: "If you don't want to be amongst the first to go to France, don't join the 69th."[71] Fran-cis P. Duffy, a Roman Catholic chaplain for the 69th's 42nd (Rainbow) Division, described the enthusiasm of the mostly Irish troops mustered at the regiment's armory to welcome volunteers on 18 August 1917: "Our 2,000 lined the walls and many perched themselves on the iron beams overhead. They cheered and cheered and cheered till the blare of the bands was unheard in the joyous din—till hearts beat so full and fast that they seemed too big for the ribs that confined them, till tears of emotion came, and something mystical was born in every breast—the soul of a Regiment. Heaven be good to the enemy when these cheering lads go forward together in battle."[72]

The marines were ready for war. "When the United States declared war on Germany, a thrill went through the Marine Corps," remarked Brigadier Gen-eral Albertus W. Catlin, "for we were fighting men all and we learned that Marines were to be rushed over to France to take their stand on the Frontier of Liberty beside the battle-scarred veterans of France and Great Britain."[73] For the most part, Americans rallied and galvanized into action when their coun-try declared war. As Corporal J. E. Rendinell and newspaper correspondent George Pattullo wrote, "The young American men with a brashness born of the ignorance of war's brutality rushed to enlist in the armed forces. . . . They exuded invincibility and exhibited their intense belief in their own immortal-ity."[74]

By the end of 1918, the government believed that the 4 million men in the services were combat ready; America sent 2 million of these soldiers overseas to the front. The majority of men went willingly as volunteers or conscripts; only a few went unwillingly as disgruntled draftees. One of the latter was Wilbur T. Brownley of Norfolk, Virginia, whose thoughts on military service were succinct: "What can't be cured, must be endured."[75] In a 16 January 1988 interview with Kerry W. Bate, David E. Davies of Kanarraville, Utah, recalled his reaction on receiving his draft notice in July 1917: "I don't believe in wars. I don't think they settle anything. . . . I didn't want to fight anybody, but I did want to stick up for our rights. . . . I figger you got to stick up fer your rights, an' I think that was the attitude, mostly."[76] Brownley and Davies, however, repre-sented the minority.

At the time of the war, Americans embraced romantic notions of combat. Many men were eager to go because they had not tasted battle; thoughts of honor, heroism, and patriotism filled their heads. Common were dreams of courageous acts that would make the doughboys heroes—and indeed, many of these dreams were fulfilled, although not necessarily in the way the soldiers imagined. The men who enlisted or responded to conscription had visions of righteous glory in battle, based on the Civil War stories their fathers, uncles, and grandfathers had regaled them with as young boys. Tales of bravery at Antietam, Fredericksburg, Gettysburg, and elsewhere spurred their desire to experience the thrill, the adventure. In addition, the exploits of Theodore Roosevelt and his Rough Riders were still vivid memories, making combat seem delectably dangerous and appealing to many young men. Thirty-one-year-old Herman R. Furr of Norfolk, Virginia, enlisted in the National Army on 15 May 1917 and "believed in preparedness, not a big standing army but a trained reserve." He added, "My father was a Confederate soldier, and have always believed it was my duty to get into military service at once in case of war."[77] Czechoslovakian Edward G. Pobuda, a resident of Willington, Connecticut, enlisted in the National Guard on 23 August 1917, his twenty-third birthday. He said, "As soon as war was declared I resigned my position and joined the ranks for a just cause against a common enemy."[78]

"I was not called, being a volunteer three days after declaration of war. Was glad to go and will go again if necessity arises," commented Joseph Ryan, a student from Putnam, Connecticut, who enlisted on 9 April 1917 at age nineteen.[79] Private Stephen J. Weston of Waterbury, Connecticut, enlisted five months before his eighteenth birthday, on 6 June 1917. Weston's zeal for military service was echoed by other young men as well: "Military service builds strong bodies, and sound minds. With military service one acquires confidence and poise. Being young and adventurous, I chose the Infantry. After all, when positions must be taken it is the Infantryman that takes them. When ground must be held, it is the Infantryman's job to hold it."[80]

Douglas C. France, a lawyer from Charlottesville, Virginia, said he "always found military life to be attractive and considered it my duty to volunteer when war was declared."[81] Twenty-three-year-old France entered the Army Ambulance Service on 28 May 1917. Millard C. Life, a twenty-seven-year-old college-educated shipping clerk from McGaheysville, Virginia, entered the service on 18 September 1917 and affirmed that he "was ready to go at any time that I might be called." Life added, "Made no effort to be exempted."[82] "My enlistment was brought about by the realization that manpower only could stop a tremendous slaughter. My country's need and the 'Great Adventure' were also

Edward G. Pobuda of Willington, Connecticut, in France, 25 April 1919. (Box 64, Connecticut State Library)

compelling items," said Theodore E. Whitney, a machine gun corporal and Hartford native.[83]

Thomas B. McDermott felt so strongly about helping his country that he left his wife and two children at home in Hartford, Connecticut, when he began his military training in Plattsburgh, New York. The twenty-seven-year-old McDermott, who enlisted in the infantry on 28 April 1917, "had no definite attitude except the firm conviction that his country would take impudence from NO ONE."[84] Alvin C. York of Pall Mall, Tennessee, reported to his local draft board on 14 November 1917. According to York, "Uncle Sam said he wanted me and he wanted me most awful bad. And I had also been brought up to believe in my country. I knowed that even in the Civil War, when Tennessee was a doubtful state, my two grandfathers had both fought straight out for the Union. I knowed that my great-great-grandfather, old Coonrod Pile, had been one of the pioneers who done helped to build up this-here country, and he hain't never hesitated to use a gun, and I kinder felt that my ancestors would want me to do whatever my country demanded of me."[85] At age seventeen,

Martin J. Hogan of New York enlisted in the Fighting 69th Regiment. Recalling his enthusiasm for answering the recruitment call, Hogan stated, "I felt that I looked old enough to pass a recruiting sergeant and that the call for men was urgent enough to justify my camouflaging my age by one year. Anyhow, I thought I can go to France and grow up with the war."[86] Hogan seemed to desire the same path taken by Crane's Henry Fleming.

Pro-war propaganda and literature also encouraged these earnest Americans to rise to the challenge of serving in the military. English poets Rudyard Kipling and Rupert Brooke, whose works were widely read in the United States, contributed to the romantic images of war held by these young men. Kipling's "For All We Have and Are" (1914) is a prime example:

> For all we have and are
> For all our children's fate,
> Stand up and take the war.
> The Hun is at the gate![87]

Equally important to the doughboys' mind-set was the influence of veterans—soldiers of past American wars who helped shape their aggressive, sometimes idealistic mentality. The charismatic Theodore Roosevelt, famous for his charge up Kettle Hill during the Spanish-American War, made fighting the enemy seem no more than a hazardous sport. Others characterized war as a glorious adventure and a way of escaping a dull or unchallenging life.

Younger educated men, especially in the northeastern United States, pushed for military training and US participation in the war. Editors and publishers of newspapers and magazines supported America's entrance into the Great War. Through the written and spoken word, men with influential positions not only perpetuated the heroism of war but also pressed for it. As early as 1914, John G. Hibben, Woodrow Wilson's successor as president of Princeton University, had begun advocating US involvement in the European conflict. As David M. Kennedy notes, Hibben spoke of "the chastening and purifying effect of armed conflict."[88] Colleges and preparatory schools contributed hundreds of volunteers for military service. Ivy League universities such as Princeton and Yale, steeped in the teachings of war as a noble cause, sent their young students off to fight the Germans. In 1925 Yale president Arthur Twining Hadley said that, during the war, "the students as a body were carried outside of themselves by visions of a larger world than that in which they had hitherto moved. . . . Thank God, the vision of 1917 and 1918 led us in the right direction. The lives of those who fell in that great struggle were not wasted." Hadley added, "It was the good fortune to die while the inspiration under which they fought was at its highest."[89] In affirming the war's purpose and praising those who had fought and died, Hadley seemed to surmise that the war and the sacrifices made by American soldiers would slip from the nation's collective memory in future years.

General Catlin noted, "Unquestionably, the intelligent, educated man makes, in the long run, the best soldier. There is no place for the mere brute in modern warfare. It is a contest of brains as well as of brawn, and the best brains win. The American colleges doubtless supposed that they were turning men into scholars; when the test came they found they had been training soldiers."[90] Catlin remarked that in the 6th Regiment, 60 percent of the soldiers were college men; two-thirds of one entire company came from the University of Minnesota. Twenty-four-year-old Washington and Lee University student William B. Yancey of Harrisonburg, Virginia, recalled, "I was not called, and as to my attitude it was not mine to question, and being a firm believer in that old but apt saying, 'May America in all her diplomatic relations be right but America right or wrong,' I went with full confidence of victory and we came home with the bacon."[91]

Joseph B. Bowen of Pawtucket, Rhode Island, was a forestry student at Yale when the United States declared war. In a letter home, Bowen wrote, "I shall enlist at the first opportunity. It is true that the aviator's job is dangerous, but death has never held any dread for me; in fact, I think I have a philosopher's point of view, and I can look on it as an interesting experience that will come sooner or later. I shall hope and pray that I may be killed outright rather than come back maimed, but God's will be done."[92]

Influential men and women of the era echoed similar sentiments when advocating US entry into the war. In addition to Hibben at Princeton, writers such as Robert Herrick and Edith Wharton spoke and wrote about the cleansing aspects of military conflict. The words of the Roman poet Horace, "Dulce et Decorum est Pro patria mori" (it is sweet and glorious to die for one's country), influenced recruiting posters, one of which showed the image of Dame Columbia or a goddess figure guarding soldiers as they marched to the front.[93] Even *Lost Generation* novelist John Dos Passos himself joined the American Volunteer Motor Ambulance Corps (Norton-Harjes Ambulance Corps) to experience adventure: "We had spent our boyhood in the afterglow of the peaceful nineteenth century. There was a war on. What was war like? We wanted to see with our own eyes. We flocked into the volunteer services. I respected the conscientious objectors, and occasionally felt I should take that course myself, but hell, I wanted to see the show."[94]

Films, novels, stories, and poems recounted glory, virility, and destiny, bringing young men to Europe even before the United States declared war. Students from prestigious colleges and sons from influential families joined French, British, and Italian forces. One such young man was poet Alan Seeger, best remembered for his poem "I Have a Rendezvous with Death." He graduated from

Harvard in 1910, traveled to Paris two years later, and joined the French Foreign Legion in 1914. Seeger recorded his war experiences in France in his poetry, letters, and diary. In a letter to his mother dated 3 July 1915, he wrote, "Had I the choice I would be nowhere else in the world than where I am. Even had I the chance to be liberated, I would not take it. Do not be sorrowful then. It is the shirkers and slackers alone in this war who are to be lamented."[95] Two months later, on 1 September, he admitted that his "sentimental and romantic nature" yearned for combat; "it is for glory alone that I engaged."[96] When Seeger died in action on 23 July 1916, he became an American hero, propelling more young men toward the European conflict.

Poet and historian Joyce Kilmer served with the Fighting 69th of New York. When Chaplain Duffy met Kilmer at training camp on 5 August 1917, he remarked that Kilmer "sees what he considers a plain duty, and he is going ahead to perform it, calm and clear eyed and without the slightest regard to what the consequences may be."[97]

New Jersey–born writer Arthur G. Empey joined British forces after the sinking of the *Lusitania*. Empey's autobiographical books *Over the Top* (1917) and *First Call* (1918) describe his experiences in the trenches with the English troops. *Over the Top* became an instant success and sold 350,000 copies. A year later, Hollywood made the book into a motion picture starring the author. Empey, who was wounded three times in combat, became a popular speaker who described his personal war adventures as one long heroic undertaking filled with camaraderie and thrills. Although he wrote of the horrors of war and the death of a close trench mate, Empey's overall message was one of adventure, manhood, and ultimate triumph. He helped convince many young American men that war was a grand adventure they should not miss: "In a worthwhile cause like ours, mud, rats, cooties, shells, wounds, or death itself, are far outweighed by the deep sense of satisfaction felt by the man who does his bit."[98] In *First Call*, Empey recounts the following story—an impassioned plea for young men to enlist:

> A friend the other day made a remark that was very helpful to me and may be helpful to you. He is a shade under forty, healthy and vigorous, but he has a large family and many responsibilities and cannot go—and oh! how he wants to! As he watched a few of the men in the office saying "Good-bye" the day before they were to leave for the training camps, he said: "No matter what we men who are left behind may do—those fellows will have it all over us."
>
> Wasn't he right? . . . Men may become rich or famous in other walks of life—but no matter what their achievements, they can be no greater than yours. You will have it "all over them." To have taken part in this great war, on the side of Right, to have been one of the struggling

soldiers who have helped to bring back to the earth Freedom and all that makes life precious, is well worth while. The sacrifice may be great, but it will not have been in vain.[99]

Jack Morris Wright, a young American who joined the French Air Service in July 1917, trained in France and obtained his pilot's license. He wrote to his mother on 20 November, expressing his enthusiasm for his role in the war: "Never has a third of a year rushed past my bewildered eyes so rapidly. It passed like a comet furious and glowing. It has been a wonderful period of youth, of adventure, of romance, that which is now the ideal I strive to attain. Thank God I am living up to my dreams. Thank God my dreams are not fancies, are not dreamt in vain, and perhaps are the forgings of a real mind and the real prospect of a man."[100] Wright became a first lieutenant at age nineteen in January 1918 and was killed that same month.

Young women, too—some born of privilege, others not—were dedicated to the war's causes. One such young woman was an American nurse—the daughter of a former medical director of the US Navy—who served as a lieutenant in a French army hospital near the trenches along the Marne. Her patients called her "Mademoiselle Miss," and a collection of her letters sent from the front was published anonymously. Working fourteen-hour days caring for the thirty-four patients in her ward, Mademoiselle Miss maintained a cheerful attitude to inspire the recovery of the wounded. In a letter home dated 19 January 1916, she described the type of woman needed for wartime nursing: "I tell you that here on the front it isn't just a mere nurse that is required; send the finest, most versatile woman that America . . . can produce, and her fineness and her gifts will not be wasted. . . . She should combine a glacial calm with unfailing, gayety . . . and a sense of humor . . . a touch as light as a watchmaker's, and strength to carry a man alone on occasion."[101]

Other women volunteered to serve as ambulance drivers, nurses, Red Cross workers, secretaries, and canteen girls before or shortly after the United States declared war. Elizabeth McCune of Salt Lake City, Utah, daughter of mining millionaire Alfred W. McCune, was determined to drive ambulances or supply vehicles at the front. She studied auto mechanics, purchased her own vehicle (a requirement for female drivers), and sailed for France aboard the *Rochambeau* on 5 November 1917.

Another Utahan from a wealthy mining family, Maud Fitch of Eureka, was an active Red Cross volunteer at home, but she wanted to serve in Europe. In February 1918 Maud went to New York, where she passed the driving and engine knowledge exams and bought her own truck and a six-month supply of fuel. She sailed for France on 7 March 1918 aboard the *Chicago*—the only female in the group. In a letter to her father, Walter, dated 9 April 1918 and sent from Paris, she expressed how excited she was about her new assignment to serve as a Red Cross driver with the French Third Army near Compiegne, an area experiencing heavy shelling: "We will get into action AT ONCE—the magic of these two words! And to think at last I shall get into the very vortex of the greatest conflict in the history of the world. . . . If only I shall have the right stuff in me to benefit by it—to go into it and come out with one's soul and heart all fire tried!"[102] Indeed, Fitch possessed the right stuff. She often worked twenty-four-hour shifts, weaving through heavy traffic to transport the wounded to hospitals behind the lines, sometimes bribing the traffic directors with cigarettes to allow her vehicle through. For her 9 June 1918 rescue of wounded soldiers during heavy fire, Fitch received the French Croix de Guerre with a Gold Star.

Once the United States entered the war, thousands of young women enrolled in nursing courses to help the wounded troops. In 1917 there were 7,000 graduate nurses available as reserves, and more were being trained, but there was still a shortage. Recruitment of nurses began across the country, and Lettie B. Welsh, supervisor of nurses for the Mountain Division of the Red Cross, traveled to Salt Lake City in April 1918 in the hopes of adding to their ranks; it was estimated that 5,000 more nurses would be needed. In her appeals at the YWCA and nursing schools at Holy Cross, St. Mark's, and Latter Day Saints Hospitals, Welsh stated, "War demands something from everyone," and "those parents who give their boys gladly and willingly for their country need to give their daughters, that their sons may be rightly cared for."[103] Utah answered the call, sending one-quarter of all its nurses to serve in the war.

As young men enlisted and left for training, their minds were filled with thoughts of doing their part for freedom and serving their country; many of them never considered the realities of war or faced their own fear of dying. Their sense of duty trumped the personal sacrifices they would soon make. Miletus B. Jarman, a twenty-six-year-old high school principal from Elkton, Virginia, remarked that he "had no definite attitude toward military service in general—until U.S. entered the war. Was then eager to serve in any capacity in which Gov't. could use me. I felt that I wanted to do my own fighting—asked for assignment to infantry when called upon to express a preference."[104]

Twenty-six-year-old Culpeper, Virginia, native John W. Covington believed it was "my duty or any American to obey the call of the country regardless for what purpose. A man who cannot serve a country where he was born and raised or nationalized is not a good specimen of citizen and if he cannot fight for it he does not deserve the right to live under the protection of that flag."[105] Empey expressed the same sentiments: "The flag flying from the front of your home is your flag, our flag; our fathers shed their blood to put it there; now it is up to every man and woman of us to shed our blood, if need be, to keep it there. If you will not do this, you are not an American and America does not want you. Go over where you belong, under the German flag of murder, rapine, dishonor and treachery."[106]

Curry P. Hutchison, a twenty-three-year-old farmer from Newport, Virginia, recalled, "While in my school life I had often felt a longing for to wear my country's uniform as a soldier never dreaming that my call was to come so suddenly. I answered my call with no feeling of remorse or regret and felt thankful that God gave me power and strength to serve my country and my people in a cause as just."[107]

The vast majority of the 30,847 Connecticut, Utah, and Virginia veterans who expressed their opinions after the armistice, even those who saw heavy combat in the closing months of the war, supported the military both before they went to war and after they came home (although perhaps a little less vigorously after the fact). "I did, and do believe that every man from 18 to 40 years of age should have at least one solid year of military service, not only to prepare him for emergencies but for the personal benefits derived therefrom," recommended William P. Nye of Radford, Virginia.[108]

Proud to Volunteer

Aspirations of heroism and manhood encouraged tens of thousands of young Americans to enlist, with the applause following President Wilson's speech still echoing in their ears. Many men proudly stated that they did not wait to be drafted; they volunteered. There were draft dodgers, however, especially in larger cities like New York. These men, referred to as "slackers," either refused to register with the Selective Service System or simply did not report for duty when drafted. Also included in the slacker group were conscientious objectors who sought exemption from combat on religious grounds; many of these men accepted noncombat roles in service of their country, thus avoiding prosecution. Society regarded slackers not only as unpatriotic and unfit citizens but also as cowards. Approximately 338,000 men eluded duty in the AEF, but by mid-1919, half had been taken into custody.[109] For the most part, though, even those who were conscripted answered the call with pride. But the doughboys were not prepared for the horrors of the Western Front; despite reading about the war for three years, most of them were oblivious to the realities of the conflict.

Raleigh A. Bagley, a twenty-six-year-old unmarried physician from Norfolk, Virginia, enlisted on 6 June 1917. "I enlisted as soon as possible after the declaration of war," he noted, "and thought every man without disqualifying diseases or dependents should do likewise."[110] Twenty-year-old Fairfield H. Hodges, an assistant rate clerk from Portsmouth, Virginia, enlisted in the 1st Virginia Ambulance Company of the National Guard on 1 June 1917 and served as a sergeant with the 104th Sanitary Train, 29th Division. Hodges recalled his desire to enter military service: "When we first went in the war I tried to enlist the second day after the declaration but owing to the fact that my eyesight was poor could not get in the artillery my favorite branch of the service, but managed after much trying to enlist in the ambulance service by June 1st, 1917."[111] Channing W. Daniel, a twenty-seven-year-old teacher and salesman with a bachelor's degree from the University of Virginia, enlisted on 28 August 1917. Daniel stated that he was "satisfied to go as volunteer, glad of opportunity for a great experience, and not inclined to consider probability of death."[112]

Hugh E. Brown, a bank clerk from Norfolk, Virginia, volunteered for military service on 24 April 1917 and described his attitude: "In general, I volunteered believing every patriotic, able-bodied man should enthusiastically answer the call of his country if necessary. 1st, unmarried men under 25 years old; 2nd, unmarried men under 35 years old; 3rd, married men under 35 years old, without children; etc. I have always been opposed to a large standing army, but should have one, between 4 and 5 hundred thousand men."[113] Twenty-five-year-old contractor James F. Bonham of Sugar Grove, Virginia, enlisted in military service on 4 August 1917 and served as a private first class with the 108th Aero Squadron. Bonham remarked, "I was never CALLED and I felt it my duty to Enlist in the army and do my BIT, so I did."[114]

Chaplain Duffy recalled an incident at camp in September 1917 that illustrated the enthusiasm of the men of the Fighting 69th:

> A soldier of Company K came to my tent one afternoon last week and stood at the entrance fumbling his hat in his hand like an Irish tenant of the old days that had not the rent to pay the landlord. "What's the matter, Tom?" "I took a dhrop too much, and Captain Hurley got very mad about it and brought me up before Major Moynahan. I wouldn't mind if they'd fine me and be through with it for I know I deserve it. But the Major and the Captain say that they're not going to stand anything like this, and that they won't lave me go to the war. And sure, Father Duffy, if I couldn't go to the war it'd kill me." The smile that came to my lips at this very Irish way of putting it was suppressed when I thought of the number of men born in the country who were worried sick lest the Draft should catch them and send them to the war.[115]

The reality of war escaped these eager and duty-bound soldiers. Their conceptions were dramatically different from the actual experience; in addition, warfare had changed from the days of the Civil War and the Spanish-American War. The first American troops arrived on the Western Front in November 1917, eight months after the United States declared war. This seemed like an eternity to the impatient Allies. European armies had mobilized much quicker than the AEF had: one month after the assassination of Francis Ferdinand on 28 June 1914, Austria-Hungary had mobilized; Germany invaded Belgium on

4 August, and France clashed with Germany three days later. Although American troops did not engage in heavy combat until March 1918, the anticipation of an overwhelming US force prompted Germany to launch major offensives in the spring of 1918.

General Pershing believed the AEF could end the stalemate on the front. The infantryman, Pershing assumed, was still the backbone of an army, and the US armed forces could show their European counterparts how war was supposed to be waged. Pershing and the AEF soon learned the hard truth: America was unprepared. The trenches, modern technology, and artillery were the champions, and infantrymen alone could not win the war—a lesson the Europeans had learned after three years of brutal combat. The Allies believed it would take more than American bravado to achieve victory in Europe. Much to Europe's surprise, however, with the aid of Allied (especially French) technology, the United States rescued the Allies. Although the cost was high, the doughboys' élan saved the Allies from defeat against the Germans' spring offensives.

Americans who craved battle did not realize the power of industrialized warfare. But even with hindsight, the majority of American soldiers still supported their initial patriotic enthusiasm for the war, the draft, and enlistment after the armistice. What these men did not know was that their country had been poorly prepared to train, equip, or transport them to the front. Throughout the war, in fact, American forces depended on the Allies for almost all their artillery, machine guns, tanks, airplanes, and other supplies. American soldiers nevertheless went headlong into the trenches of Europe, their idealism buoying their spirits and inspiring them to overcome the actuality of modern war. Many doughboys acknowledged that their Judeo-Christian beliefs helped get them through their ordeal, along with a belief in their country and the support of family at home and their fellow soldiers. These vital factors enabled the men to endure with their convictions intact.

2

"Gimme da Gun"

The enduring popular image of the doughboy is that of a disillusioned, shell-shocked soldier who returned home only to find himself out of place, broken in spirit, and robbed of his manhood by the gruesome war. Nearly 100 years later, the term the *Lost Generation*, attributed to Gertrude Stein and made famous by Ernest Hemingway, continues to define the doughboy.[1] The Lost Generation myth is not exclusive to America. European countries have their own Lost Generation poets and novelists, the most famous being the British trio of Siegfried Sassoon, Robert Graves, and Edmund Blunden. The genesis of the Lost Generation movement, however, occurred in France with the publication of Henri Barbusse's *Le Feu* (Under Fire) in 1916. That novel attacks the war and everything it stands for, exemplified by one French soldier's statement: "Shame on military glory, shame on armies, shame on the soldier's profession, which changes men, some into stupid victims, others into base executioners."[2]

The interpretation of doughboys as "stupid victims" and "base executioners" is best captured by two American Lost Generation novelists who were also combat veterans: William March and Thomas Boyd. In March's book, *Company K* (1933), Private Joseph Delaney (representing March) hopes his collection of stories form "an unending circle of pain," which, for Delaney, defines the war.[3] The stories in *Company K* depict a war of infinite horror, crime, and barbarity, typified by a vignette on the "Unknown Soldier." In this tale, an unidentified doughboy, gored and entwined by barbed wire in No-Man's-Land, disposes of every item he has that might identify him, thus ensuring his anonymity so that he will not be honored for what he believes is a meaningless sacrifice. With his dying breath he whispers, "I have broken the chain . . . I have defeated the inherent stupidity of life."[4] Ironically, in reality, America honored the Unknown Soldier with his own tomb at Arlington National Cemetery on 11 November 1921.

Ten years before March's novel, former marine and combat veteran Thomas Boyd published *Through the Wheat* (1923), which depicts war as something that wears a man down until he is just an empty shell. The book's protagonist, William Hicks (representing Boyd), becomes less and less human as the novel progresses and he turns to alcohol to escape reality. What eventually breaks Hicks, however, is the death of a fellow doughboy who is killed by a tree branch while resting. To Hicks, "it seemed the height of cruelty . . . an act of vengeance, and he believed it to be the vengeance of an angry God." The event turns Hicks into a mindless automaton, and in the end, "the soul of Hicks was numb."[5]

The themes examined by March and Boyd—brutality, futility, emptiness— were also prevalent among the most famous American Lost Generation novelists: John Dos Passos, E. E. Cummings, F. Scott Fitzgerald, William Faulkner, and Ernest Hemingway. None of these five men experienced actual combat (unlike March and Boyd), yet their works played a major role in sculpting society's understanding of the doughboy.[6] As Keith Gandal concludes, these writers "were geniuses of self-styling and self-promotion, and they also got unusually lucky in their project of self-definition."[7]

Harvard University graduate John Dos Passos drove ambulances with the American Volunteer Motor Ambulance Corps (Norton-Harjes Ambulance Corps) and the Red Cross in 1917 and 1918 but was forced to resign owing to the defeatist tone of his letters about the war. Dos Passos had reenlisted with the Army Medical Corps in October 1918 and was on his way across the Atlantic when the war ended the following month. In Dos Passos's *One Man's Initiation: 1917* (1920) and *Three Soldiers* (1921), the forces of industry and the army—a monstrous machine—strip man of his humanity. In *Three Soldiers*, a trio of doughboys—Dan Fuselli, Chris Chrisfield, and John Andrews (representing Dos Passos)—are crushed by the machine by the end of the novel, in particular the sensitive, cultured Andrews.

Like Dos Passos, E. E. Cummings was a Harvard graduate and drove an ambulance in the American Volunteer Motor Ambulance Corps. Cummings, however, was actually sent to La Ferté-Macé prison for the defeatist letters he wrote to his friend William Slater Brown. After he was released, Cummings arrived back in America on 1 January 1918 and was drafted a few months later. However, he remained at Camp Devens in Ayer, Massachusetts, until his discharge on 18 January 1919. Cummings's autobiographical novel *The Enormous Room* (1922) is a mocking depiction of war and its futility.

F. Scott Fitzgerald dropped out of Princeton University and enlisted in the army, becoming a second lieutenant. While stationed at Camp Sheridan in Montgomery, Alabama, he began to write his first novel, and he was never sent overseas. The protagonists of Fitzgerald's most famous book, *The Great Gatsby* (1925), are two veteran doughboys: Jay Gatsby and Nick Carraway. The former, a decorated combat veteran, has made his fortune in bootlegging and other corrupt businesses, driven by his attraction to high society and an obsession with the enchanting Daisy Buchanan, whose voice, Gatsby confesses "is full of money."[8] In the end, Carraway becomes disillusioned, and Gatsby's fixation with Daisy leads to his death.

William Faulkner's great-grandfather, Colonel William C. Falkner, lived a storied life and served in both the Mexican-American War (1846–1848) and the Civil War. In addition, Colonel Falkner founded a railroad company and wrote *The White Rose of Memphis* in 1880, which became a best seller. Haunted by the shadow of his great-grandfather, Faulkner attempted to join the US Army Air Corps but was rejected. He eventually joined the Canadian air force, but the war ended while he was still in training. Faulkner then concocted a phony war record, purchased medals, and walked with a manufactured limp. His novel *Soldiers' Pay* (1926) chronicles the return of a crippled, shattered veteran named Donald Mahan (representing a fantasied Faulkner).[9]

Like Dos Passos and Cummings, Ernest Hemingway also served in an ambulance unit. He was wounded by mortar fire while delivering chocolate and cigarettes to Italian soldiers on the Italian front. Two of the author's most famous protagonists, Jake Barnes and Frederick Henry, represent Hemingway's bitterness and disillusionment. In *The Sun Also Rises* (1926), Jake Barnes has been destroyed by the war, both physically and emotionally. It has robbed him of his manhood, making him incapable of consummating his relationship with Brett Ashley. In *A Farewell to Arms* (1929), Frederick Henry is wounded and his friend Passini is killed by mortar fire while the two of them relax, eating cold macaroni (spaghetti). This pivotal scene parallels the one in which a tree branch kills Hicks's fellow doughboy in *Through the Wheat*. For Hemingway and Boyd (and the entire Lost Generation), modern war is senseless; it brings anonymous, random death, and the soldier has no chance to perform heroic deeds. After Passini's death, Henry muses, "I was always embarrassed by the words sacred, glorious, and sacrifice . . . and I had seen nothing sacred, and the things that were glorious had no glory and the sacrifices were like the stockyards at Chicago if nothing was done with the meat except to bury it." He continues, "Abstract words such as glory, honor, courage, or hallow were obscene beside the concrete names of villages, the numbers of roads, the names of rivers, the numbers of regiments and the dates."[10]

Some contemporary literary critics voiced their disapproval of the Lost Generation novels. Heywood Broun disagreed with the writers who railed against the armed forces in their narratives and created characters who had been dehumanized by the military machine. According to Broun, army life "actually did nothing of the sort to huge numbers of men . . . the most terrific adventure the world had ever known lifted its hordes into the air and when it set them down again vast numbers had not been changed spiritually by so much as a single hair." Clennell Wilkinson agreed with Broun and asserted that the disillusionment novelist was an "amateur soldier" who "thought it wrong to say a word that might seem to be in favour of war. He therefore shut his eyes to half the facts—the comradeship, the self-sacrifice."[11]

Montgomery Belgion terms the Lost Generation writers the "School of Despair" and reminds readers that in war "men are enriched by what they undergo, made more human, not more mechanical." Belgion concludes that novelists such as Dos Passos and Hemingway are "untypical as soldiers."[12] In a review of Dos Passos's *Three Soldiers*, Coningsby Dawson, a World War I combat veteran and novelist, concludes:

> I remember a discussion which I had with a Russian who had served in the French Foreign Legion, as to what the individual man who had been part of the war had got out of it. On the one hand, you had Barbusse declaring that all the war did to a man was to deprave him. On the other hand, you had Alan Seeger and a throng of idealists of all nations declaring that they had found the purpose of their lives in the sacrifice. What was the explanation of these irreconcilable points of view? My Russian gave an answer that was very true. "Men get out of the war," he said, "what they brought to it. The hero found heroism; the coward found cowardice. Except in rare instances the war did not recreate men; it only made emphatic in them tendencies that had been latent. Now that the war's ended, bad men are a little worse for their experience; honorable men are a little more good."
>
> The men depicted in "Three Soldiers" got out of the war what they brought to it—low ideals and bitterness. . . . The voice of righteousness is never once sounded; the only voice heard is the voice of complaint and petty recrimination.[13]

The loudest and most interesting declarations rose above and silenced the true tales of duty, courage, and survival. The literature of the Lost Generation does not answer why the doughboys fought or how their experiences affected them. To understand the doughboy, like any soldier, one must examine the individual. The prewar life experience and personality of a soldier dictate how that soldier will react to battle. Individual predispositions shape a soldier's experience. When gathered en masse, these individual voices become a collective narrative of warrior motivation and reaction to war. What factors shaped the AEF soldier? To start, each man's experience depended on his ethnic, religious, and educational background.

The doughboys, united in purpose, formed a diverse group in other ways.

Most were young, some barely eighteen years old when they enlisted or were drafted into service, but older soldiers served as well. The majority were US citizens, but large numbers were foreign-born from Russia, Italy, Greece, and other European countries.[14] Their occupations included farmers, lawyers, sales clerks, college professors, and bartenders. They identified themselves as Roman Catholics, Jews, Baptists, or Mormons or with no religious affiliation at all. Leaving their civilian lives and families behind, the doughboys served what they believed to be a worthy cause. The Lost Generation novelists fictionalized the experiences of the doughboys. The voices of the actual soldiers need to be heard. Their words, thoughts, and opinions—often written with intense emotion—convey what the front was like, what it meant to serve in the AEF, and, most important, what stirred their spirits.

"We Want Men, Men, Men"

Future historian William L. Langer, a young volunteer soldier in 1917, was eager to join the fight at the front: "We and many thousands of others volunteered. . . . We men, most of us young, were simply fascinated by the prospect of adventure and heroism. Most of us, I think, had the feeling that life, if we survived, would run in the familiar, routine channel. Here was our one great chance for excitement and risk. We could not afford to pass it up."[15] Langer's words explain the motivation of many men who enlisted for military duty during the war, including Douglas B. Green, a 1904 graduate of Yale University. "There isn't anything that I would rather do than go over and fight the Germans," he wrote to his sister. "So whatever you may think about it, just remember that I'm doing what I want to do, and something that I wouldn't give up my chance of doing for all the rest of my natural life."[16] Major General J. Franklin Bell, first commander of the 77th Division at Camp Upton, Long Island, New York, spoke for many officers and enlisted men in August 1917 when he declared, "I would rather die at the front than spend the rest of my life explaining why I was not there."[17]

Even before men like Langer enlisted, some Americans served in France as volunteers with the Allies, and their dedication influenced others. William Y. Stevenson of Philadelphia was with Section No. 1 of the American Ambulance Field Service volunteers, serving with the French army, before the United States declared war. Stevenson remarked, "The Ambulance men, who had volunteered long before the United States had entered the war, were each and every one a small but vital factor in bringing America in. Every time a man volunteered, he carried with him the hopes and sympathies of all his relatives and friends; and as the Ambulance grew, so did the pro-Ally sentiment grow by leaps and bounds in the United States."[18]

This sympathy for the Allies, coupled with Americans' preconceived romantic attitudes about combat, inspired thousands to enlist. Unlike the European belligerents, Americans had already had a taste of the war through newspaper headlines and photographs. But rather than taking these words and pictures as warnings, the doughboys saw mainly adventure and were ready to go as soon as America declared war. Thanks to the new rotogravure printing process, the *New York Times* carried a twelve-page pictorial section every Sunday, with several pages usually devoted to war images. These photographs demonstrated the destructive power of modern combat and the ruthless conditions it imposed: the ruins of the Belgian city Louvain (Leuven), annihilated by artillery, and Polish soldiers crawling through muddy rifle pits on the Eastern Front.[19] But due to the heroic legacy of warfare, young men overlooked these images and focused on others that depicted more grandiose scenes, such as the one captioned: "Australian soldiers, sent to protect Egypt against the Turks, in camp at the foot of the pyramids."[20] Before the US declaration of war, the pictorial captions and journalistic reports published by the *New York Times* and other newspapers had been relatively unbiased. Afterward, pictures of Germans, Turks, and Austro-Hungarian forces—in fact, all combat-oriented photographs—became rare, replaced with scenes of President Wilson, doughboys in training, and patriotic parades.

The hot-blooded doughboys and the United States in general were not prepared for war: the Regular Army consisted of 127,588 officers and men, while the National Guard totaled 80,446 officers and men.[21] These low numbers necessitated a national draft, although many men volunteered rather than waiting for their draft numbers to be called. One such individual was Daniel R. Edwards, a rancher from Taylor County, Texas, who recounted his enlistment day: "When the U.S. entered the World War I knew I would be called from reserve. But without waiting I reenlisted—in fact, I joined up that same day, April 6, 1917." Edwards's enthusiasm was contagious:

> All of the men at the ranch wanted to go along with me. Half of them barely knew where the war was and didn't give a damn. A few couldn't possibly get into the service, on account of bad teeth, age, and other disabilities. So I persuaded these chaps to stay on the ranch and look after it. The rest of us saddled up and beat it for the railroad, thirty-five miles away, whooping it up as we went. We caught the train to Waco, and soon as we got there all of us, thirty-two strong, trotted right up to the recruiting office and took the oath. That was sure one happy crowd.[22]

Nineteen-year-old Harvey G. Callahan, born in Brooklyn, New York, enlisted in the army on 31 October 1914. He "favored an early American participation in the War, and was of the opinion that the draft was a necessary measure after the declaration of hostilities." He added, "My own case was voluntary."[23] When America entered the war, the Allies made it clear that they needed AEF soldiers to fight with the British and French. During a visit to the United States in April 1917, former French commander in chief Joseph Joffre had expressed his country's needs with this famous line: "We want men, men, men." To meet the demand for troops, President Wilson elected to use conscription rather than rely on volunteerism—a decision influenced by events in Great Britain at the start of the war. At first, Britain had depended on a volunteer army, but heavy casualties depleted the number of troops. In addition, volunteerism had taken many skilled workers away from important jobs in war-related industries. Wilson did not want this to happen in the United States. The president recommended draft legislation to increase the size of the new National Army, from which 77 percent of wartime servicemen would come.[24] Despite a few obstacles, such as Theodore Roosevelt's proposal to command a volunteer force in France, Congress passed a draft bill, and the president signed it on 18 May 1917.

Congress designated 5 June 1917 as draft registration day across the country, and more than 9.5 million men aged twenty-one to thirty registered for the selective service process. On 20 July 1917, a blindfolded Newton D. Baker, Wilson's secretary of war, began the selection process by drawing the first number: 258. Each man who held number 258 was required to report for military service.[25] Two additional draft registration dates were set during the war, necessitated by Russia's withdrawal, large British losses, and the low morale of French troops. On 5 June 1918, men who had attained age twenty-one after June 1917 were required to register. Three months later, on 12 September 1918, men aged eighteen to forty-five signed up for the selective service process. In total, during the three stages of the draft, the Selective Service System (SSS) inducted 2,810,296 men out of the 24,234,021 who had registered with the 4,650 local draft boards across the country.[26] The draft succeeded in dramatically increasing the size of US military forces.

The National Guard from each state served as the backbone of the American army until the massive wave of enlistees and volunteers bolstered its combat strength. In Connecticut, the National Guard could trace its origins to the days of the colonial militia, organized to "beare armes" and protect the settlers from hostile Native Americans. In 1636 all men aged sixteen or older were trained under the direction of Captain Mason, the public military officer; the militia met once a month for instruction and practice, and it gathered for ten days once a year. The 1st Connecticut Infantry, which became part of the 102nd Infantry, was organized in 1689.[27] Connecticut governor Marcus H. Holcomb acknowledged this history when he addressed the state legislature in 1917: "Such has been the steadfast spirit of the sons of Connecticut in every hour of peril. Marching in company with the heroic past let us in this untoward hour of world agony, face unflinchingly the menacing tide of events."[28] In times of danger and need, the Connecticut militia had always responded, lending aid to surrounding settlements and, after 1783, to nearby states. So when the call from President Wilson came, the Connecticut National Guard answered, and the 102nd Regiment prepared for war. The tradition of serving in the National Guard gave the doughboys a community spirit as they combined forces with the Regular Army and formed the 26th (Yankee) Division, which drew soldiers from all the New England states.

Like Connecticut and other states across the nation, Utah's National Guard responded to the call to arms. At the behest of the federal government, Governor Simon Bamberger called for more National Guard volunteers in March 1917, in preparation for US entry into the war. Parades and military demonstrations inspired many to volunteer. While training at Camp Kearney, California, the 42nd, 43rd, and 20th Infantry Regiments joined with National Guard units from California, Nevada, Arizona, and Colorado to form the 40th Division. The 40th became known as the Sunshine Division because its insignia was a gold sunburst displayed on a blue background, symbolizing the sunny weather in the western states. In December 1917 Major General Frederick S. Strong of the Regular Army became commander of the 40th Division, serving until the armistice.[29]

Melting-Pot Doughboys

While the National Guardsmen formed bonds within the Regular Army, the new divisions of the National Army, made up of drafted and enlisted men, were strengthened by the links between their foreign-born members. These new divisions contained a diverse array of nationalities, especially from the multiethnic Northeast and Great Lakes regions; the parents of many soldiers had been born in Greece, Russia, Sweden, and Italy, to name but a few countries. Some of the men were foreign-born themselves but viewed America as their home and were willing to fight and die for their new country. One such immigrant was Tony Monanco, "a diminutive Italian" who appeared at the Selective Service Office in Buffalo, New York, one morning. When a clerk at the desk asked him, "What can I do for you?" he responded, "Ma name Tony Monanco. In dees countra seex months. Gimme da gun."[30]

In addition to the foreign-born volunteers, nearly one-fifth of America's inductees were aliens; they spoke forty-nine different languages, and 31 percent were illiterate.[31] Of the 487,434 alien draftees, 200,000 waived their exception status so they could join the AEF, even though they had not yet declared their desire to become American citizens. Due to the war, the government streamlined the naturalization process, and approximately 280,000 immigrants became US citizens and served in the armed forces.[32] After the United States declared war, foreign-born men were anxious to serve, especially, it seemed, the Poles.

At the time, Poles made up only 4 percent of the US population, yet 40 percent of the first 100,000 volunteers were Polish.[33] Since so many alien recruits were non-English speakers, morale among the foreign-born at training camps was low because they could neither understand their noncommissioned officers (NCOs) nor explain any problems to their commanders. To address this situation, the army established the Foreign-Speaking Soldier Subsection, which placed aliens in appropriate battalions and provided them with intensive English instruction, as well as courses in US history, civics, and patriotism.[34]

General William "Billy" Mitchell remarked, "It seemed strange how many Germans we had who distinguished themselves in our service, and what efficient officers and patriotic Americans they were." In particular, Mitchell remembered General J. T. Dickman, who spoke fluent German.[35] Twenty-four-year-old railroad worker Joseph R. Cooke of Atlanta, Georgia, joined the military on 11 May 1917 and praised the foreign-born soldiers of the AEF: "The so called 'foreign element,' when properly 'educated' (trained) will not only respond to the country's call, but will equal the best of our fighters. (Particularly, Italians and Greeks)."[36] From Norfolk, Virginia, Captain James W. Anderson (whose father had been born in Scotland) also expressed his admiration for the foreign-born soldiers fighting with the AEF: "The foreign-born Americans obeyed orders better and were less complaining than the native-born Americans."[37]

Many veterans from Connecticut, especially Italian Americans, had difficulty responding to their 1919 questionnaires due to the language barrier. Private Nicola Andreozzi, a twenty-six-year-old baker from New Haven, wrote his in Italian:

> I am very ashamed to have to ask someone to write this for me in English. For this reason I will write in Italian, but I promise that very soon I will learn to write in English. Now I will hurry to explain what I understood in the questionnaire, but I was not able to reply because I cannot write in English. Well, I joined military service with all my heart. In fact I was so eager to join that originally I volunteered, but my wife reported me. I therefore had to wait to be drafted. I was so eager to serve that I falsely declared that I had no one to support, when in reality I had a mother, wife, and sister. I was in one of the first training classes, and thirty days later I was on my way to France. When I reached the front, I was scared and had never seen such a terrible disaster. But, once I convinced myself we were fighting for liberty, nothing scared me anymore, not even the Devil, or death. I was always ready to fight the coward enemy. I am very proud I did my duty, and I learned and gained respect. May God bless our Flag and our Land of Liberty. Forgive me if I made a few mistakes. Thank you, Soldier Andreozzi.[38]

Twenty-six-year-old baker Nicola Andreozzi from New Haven, Connecticut, in France, 1918. (Box 29, Connecticut State Library)

Tennessee native Alvin C. York of the 82nd Division related his experiences with an ethnically and culturally diverse unit:

> The Eighty-second Division was known as the All-American Division. . . .
> We were made up of boys from 'most every state in the Union. . . . There
> were Jews from the East Side of New York; there were English and Irish
> boys from the mill towns of New England; there were Greeks and
> Italians from some of the big cities in the East; there were Poles and Slavs
> from the coal mines of Pennsylvania . . . and there were even some

German boys. . . . A right-smart number of them couldn't speak or understand the American language.[39]

York had more to say about the men he fought with:

> My own platoon was made up of a gang of the toughest and most hard-boiled doughboys I ever heard tell of. There were bartenders, saloon bouncers, ice men, coal miners, dirt farmers, actors, mill hands, and city boys who had growed up in the back alleys and learned to scrap ever since they were knee high to a duck. They were mixed up from 'most every country. . . . They could out-swear, out-drink, and out-cuss any crowd of men I have ever knowed. . . . They were fighters and that's all about it. . . . A heap of them couldn't talk our own language at all, and any number of them couldn't sign their own names.[40]

Lieutenant Colonel Frederick M. Wise, 5th Marines, 2nd Division, also commented on the diversity of the men in his command:

> That regiment was an amazing jumble of races and classes. My personal orderly was a French Canadian who had been a cornet player in the orchestra at Keith's in Boston. My horse orderly was a cow-puncher from somewhere near Cody, Wyoming. My cook, George the Greek, who had ruined my birthday pâté, came from a short order restaurant of which he was the proprietor, in Denver. My sergeant major had been a court stenographer in Rochester, New York. My chauffeur was a mechanic from the Packard factory in Detroit. Another orderly was a farm boy from Iowa. He was only five feet tall, had tried to volunteer, had been turned down on account of his short stature—and then had been drafted![41]

Almost 500,000 immigrant doughboys from forty-six countries—constituting more than 18 percent of the AEF's total strength—charged forward with their American-born compatriots.[42] Whether Russian Jew, Italian Roman Catholic, African American Baptist, or fourth-generation northeasterner, each man believed he would earn his honor on the Western Front.

Domestic Doughboys

US-born doughboys were equally diverse. They were farmers, store clerks, sales clerks, machinists, bank clerks, laborers, cigar makers, letter carriers, attorneys, college professors, and self-employed workers. Many attended churches in a variety of Christian faiths, others were Jewish, and several listed no religion at all on their war records. Some, such as Alvin C. York, considered declaring themselves conscientious objectors to the war as a matter of personal and religious belief. In March 1918, five weeks before he was scheduled to set sail for France, York went home on leave to Pall Mall, Tennessee. During that time, he reflected on a nearby mountainside and penned in his diary: "I knelt down and I prayed and I prayed all the afternoon, through the night and through part of the next day. . . . I didn't want to be a fighter or a killin' man. . . . And yet I wanted to do what my country wanted me to do. I wanted to serve God and my country, too. . . . I begun to understand that no matter what a man is forced to do, so long as he is right in his own soul he remains a righteous man."[43]

Mormons accounted for 75 percent of one Utah regiment—the 145th Field Artillery, 64th Artillery Brigade, 40th Division. The 145th achieved an outstanding performance record, boasting the best health and fewest deserters, as well as skillful and accurate shooting and solid moral habits. While in training, Mormon recruits—strict in their obedience to authority, cleanliness, and reluctance to patronize prostitutes—inspired a major at Camp Lewis to comment: "I wish that all the boys were Mormons, as they are the boys looked to for good, clean moral bodies, and they are the ones that are capable of doing things efficiently."[44]

In age, the doughboys ranged from eighteen to their mid-forties, although most were in their early twenties and unmarried. They were young men who hungered for excitement and believed that serving their country would fulfill their desire for adventure and their quest for manhood. Twenty-seven-year-old Arlie I. Day of Linville Depot, Virginia, entered the Regular Army on 24 October 1917. Employed as a general laborer, Day "could not wait until I got over there to kill every Durn Hun that was in Germany."[45] Private Moses Randolph of the 369th Infantry, a nineteen-year-old African American from Farmville, Virginia, entered the army on 27 October 1917. Randolph, a section hand for the Norfolk and Western Railroad with seven or eight years of education, explained, "Did not mind going except that it left my aged mother alone."[46] Wylie R. Cooke, a wholesale lumber secretary from Norfolk, Virginia, entered the service on 25 August 1917 at age twenty-seven. Cooke held a bachelor's degree from the University of Virginia and stated, "Got no use for military service in any form but it is only way know of to fight a war. Went into this fight because wanted to help clean up the hun, and see a little excitement at the same time."[47]

Men who were older than the recommended age for soldiers enlisted too. "On account of being 43 years old, I had to get a special dispensation from the War Department to re-enlist," reported Corporal Robert W. Marshall of New Haven, Connecticut.[48] Private Zoil A. Beaudoin was "glad to fight for U.S. and enlisted at age of 38 years." Beaudoin spoke French and served as an interpreter for American officers in France.[49] Alden Bell, a fifty-three-year-old veteran of the Spanish-American War, was a lawyer and judge in Culpeper, Virginia, when he volunteered for service. Bell declared, "I thought when I volunteered that all male citizens should stand in the ranks of one's country, and bear his bosom to the front in its defense." Despite his age and poor eyesight, Bell persisted and entered the service on 16 November 1917, proudly stating, "I am the third case on record, on file at the War Dept. at Wash. D.C. where the War Dept. has removed both the age limit and defective vision for volunteering in the 'world's war.'"[50]

Physically, the average recruit was five feet nine inches tall and weighed 141.5 pounds; he wore a size 7 hat and a size 9C shoe, had a chest measurement of thirty-seven inches, a waist measurement of thirty-four inches, and a collar size of fifteen and a half inches.[51] But like Bell, some men attempted to enlist despite physical disabilities. James J. Marooney, a sergeant in the infantry from New Haven, Connecticut, stressed, "Had five rejection slips, including two from Plattsburg for physical disability before being accepted for the National Army." Sergeant Marooney went on to say that his "physical condition improved under training."[52] Twenty-three-year-old Bridgeport, Connecticut, resident Charles S. Pemburn Jr. entered the National Army on 3 October 1917 and emphasized, "Afraid the war would end before I could get in and accross. Was put on reserve from 71st Inf. on account of broken arm but took plaster caste off and got by draft board. It was easy."[53]

For some doughboys, the motivation to fight involved familial bonds. If a man enlisted or was drafted by the SSS, his brother often followed suit. This was the case with Ensworth M. Godard, age twenty-five, and his brother Jewell W. Godard, age twenty-four. Ensworth enlisted on 3 July 1917 at the State Armory in Hartford, Connecticut, and was assigned to the 102nd Regiment, 26th Division. He saw action at Chemin des Dames and the Marne and received a citation for bravery after volunteering to carry sealed messages to a battalion two miles away. He fought in the front-line trenches from 10 February to 16 March 1918 and again from 8 June to 10 July 1918. He suffered a fractured ankle and broken arches in his feet and was gassed. Ensworth returned home partially disabled and skeptical of future wars: "I am positive that the United States should avoid all entangling alliances. Washington was right."[54] His younger brother Jewell left his job as a clerk at Aetna Life Insurance Company to enlist on 23 August 1917. Jewell was assigned to the Sanitary Detachment, 101st Machine Gun Battalion, 26th Division. He first saw action in February 1918 and was later engaged in combat at Château-Thierry, Soissons, Saint-Mihiel, and Verdun. Jewell was more fortunate than his older brother and was not wounded, although he was hospitalized in France for an illness. Jewell returned to civilian life and resumed his occupation as an insurance clerk after his discharge on 29 April 1919. Like his brother, Jewell was not impressed by army life. He did, however, have high praise for Major General Clarence R. Edwards of the Yankee Division, saying, "If all the officers were like General Edwards the army would have been something to be proud of."[55]

"Go Forward! Go Forward!"

One strong influence among US-born soldiers, particularly those from the same family or the same region, was the sense of following in the path of previous soldiers, especially Civil War veterans. Albert S. Voight of Norfolk, Virginia, enlisted on 12 June 1917, one month before his twentieth birthday, and commented, "Being an American citizen, I felt it my duty to fight for my country as my mother and father brought me up in that manner from childhood."[56] Said Joseph R. Cooke of Atlanta, Georgia, "My childhood reading was of the accomplishments of my forefathers during war times and my ambition to fight for my country during a time of need was accomplished."[57]

An incident that took place on 19 September 1918 at the Court House Green in Goochland County, Virginia, illustrates that sense of duty and honor. Mrs. O. B. Taylor describes what happened as twenty-three draftees prepared to leave for Camp Lee:

> A hoary headed veteran of the War between the States, inspired by the occasion again felt the fire of youth coursing through his veins and asked for the privilege of saying a few words. Borne on the swift wings of memory, he lived for a time in the past, recalling how fifty-six years ago he with his comrades (many of whom were relatives of the drafted men) in the same place and manner answered the roll call and went forth to serve their country for a noble cause. As Goochland men had always met their duties bravely, he felt that these soon to be veterans would also acquit themselves in such manner as to bring added honor and glory to "old Goochland." In conclusion, he asked that they bear in mind the words of General Lee who said that "duty" was the most sublime word in the English language and to adopt for their watchword "Go Forward! Go Forward!"[58]

This strong feeling was not an anomaly. Reverence for the Civil War was found in every corner of the country. As Drew Gilpin Faust explains, "The war's staggering human cost demanded a new sense of national destiny, one designed to ensure that lives had been sacrificed for appropriately lofty ends."[59] By the time that war ended in 1865, it had claimed 752,000 soldiers' lives and devastated America; yet, when the doughboys remembered the fallen, saw the cemeteries, and heard the stories, they felt a responsibility to uphold that tradition. These young men sought to emulate what their relatives had done fifty years ago. The doughboys themselves were not an unusual generation; they were akin to their antebellum brethren. As Eric T. Dean Jr. stresses: "Young men were often anxious to prove themselves and feared that hostilities would end before they had a chance to participate in the glory."[60] The Civil War dead united the nation. People memorialized the war and then, as it became memory, glorified it. For some, this glorification aggrandized war fever in 1917; however, for most, the Civil War defined what must be done when the country declares war.

Common Threads

No matter their differences, the doughboys had one critical thing in common: a desire to serve their country. Regardless of his background or ethnicity, the AEF soldier was patriotic to the core. Chaplain Francis P. Duffy of the Fighting 69th declared: "I am a very Irish, very Catholic, very American person if anybody challenges my convictions. But normally, and let alone, I am just plain human. My appreciation of patriotism, or courage, or any other attractive human trait, is not limited in any degree by racial or religious or sectional prejudice. That was the spirit of our Army; may it always be the spirit of our Republic."[61]

Among the 30,847 questionnaires surveyed from Connecticut, Utah, and Virginia, the dominant theme is an undying love of country: duty and patriotism were on the minds of the soldiers who fought in Europe. "The thought of army life appealed to me as being exciting and of course a right good size spark of patriotism," declared Curtis R. Davis, a typewriter repairman from South Richmond, Virginia. Davis, who enlisted five months before his eighteenth birthday, served as a private first class with the "42nd (Rainbow) Division from the time it was mobilized at Camp Mills, New York in August 1917 until it was demobilized at Camp Merritt, New Jersey in April 1919."[62]

Upon returning home in 1919, Walter C. Sage of Hartford, Connecticut, called military service in wartime "the finest thing in the world for any young man."[63] Seward H. Strickland, also of Hartford, spoke for many when he wrote that enlistment was "the best and only way to protect and uphold our American Flag and this Christian nation."[64] Twenty-seven-year-old Nelson C. Overton, an unmarried lawyer from Newport News, Virginia, enlisted on 11 May 1917 and stated, "I chose to go before I was called. Would have been called perhaps, but did not care to wait. I was in favor of military service for every man who could lift the weight of a rifle without complete exhaustion."[65] Raymond J. Queenin of New Britain, Connecticut, was a twenty-two-year-old salesman when he enlisted in the National Guard on 25 January 1915. "I was anxious to go," he said. "Wanted to see what war was like (and did) I would have been ashamed to have been drafted. I saw the need and didn't believe in waiting for a 'personal invitation.'"[66]

Even among those who were drafted, the prevailing attitude was a determination to "do their bit." Many men who tried to enlist were rejected at first, so they waited until their draft numbers were called and then gladly went to war. Men who had no National Guard training were just as willing to fight as those with military experience. Joseph R. Schadel of Hartford was twenty-two years old when he was inducted on 28 March 1918. A clerk at the First National Bank, Private Schadel stated, "I felt that if my country was in need of military support I should respond as soon as I possibly could."[67]

Albert M. Simons, a Hartford city assessor whose parents had been born in Austria, had a definite viewpoint on joining the army. Thirty-six years old, married, and the father of two children, Simons volunteered a month after the United States entered the war because he was "convinced that the United States is the best country in the world."[68] A candidate for a commission because he had served in the Connecticut National Guard, Simons became a second lieutenant and later a first lieutenant during his service in France.

The doughboys of Connecticut, Utah, and Virginia were anxious to defend democracy. In fact, on page two of the 1919 Military Service Record, where it reads "Inducted into service or enlisted on . . . ," many men crossed out the first four words, leaving only "enlisted on," and then wrote in their enlistment dates. Private First Class Alexander J. Flynn, who had enlisted in the Connecticut National Guard on 22 June 1916, wrote that he volunteered "as a duty to my country."[69] A New Haven native, Flynn left his job as a clerk for the New York, New Haven, and Hartford Railroad Company and joined the army just before his twenty-second birthday.

Private Frederick J. Burke, also of New Haven, volunteered because "I felt like doing my duty toward my country and took a chance and enlisted for the duration of the war and am alive to tell the tale."[70] Another New Haven soldier, Arthur L. Cartier, served in the infantry as a second lieutenant; he described military service as "a debt I owed the country I make my living in and was born in."[71] Just twenty-one years old, John M. Jacobs of Morrison, Virginia, son of an Irish immigrant, enlisted in the infantry on 26 September 1917 and called it "a sacrifice." But, Jacobs added, "Please note: I enlisted from a sense of duty, not because I would have been drafted or because the Army had any attraction for me."[72]

Sergeant Joseph Cosenzo, 102nd Machine Gun Company, enlisted with great enthusiasm: "I always loved the army and when my call came I was almost first to be at the Armory. Will go again if U.S. should ever be in danger of another war." Cosenzo, who saw combat, said he wanted to "get over there as soon as possible to prevent them from coming over here."[73] "Each man who was called owed to his country and his honor to respond. I was, and am glad that I was physically able to take my place so that no other fellow would have to take it," explained John D. Kinzer, a twenty-three-year-old farmer from Bedford, Virginia, who entered the service on 10 May 1918.[74] Thirty-year-old cigar salesman Dale M. Hoyt of Salt Lake City, Utah, volunteered for the army on 26 July 1918 and served with the 317th Reserve Tank Corps. He trained briefly at Camp Colt in Gettysburg, Pennsylvania, and embarked for France on 23 September 1918. On his return to Utah, Hoyt remarked, "These were the happiest days of my life."[75]

On 17 November 1917, one month before his twentieth birthday, Edward H. Roesch of Salt Lake City volunteered for the army and was assigned to Supply Company, 18th Field Artillery, 3rd Division. A pipe fitter by trade, Roesch trained at Fort Logan, Colorado; at Fort Bliss, Texas; and briefly at Camp Merritt, New Jersey, before leaving for France on 23 April 1918. Roesch served as a private and then a wagoner; he saw action in the Battles of Metz, Saint-Mihiel, and the Marne and served for six weeks in the Argonne Forest. In letters home to his parents, Louis and Etta Roesch, he professed, "I would not take a million dollars for my experiences and I am proud of the record of my division. . . . I never will regret that I volunteered, and smiled all through the war. . . . I am one of the luckey ones because I had a chance to fight for my country, and my Flag. So smile, smile, for me, as I am smiling for you."[76]

"I entered the military service solely from a sense of duty to my country without any thought or hope of personal aggrandizement or gain. Neither the spirit of adventure nor the love of the military lured me," explained Thomas B. Taliaferro of Caret, Virginia.[77] A twenty-four-year-old graduate student with a bachelor's degree from the University of Richmond, Taliaferro entered the service on 13 May 1917 and attended the Reserve Officers' Training Camp, emerging as a first lieutenant.

"I thought every male person physically fit, should serve his country in time of war," observed Hartford native and artillery sergeant Raymond E. Landmesser.[78] Likewise, machine gun sergeant Byron P. Graff of Hartford was a "firm believer in universal training" and "simply did what I thought every American would do—enlist when the Country asked for men."[79] Twenty-eight-year-old Thomas N. Williams, a clerk from Berryville, Virginia, entered the service on 14 May 1917 and received a commission as a second lieutenant in the infantry on 15 August 1917. Williams responded, "I believe that military service will prove a great benefit to all who served. I took it as a matter of fact that as the country was at war I must go."[80]

"Military Service, I think every young man should have some experience about it. I believe that I was doing right when I answered the call at once," observed Harry E. Curry, an African American student from Hampton, Virginia.[81] Curry, who had joined the National Guard on 23 May 1915, four months prior to his sixteenth birthday, was one of about 5,000 African Americans serving in the National Guard at the time of the First World War.[82] The United States created two African American divisions: the 92nd (the Buffalo Soldiers) and the 93rd (the Blue Helmets). The four regiments of the 93rd Division (369th, 370th,

371st, and 372nd) all fought with the French. In total, 380,000 African American men served (10,000 from the Regular Army and 370,000 draftees), and the AEF deployed 200,000 African Americans to France, 40,000 of whom participated in combat. Although black divisions in World War I were usually commanded by white officers, the 93rd began with five black officers. The army had established Fort Des Moines in Iowa to train black officers, and the AEF sent black officers overseas with the 92nd and 93rd Divisions.[83]

"I saw that the United States would need men, after she broke Diplomatic Relations with Germany, so I enlisted before she called. Otherwise I should have considered myself a slacker,"[84] declared Clifford R. Haskins, who served with the 26th Division. Whether young or older, educated or uneducated, married or single, the men who answered the call to duty and served in the AEF were willing and anxious to do so. For many, combat changed their perspective; others remained just as determined and patriotic upon their return from the war. Hugh H. Bishop of Marion, Ohio, a silk weaver with an eighth-grade education, enlisted in the Coast Artillery Corps on 13 February 1917 at age eighteen and recounted his feelings about his service: "As far as my attitude was toward military service, it is all right for a young person to enlist in it, but if I had to go over the same experiences again I would try my best to get out of it."[85] Perhaps his combat experiences had prematurely aged Bishop, who would have been only twenty-two at the time of his statement.

Others expressed no regrets. "I always cared for military service and was more than glad to have been able to answer my call," offered Willis B. Godwin, an African American student from Smithfield, Virginia, who entered the service on 28 October 1917 at age twenty-two.[86] Infantry Sergeant First Class George L. Ayotte of Waterbury, Connecticut, said, "When President Wilson called for volunteers I felt it my duty as an American citizen and a soldier to enlist at once."[87]

"I was quite pleased when I was called in '17 it meant business. . . . I was very anxious to get in to action," explained Private Nelson F. Waters, 2nd Connecticut Infantry, National Guard. Waters, who was barely eighteen years old when he started his training, had been employed as a salesman at the New Haven Shoe Company. Wounded in his arm, hand, and leg at Seicheprey on 20 April 1918, Waters became a prisoner of war and was not released until 9 December 1918. While imprisoned in Germany, Waters contracted typhoid fever in May and influenza in November. In spite of all he endured, Waters maintained his spirit, saying, "I believed in the War before I fought and much more after."[88]

Not every man entered the military eagerly or with noble motives, however. New Haven native Louis J. Popolizio, who served as a corporal in the 102nd Infantry, remarked, "When America entered the war I knew if I didn't go they would get me so I enlisted right away. May 8, 1917. With my whole heart and soul. And I was going to travel the world at the government's expense."[89] Travel he did—all the way to the front lines in France. Drafted at age twenty-three, Hezekiah E. Lofland of Melfa, Virginia, an African American farmer with a grade-school education, felt a "fear of not returning home again. It seemed too much to be drafted for another Country."[90] Not every man liked the military or felt compelled to serve, but the majority did.

"It Costs to Be Patriotic"

Patriotism came at a great cost for many. That was true for Utahan Albert W. Stone, whose writings stressed the sacrifices made for the war. Stone, from Ogden, was inducted into the army on 28 August 1918 and served in the infantry until his discharge on 9 April 1919. In the following poem, titled "His Bit," Stone includes motifs from the Four Minute Men's poem "It's Duty Boy," but rather than praising the act of duty, Stone echoes Wilfred Owen's famous "Dulce et Decorum est":[91]

> "It Costs to be patriotic."
> The aged man swayed on his feet
> As he pleaded for funds to battle the Huns
> From the throngs as they passed on the street.
> "It costs to be patriotic
> When we're fighting on land and on sea;
> Nor can the expense in dollars and cents
> Be reckoned by you or me."
> "How much are *you* giving?" a stranger
> Sardonically voiced a demand.
> "The city's drained dry from this ev'ry-day cry
> For our coin—say, where do *you* stand?"
> "Why, I've done my bit," said the ancient,
> "Or we've done it—mother and I,
> Don't you think that a man's doing all that he can
> When he gives up his son—to die?"[92]

Numerous young men sailed off to Europe with old-fashioned ideas about war, and the soldiers of the AEF were no exception. Like the majority of young men in Europe who celebrated their countries' declarations of war in 1914, the Americans did the same in 1917. But the enthusiasm of both groups would be tested when they witnessed the true nature of modern combat.

As a whole, the men of the AEF, whether they belonged to the Regular Army, enlisted voluntarily, or waited to be drafted, were ready to serve the United

States and fulfill their duty. Some soldiers were anxious to enter the fray; a few were less enthusiastic. As they prepared to depart for Europe, the doughboys reported to various training camps around the country, where their romantic notions of warfare continued. As James E. Chenault of Richmond, Virginia, declared, "Intensive training meant nothing me as I was to anxious to get a crack at those tretcherious Huns!"[93] The doughboys wanted the army to "gimme da gun," but the army had few guns to give.

3

Wooden Weapons

For many of the doughboys, life in an army camp was a new experience. Only those with National Guard or comparable military service knew what to expect when they arrived at training camp. The army had established thirty-two such camps, located predominantly in the eastern and southern states, each named after a famous American commander; additional camps were set up for officers, marines, and aviators.[1] The majority of New Englanders received their training at Camp Devens in Ayer, Massachusetts, while most officers trained in Plattsburgh, New York. Almost all Virginians trained at Camp Lee in Petersburg, Virginia. Several states had additional smaller camps for specific troops, such as engineers or aviators; for example, some Connecticut soldiers went to Camp Greene in North Carolina, and others went to Camp Bowie in Fort Worth, Texas. Connecticut also had Camp Yale (or Yale Field) in New Haven and a training camp in Niantic. In Utah, most recruits were sent to Camp Lewis, located on American Lake in Washington; others trained at Camp Kearney, near San Diego, California.

Training the Troops

The typical new American soldier was white and in his early twenties, had a minimal education and no military experience, but was ready to do his bit for the United States. For the most part, these men were factory workers, laborers, and farmers. Students and professional men, quickly trained as officers, were often as ill prepared as the troops they were supposed to command.

Although the army intended the training camps to prepare the doughboys for combat, they lacked equipment and adequate supplies. Many of the doughboys sent overseas had never even handled a rifle because the camps did not have enough real weapons; instead, the army provided wooden rifles and artillery replicas for training, and some men drilled with wooden sticks. Men of the 82nd Division dubbed their wooden rifles the "Camp Gordon 1917 Model Rifle."[2] Although most camps provided training in going over the top of trenches, grenade throwing, and bayonet practice, many soldiers did not experience live-fire exercises. "As regards preparation for meeting the enemy, I consider the training at Camp McClellan below par. We were only trained in discipline and in Civil War tactics. Very few of our men saw an automatic rifle, live grenade or had any idea of formations for a modern attack," emphasized Captain Charles T. Holtzman Jr. of the 29th Division.[3] A resident of Huntington, West Virginia, Holtzman was twenty-four years old when he began his training in Alabama. Lieutenant Joe Roddy described his unit's training: "Our trench mortar battery was organized at Camp Jackson where we did practically all of our training with wooden sticks. It was not until the last of our training that we got a chance to use the guns themselves which we fired once or twice with a small charge and dummy shells."[4]

Sergeant Philip W. Higgins was eighteen years old when he enlisted on 14 May 1917. Raised in Clinton, Connecticut, he was a student at Harvard University before entering the service and being assigned to the Signal Corps. Higgins spent nine months at Camp Devens and commented, "Developed a feeling of disgust at seeing so much time wasted in obsolete training methods. Saw many men lose all interest and enthusiasm for the same reason."[5] Corporal Jacklin M. Holmes of the 80th Division, a farmer from Fauquier, Virginia, described Camp Lee as "great mental and physical training if you get the proper amount of it—about 8–12 months. But I was unfortunate enough to get only about 7 weeks in camp—about 10 hours a day."[6] This brief time spent in training would prove costly once the American Expeditionary Forces (AEF) reached the front.

While the army ensured that its soldiers would be physically strong, it did not harden their minds to the horrors of the front. These men had never heard the sounds of a Maxim machine gun or the rumble of the earth during an artillery shelling. They barely had time to learn the fundamentals before the army shipped them off to France. This was basic training at its most basic. But their inadequate training did not worry most soldiers; they were too eager to cross the Atlantic and win the war. Many doughboys believed the Germans were inept brutes who would be easy to defeat. "I only had six weeks of [training]," stated Private Richard H. Baker Jr. of Norfolk, and "mentally I was tired of it and wanted to get away as soon as possible."[7] Baker, who served in the Medical Corps, was twenty years old and a student at the University of Virginia when he enlisted; he trained at Allentown, Pennsylvania. Like Baker, twenty-six-year-old Virginian Emory P. Barrow, a corporal with the 6th Division, soon grew restless: "After a month at Camp Wadsworth I craved the front line trenches, for I knew the rains and cooties of France couldn't be any worse than the heat and flies of South Carolina."[8] Twenty-seven-year-old Private First Class Arlie I. Day from Rockingham, Virginia, declared, "I was a regular pack mule, a doughboy, did anything that was to do." He later added, "I had good health and liked it fin in camp."[9] Thirty-eight-year-old Samuel L. Alexander of Leeds, Utah, wrote to his mother from Camp Meade, Maryland:

> Now mother listen, do not worry over me for we have the finest officers here. They could not be nicer and everyone is treated fine here and you or anyone else must not think any of the soldiers are mistreated anywhere in the U.S. Army. The boys who write home and say they are not treated good are not true Americans. They are would be slackers who do not love the flag. . . . It makes my blood boil to think there is such boobs born in the U.S. . . . I'll spill lots of German sauerkraut. . . . Tell Ed the 27th Engineers are busy knitting a Barbed wire sweater for Kiser bill and we intend to make Kiser a nice soft pillow out of catclaws . . . we are going to show Kiser the time of his life because his life will be short when the Yankees get a hold of him. . . . The army is the only life on earth and I shall always belong to it, even after it is over. I will work for U.S. somewhere I never enjoyed anything better. It is such a grand system.[10]

There is no doubt the doughboys had the spirit to fight, but were there enough officers to properly train and lead them? When the United States declared war on 6 April 1917, the number of officers and men in the Regular Army and the National Guard was low. Even the General Staff had only forty-one officers.[11] Although draftees and volunteers filled the shortage of troops, the deficiency in experienced commissioned officers was problematic. Prior to World War I, General Leonard Wood had initiated the Military Training Camps Association, also known as the Plattsburgh training camps, where aspiring young officers, most of them from upper-middle-class families, spent a month in training. When the United States declared war, the Plattsburgh camps served as models for the officer training camps established across the country. Potential commissioned officers spent ninety days in training and then, in most cases, joined military units. These officers, often called ninety-day wonders by the soldiers they commanded, were not always prepared for the realities of combat.

Many doughboys complained about these new officers and criticized their ability to lead. Sergeant Major Ralph P. Howard, a thirty-year-old banker from Fairfield, Connecticut, trained at Fort Terry, New York, for eight months before embarking for France in March 1918. He stated, "Large numbers of men were commissioned officers who had no ability to handle large companies of men in the field, technical ability they had, but so many of them were arrogant, boorish and impractical, that most of the enlisted men were happy when they received their discharge."[12] Twenty-four-year-old artilleryman Private Harold T. Lyons, a chauffeur from Kent, Connecticut, enlisted on 24 October 1917 and spent barely a month in training at Fort Myer, Virginia, before boarding a ship for France on 9 January 1918. Lyons observed, "The older Regular Army officers were fine officers and knew what they were doing. I was disgusted with the conduct of the 90-day officers."[13] Twenty-year-old Private Brack M. Osborne from Grayson, Virginia, stated, "I improved physically but cannot say that I gained mentally at Camp Lee. The officers were perfectly unfair."[14] Regardless of their quality, less than half of the Regular Army's officers went to France; the majority of them remained in the United States to instruct new officers.

General John J. Pershing, commander of the AEF, requested that American troops receive six months of training in the United States and two additional months of training when they arrived in France, followed by a month in a quiet sector before taking part in combat. In this way, Pershing believed his forces would be ready to make a positive contribution to the war effort. In reality, many of the soldiers drafted in July 1917 were at the front by November. The average American soldier had only four months of inadequate training, and many had only a few weeks. Men who never handled a rifle received ten days of instruction when they arrived in France. Pershing ignored his own timetable for training when the Allies pressed the United States for troops; he called for a large American force to arrive at the front as quickly as possible.[15] As Richard S. Faulkner argues, "The sad reality was that the AEF was an army of 1914 thrust into 1918."[16] The AEF lacked time, technology, and training. The United States' unpreparedness would be measured by the number of lives lost in Europe.

Camp Life

In spite of inadequate training, some soldiers reported positive camp experiences in the United States. Private Ensworth M. Godard spent several weeks at Camp Yale and another month at Fort Totten, Long Island. Godard described his camp experience as "beneficial." He continued, "I believe in a short period of compulsory military training between ages 17 and 21 under military discipline. But I do not believe in a large standing army."[17] Godard's younger brother Jewell trained in Niantic, Connecticut, from 23 August to 9 October 1917 and reported, "Improved physically, but mentally indifferent."[18]

Albert M. Simons of Hartford, Connecticut, spent nearly three months in training at Plattsburgh, New York. "I am convinced that mentally camp broadens a man giving him a better view of the world at large, and men in particular," Simons commented. "Physically it is splendid."[19] Second Lieutenant Simons left for the front on 5 September 1917. Private First Class Afanariy Boyko, 153rd Machine Gun Company, echoed these sentiments: "Went into the Service a raw recruit and emerged from same a well qualified Soldier fit for any duty both mentally and physically."[20] First Lieutenant John W. Covington, a twenty-six-year-old from Culpeper, Virginia, trained at Camp Funston in Kansas; after two months, he became an instructor of new officers there. Said Covington, "Could not expect better living conditions for soldiering. Mentally and physically I benefited a great deal."[21]

Some soldiers made lasting friendships that survived the war. This camaraderie bolstered their spirits and helped the men improve their health and fitness. Thomas J. Bannigan of Hartford said, "The experience was one that money could not buy, nor could it be obtained in books. . . . Met the finest type of American manhood in associations with brother officers from all over the United States."[22] First Lieutenant Max Climon of Hartford, who served in the Medical Corps, remarked, "Camp experiences in the United States were a great stimulus for the reason that it brought me into intimate contact with the great men of my profession. Physically I was improved by outdoor living and exercise."[23] "Since my childhood I always wanted to be a Soldier boy and my dreams came true. I am satisfied now," commented Corporal Stanley W. Elovetsky of Wallingford, Connecticut. Elovetsky said of his camp training, "I think I was in the best college in the world."[24]

Twenty-two-year-old Corporal Curry P. Hutchison, an unmarried farmer from Newport, Virginia, trained at Camp Lee from 10 October 1917 to 25 May 1918 before embarking for France. Hutchison noted, "I was much improved physically and mentally. Trained to think and act without hesitation. I met with men from every walk of life therefore having an opportunity to study life and men as I had never before."[25] For the most part, doughboys enjoyed the camaraderie of training in America, and the closeness they developed would be crucial to their survival on the front.

The camaraderie of camp life belied the problems inherent in getting a large force ready for war. During the summer of 1917, the army had to construct temporary quarters to house the new soldiers; both wooden barracks and tents, along with roads and sewer systems, had to be in place. There was no time for army officials to follow the usual procedure of soliciting bids for the construction of camps, since the Allies needed soldiers at the front immediately. Therefore, the army expanded old camps and set up new ones to accommodate the growing number of troops. Camp construction in the southern states did not take into account the possibility of cold winter weather, and the men assigned to these quarters suffered the effects. First Lieutenant Albert J. Engelberg, of Austro-Hungarian descent, stated, "Camp Austin wasn't as agreeable a place as one would like, but was the best the government could give during the crisis and although very muddy my battalion and I were in excellent condition when we arrived at the port of embarkation at Newport News."[26]

Recruits from rural Utah discovered that their training camps were more

Several of the barracks and other buildings at Camp Devens in Ayer, Massachusetts, which was built by about 5,000 workers in only ten weeks. (Camp Devens, box 131, Historical Data File, Connecticut State Library)

modern than most of their homes, where running water, electricity, and sewage disposal were often lacking and paved roads were nonexistent. Camp Kearney was newly constructed and well equipped, prompting an unnamed soldier to write to the local newspaper in Blanding: "We are enjoying good health and everything else that falls to the lot of the soldier . . . good quarters, good food, good clothing and best of all, we are in with a good lot of men."[27]

Camp Lewis in the state of Washington received high praise from Private Bert Swindlehurst of Beaver City, Utah. The twenty-two-year-old unmarried farmer, who had completed two years of high school, was drafted on 3 October 1917 and served in the 326th Regiment of the 91st (Wild West) Division. Concerning his nine months of training, Swindlehurst stressed, "From what I can learn Camp Lewis was the Best training camp in the U.S. the cleanest morally and physically."[28]

Once the United States declared war, camps appeared almost overnight to meet the demand for training sites. One such camp was built in Ayer, Massachusetts, where numerous New Englanders received their military training prior to going overseas. Before the army descended on Ayer, it was a quiet town consisting of 200 to 300 cottages surrounded by wide-open spaces. Construction of Camp Devens (named after General Charles Devens, a Civil War officer from Worcester County, Massachusetts) began on 18 June 1917. Ten weeks later, 9,000 acres of backwoods and marshes had been transformed into a training camp. Five thousand workers constructed the 1,400 buildings, 20 miles of road,

Soldiers relax, read, and play table tennis in the American Red Cross building at Camp Devens. (Camp Devens, box 131, Historical Data File, Connecticut State Library)

and 2,200 showers using 400 miles of electrical wire, 60 miles of heating pipes, and 3,320,000 cubic feet of lumber.[29] When the contractors pronounced Camp Devens ready for occupancy on 1 September 1917, New England became the first part of the country to provide military training at a new facility. Recruits from Connecticut destined for the 304th Infantry and Machine Gun Battalions were among the first to arrive at the camp. Similar to other training camps, Devens resembled a small city, with anywhere from 30,000 to 48,000 men living there during 1917 and 1918.[30] The men at Devens were fortunate because they slept in wood barracks. At other military camps, such as Camp Wadsworth in South Carolina and others in the South, the troops had to make do with tents.

Elsewhere, while awaiting the completion of new camps, training took place at parks, armories, and college campuses. For example, by 15 July 1917, many Connecticut infantrymen had arrived at Camp Yale to begin their training. The camp had no barracks; the men slept in canvas tents and spent their days drilling in the hot summer sun. There were 52 officers and 1,750 enlisted men at Camp Yale, under the command of Colonel Ernest L. Isbell of New Haven; with new recruits coming in, the regiment expanded to 4,000.[31] In September 1917 Company D of Camp Yale took a steamer to New York and boarded the *Adriatic*, bound for Liverpool, England, and then Le Havre, France. Throughout September and into October, the remaining soldiers from Camp Yale made the same journey.

On the other side of the country, in American Lake, Washington, Camp Lewis (named after Captain Meriwether Lewis of the Lewis and Clark Expedition) opened for new recruits on 5 September 1917, and the 91st Division trained there. At the time, it was the largest training camp in the country; it took ninety days and 10,000 men to build the 1,757 buildings and 422 other structures.

On arrival at their respective camps, the newly inducted soldiers underwent medical exams, received their uniforms and supplies, and located their barracks. After that, army life consisted of exercise drills, rifle instruction, bayonet training, grenade practice, and training in trench warfare (soldiers dug actual trenches). The army also provided time for organized recreational activities and religious services. Every morning before breakfast and right after roll call, each company performed calisthenics, which were intended to build the soldiers' muscles. "The calisthenics, hikes and regular habits were essential for the endurance which followed," stated twenty-nine-year-old Private Charles R. Goddard, an attorney from Hartford.[32] Twenty-three-year-old Sergeant Hamilton Du Trienille Jr. of New Haven remarked, "The daily drill and exercise made me much stronger than heretofore. It also made me alert to all things."[33] Sergeant Dennis F. Flynn of the 102nd Infantry, also from New Haven, declared, "My experience of camp life in the U.S. were the drills and execises while not laborious were good for the devolepement the body and muscles."[34]

Nineteen-year-old miner Thomas Myers of Parowan City, Utah, was drafted on 19 September 1917 and served with the 346th Machine Gun Battalion, 91st Division, in France and Belgium. While in training at Camp Lewis, he wrote to his father: "We are getting plenty of exercise out here and we get it regular. Every day about eight hours of good hard drill. If we keep on for six months we will be in good order for France. I have just come in from a six or eight mile hike. We certainly do hit the road. I wish this old war would end tomorrow for my part I am sure not at all in love with this kind of work. But, now I am here I am going to do what I can to help to protect the country."[35]

Another important part of training was bayonet practice; each man had to master the use of the bayonet both offensively and defensively prior to leaving for the front. Grenade throwing was another aspect of warfare the doughboys practiced at training camps. They were also taught methods of signaling, learning to use the semaphore code by waving flags or merely their arms. In addition, there was rifle and artillery drill, which was usually accomplished with wooden imitations, as real guns were in short supply. With thousands of men inhabiting a camp, trash accumulated quickly, so policing the grounds was another daily activity carried out by the soldiers.

As men arrived at Camp Devens, their commanders assigned them to various units until each reached its quota. There were four regiments of infantry: 301st, 302nd, 303rd, and 304th. A depot brigade of thirteen battalions was formed, as well as three regiments of field artillery, three machine gun battalions, the Headquarters Train, the Engineers' Train, and the Sanitary Train.

Table 3.1. Origin of Units Formed at Camp Devens, Ayer, Massachusetts

Unit	Region of Origin
301st Infantry	Boston
302nd Infantry	Southeastern Massachusetts
303rd Infantry	Eastern New York
304th Infantry	Connecticut
Field artillery	Maine, New Hampshire, Vermont
Depot brigade	Western Massachusetts
Machine gun battalions	Connecticut, northeastern Massachusetts
301st Engineers	Rhode Island
Headquarters Train	Central Massachusetts

Source: Roger Batchelder, *Camp Devens* (Boston: Small, Maynard, 1917), 9–10.

Table 3.1 shows these assignments based on place of origin. For example, the 304th Infantry comprised Connecticut troops commanded by Colonel Samuel J. Herron. The majority of men in the 304th were former factory workers from Hartford, Bridgeport, and Waterbury. Many were immigrants who could not speak English; some could not write. Well aware of this fact, the army established schools at Camp Devens to teach English so that the soldiers could understand instructions. Most were grateful for the opportunity.

Others also felt their military training helped prepare them for life. Private Mifflin T. Gibbs of Ansonia, Connecticut, did not serve overseas but said, "I received from my experience in the camp valuable training which has contributed to my sucess since returning from camp. I am much stronger physically and better prepare to meet life struggles."[36] Howard J. Dunn of New Haven, a mechanic in the air service, stated, "Increased in weight and felt better physically in general. Also learned considerable in my civil occupation."[37] Most factory workers, farmers, and laborers learned vital skills, so it is understandable that they would commend their training camp experiences.

Physical and Mental Fitness

Physically, the majority of enlisted men left the training camps in better shape than when they arrived. Soldiers put on weight and gained strength. Many men claimed they gained ten, twenty, or even thirty pounds of muscle. "Weighed 156 pounds when examined in July 1917—weighed 190 lbs. when discharged July 1919—Wore shoe size 8½ July 1917—wore shoe size 10, July 1919. General health improved very much during the two years service," stated Miletus B. Jarman, age twenty-six, of Elkton, Virginia.[38]

Private Charles L. Hogue, a thirty-one-year-old African American freight handler from Norfolk, concluded, "Camp experience was very severe. But it was very necessary. My mental capacity was broadened in many forms. Gained excellent knowledge physically."[39] Artilleryman and bugler Leo J. Hill of East Haven, Connecticut, commented, "Didn't note any great mental improvement but gained weight and strength which came in handy later at the front."[40] Twenty-two-year-old Private Ulysses S. G. Mayo, an African American from Cumberland, Virginia, explained, "The association of men, condition and the Study of different types of men increased my mental power 100%. The recreation exercises that I had caused me to gain 15 lbs."[41]

Sergeant Byron P. Graff, a Hartford native who served in a machine gun battalion, gave specific numbers: "Weighed 141 pounds when examined for service. Weighed 175 pounds in service. Present weight about 165. Figures tell the story."[42] Graff represents the majority of doughboys, who noticed an increase in muscle and strength and were proud of their weight gain—more weight meant better health. Seward H. Strickland of Hartford declared, "I had only a short experience in American camp but find the mental atmosphere uplifting and physical conditions and living unequalled."[43]

Infantryman Private Frederick J. Burke of New Haven commented, "A man couldn't want any better place for building up his health."[44] "My camp experience was very pleasing and I got a lot out of it. Physically I was of the best," said infantry bugler Nelson F. Waters of New Haven.[45] He trained at Camp Yale from 28 February to 9 August 1917, when he boarded the *Adriatic* in Hoboken, New Jersey. Twenty-four-year-old Private James O. McKarney of Washington County, Virginia, reiterated, "I believe that camp life helped to build a man up and make him stronger than any other kind of life."[46] Sergeant Harry E. Curry, an African American from Hampton, Virginia, reflected, "I experienced a great deal in camp. I learned that out-door-life was best for my health. I did not know that at first."[47] The growth in physical prowess enhanced most young Americans' hunger for the front.

Physically, the army prepared the doughboy for war. Mentally, it was a different story. Although numerous soldiers cited the mental and physical benefits of camp life, some complained of intellectual stagnation. According to Captain James R. Miller of Hartford, who served in the Medical Corps, "Physically I was greatly benefited by my training camp experience. Mentally I was greatly depressed by having to learn many things that I knew at the time, and found out later, to be not only useless, but incorrect."[48]

Virginian Jack M. Bowen, a private with the 80th Division, agreed: "I improved slightly, physically, but I cannot see where the army improves any one mentally—unless he is an absolute blockhead to begin with."[49] Another Virginian from Portsmouth, Second Lieutenant Marshall W. Butt, had similar negative thoughts: "No physical change of note, mentally I was disgusted with the methods used in the United States."[50] Artilleryman Private Frederick E. Benjamin of New Haven stated, "Detrimental, absolutely, to mental faculties; improved somewhat physically."[51]

Whether a doughboy's opinion of his training was positive or negative, time at camp guaranteed that he would have the strength to go over the top and charge across No-Man's-Land. But he did not know how to engage in trench warfare or how to counterattack on the Western Front. Nor did the army prepare its soldiers for the psychological aspects of combat. Making the same fatal error as their European counterparts, the US high command believed that the infantry alone, in classic pitched battles on open fields, could win the war. They would soon realize that, this time, combat would be different. The Allies were still attempting to master trench warfare as the first American troops arrived in November 1917.

Supplying the Troops

Supplies for the AEF were another problem area. The doughboys needed uniforms, weapons, medical supplies, field glasses, helmets, ammunition, mess kits, horses' equipment—the list went on. There was little surplus due to the 1916–1917 mission to Mexico and the lack of industrial preparation for war. Demand for uniforms, ammunition, and food was especially high. The army turned to American executives for advice on where to obtain the best quality for their money. To supply such a vast number of soldiers in such a short time took a great deal of effort by the various bureaus of the army. The Quartermaster Corps alone supplied the army with 17,000,000 woolen trousers and breeches, 22,198,000 flannel shirts, and 26,423,000 shoes.[52] Once again, soldiers who trained at Camp Devens were fortunate. They received straw mattresses and as many blankets as they needed to place on their iron cots equipped with springs; the Quartermaster Corps, however, did not provide pillows. The army had little difficulty purchasing food for the camps, but there were not enough trained cooks and bakers to prepare it. Civilian chefs were hired to cook for the troops at the camps while the army schooled its own.

The supply situation seemed to go unnoticed by many soldiers. First Lieutenant Dryden L. Phelps, an army chaplain from New Haven, described his camp experience as "most beneficial. . . . We received first class food; barracks in good condition; the highest type of mental and physical training."[53] English-born Private Wilson H. Whitehouse, who lived in Wallingford, Connecticut, when he enlisted in the army on 5 May 1917 at age nineteen, observed, "They were of the best as far as mental and physical conditions were concerned. But they might have been more lenient with their passes."[54]

Doughboys were often crowded together due to a lack of barracks or tents, and since uniforms were in short supply, soldiers reported for drill dressed in a combination of military attire and civilian clothing. Men without previous mili-

Yale University student Humbert F. Cofrancesco from New Haven, Connecticut, in December 1917. (Box 30, Connecticut State Library)

tary experience quickly learned that the army ran on discipline and drill; their seventeen-hour days were typically filled with marching, calisthenics, classes, and practice. "Camp experience was of the best. I could get up with the bugle at 4:30 where now an alarm clock has a hard job awakening me at 7:30," said Second Lieutenant Francis P. Pallotti of Hartford.[55]

The recruits received three army-style meals a day. They may not have appreciated all the items on the menu or the way their food was prepared, but there was a lot of it. Each soldier's daily ration was 4,761 calories.[56] The entrée differed each day, but a typical menu from Fort Riley, Kansas, in the summer of 1917 included the following: for breakfast, cantaloupes, corn flakes with sugar and milk, fried liver with bacon and onions, bread, and coffee; for lunch, beef à la mode, boiled potatoes, creamed cauliflower, pickles, tapioca pudding with vanilla sauce, bread, and iced tea; and for dinner, chili con carne, hot biscuits, stewed peaches, and iced tea.[57] The army's heavy calorie and exercise regimen enabled doughboys to pack on pounds of muscle. Private Harvey E. Braxton, an African American farmer from Accomack, Virginia, felt that "plenty of exercise, pure air, pure food enabled me to think quick, act and be ready for service."[58]

Eighteen-year-old Private Humbert F. Cofrancesco, a field artilleryman of Italian descent from New Haven, remarked, "The most pronounced effect on me was physical. The human body was a living engine in the army. With painstaking care, every precaution was taken to safe guard the men's health, especially during the influenza epidemic. Every man was upon his discharge, healthier—stronger and stouter. All weaknesses and feebleness were eliminated. Backs were straightened; round shoulders disappeared." Cofrancesco added, "Military training was beneficial mentally, as well as physically. One had to be alert, energetic, attentive and responsive to any duty. The drills in particular demanded a steady concentrated mental effort. Military topography taught the man to be keen, observant, appreciative of details under unusual, and sometimes, discomforting circumstances."[59]

Health and Welfare

In spite of their improved physical fitness, numerous American soldiers contracted diseases before being deployed overseas. Influenza hospitalized 25 to 40 percent of the men in the training camps, and 30,000 died of it.[60] Others became sick with various other ailments: measles, mumps, chicken pox, meningitis, typhoid, smallpox, and tuberculosis. Army medical officers kept the camps in the United States sanitary, and the Public Health Service kept nearby towns as clean as possible. Nonetheless, living in such close quarters contributed to the spread of illnesses.

Thirty-four-year-old nurse Nora B. Sanford of Roanoke, Virginia, worked at Camp Jackson's hospital in Columbia, South Carolina. "My first duty," she recalled, "was with colored pneumonia patients, there being thirty-six at most, most of whom were seriously ill. . . . The work was of course very heavy, but one enjoyed it as the patients were mostly Southern darkies and very humble and grateful—and pitiful. From there I went to a measles ward—where the greater number of boys were from the country and so genuine and unselfish. But to my regret I didn't stay with them long."[61] Sergeant William A. Bergen of the 102nd Infantry, a native of Waterbury, Connecticut, suffered "chest pains, deafness, respiratory problems, and anxiety" while in camp in the United States, and he felt "nervous, irritable, and shifty."[62]

Influenza was the worst disease to attack the men. The origin of the pandemic remains unclear. It may have originated at Fort Riley, Kansas, where 1,100 soldiers became ill after inhaling dust and smoke from burning manure, and 46 died. When some of these Fort Riley–trained doughboys deployed to France, they carried the virus with them. In France, influenza spread quickly throughout the ranks of Allied and enemy forces alike and then traveled back to the United States as the troops returned home.[63]

A global influenza epidemic raged from March 1918 to August 1919. More than 25 percent of the army contracted influenza during the war.[64] In September 1918, 25,000 French troops and 37,000 doughboys came down with the flu.[65] Civilians suffered from the rapid spread of the disease as well, and the epidemic caused businesses and schools to close. Pneumonia, a complication of influenza, contributed to the number of flu-related deaths. Soldiers in training camps or those stationed in the rear were more susceptible to the disease due to the crowded conditions and the lack of food and rest.

The 1918 influenza pandemic attacked people of all ages; however, young adults between the ages of twenty-five and thirty-four suffered the highest mortality rate.[66] Approximately 50 percent of those who died due to influenza were men and women in their twenties. Draft calls and military training ceased for nearly a month during October 1918, when four of every thousand soldiers in US training camps died of influenza.[67] The War Department even curtailed the deployment of doughboys to France until the epidemic subsided. The flu proved to be as formidable an enemy as the Germans, accounting for nearly half the soldiers who died in Europe during the war.[68] After the war, the US Army reported 46,992 deaths due to influenza and pneumonia—only 3,500 fewer than the total number of men who died in battle during World War I.[69]

Thirteen doughboys of the Utah 145th Field Artillery died in France of influenza. In early February 1919, at the War Mothers' Service Flag Ceremony in Deseret, Chaplain B. H. Roberts spoke of the sacrifice of Utah's soldiers, including those who succumbed to influenza: "The heroism of the soldier consists in the fact that he offers his life to his country with full interest to meet whatever fate may befall him. It is not his prerogative to choose his place in the line of battle, or to say when or how or where or in what manner he will fall, if fall he must. He does his part when in response to his country's call for service he says, 'Here I am, send me.'"[70]

At some camps, soldiers escaped influenza due to wide-open spaces, well-constructed housing, and trees planted throughout the facilities, all of which contributed to the health of the troops. For example, the sanitary officer at Camp Devens ordered the men to hang all mattresses and blankets outside the barracks windows and to keep all windows open during morning drill, to prevent the spread of viruses. In addition, companies whose troops developed illnesses such as measles or influenza were subject to quarantine until the infected soldiers recovered.[71]

Dr. Roy, an army doctor stationed in Surgical Ward No. 16 at Camp Devens, wrote to a friend and fellow physician on 29 September 1918 and described the severity of the influenza epidemic and its effect on the camp. He explained that the camp had suspended all drills, assemblies, and other normal activities, in an attempt to halt the spread of the illness. But in spite of all precautions, Roy lamented, "We have been averaging about 100 deaths per day, and still keeping it up." Located near Boston, Devens housed approximately 50,000 men as well as serving as a base hospital. The army assigned 250 doctors to the camp, and they put in sixteen-hour workdays. Roy described the suffering of his patients when flu became pneumonia: "It is only a matter of a few hours then until death comes, and it is simply a struggle for air until they suffocate. It is horrible. One can stand it to see one, two or twenty men die, but to see these poor devils dropping like flies sort of gets on your nerves." Roy concluded, "It takes special trains to carry away the dead. For several days there were no coffins and the bodies piled up something fierce, we used to go down to the morgue . . . and look at the boys laid out in long rows. It beats any sight they ever had in France after a battle."[72]

Influenza was not the only threat to the army. President Woodrow Wilson and Secretary of War Newton D. Baker took steps to protect the troops from the vices of liquor and prostitution. Wilson wanted the AEF to be more sober and more moral than past armies. For instance, during the mobilization of troops on the Mexican border, drunkenness and prostitution had been rampant. To combat these temptations, Baker established the Commission on Training Camp Activities, sanctioned by the War Department but privately funded. He appointed Raymond B. Fosdick, a lawyer and social worker, as the director of the newly formed commission. Fosdick, a Princeton University graduate, was committed to public service and to eradicating corruption and immorality in city government. He had served on a commission under John D. Rockefeller Jr. and had established a reputation as a foe of prostitution and graft. It became Fosdick's duty to advise the army on providing appropriate recreational facilities at the training camps.

First, the areas around the camps were to be free of saloons and brothels, and the commission prohibited the sale of liquor to servicemen in uniform. The army also provided instruction on venereal diseases in the form of lectures, movies, pamphlets, and posters. Before Sir Alexander Fleming discovered penicillin in 1928, there was no effective treatment for venereal disease, and it disabled thousands of soldiers. The British and French armies had lost too many troops to syphilis and gonorrhea, and the United States was determined not to waste valuable manpower in this manner. Education was the army's chief weapon against venereal diseases.

The Commission on Training Camp Activities supervised the work of organizations such as the YMCA, Jewish Welfare Board, Salvation Army, and Red Cross, which were of great support and aid to the doughboys. These groups worked with the commission to improve camp life. Libraries, theater productions, and sports activities provided a respite from their training regimen—the soldiers had half a day Saturday and all day Sunday off. Fosdick also introduced group singing to the military men; there was some initial resistance, but once singing caught on, the soldiers became enthusiastic and sang while they worked. Songs such as "Over There" and "We'll Hang Kaiser Bill to a Sour-Apple Tree" became army favorites. At most training camps, the army made sports a top priority and provided equipment and fields for football, tennis, baseball, soccer, and boxing—the most popular sport. College coaches even formed and supervised intramural teams. The army designed these activities not only to boost morale but also to discourage immoral and degrading behavior.

In spite of the army's efforts to make camp life agreeable, not all soldiers had positive experiences, whether owing to a dislike of the military, boredom, or illness. Private David Fransen, an artilleryman from Hartford, stated, "Made me hate an Army Officer but it taught me to do as I was told."[73] Private Frederick E. Benjamin of New Haven said, "Accepted my duty and performed it to the best of my ability but think military service is·the nearest vocation to barbarism possible—at least for an intelligent enlisted man who does the thinking for a lot of numbskulls."[74] Private Donald L. Jacobno of New Haven, who trained at Camp Upton in Yaphank, New York, and later at Camp Hancock in Augusta, Georgia, commented, "At Upton the barrenness and ugliness of the camp structures and surroundings were mentally depressing. So was the monotony of camp life; at Hancock they permitted a few trees to grow, so it was not so bad there."[75] Private William J. B. Morris, a twenty-four-year-old traffic manager from Mappsville, Virginia, trained at Camp Wadsworth, South Carolina, from 17 May to 28 June 1918. After this brief time in camp, Morris recounted, "Mentally I wasn't living as everything was so new and different from what I was used to and we were kept on the jump all the time to such extent that I hadn't time to think. I was learning to be a mechanical machine, never allowed to think for yourself just obey . . . physically, I nearly became a wreck until I got hardened to that type of life. I lost 20 pounds in 3 weeks."[76] Private Charles A. Cormier of Ansonia, Connecticut, said, "I had never been ill before enlisting but during my various illnesses received every care. I am not as well physically as before and mentally I have aged about ten years."[77] Private Jacobno also suffered from the flu during his military service, stating, "All physical improvement was offset by the effects of the Spanish Influenza."[78]

When men died from influenza or pneumonia while en route to Europe, the army sent letters to notify their families. Mary Costello of New Haven received such a letter in October 1918, conveying the news that her son Frank had died while sailing to England. Army chaplain Lieutenant George F. Finnigan wrote to Mrs. Costello: "His death was not hard. The cold had settled on his lungs and the doctors could do no more for him than they did. We buried him at sea. . . . The stars and stripes were around him."[79]

Other soldiers died in training camp or while on duty in America. First Lieutenant William C. Brown Jr., who served in the Quartermaster Department, had attended Harvard University and Harvard Law School before enlisting. In a letter to his family, the resident of Manchester, Connecticut, voiced his excitement: "Right here in camp, 40,000 of the finest soldiers in the world are being put in shape." Brown's enthusiasm for military service did not carry him overseas, however; he was assigned to the Admiralty Section of the Water Transport Branch of the Embarkation Service in Washington, D.C. Lieutenant Brown contracted influenza and died on 19 January 1919.[80]

Edgar O. Shirley, a twenty-three-year-old Hartford resident, was notified to appear before his local draft board at the Old Hall of Records on 1 September 1918. But that same day, Shirley was "taken ill . . . and removed to Hartford Hospital, where he died 5 September, with bronchial pneumonia, being the first to die in Hartford with the 'flu.'"[81] Shirley had tried to enlist prior to being drafted, but the examining physician had rejected him. Soon after his appointment, First Lieutenant Julian C. Warner, a 1916 Yale graduate, was stricken with a "fatal malady" and died before he had an opportunity to serve in the military.[82] Utahan volunteer Private Clarence Anderson fell ill with the Spanish flu while training at Camp Lewis, Washington; he dictated his last letter home to a nurse before he died: "I am very sick and may not recover, but in case I should cross the Great Beyond I want you to all know that I am a Christian and am prepared to meet my maker. I didn't like to drill at first, but I got so I liked it, and I love the army life. If I had a thousand lives I would give them all for the U.S.A."[83]

Were the doughboys prepared to fight? Physically, they were ready; psychologically, they were not. Even if they were subjected to live-fire exercises and simulated trench conditions, this type of training was not enough to overcome the American military unpreparedness or the Civil War romanticism that informed the doughboys' perception of combat. Filled with enthusiasm, the doughboys were eager to get to the front, and nothing, it seemed, could stop them. Utahan Harry Keyes, a twenty-one-year-old married foreman for the Union Pacific Railroad, volunteered for service on 3 July 1917 and served with Battery F, 145th Field Artillery, 40th (Sunshine) Division. After completing most of his training at Camp Kearney, Keyes embarked for France on 14 August 1918. "Shure was anxious to get overseas," he remarked, "so we did lots of hard training getting ready." But Keyes contracted influenza in France and never saw action. He returned home and was discharged on 22 January 1919.[84] John P. Dwyer, a machinist for Manville's Machine in Waterbury, Connecticut, enlisted on 17 June 1917 at age twenty-three; the army assigned him to the 102nd Infantry in the National Guard. "I think the training etc. done me good," he declared, "but was more interested in getting across the pond than anything else."[85] The Western Front would put the doughboys' training to the test. Prepared or not, they were going. It was a matter of duty.

4

Across the Pond

The Atlantic was U-boat territory. German submarines made the seas a dangerous battleground during the war, above all for Allied merchant shipping. This was especially true after 18 February 1915, when Germany allowed its U-boats to sink Allied merchant ships at will. This tactic had devastating results. In 1915, after the sinking of the *Lusitania* on 7 May and the *Arabic* on 19 August (both carrying American passengers), Germany discontinued unrestricted submarine warfare, for fear of American reprisal. As the war progressed, Allied shipping increased, while the Allied naval blockade constricted the Central Powers; Germany reinstated unrestricted submarine warfare on 1 February 1917.

Once again, German U-boats wreaked havoc on Allied shipping; this time, however, the Allies developed and employed the convoy system. Instead of traveling alone, merchant ships and troop transports were escorted to their destinations by destroyers. By the summer of 1917, the submarine threat had decreased, but the waters were still not completely safe as the doughboys made their way to France. Precautions were taken to avoid submarines, such as following a zigzag course and keeping the transports unlit after dark. The men took turns keeping watch for submarines, and when they were off duty, they relaxed by playing card games, practicing their French, or singing. Many doughboys from the Midwest got their first look at the ocean and spent time on deck, basking in the sun, wherever they could find room to stretch out.

General Johnson Hagood, chief of staff of the Services of Supply in France, crossed the Atlantic aboard the *Aurania* out of Hoboken, New Jersey. While in transit, Hagood made the following observations on 18 August 1917: "The trip across was uneventful. A submarine took a pot shot at one of the other ships of the convoy, but missed. We got a radio that a merchantman had gone down twenty miles to our southward. But the sea was calm, the nights were clear, and we zigzagged along like house flies playing tag on a summer day."[1]

Leland C. Stapley of Kanarra, Utah, was inducted on 19 September 1917, trained at Camp Lewis and Camp Merritt, and sailed for France aboard the *Dano*, arriving on 22 July 1918. In his diary, Stapley described his trip across the pond as part of a twenty-two-ship convoy: "Life on board was one continual jam. We had daily inspections which are the curse of a soldier's life. The trip across was one hard knock with another. The main excitement was the sighting of a whale now and then, and the rush for the canteen when it opened."[2]

For men unused to ocean travel, seasickness was a problem. First Lieutenant James McBrayer Sellers, 4th Marine Brigade, 2nd Division, of Lexington, Missouri, boarded the *Henderson* in New York on 24 January 1918. On 25 January rough weather took its toll on the men. Sellers, who escaped the ill effects of the tumbling sea, went belowdecks to check on the enlisted men. He reported:

> They were jammed up so tight down below that when we wanted to inspect their compartments, we had to run them all up on deck. Their bunks were arranged in three tiers, and there was barely room for two people to pass between the tiers. During the rougher weather, it was an awful sight to behold down below. About three quarters of them wished they were dead; some said that they didn't intend to go back to America unless they could fly. But even the sickest of them could always get up courage to laugh at the other guy and not a one failed to come up at the proper times.[3]

Despite their escorts, there were times when the transport ships were in danger of attack. Twice-wounded combat veteran Louis M. Lindsay, a bookkeeper and waiter from Eureka, Utah, was twenty-four when he volunteered for service on 26 February 1918. About his overseas journey, Lindsay noted, "On 23rd May at 2 a.m. within twelve hours run from England the boat on which I was transported, the 'Moldavia,' was torpedoed and had to be abandoned. 20 percent of Co. 'B' 58th were lost."[4]

One enemy greater than the German U-boats was disease. The trip across the Atlantic took about two weeks, and transport ships were scarce, so American troops were packed like sardines. This gave the Spanish flu plenty of opportunity to spread throughout a ship. Many soldiers became ill, and many died on the voyage. In October 1918 "the *Leviathan* alone arrived with 514 cases of 'flu,' 463 cases of pneumonia, and 68 dead."[5] When reflecting on his Atlantic journey, Walter H. Anderson, a farmer from Toquerville, Utah, said, "We got on the boat July 13th last and sailed the 14th. We had a great convoy of four-

Men aboard the *Northern Pacific*, near the English Channel, watch shells being fired at a U-boat. (Photograph Collection, box 131, Historical Data File, Connecticut State Library)

teen ships, including great battleships and men of war. Well, we traveled a zig zag course way up in the artic regions. We landed in Liverpool after twelve long, tiresome, hungry days."[6]

Over There

After braving the U-boats, seasickness, and influenza, the doughboys found that European camp life did not match the comforts of camps at home. Thousands of soldiers arrived in Liverpool, England, and then traveled by train to a "rest camp" in Southampton before continuing on to France. That camp, and others like it, was anything but restful. Colonel Ernest L. Isbell, commanding officer of the 102nd Infantry, 26th Division, described the situation in a letter to General Peter E. Traub, commander of the 51st Infantry Brigade: "At the rest camp the men were sheltered in tents. The place was wet and muddy; there was . . . an entire lack of organization, system or method. For the first day the entire subsistence provided was a piece of bread with some jam."[7] Thieves stole part of their baggage; shoes, shirts, socks, and other articles of clothing were in short supply.

American soldiers had similar experiences at other English rest camps. Private Stanley J. Herzog, a telephone operator from the 103rd Field Artillery, 26th Division, described the conditions at his camp: "Here we were packed fourteen in a tent which could only accommodate seven men." There was very little food, according to Herzog, and "to make it worse, a very few of the boys had any money as we did not get paid before leaving good old U.S., so we could not buy any food. . . . I sold a pair of gloves to an English soldier for a half crown, for which I bought a package of cigarettes and a little fruit." After a brief stay in England, the doughboys traveled to France, growing more enthusiastic about meeting the enemy. Herzog recounted, "It was bright and early when we landed in Le Havre, France. I could hear the boys say: 'show me the Hun and we will clean out all of the Kaiser's army.'"[8]

Private Martin G. Gulberg, 4th Marine Brigade, 2nd Division, sailed out of New York aboard the *Henderson* on 23 September 1917. When his transport docked in Saint-Nazaire on 5 October, the French countryside was a welcome sight. Gulberg recounted, "Some of our brother Marines who had landed in June, came down to the docks and started to hang crepe. They told us what a hell of a place France was; and that we would have our bellies full in a month's time. But that didn't discourage us a bit. Any kind of land was good enough for us, as long as we got off the ship. Anyway a soldier is never satisfied no matter where you put him."[9]

In spite of the inhospitable conditions and cramped quarters, most soldiers welcomed the opportunity to travel and see new sights. To some, it was an exciting foreign excursion. Joseph J. O'Connell, an infantry corporal from Manchester, Connecticut, said the training overseas was "hard work but the traveling which we did gave us an opportunity to see many things which we would not see otherwise." O'Connell added that he had "learned a great deal due to these experiences."[10] Second Lieutenant George S. Crockett, a twenty-one-year-old student at the Virginia Military Institute, entered the Air Service of the National Army on 7 August 1917. Crockett, of Accomack, Virginia, considered his time overseas "an educational experience that could not be given any other way."[11] Others viewed their time in Europe as an occasion to broaden themselves intellectually or even spiritually. The American Church of the Holy Trinity in Paris distributed a map to help doughboys locate the church.

Ordnance Sergeant Maurice M. Condon of Hartford, Connecticut, said, "I had the pleasure of mixing among strange people observing their habits and customs. I also saw most of the large cities of France, their different works of art, cathedrals, castles and châteaux."[12] Twenty-six-year-old First Lieutenant Miletus B. Jarman, a high school principal in Elkton, Virginia, joined the army on 20 August 1917. About his experiences in Europe, Jarman wrote, "I have been broadened by meeting many men under unusual conditions, by travel in France, Luxembourg and Germany, and by just naturally growing mentally by virtue of being two years older than I was when I entered the service. Some illusions about France and the French, Germany and the Germans, were shattered."[13]

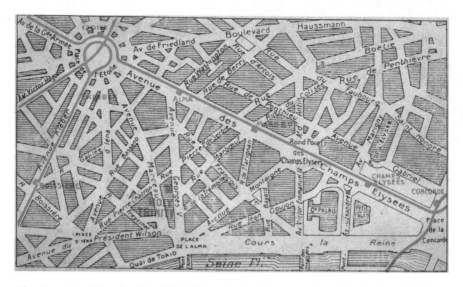

The American Church of the Holy Trinity (today known as the American Cathedral in Paris) supplied this map for Americans. The map highlights Holy Trinity's location at 23 avenue George V. The red lines denote four Paris Métro lines and seven stops along those routes. All four lines (M1, M2, M6, and M8) still exist today, but along L'avenue des Champs-Élysées (M1), the Alma and Marbeuf were renamed George V and Franklin D. Roosevelt, respectively. (Map File, World War I, 1917–1920, Connecticut State Library)

     Another twenty-six-year-old, First Lieutenant Edgar C. Outten of Hampton, Virginia, described his training overseas as "a wonderful and broadening experience, the value of which cannot be reckoned in terms of dollars and cents."[14] New Haven native Sergeant Matthew M. Quinn, 302nd Field Artillery, said, "Used my trip as a tour of sightseeing and travel."[15] Quartermaster Corps Corporal Charles H. Henderling, also of New Haven, wrote, "I gained considerably in my experiences overseas and will never forget what I have seen and learned by the trip."[16] Thirty-four-year-old First Lieutenant Arthur A. Grove, 116th Infantry, 29th Division, a merchant from Luray, Virginia, called his training overseas "very beneficial. It was a wonderful experience—one that I can look back upon with a great deal of satisfaction."[17]

     Field artilleryman Second Lieutenant Leslie A. Tracy of Hartford did not train in the United States; he was immediately shipped to France and said his overseas training was "an experience never to be equaled. It was an opportunity to associate with men of every station in life."[18] Pleased with his service, Paul T. Wysocki of Norfolk, Virginia, wrote, "My overseas experience broadened my mind and made me take notice of things I would not have noticed without my army experience."[19] Captain Thomas B. McDermott of Hartford,

Major General Clarence R. Edwards inspecting the 101st Infantry, Neufchâteau, France, 1918. (Photograph Collection, box 131, Historical Data File, Connecticut State Library)

twenty-seven years old and a former statistician for the Rossia Insurance Company, was married and the father of two children. He said, "Had a chance to see France, Belgium, Italy, Luxembourg and Germany, and I am firmly convinced that 80% of them are a gang of 'furriners,' the other 20% would undoubtedly do this country a lot of good if it had them."[20] John E. Barnes, an eighteen-year-old shipping clerk from Norfolk, recalled, "Overseas experience caused me to feel I had lived and gained more in a month than I ordinarily would in years."[21] "I learned that America, though the greatest country in the world, can learn much from other countries," said Leslie H. Patterson, age twenty-three, of Bedford, Virginia.[22]

Jack Wright, a young American who flew with the French air service, wrote to his mother on 7 January 1918 from Paris, lauding the French attitude and the city's essence:

> There seems to be a spirit of friendship unknown to peace-times, and it draws you closer to the gray houses, their balconies, and windows; to the towers and curving bridges—to all the silent, smiling soul of Paris, the city of War. There is where I hold a great deal of pity for you all—at home. You are not, in your limits even, finding the new spirit that the War has brought. Paris has not all been able to fight, but all of it has been saturated with the holy spirit of fraternization which the Great War has

brought. That spirit will die away, and you shall not have been caressed by it; you shall not have had the blessed opportunity of finding a sort of Paradise, ephemeral but beautiful, ruling the hearts of men.[23]

The doughboys would begin their European education when they arrived at their training camps in France, such as Neufchâteau in the Meuse River valley in the Lorraine region, Vosges department, of eastern France.[24] Conditions there were no better than they had been in England, and France did not resemble the country the doughboys had imagined. The photographs they had seen of the Eiffel Tower and the picturesque Parisian streets along the Seine were quite different from the cold, rainy, muddy countryside they found themselves in—a collection of small farmhouses and tiny villages located along the roads crossing through Neufchâteau. As Daniel W. Strickland of New Haven remembered, the constant rain made "the ever present damnable mud all about . . . clinging to shoes, boots, and clothes so that a soldier worked, drilled or paraded with anywhere from one to five pounds of mud attached to each foot."[25] Corporal Virginius L. Bland, 318th Regiment, 80th Division, a twenty-four-year-old farmer from Shanghai, Virginia, remarked, "I found that France wasn't like it had been said. It made me think, Look! The cooties."[26]

Initially, the doughboys believed the only foe they would face in Europe would be the Germans. They were wrong. The cold, damp climate, poor food, and lack of supplies, coupled with mud, grime, and the omnipresent louse, all combined to wear down the AEF even before they faced any human opponents. The louse—or cootie, as the soldiers called it—was a tiny parasite that caused not only intense itching and discomfort but also trench fever, which could incapacitate a soldier for days with a high fever and general weakness. To combat cooties, the army sent a steam generator and tank truck around the camps. The doughboys undressed and threw their bundled clothes into the tank, where the steam killed the lice. Of course, this relief was only temporary, since the cooties infested the hay on which the troops slept.

The men of the AEF managed to keep their spirits up despite the continuous assault of lice, as evidenced by the many poems and jokes appearing in *Stars and Stripes*.[27] In a 29 November 1918 letter to the editor, Jimmy Murrin of Headquarters Company, 112th Infantry, remarked, "Machine gunners, who know how to sweep the enemy's front with their rat-tat-tat machines, have yet to learn the law of separation—for neither Hun, shrapnel nor changing weather conditions can subdue the same old cootie. He is there to the last." Murrin ended his letter with a quote from a front-line soldier: "I have not seen a single cootie in France. . . . They are all married and have large families."[28] Sergeant A. P. Bowen, a radiotelephone operator, wrote a poem entitled "If I Were a Cootie" that was published in the 1 November 1918 issue:

If I were a cootie (pro-Ally, of course),
I'd hie me away on a Potsdam-bound horse,
And I'd seek out the Kaiser (the war-maddened cuss),
And I'd be a bum cootie if I didn't muss
His Imperial hide from his head to his toe!
He might hide from the bombs, but I'd give him no show!
If I were a cootie, I'd deem it my duty
To thus treat the Kaiser,
Ah, oui![29]

Private George C. Pierce was a farmer in Wellington, Utah, when he was inducted on 4 October 1917. After completing ten months at Camp Lewis and an additional month at Camp Merritt, Pierce arrived in France on 1 August 1918. In a letter dated 28 December 1918, Pierce wrote to his parents about some of his wartime experiences while serving with the 321st Infantry, 81st Division. About the omnipresent lice, he jested, "I will tell you about our little cooties. I have just two regiments on me now. Nearly all of them have service stripes across the back, and I will give them war crosses because they have stayed with me all during the war."[30]

Lice were a terrible mental and physical drain on all the troops, yet like Pierce, many of the doughboys made light of the situation (at least in letters home). At the time of the armistice, lice infested 90 percent of all AEF divisions, but by the next spring, that figure had dropped to 10 percent.[31] This was due to the army's aggressive delousing programs, which included better living and bathing conditions for the soldiers, and more stringent policies instituted by the navy to rid the troop transports of lice.

Besides lice, the AEF found the weather conditions in England and France difficult to handle. A thirty-year-old veteran of the Border Service, Walter T. Spencer of Fort Mitchell, Virginia, was stationed in Blazy, France, from 21 April to 21 May 1918. A supply sergeant, Spencer commented that his "health has never been good since exposure to weather" in France.[32] The cold weather and mud resulted in feet that were constantly wet, frozen, and sore. Colonel Isbell issued a memorandum on 31 October 1917 that included a list of suggestions to help his men stay healthy under such adverse conditions:

Thorough daily drying and greasing of shoes.
Saving fat for shoe grease.
Wearing cardboard insoles if shoes are bad.
Frequent washing and rubbing the feet, with camphorated oil.
Frequent changes of socks and wearing of several pairs at a time.
Frequent washing and changing of underwear.

Drying and airing of clothing.

Use of papers, poncho, shelter tent half or rain coat with poncho underneath blankets and rain coat or shelter half on poncho over blankets to keep out cold.

Drying and airing of bedding.

Folding blankets to make a sort of sleeping bag.

Cleaning billets and barracks.

Stopping holes in barracks roofs and walls with paper, straw, etc.

Bathing and personal cleanliness.

Moderation in eating and drinking.

Proper regulation of bowels.

Temperance, avoidance of all excesses.

Avoidance of inactivity, while wet, especially in draft or wind or when it's cold.

Avoiding commission of nuisances.

Washing of hands after visiting latrines.

Drinking no unboiled water save that treated by chlorated lime.

Getting ample rest and sleep.

Avoiding needless exposure to bad weather.

Constructing drains.

Constructing hardened paths.

Constructing weather protected latrines.[33]

The unfavorable weather conditions, coupled with long hours of training, resulted in illness and even death for some AEF troops. Russel Muir was a twenty-two-year-old farmer and rancher in Heber, Utah, when he volunteered for service on 13 May 1918. Assigned as a mechanic in the 339th Field Artillery, 88th Division, Muir trained Stateside at the University of Colorado–Boulder and at Camp Dodge, Iowa, before arriving in France in August 1918. While attending a course in motors at a camp near Clermont, France, Muir contracted pneumonia and died on 29 October. In his last letter home, written to his mother on 8 October, Muir urged people on the home front to support the troops: "Keep up spirit and work for we need all of your help. I am going ahead and doing my best every day we work, but that is nothing compared to what is in head of us. We are all willing to work and fight if only you all stay behind us. Every boy in this army of ours feels it is his duty to protect his rights. If we lose, we have lost everything, but we are not going to lose. We are going to win."[34] Russel Muir was buried in the American Cemetery at Clermont.

Besides trying to avoid sickness, the soldiers worked nearly nonstop under the guidance of French officers to learn the skills they would need at the front. A typical day for a doughboy went something like this: After sleeping in a hayloft, he was up at dawn, washed in cold water from a horse trough, ate boiled salt pork and bread for breakfast, and washed it down with black coffee. He worked and trained all day, ate supper after dark, slept, and started again the following day.

Doughboys learned the tactics of trench warfare and offensive combat from seasoned British and French soldiers. For instance, Colonel Bertrand, commander of the French 162nd Regiment of Infantry, instructed the Americans at Neufchâteau. As Frank P. Sibley remembered, these French soldiers "were remarkable examples of professional efficiency and teaching ability."[35] Allied officers instructed Americans in the use of gas masks, hand grenades, the Chauchat 8mm machine gun (an unpopular French light machine gun), and the Stokes mortar. Brigadier General Albertus W. Catlin recounted the constant drilling of the 6th Marines Regiment, regardless of weather conditions: "They were drilled constantly in trench organization, signal systems, and all the details of trench warfare as it existed at the front. And all this in addition to the routine drill of the Marines."[36]

Lieutenant Colonel Frederick M. Wise, 5th Marines, 2nd Division, described the French training camps located between the towns of Chenevier and Menaucourt during July and August 1917. As Wise explained, the 1st Division was also billeted in small towns and participated in similar training exercises, which included digging trenches and practicing bayonet fighting:

> Long lines of straw-stuffed figures hanging from a crossbeam between two upright posts were set up. The men fixed bayonets and charged them. British instructors, who had arrived shortly after us, stood over them and urged them on. The men had to scramble in and out a series of trenches before they got to the swinging dummies. That was to improve their wind. When the dummies were reached, according to the British instructors, you must put on a fighting face, grunt and curse as you lunged and literally try to tear the dummy to pieces with the thrust. There was special instruction to bayonet them in the belly whenever possible. If you bayoneted a man you were chasing, you must get him through the kidneys and not in the rump. If your bayonet stuck, shoot it out.[37]

The bayonet received high praise from the Europeans during the war, especially the British; however, it was considered more of a psychological weapon than a physical one. Due to the perception that this weapon caused negligible casualties, the armies kept no statistics; however, Rob Engen estimates that among the Germans alone, 199,808 men died by bayonet.[38]

In addition to practice sessions and drilling with weapons, soldiers dug latrines and trenches, cleaned up livestock manure piles, and struggled with the gloomy mud and cold. The first American arrivals in France spent the winter of 1917–1918 dealing with daily rain or snow in places such as Camp de

Coëtquidan, dubbed by the AEF as "Camp Quityourkiddin."[39] "Certain camps in France were nothing more than death traps; no stoves, no wooden floors for tents; general disregard for enlisted men's health by the officers in command," wrote Harold T. Lyons, a twenty-four-year-old chauffeur from Kent, Connecticut.[40] They also constructed barracks, hospitals, and telephone lines; cut firewood; and kept the villages clean. Doughboys did all this in addition to training for combat.

Since the French army did not have time to construct barracks for the arriving American troops, many of the doughboys were billeted in farmhouses in the countryside; others were relegated to the barns, sleeping alongside the French farmers' cattle or in haylofts. No heat, no electricity, an inability to communicate with the locals, and problems figuring out the French currency all added to the soldiers' anxiety. It took time, but some Americans eventually befriended the French citizens, particularly the children, with whom they played games and shared candy. Two months before his twentieth birthday, Sergeant Fairfield H. Hodges, 104th Sanitary Train, 29th Division, had enlisted in the National Guard; the assistant rate clerk from Portsmouth, Virginia, stated: "I learned much. The countries I visited were strange and interesting and the people I shall never forget. The French treating me in every instance fine."[41]

The majority of AEF soldiers enjoyed their overseas camp experiences, despite the hardships they endured. Corporal Theodore E. Whitney, a machine gun infantryman from Hartford, commented that his overseas training made him realize "that every man, no matter what his wealth, creed or nationality, was equally as good as myself."[42] Corporal Hugh E. Brown, 166th Aero Squadron, a bank clerk from Norfolk who arrived in Brest on 18 June 1918, remarked, "Physically, I lost some flesh, but I was generally well, and came home in good health. Mentally, I gained in knowledge of people and their customs and tempered my mind more to the sympathy of my fellow man in distress."[43]

Captain Nelson C. Overton, 325th Infantry, 82nd Division, found it "very difficult to describe" his training overseas. "I think that among the effects are these: more tolerant of other people's opinions and less liable to judge them entirely upon what they may say."[44] Sergeant Philip W. Higgins of Clinton, Connecticut, served with the 301st Field Signal Corps and arrived in France on 4 August 1918 aboard the *Durham Castle* out of Montreal. His time overseas gave him "interest and deep admiration for the spirit of France. . . . I became surer of my own ability, more assertive, learned to endure discomforts, and to make the best of any situation."[45]

Some men believed the camps in Europe and the training they received there were inferior to those in the United States. "The English camps made me feel bitter toward the arrangements my country has made for our welfare and when in France the feeling grew to open condamnation. But the experience is worth much," said Private First Class Eugene M. Kelcy, Signal Corps, Photographic Division. Although the Hartford native did not like the training camps, he did enjoy interacting with the people of France. Kelcy stated, "In Paris I had the chance to study the French people in an intimate way. I found them of high ideals and sympathetic, very hospitable and easily pleased. Intellectually they feel a certain superiority to all other people."[46] Other soldiers expressed affection for France and dislike for England, perhaps due to their brief time there. The soldiers' stay in France was a good deal longer, and they became well acquainted with the French troops who trained them. Second Lieutenant John M. Ross, an African American soldier from New Haven who served in the Field Artillery Reserve, had "the feeling of love toward the French as a people, and a distrust of England as a nation."[47] Russian-born Jew Abraham Miskin was nearly twenty-seven years old when he enlisted. Reflecting on his travels, Miskin remarked:

> I have been in England a short time, but in that very short time I have learned that the people from England are more or less to themselves. I have noticed that when we Americans were walking and they would pass us by, they would never greet us. When we Americans first came, we thought that everybody would welcome us. I was very much disappointed. The French people are very friendly; they like to know everything about you and your family. Well, I can forgive everything, but oh! Why are the villages in France so dirty, the richer the family, the more dirt there was piled around the doors and windows. The manure piled up in front of their windows, and you can imagine how we felt about that, and in general it looked more like a fiftcenth century instead of a twentieth century village.[48]

Bugler Leo J. Hill, a New Haven resident, said, "Didn't see much of England and don't care to if the English crew on the transport is a sample. The French I like, and would like to see more of."[49]

Numerous men expressed compassion for the difficulties faced by the citizens of the Allied nations. Private Jacob Salovitz of New Haven remarked, "Gave me a chance to see the sufferings of the people over there, and that alone made me proud to think that I could do a little to help those poor, suffering souls."[50] Manchester, Connecticut, native Captain George W. Cheney said, "It was brought home to me very forcibly how little we had suffered in comparison with the French and British. They had stood the brunt of the fighting for four years whereas we were engaged less than a year."[51]

New Haven resident Sergeant Joseph Cosenzo, 102nd Machine Gun Company, wrote, "My experience overseas was most wonderful, both in France and England. It showed me people of other nations, how they lived and how they suffered from the war. . . . I found myself with more and better feelings towards mankind."[52] Austrian-born Corporal Henry Evanier, a resident of Hartford, enlisted in the National Guard on 14 April 1914 at age nineteen; for Evanier, his time spent in France "made my love for fellow men much more."[53] A clerk at Aetna Life Insurance Company, Evanier had served with the Border Service in Mexico prior to the war. Private First Class John D. Kinzer, 8th Division Military Police, left his Bedford, Virginia, farm and joined the service on 10 May 1918—his twenty-third birthday. Kinzer said his time in France "showed me distinctly how small one man really is in this world."[54] Clearly, the doughboys developed empathy for the people of Europe, especially the French.

Nostalgia

Travel to Europe increased the doughboys' love of America. Although their overseas experiences enriched their lives, many felt that the United States eclipsed anything offered in Europe. Private First Class Frank E. Murphy, 101st Machine Gun Battalion, expressed the feelings of other servicemen when he said, "The chief effect of my eighteen months in France was that it brought out strongly the advantages of living in America and how little I had appreciated my home [in Hartford]."[55] Through his overseas experiences, twenty-seven-year-old physician Captain Thomas G. Hardy of Farmville, Virginia, "learned to love America better and to hate war more."[56]

First Lieutenant Albert M. Simons, 104th Regiment, 26th Division, stated, "I am convinced the US is the best country in the world. We are far advanced in our method of living both in sanitation and methods. The French and English are very interesting people, but they are not as energetic as Americans."[57] Private John N. Dickerson, a cigar maker from New Haven, valued his time in France, which allowed him to undertake "a study of classes, or of nations, which I consider very important to a man's education."[58] New Haven native Sergeant Horton J. Dorkendorff, 102nd Machine Gun Battalion, commented, "I am sure that my overseas service has helped me to be more self-reliant, broadened my knowledge of this world and made me more appreciative of my own country."[59]

"I love my country better, I know what a good home we have," wrote twenty-year-old African American Corporal Thomas M. Clary, 369th Regiment, a native of White Plains, Virginia.[60] A teacher and salesman from Richmond, Captain Channing W. Daniel said his "vision was broadened by travel and experience . . . increase of human sympathy, and greater appreciation of home materially and of France ethnically."[61]

Hartford native Private William G. B. Augermann, 104th Ambulance Company, 26th Division, stressed, "I despise from the bottom of my soul a system as was practiced in Germany, but when I volunteered in the USA I could hardly await the call that would summon me to the cause. The more I saw of England

and France, the better I liked the US which is a fact of truth with every soldier I ever met and mentioned the subject to."[62] Private Lawrence W. Porter of New Haven observed, "If there is an army better than ours I want to see it. It is better drilled and better kept than any I have seen. . . . The army will make a man out of you. I think that it has almost made one out of me. France may be a nice country to visit but a place to live give me the USA."[63] Longing for home seemed to increase in proportion to the hardships the men endured.

First Lieutenant John R. Castleman of the Army Air Service, a twenty-two-year-old from Roanoke, Virginia, enlisted on 14 May 1917 during his sophomore year in college. After attending Wilbur Wright Aviation School in Ohio, Castleman embarked for France on 2 November 1917. His words illustrate the mindset of the majority of AEF soldiers as they arrived in France or England: "I wanted to do the duty of a soldier, and naturally there were many things we did not like to do, and even grumbled among ourselves about some things, but the spirit was very good." Writing about how being overseas affected him personally, Castleman said, "It left me in the most restless sort of condition, the excitement which had keyed me to a high pitch, when taken away I did not want to do anything but dream and wander over the country."[64]

A Richmond native, thirty-year-old First Lieutenant Robert C. Duval Jr. was a practicing attorney when he enlisted in the National Army as an officer candidate on 14 May 1917. He noted that "the spirit of the AEF was very fine, and there was an inspiration and an uplifting of ideals that the after-war period can hardly efface."[65] Private William J. B. Morris of Mappsville, Virginia, said his overseas experience "proved to me that I was a man physically and mentally as nothing but a man could withstand the hardships."[66]

Captain Anson T. McCook of Hartford described his camp in France as "not so good. Exposure and exhaustion were often extreme, although the outdoor life counter balanced many hardships." McCook felt indebted to the civilians who supported the war effort, and especially the groups that aided and comforted the doughboys overseas. McCook stressed, "I wish to record my gratitude to the men and women who backed us at home and above all to the Welfare Organizations, particularly their women workers, who made our work more efficient and our life more endurable."[67]

Auxiliaries

Three organizations that accompanied the AEF overseas were the YMCA, the Red Cross, and the Salvation Army; of these, the American veterans praised the last group most highly. During the war, unselfish individuals, mostly women, journeyed with the Salvation Army to England, France, and, after the armistice, Germany to lend support and bring a small touch of home to the AEF. Lieutenant Florence Turkington from Manchester, Connecticut, along with twenty other Salvation Army "lassies," as the doughboys called them, served coffee, sandwiches, and doughnuts to soldiers on the Metz front. She remembered, "At night, you could hear the shells whistling through the air in the darkness, you knew they could land close to you. You didn't think of that though. You thought only of those poor doughboys in the trenches only a few miles away, and what they were enduring. You prayed for them."[68] The Salvation Army's dedication and concern remained constant as its members toiled for the benefit of the doughboys at the front and elsewhere in Europe. The lassies also visited soldiers in hospitals and wrote letters for the wounded.

Doris Kellogg of Buffalo, New York, volunteered as a canteen girl with the Red Cross. In a letter home to her mother on 8 June 1918, Kellogg expressed her joy at being able to assist at the Vanderbilt Hospital in Neuilly-sur-Seine: "I shall never be able to thank my stars enough for having been able to get over here just when I did and for the way things have turned out. If you could half realize what it means to these Sammies to have American girls here to comfort and cheer them you would be building special ships to send more and more overseas. Being here is a privilege for which I shall never cease to be grateful."[69] The wife of William Kissam Vanderbilt II had established the hospital in Neuilly-sur-Seine before America entered the war. After the armistice, Mrs. Vanderbilt declared, "I wonder, whether the American people really can visualize what their boys at the front have been through? I wonder if they realize how fine they've been?"[70] Corporal Fred W. Chitty from New Haven was eternally grateful to the Red Cross: "I was taken a prisoner at Seicheprey. For four long months I was in a prisoner hospital in Germany with just enough to eat to keep myself alive. In September 1918 my Red Cross food boxes reached me."[71]

Even with aid from organizations such as the Salvation Army and the Red Cross, some men could not withstand the rigors of military life in France. Private Samuel Dunn, a twenty-four-year-old Russian, had worked at the G. Fox and Company department store in downtown Hartford before entering the service. Dunn described his time in France as "very poor, officers poor, mistreatment, hunger, and hell in general."[72] At age twenty-nine, Private Charles R. Goddard, a lawyer from Hartford, was inducted into the National Army on 19 September 1917. Concerning his training in France, Goddard recalled that the "drills and marches were very strenuous; I was near the point of exhaustion many times."[73]

Censorship

If the doughboys wanted to express their bitter feelings, they had to be careful: the letters and postcards they sent to their families and friends back home were censored. Although there had been some censoring of soldiers' letters during the Civil War, it was not until the Great War that censorship became more thorough. An officer or a chaplain worked as a censor for each unit. These men checked the troops' letters to ensure they did not contain any information the enemy would find useful. Careful proofreaders removed information such as the location of the soldier's unit, troop strength, and movements. Officers also read the doughboys' letters to determine the morale in their units. Soldiers were instructed what to exclude from their letters home, but they sometimes made mistakes, and officers redacted parts of their correspondence by cutting them out or blotting them with ink. Most doughboys complied, and the words "somewhere in France" often appeared at the top of their letters. Although the doughboys might not necessarily write what was actually on their minds at the time, and although they varied their remarks, depending on who would be receiving the message, above all, they attempted to stay upbeat in their discussions of the war.

Private Carl C. Senkbeil wrote a postcard to John Knoll of Manchester, Connecticut, in June 1918. His words masked his actual reason for being overseas; he seemed to be just a tourist: "Just a few lines to let you know I am well and happy and enjoying life over here. The country here is a fine sight and I like the conditions here better than I thought I would. We are at work at present but not at our own trade but expect to get it in the near future. Our trip across was a very quiet one and we enjoyed it. I went to the city of Bordeaux on a sight seeing trip and found it to be a very noted place."[74] When he wrote this postcard, Senkbeil had yet to experience the front and still had a sense of wanderlust. Second Lieutenant Julius I. Twiss of Hartford spoke out against the censorship: "The next war it might be advisable to let the soldiers keep in touch with the folks at home and not have all their letters chopped into hash. Then the US wouldn't have to put out so much propaganda."[75]

Day-to-Day Experiences

Keeping a diary during wartime was strictly against army regulations, for if a diary fell into the wrong hands, the enemy could learn a great deal about troop formations, unit strength, and attack plans. Nonetheless, some soldiers kept journals or diaries of their day-to-day experiences. If they did not have notebooks, the men might number loose pieces of paper to organize them into a journal; others numbered their letters home so that their loved ones could read them in the proper sequence. Solomon Wollman maintained a diary from 15 September 1917 to 4 July 1918; it offers glimpses of a doughboy's life overseas and is particularly valuable due to the army's censorship policies. Wollman was killed in action on 20 July 1918 at the Battle of Château-Thierry.

The question of whether Wollman received proper training for combat is difficult to answer, but Wollman's mother reflected, "Had only been at the Range for training a few times. Had not done much shooting on the Range, but was in action just the same."[76] Like so many of his fellow doughboys, especially those from the North, Wollman did not receive appropriate rifle training. Southern and western men were generally more accustomed to using firearms due to their upbringing and country lifestyles. As Tennessean Alvin C. York observed in March 1918, "Some of the boys from the big cities hadn't been used to handling guns. Some of them didn't even know how to load them, and when they fired they not only missed the targets, they missed the backgrounds on which the targets were fixed. They missed everything but the sky. It shore was dangerous scoring for them boys. Of course, it weren't no trouble nohow for me to hit them great big army targets. They were so much bigger than turkeys' heads."[77]

Wollman left the United States on 15 September 1917 and fired his rifle for the first time on 22 December. The following excerpts from his diary illustrate the conditions in France:

October 9. After breakfast went out and carried stones all day on our shoulders to help build a walk. It is raining now and we are full of mud. Went to bed at 6 PM.

October 13. It rained all day and most all of the boys are disgusted with so much mud around.

October 14. We are all disgusted with the food; we get stew for dinner and stew for supper with hard tack. An American officer gave us a lecture at the YMCA. He had been in the trenches and he gave us a little information. Some of the things he told us were very discouraging but the boys all took it with a smile.

October 26. We worked on detail all day digging around our barracks so that the water would run down in the stream nearby.

October 27. One of our boys died of pneumonia, which he got from the mud around here. It rained all that day and night too.

Wollman and his fellow soldiers spent most days digging, carrying rocks, bringing wood into camp, and occasionally going into the nearby village, which was three miles from the camp. His diary continues:

November 9. Got up at six and had breakfast; went out to drill at 7 a.m. and we had some drill. It rained all the time while we were drilling. We were shown the French style of trench warfare. It made all of us tired. After a hard morning drill we had a very poor dinner which consisted of hard-tack and a piece of cheese. After dinner we hiked back to camp and they gave us our new trench hats which weigh about five pounds.

November 16. We had a lecture from General Edwards on a subject about the trenches and army discipline. He told us that in the trenches the mud is waist deep, yet the soldiers just smile and don't complain.

December 22. We went through some bayonet and rifle practice for about
two hours. I shot my rifle for the first time since I received it and didn't
make any hits out of five shots.

There were times during that winter when the men drilled in snow up to
their waists. Measles, spinal meningitis, pneumonia, and colds were among the
maladies afflicting the soldiers in camp. Wollman writes in his diary of men
standing around the stove for more than an hour at a time, trying to keep warm.
It was now 1918, and Wollman wrote:

January 21. Went out to drill with our packs on and got a lecture from our
new Colonel telling us that we would be in the trenches within ten days.
All the boys sure did cheer.
January 26. I shot my Springfield and a rifle grenade and smoke bombs. In
the afternoon I started out to the gas chamber and stood around until
2:45 without going in the chamber.
February 8. After breakfast got ready to move and at 7:30 started out to hike
for Châtenois, which is about 8 miles. Arrived at 12:20 and it sure was
some hike. Got on the train after dinner and pulled out at 2:30. Rode all
day in box cars; we had 48 men in our car and we couldn't sleep because
it was too crowded to move. We got coffee at 11:20 p.m. and then 8 of us
moved to another car.
February 9. Woke up at 5:20. It was raining but it stopped about 8:30 then we
opened up the doors. When we stopped I went in the other car and got
rations for us all. We got off at 10:20, stood around the depot until after
dinner when we hiked to a village about five miles. We found the place
all shot. Slept in barracks for tonight.

On 10 February, Wollman and his fellow soldiers reached their destination, a
village a few miles from the front.[78]
As Wollman's diary illustrates, the AEF soldiers had trouble adjusting to
the French climate—bitter cold accompanied by rain and snow. The inability to
stay warm dampened the spirits of many soldiers. Yet Corporal Fred W. Chitty
from New Haven said, "The training in France during the winter of 1918 made
me fit to stand the cold and hardships of the trenches when we took them over
in 1918."[79] Like many others, Corporal Louis J. Popolizio of New Haven found
the French winter uncompromising: "The first few months in France were hard
ones; cold winter nights. We couldn't keep warm. Cold feet, lots of hard training. On the go all the time. That's where I learned to swear."[80] After four
months in camp in France, twenty-four-year-old Captain Charles T. Lawson, a
marine from White Stone, Virginia, reflected that "the months spent in the
mud, water, cold and no rest probably aged me as many years."[81] "I went over-

seas weighing 158 pounds, four months later I weighed 119," wrote Sergeant Clarence H. Brinkley, 317th Regiment, 80th Division.[82]

"Every thing Over-seas, was very bad in many ways, for Instance FOOD was very Short, Caused by Mr. Hoover's, SAVE FOOD and WIN the WAR," wrote Private First Class James F. Bonham, 108th Aero Squadron.[83] Woodrow Wilson had appointed Herbert Hoover chief of the United States Food Administration after the country declared war. Hoover enacted policies on the home front to save food for the doughboys, such as observing meatless Mondays and wheatless Wednesdays and encouraging Americans to grow their own fruits and vegetables in war gardens. Besides blaming Hoover for the food shortages at the front, Bonham detested the entire experience; perhaps he was looking for a fantastic escapade but found a fierce struggle instead.

First Lieutenant Wylie R. Cooke, a twenty-seven-year-old graduate of the University of Virginia, professed that, after serving abroad, he "learned to cuss a little more fluently and came out with a poorer opinion of the Military Service as exemplified by the U.S. Army."[84] Captain Herman R. White did not receive any training in the United States and spent only three weeks training with the Royal Army Medical Corps at Blackpool, England. White remarked, "Physically improved. Learned to carry on even when hungry, thirsty, cold, tired, sleepy and even somewhat frightened."[85] Private First Class Walter B. Haislip, a Lynnhaven, Virginia, native and twenty-nine-year-old high school principal, explained that the effects of his training in Europe were "many and complex, but the strongest perhaps the ingraining of hatred of war."[86] Others, such as Private First Class Max L. Cohen, born in Orange, Connecticut, and assigned to US Base Hospital No. 1, developed a close comradeship with their fellow soldiers. Cohen concluded, "We might forget the terrors of the war, we might forgive and forget our wrongs in the service, but never forget the new friends we made and the new visions of life."[87]

Once they were in France, the doughboys were anxious to defeat the Central Powers. "I have just completed my course at the Clermont School. I have enjoyed myself while here and have been interested in my work. I figure that I am better qualified to meet the hun," remarked farmer Harlin Blair of St. George, Utah, in a letter to his parents dated 15 September 1918.[88] Ready for combat but perhaps nervous about what lay ahead, the young doughboys prepared themselves as best they could.

A twenty-one-year-old farmer with a sixth-grade education, Ralph L. Goodrich of Bicknell, Utah, was inducted into the army on 22 September 1917. He was promoted to corporal while in training at Camp Funston with the 431st Field Artillery, 89th Division, and left for France in June 1918. Goodrich underwent further training at Camps Castelnau-de-Médoc and de Souge in France, and before he arrived at the Toul sector of the front on 18 September 1918, he revealed his emotions in a letter to his mother: "I know I hadn't ought to use it but mother its going to be hard out on the field fighting and not have any thing to settle our nerves so I wish you would ask Mr. Porter if he would send me some horseshoe chewing tobacco. We can't get any over here. We can get some but its so strong you can't bear it. I suppose I can get along without it if I have to."[89] Goodrich survived the war, and after the armistice, the army assigned him to Dusseldorf, Germany.

Military policeman Corporal Emory P. Barrow of Alberta, Virginia, expressed a typical sentiment while in training: "Didn't mind it as long as the fight was on," he explained, "but became very impatient waiting so long for the command: Westward, march."[90] Like so many others, Barrow received his wish.

5

The Supreme Test

Vera Brittain, a young British woman from an affluent family, left Oxford in 1915 to serve as a nurse during the war. While working at a hospital in France, she watched as soldiers marched along the road that ran through the hospital's camp. At first, Brittain believed the troops to be colonial or British, but something about their "unusual quality of bold vigour" made her observe them more closely. "They looked larger than ordinary men," she recalled. "Their tall, straight figures were in vivid contrast to the under-sized armies of pale recruits to which we had grown accustomed." As Brittain pondered the identity of these soldiers, someone cried out, "Look! Look! Here are the Americans!" A group had gathered to watch "the United States physically entering the War, so god-like, so magnificent, so splendidly unimpaired in comparison with the tired nerve-racked men of the British Army. So these were our deliverers at last." The sight of the "confident Americans going to the front" brought tears to Brittain's eyes. The fear of German victory left her, and Brittain realized that "we were not, after all defeated."[1]

The Deliverers

American soldiers arrived at the front eager and ready to do battle, strengthened by duty, and with Civil War images in their minds. But combat and the dire conditions of life at the front were not what the men had envisioned. French officers taught the doughboys how to dig trenches, operate new weapons, and use gas masks, but nothing could prepare them for the filthy living conditions, the lack of food, the rats, and the stench of death emanating from the corpses of the fallen. They had imagined war as a great adventure, but the reality of the front was an experience of another kind. Combat changed the men. As Frank P.

Ground Gained by American Divisions on the Western Front in 1918.

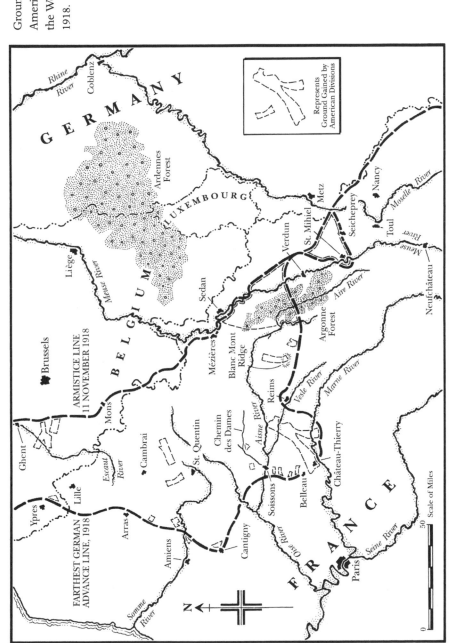

Sibley witnessed firsthand, "They no longer howled with ignorant enthusiasm for the chance to go against anything that might turn up. Nevertheless, they had a quiet confidence in their ability to handle anything the Boche might offer. And they had the steady look in their eyes of men who have seen their comrades killed and have felt death brush by them."[2]

For the doughboys who survived combat, General William Tecumseh Sherman's words became a maxim: "There is many a boy here today who looks on war as all glory, but, boys, it is all hell."[3] The American Expeditionary Forces (AEF) engaged in heavy combat for about eight months on the Western Front—from the start of the German offensives on 21 March to the armistice on 11 November 1918. Doughboys also saw action in Italy in 1918 and in the Russian campaigns (in northern Russia and Siberia) from September 1918 to April 1920. During that time, 53,402 men were killed in action, and another 204,002 men were wounded.[4] These losses represent a combination of AEF unpreparedness and a formidable German opponent.

By the time the AEF arrived at the Western Front in November 1917, German morale had received a massive boost from Russia's capitulation. Germany knew the United States' entry into the war would turn the tide. As it had in 1914, Germany seized the initiative and launched massive offensives in the spring and summer of 1918. Sixty-two divisions of the German army began an offensive drive against the Somme front held by the British on 21 March 1918. General John J. Pershing sent the four combat-ready AEF divisions to assist the French in defending the lines broken by the Germans. Although the French employed only about 2,200 Americans, the Allies stopped the German advance by 6 April. Not utilizing all four American divisions could have been costly; however, the Germans failed to capitalize on their early success owing to a lack of reserves.

Another major German offensive began on 27 May along the Aisne River, in an attempt to divert the Allied reserves southward. Taking the British and French forces by surprise, the Germans overran them along a forty-mile front. The German army occupied Soissons, and by 31 May it was within forty miles of Paris, near Château-Thierry on the Marne River. This was only ten miles short of the distance the Germans had reached in 1914. Once again, doubt crept into the minds of the Allies: Paris might fall.

The German attack overwhelmed the French, and they began to retreat. As the German forces attempted to widen their positions, 27,500 AEF soldiers advanced to halt them. In early June the 3rd Division prevented the Germans from establishing a secure position on the Marne at Château-Thierry, while the 2nd Division defended the road to Paris. Fighting with the 2nd Division was the 4th Marine Brigade. On 3 June, in the midst of the French retreat, a French officer sent a written order to Captain Lloyd W. Williams to have his marines join the withdrawal. Williams ignored the order and growled, "Retreat, hell! We just got here."[5] Two days later, against devastating German firepower, First Sergeant Daniel Daly rallied his men and barked, "Come on, you sons-o'-bitches! Do you want to live forever?"[6] The doughboys advanced and prevailed against fortified German positions at Belleau Wood.[7] The legendary lines uttered by Williams and Daly represent the feelings of many doughboys and embody their sense of duty.

Since the end of the war, official European histories and many scholars have downplayed the contribution of the AEF, but without the Americans, Paris might have fallen. The doughboys became a footnote, a simple morale booster and nothing more, in most major volumes on the war. Sir John Keegan best encapsulates these sentiments. With only four pages devoted to the AEF, he scoffs, "It was indeed immaterial whether the doughboys fought well or not. Though the professional opinion of veteran French and British officers that they were enthusiastic rather than efficient was correct, the critical issue was the effect of their arrival on the enemy."[8] At the time, however, the French credited the marines with saving Paris and halting the Germans and even renamed Belleau Wood in their honor: Bois de la Brigade de Marine. According to AEF General Robert L. Bullard, "The marines didn't 'win the war' here. *But they saved the Allies from defeat.*"[9] Quartermaster General Erich Ludendorff, joint commander of the German army, agreed with Bullard. In his memoirs, Ludendorff admits:

As long as our troops maintained their morale they would be able to cope with any enemy, even with the strong American divisions, whose nerves were less shaken than those of our men who had been in action continually for a long time. But the fact that these new American reinforcements could release English and French divisions on quiet sectors weighed heavily in the balance against us. This was of the greatest importance and helps explain the influence exerted by the American contingent on the issue of the conflict. It was for this reason that America became the deciding factor in the war.[10]

Even after the defeat at Belleau Wood, Ludendorff continued his drive for victory. But this time, when the Germans attacked on both sides of Rheims on 15 July, they found the Allies ready and waiting. As German troops drove across the Marne River close to Château-Thierry, French and American units stopped them. The 3rd, 26th, 28th, and 42nd Divisions of the AEF, as well as the 369th Infantry, furnished crucial support in thwarting the German advance. The 3rd Division's 38th Infantry held the line against a lethal German onslaught, earning the appellation "Rock of the Marne."

The arrival of increasing numbers of AEF troops at the front made up for Allied losses during the Germans' spring and summer offensives. Germany was unable to replace its lost soldiers, but the Allies could do so because of the fresh

The remains of Bois des Éparges after four years of war, looking southwest toward Saint-Mihiel, 3 February 1919. (Photograph Collection, box 150, Historical Data File, Connecticut State Library)

American troops. German morale began to decline, and by the end of July 1918, the Allies—with the AEF bolstering their ranks—clearly outnumbered the Germans on the Western Front. The Allies now seized the initiative.

The AEF once again proved its capabilities during the Aisne-Marne offensive, which lasted from 18 July to 6 August. French forces and the 1st and 2nd Divisions of the AEF launched an attack on the German position near Soissons. The AEF's 3rd, 4th, 28th, and 42nd Divisions then joined French forces and succeeded in pushing the Germans back across the Aisne and Vesle Rivers. The breaking of the Marne salient eliminated the German threat to Paris. After the Aisne-Marne offensive, the German army lost its advantage and would never regain it.

General Pershing's First Army, organized on 10 August 1918, prepared for an attack on the German salient at Saint-Mihiel. Employing French artillery, tanks, and airplanes, the Americans and four French divisions unleashed a three-pronged attack to cut the salient off from the Germans' defensive line. The Saint-Mihiel offensive marked the AEF's first major operation under American command, and the Allies attained their objectives after the second day—taking a salient the Germans had held for four years (although Ludendorff was in the process of withdrawing).

The final campaign of the war was the forty-seven-day Meuse-Argonne of-

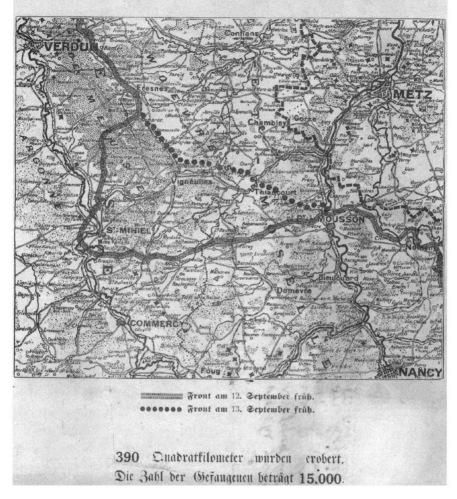

Der Bogen, wo sich die Deutschen
4 Jahre lang behauptet hatten, wurde in 27 Stunden
von den Amerikanern eingenommen.

━━━━━ Front am 12. September früh.
●●●●●●● Front am 13. September früh.

390 Quadratkilometer wurden erobert.
Die Zahl der Gefangenen beträgt 15,000.

As part of its psychological warfare campaign, the AEF dropped this map inside German territory to show what had been gained by the doughboys. The top reads, "The Salient, that the Germans occupied for 4 long years was seized by the Americans in 27 hours." The bottom reads, "390 square kilometers were conquered. 15,000 prisoners taken." (Map of Saint-Mihiel, Map File, Connecticut State Library) fensive. Supreme Allied commander, French Marshal Ferdinand Foch, and his subordinate commanders sought to drive German forces out of France and precipitate the end of the war by spring 1919. Beginning on 26 September 1918, the Allied offensive placed Pershing's troops in position to strike a twenty-mile front between the dense Argonne Forest and the Meuse River, where the Germans still maintained excellent positions. Pershing sent 1.2 million doughboys into action during the Meuse-Argonne offensive. The Americans advanced along a considerable stretch of territory and met stiff resistance in the southern Meuse-Argonne area. The AEF captured two defensive positions, but unpreparedness and a lack of tank support contributed to the failure to secure a third German position. During the second phase of the campaign, with more experienced AEF troops, First Army pushed the Germans out of the Argonne Forest. In the final stage of the campaign, from 1 to 11 November, First Army prevented the Germans' escape to the Sedan-Mézières railway. Outnumbered and overwhelmed, Germany knew the war was lost.

American casualties were high—but imagine what they might have been if German combat effectiveness had been at its 1914 level. Captain Clarence M. Thompson of Hartford, Connecticut, remarked, "It was mighty fortunate we entered the war after the enemy was weary. The dash of the American carried him thru but at terrible expense for what was accomplished. What would it have cost if our untrained men had met that enemy two years earlier?"[11] Thompson was one of the rare doughboys who acknowledged the quality of the German army so soon after the war. The majority of AEF veterans recognized the Germans' superiority only after decades of reflection.

The Individual Experience

The first AEF combat deaths occurred in the trenches located northwest of Toul at approximately 3:00 a.m. on 3 November 1917. Sergeant Edgar Halyburton, 16th Infantry, 1st Division, described the German assault on his men: "I saw a wall of fire rear itself in the fog and darkness. Extending to right and left a couple of hundred yards, it moved upon us with a roar, above which I could not hear my own voice. The earth shuddered . . . sections of the trench began to give way. Then the explosives were falling all around me. The air was filled with mud, water, pieces of duckboard and shell splinters."[12] Halyburton was knocked out, and when he regained consciousness, German soldiers atop the parapet were holding him prisoner. By that time, he realized, "My men were no longer offering any resistance. I concluded that they had all been wounded or killed. I could hear some of them screaming in agony."[13]

Some soldiers had difficulty putting their experiences into words, while others used blunt terms to capture the effects of combat. Brigadier General William "Billy" Mitchell, who was instrumental in advancing the concept of airpower, observed, "During a war of this kind, one's nerves, passions and whole physical and mental make-up are tremendously overwrought and one's outlook is somewhat different than it would be ordinarily."[14] Mitchell's words describe how the majority of American soldiers felt: combat changed them, their views on life, and their opinions about war. The Civil War stories of their youth, Roosevelt's charge up Kettle Hill, the articles in local newspapers, and the remarkable rotogravure photographs they had seen only months earlier began to turn a different color. "From the newspapers we learn how the battle goes," stated Brigadier General Albertus W. Catlin, but "it is only from the individual soldier that we can learn how the war appears to the man who is doing the fighting."[15]

Initially, the doughboys thought the war in Europe would be a glorious escapade: the Germans would be easy targets, and the doughboys would save the world from autocracy. The men who participated in heavy combat and lived through intense shelling learned otherwise. A significant number of doughboys described their combat experience by quoting General Sherman. Machine gunner Sergeant Byron P. Graff of Hartford was one of many who referred to the Civil War commander: "I had often heard what Sherman said and I found out he didn't exaggerate one bit."[16] Fellow Hartford resident, Private Carl J. Schultze of the 103rd Engineers, remarked, "I took part in the fighting and was exposed to shell fire five months steady so I agree with Gen. Sherman that War is 'H.' but I'm thankful I came out alive."[17]

Twenty-year-old Private First Class Robert E. Livingston of Salt Lake City, Utah, volunteered on 2 October 1917. In a letter to a friend written after the armistice, Livingston described his unit's participation at Saint-Mihiel:

> For days and days we fought the Germans, trying to get them out of the woods. I never heard so much noise in all my life. . . . You could hear the six-foot aeroplane bombs for a long time, each coming with its peculiar whistle of death and sounding as though it were speeding directly at the spot where you are flattened against the earth. When they explode you are lifted some two feet from the ground and your hair rises almost out of your head. At times I did not consider my life worth ten cents . . . but I came out of this living hell safe and sound.[18]

After helping to return French and Belgian prisoners of war, Livingston returned Stateside, and the army discharged him on 24 June 1919.

Leonard R. Bennett of Hartford, a private in the 12th Field Artillery, agreed: "War is all that Sherman said it was—and then some."[19] Twenty-seven-year-old Corporal Emory P. Barrow, a student from Alberta, Virginia, also invoked the Civil War general: "Sherman only half said it when he said, 'War is Hell.' Stay out of it until there is no other recourse, as was the case in this great conflict."[20]

Participation in combat "gave one a love for excitement. Death was not taken serious. Sherman was right," said infantryman Sergeant Marcel W. Rice of New Haven. According to Rice, combat gave him "the desire to do unto Germany as she had done unto France."[21] Hartford native Captain James B. Moody Jr., 301st Supply Train, stressed, "What I saw in the Advance Section was sufficient for decision that Sherman did not realize how terrible war might be fought in the twentieth century when he said: 'War is h——!'"[22] Thirty-year-old Walter T. Spencer, a native of Fort Mitchell, Virginia, declared, "Hell could not be a worse place than this."[23] Sergeant John McDaniel, age twenty-nine, of Roswell, Utah, volunteered on 15 July 1917 and, upon completion of his training at Fort Douglas, shipped out for France on 17 November 1917. In a letter to his father dated 20 November 1918, McDaniel devoted a few lines to his experiences at the front, where he had served for eleven months with the 304th Tank Regiment. "We were raided almost every good night and at times it seemed like Hell was turned loose but we got it so often we got used to it. That's if it's possible to get used to a thing like that."[24]

New Haven resident Alexander J. Flynn, a clerk for the New York, New Haven, and Hartford Railroad Company, enlisted in the National Guard on 22 June 1916 "as a duty to my country." Flynn summed up his combat experiences in one brief phrase: "That Sherman was right."[25] "I felt as though I had experienced the whole alphabet, while Sherman had scarcely experienced the first letter," said Private First Class Garnett D. Claman, a nineteen-year-old farmer from Bristol, Virginia.[26] Twenty-six-year-old First Lieutenant Miletus B. Jarman entered combat on 25 July 1918 at the second Battle of the Marne and remarked, "War in general is more or less Hell."[27] George A. Fordham, a twenty-six-year-old teacher and farmer from Santa Clara, Utah, was inducted on 3 September 1917. He served with the 26th Infantry, 1st Division, and "saw heavy fighting on eight fronts." In a 24 November 1918 letter to his father-in-law, by which time "the censor allows us to write about most everything," Fordham explained "going over the top": "It means that we advance toward the enemy while he is sending machine gun bullets, rifle bullets . . . large shells and all other kinds of explosives are coming towards us, and we are sending shells toward them to beat hell at his own game. You know how fast rain drops fall on a house during a shower well our shells go over about that fast. It sure is and sounds like arterial hell."[28]

Survival in the Trenches

Men were wounded or gassed or died in battle, but the Germans were not the only threat to American soldiers. Scarlet fever, trench cave-ins, pneumonia, premature grenade explosions, and trench fever contracted from lice killed many men. Clean, dry uniforms and socks were rare; food was sometimes spoiled; and sleeping conditions were poor: all these things contributed to the

AEF soldiers' misery. The winter of 1917–1918 in Europe was cold and cruel, especially for the doughboys, who were short on supplies and had to withstand rain, mud, snow, and freezing temperatures.[29]

Captain James T. Duane remembered that, overnight, the soldiers' "shoes would freeze and on several mornings when they could not get them on they were compelled to put a piece of paper in the shoes and set it on fire to melt the ice. They could then pour out the water and put them on."[30] The American-made shoes issued to the AEF were inadequate for the severe French winter. "The men called them 'hen's skins' and 'tango shoes,'" wrote Billy Mitchell. "Marching on the roads with full packs tore them to pieces in a day. I saw a division go by . . . with the men practically barefooted, many leaving blood marks in the snow."[31] Private John J. Sullivan, 151st Depot Brigade, characterized the conditions as akin to "the life of a tramp sleeping in dirty and filthy barns at times and other times in holes of water." The Hartford native summed up his impressions: "As Sherman said, War is Hell."[32]

For Corporal Joseph J. O'Connell of Manchester, Connecticut, combat caused "a nervousness which increases as the time draws near for an engagement which soon wears away to an indifference to any danger, upon getting tired out and lack of food with nothing but mud to sleep in. I have often prayed to get wounded and so reach a hospital where I could get rest and a good meal."[33] Beaver City, Utah, native Private First Class Bert Swindlehurst of the 91st Division reflected, "I have suffered cold and hunger, and have been so thirsty could not speak. . . . I seen my comrades blown to pieces." Swindlehurst was wounded in the neck and left leg on 29 September 1918 in the Argonne Forest and recalled, "I was 24 hours reaching hospital, after I was wounded, but oh how good to get a bed when I reached it—it was heaven for sure."[34] Swindlehurst received his discharge on 3 May 1919.

Twenty-one-year-old Raymond S. Jackson of Fremont, Utah, was drafted on 3 October 1917; served with the 145th Field Artillery, 40th Division; and spent three months fighting on the front lines. He contracted influenza and pneumonia after the armistice and was hospitalized for five months. Upon his recovery, Jackson detailed some of his combat experiences in a letter to his mother dated April 1919: "I've hiked many a night all night in the rain with my pack on my back . . . and went three days without a bite to eat and a very little to drink. I have seen the time when there wasn't much hopes for life when men were getting killed all around me. . . . I could hear the cannons roar and the bullets sing and see the shells coming toward me."[35] In a letter home, Evern E. Saville of Salt Lake City said he was looking forward to returning to the United States and taking a trip "where you really know that there is no one on the side of the road laying for you or someone behind a tree shooting at you or an airplane dropping a bomb on you. That is what we put up with."[36]

The dirt and vermin in the trenches combined to make conditions nearly unlivable for the doughboys. The men could do little about the ever-present mud and the rats, which grew fat from gnawing on corpses. Lieutenant Colonel Frederick M. Wise, 5th Marines, 2nd Division, vividly described the rodent problem: "I never saw such rats. Some of them were a foot long, not counting the tail. They were fat, arrogant and full of fight. One of my men was bitten through the lips by a rat that started to make a meal off his face as the man slept."[37] Corporal Wilson H. Whitehouse of Wallingford, Connecticut, who served with the 102nd Infantry, 26th Division, added a twist to General Sherman's words by observing that "Sherman was more than right, but then he didn't have so much mud & such large rats to contend with."[38]

Reactions to Combat Violence

The French and British soldiers had survived the trenches far longer than the Americans, but it did not take long for the AEF to appreciate the reality of modern, industrialized warfare. Doughboys differed in their responses to the unrelenting violence that surrounded them, but patterns emerge from their MSR questionnaires, diary entries, and letters home. In general, US soldiers were frustrated because the enemy remained invisible, hidden in their own trenches, and bombardment from an unseen enemy made life at the front even more disheartening. When AEF soldiers fought Germans in hand-to-hand combat, they felt like they were making a greater difference and accomplishing their goals. But at the same time, most men found it difficult to kill another human being, even when that other human being was an enemy intent on killing them. The doughboys' former lives—as postal clerks, farmers, students, attorneys, and family members—seemed a world away.

The soldiers' responses reveal a wide range of emotions. Combat caused numerous soldiers to take more pride in their country, even while it increased their dislike of war. For some men, combat brought out a deep courage they did not know they possessed. For many, the war caused them to feel more empathy toward their fellow human beings and to become more humane themselves. The exposure to violence altered each man in a different way, depending on his background. But whether they embraced combat or attempted to avoid it, the war—especially front-line combat—often left an irrevocable mark, both physical and mental.

Kill or Be Killed

The sight of wounded and dead Americans spurred many soldiers to fight. As Sergeant Samuel B. Yaffo of Hartford asserted, "At first I could not get angry enough at the Huns to want to kill them, after I saw my pals fall in agony from their shells, I did the rest."[39] Corporal John A. Rosner, also of Hartford, was moved by the sight of "the young American men who lay dead in a pool of there own blood on the Battlefields," and it made him feel "that they who are responsible" should "be hung."[40] Infantryman Private James O. McKarney, a twenty-four-year-old farmer from Washington County, Virginia, who entered action on 20 June 1918, declared, "I saw some pretty bad things happen overseas. When we were fighting and my comrade was killed by my side, I would get so mad I could have killed every German there was in Europe."[41] Hartford native Private Edward F. Plumridge observed, "I found that when a man gets excited in the heat of battle he has no thought of getting hurt himself, all he wants to do is kill."[42] Marine brigadier general Albertus W. Catlin, who led the attack on Belleau Wood on 6 June 1918, reflected, "You may be a perfect gentleman by inheritance and training, but the sight of a dead comrade's upturned face makes you want to kill."[43] Leo J. Hill, an artillery bugler from New Haven, commented, "What impressed me was how quickly an ordinary being like myself could get over being afraid and become bloodthirsty after being shot at."[44]

Salt Lake City resident Lamar H. Deming volunteered on 28 February 1918 and served in the field artillery. In a letter to his father written after the armistice, Deming recounted his experience with the 2nd Division in September 1918 as they moved through Verdun, where the 1st Division had battled the Germans two hours earlier: "The fields were covered with dead," Deming noted. "They were still warm and still dripping blood. I'll never forget those Marines."[45] Sergeant John J. Eckels from Hartford spoke about the transformation necessary to take another man's life: "In order to arrive at the point where you can stick a bayonet in another you have to slough off all civilization has built up since the Stone Age."[46] Samuel C. McDaniel, a twenty-year-old welder from Blackstone, Virginia, who first saw combat on 5 August 1918 at Vosges, said, "I learned that war over there was not what they put in the papers, that a man, after he smells powder or blood is not a civilized person, he is a beast."[47]

"The experiences were unlike anything I had known before, though I believe that part of the time due to the excitement it is very hard to say what one's feelings were. One seemed to act much by instinct. But the whole thing, one idea dominating was, get your opponent before he had the chance to get you. Chivalry died fifty years ago, neither did I see any displayed during the fighting," concluded Distinguished Service Cross awardee First Lieutenant John R. Castleman of Berrysville, Virginia.[48]

First Lieutenant Albert M. Simons first saw action at Chemin des Dames on 1 February 1918 and engaged in combat at Château-Thierry, where he was wounded in the left leg on 21 July; he was wounded again, in the right hip and ankle, at Saint-Mihiel on 12 September. After sustaining these wounds, Simons spent a month at Base Hospital No. 25 in Allerey, France. He reflected, "It is human to fight for what one believes is right. Fighting becomes part of a day's work. The animal nature predominates. A man goes back to the days of the cave man. Civilization is nothing more than a polish, which loses its luster when

Ernest C. Porter on horseback at Fort Myer, Virginia. Porter thought his war experience strengthened his religious beliefs. He "would pray every day particularly during battle, remembering Stonewall Jackson. Prayers answered by being sent home without a scratch." (Ernest C. Porter, 24 August 1919, box 14, Library of Virginia)

exposed to the elements. It is a matter of environment. It is a question of kill or be killed, and you do not hesitate to kill."[49]

Courage Trumps Fear

A recurring theme among the veterans was that selflessness and bravery often replaced terror during the heat of battle. When Sergeant Edward Wilson from Manchester, Connecticut, was asked if he took part in the fighting, he replied, "'If I took part in fighting,' where do you get that 'if' stuff? I did take part in some fighting and it scared the hell out of me." But, Wilson added, "I will go through it again tomorrow for the same purposes, the same ideals and the same flag."[50] Ordnance sergeant John E. Howell of Alexandria, Virginia, was a college-educated salesman when he entered the service at age twenty-five. Howell saw action at La Ferté-sous-Jouarre and was gassed, which severely injured his eyesight. "Going into battle for the first time at night with everything dark and the noise of continual gun fire and being with a French outfit instead of American I was very frightened," he recalled, "but after the first few hours everything became a matter of course and all fear left me."[51]

In an undated letter to his mother, Corporal Ray Van Cott Madsen of Ephraim, Utah, described his feelings about front-line combat: "There's something fascinating about going in the front line trenches. It's like a swimming hole. A fellow dreads it until he is wet all over, and then he likes it and finds pleasure in it until he is tired out."[52] Madsen was a twenty-four-year-old farmer when the army drafted him on 17 September 1917. One of four brothers serving with the AEF, Madsen was a member of the 41st Division; he was killed in action on 5 October 1918 and was buried in the Meuse-Argonne American Cemetery.

At twenty-two years of age, Ernest C. Porter of Norfolk was a cadet at the Virginia Military Institute when he enlisted on 14 May 1917. Porter first saw action on 6 February 1918, and he participated in engagements at Toul in April and June 1918 and at Château-Thierry from July to August 1918. Porter said combat "gave me courage and made me about fearless . . . look upon death as nothing to be feared, the dead seem as any inanimate object & nothing of the superstition ideas of spirits hovering over the dead." He was cited for bravery in action when "two gun crews were blown to pieces, several men wounded, the Captain and myself remained through it all, called back to fire barrage and walked over dead comrades."[53]

Leland C. Stapley of Kanarraville, Utah, arrived in France on 22 July 1918; by September, he was immersed in combat. He recorded the following in his diary at 3:00 p.m. on 26 September:

Zero hour. It is impossible to describe the noise made by the cannon. Hundreds of them firing at the same time with huge shells bursting all around. The lights of Broadway are mere glimmers when compared with the lights of battle. The flashes of the guns, star shell lights and signal rockets lighted up the horizon in one continuous stream of fire. In marching over no-man's land, which had been in the hands of the Germans for four years, we had to cross one large shell hole after another. No farmer ever turned over the soil more thoroughly than the artillery had plowed up the forest of Cheppie. Some of the sights along the road would make a strong man weak. That march was the hardest part of the fight for it looked like a death trap to me, as men were falling here and there, with shells on all sides of us, but we marched right through . . . the second night in the rain with only a rain coat.[54]

Private First Class Henry A. Isleib made similar observations: "Fighting is a terrible thing and after you did it for a few days you got hardened to the most horrible sights. When I was discharged from the Army I felt ten years older in thoughts than I did before entering it." Isleib was cited for conspicuous bravery at Saint-Juvin, France, in October 1918 for "fearlessly exposing myself as a stretcher bearer to carry off wounded until I myself was wounded." He was also gassed in the Argonne Forest that same month.[55] Corporal Mark N. Holmes mused, "If a fellow ever died and went to H—L he certainly would be use to it. It seems almost impossible to get out of it alive, and I wonder many times why I am not pushing up daisys in France now."[56] Captain Thomas B. McDermott of Hartford called himself "lucky" to have avoided injury during combat, although he was "scared to death most of the time and wished I was in Honolulu. When it was over I wanted to be in again and when in again scared again. Left with a profound regard for the wonderful bravery of all the rest of the American soldiers. They have no equals." McDermott added, "Have become blasé as regards life in general; there are no more thrills."[57]

Channing W. Daniel stressed "the magnitude of the effort, the somber glory of battle, the thrill of the fight, the utter disinterestedness of the participants, the instinct of self-preservation reduced from feeling to automatic action, the beauty of sacrifice, the crime of slaughter and destruction."[58] Educated at the University of Virginia, Daniel was a teacher and a salesman before serving in the army.

LeRoy H. Cox was a twenty-two-year-old college student from St. George, Utah, when he was drafted on 1 November 1917. Cox served with the 148th Field Artillery, saw action at Château-Thierry and Saint-Mihiel, and took part in the drive that broke the Hindenburg Line.[59] In a letter home on 26 September 1918, Cox wrote about the soldiers' motivations:

> A few things which fill the soldiers hearts with determination to carry things through and stand the hardships of the battlefield. The first is the satisfaction we get that we are in the right and that everybody is backing us at home in every way possible; the next stimuli is to see your comrades lying dead and dying upon the battlefield: this hardens our hearts with determination to see things through. Among other things are the cruelties that we have seen that have been committed by the Germans. I know that upon one occasion our boys found French girls and women who were compelled to live in German dugouts with German officers. This is just one example of the many crimes they have committed. Before the war I read of these but thought they were exaggerated, but now I can bear witness that they are true. . . . I am proud of the fact that I helped in stopping the German drive for Paris at Château-Thierry and helped in the late Saint Mihiel drive and hope to be in more.[60]

A student at Yale University before the war, twenty-three-year-old First Lieutenant Clarke O. Kimberly, 12th Field Artillery, entered combat at Verdun on 15 March 1918. Kimberly, from Elizabeth City, Virginia, also participated in the offensives at Aisne-Marne, Saint-Mihiel, Champagne, and Meuse-Argonne. He commented, "One never knows what superb qualities a man may have until the supreme test comes. American soldiers went into battle as if they were going on a lark, realizing the horror of it all but with the determination that carried all before them."[61]

On 8 August 1918 Swedish-born Corporal Fred Lindbeck of Salt Lake City was wounded in action west of Soissons. While recovering in a French hospital, Lindbeck wrote to his sister, "You might think we see many things, but we haven't time to stop and think about them. Just so we get the Germans to run we don't care, and run they do. I am going back to my comrades in the trenches in a week and I long for the time to come . . . it is lonesome in this hospital." Lindbeck, twenty-four, also informed his sister that he was sending her "a German helmet for a souvenir . . . very worn, weighs 3½ lbs, bullet hole in back part of rim indicating wearer was in full retreat towards Berlin when last seen alive."[62]

Postal clerk Herbert D. May of Culpeper, Virginia, joined the National Guard on 22 September 1908, two weeks after his sixteenth birthday. When the United States declared war, he "took the additional oath for foreign service as soon as could be arranged by the federal government." May had two main impressions of combat: "First—that the American soldier as a whole is more willing to make sacrifices than the average American citizen believes. Second—that to do battle in defense of one's country is an honor of the highest, and the duty every man owes. Nevertheless war is horrible and indescribable."[63] May entered action on 26 July 1918; he fought at Argonne, was wounded by shell splinters, and had his legs crushed in a motor accident in France on 4 April 1919.

Twenty-eight-year-old John A. Holt of Salt Lake City volunteered on 11 April 1917; his younger brother, eighteen-year-old Leland, volunteered twelve days later. John served at the front beginning in June 1918 and acknowledged that it is difficult to grasp the brutality of war without experiencing it firsthand. In an undated letter to his parents, Holt expressed his determination to do his part:

> After looking at the ruin on the way up to the front, it makes a fellow feel more than ever like doing his bit for a cause like this. Gee! it makes one feel like giving the Huns hell for what they have done to this once beautiful country. Those in America do not know what the war is—only her fighting men can know. I have been on some of the big battle fronts, and it certainly is horrible to go over the ground and hear the death-calls. Still we can only go on and give Germany what she has given our allies for the past four years.[64]

Both Holt brothers survived the war.

Echoing the sentiments of Holt, fellow Utahan Walter H. Anderson wrote a letter home two weeks after the armistice:

Our famous old 91st Division fought the most wicked battle in the war, and we drove those Huns through the great forest and barbed wire and we went through ten days of hell that I pray to God that I never have to go through again, nor my children. For five days and nights I lived in a little hole with mud and water in it. It's too awful to write about. But, dad, you folks at home don't realize what war is. After that we came up here and opened the famous Flanders Front. Well, our hell ended. . . . I am ready to settle down now for I have kept myself clean and lived like a man since I came into the army.[65]

Despite their courage, homesickness afflicted the doughboys. Private First Class Millard C. Life, a twenty-seven-year-old college-educated shipping clerk from McGaheysville, Virginia, entered the service on 18 September 1917. He commented, "War is awful. It kept us constantly thinking of loved ones at home and friends. The bravery, courage and grit of all the boys was great."[66] Life entered action on 23 July 1918 near Albert and participated in the Saint-Mihiel drive; he was burned by mustard gas at Meuse-Argonne on 3 October 1918.

Private John P. Dwyer from Waterbury, Connecticut, served with the 102nd Regiment, 26th Division. He arrived at the front on 4 February 1918 and immediately went into action at Chemin des Dames; later, he saw action at Toul, Château-Thierry, Saint-Mihiel, and the Argonne Forest. Dwyer was recommended for the Distinguished Service Cross for acts of bravery at Toul. He recalled those events: "Sergeant Singer of Ansonia was very dangerously wounded, and it was essential that he be moved from the front line to Beaumont, where they would better be able to take care of him. Another man named Tournard and myself undertook to do the job, it was on the 21st of April about 11 in the morning, a nice bright day, and we had to carry him about ½ mile in plain sight of the Germans. Lieutenant Thomson, of the 2nd Battalion Snipers recommended us for the Medal but he did not have any luck or rather we didn't. Well, Ce La Guerre."[67] Dwyer, wounded in the left hand at Château-Thierry on 21 July 1918, underwent three unsuccessful surgeries after the armistice and was permanently disabled. He had received two promotions during his tour of duty overseas and left the National Guard as a sergeant.

Earle T. W. Gronk of Pembroke, Virginia, enlisted in the National Army at age twenty-one on 10 October 1917. Since he held a bachelor's degree in electronic engineering, Gronk, along with three other Virginians, was assigned to the First Army's 21st Engineers. He entered the front lines in February 1918 and participated in the fighting at Toul and Meuse-Argonne from 17 March to 11 November 1918. During his eight months at the front, during which time he was wounded, Gronk was "impressed by the magnitude of the government's operations, the necessity of organization and training, the spirit of his comrades in arms, the excellent morale of the American soldiers and their desire to come through but win first."[68]

Private Joseph R. Schadel, 28th Division, said, "Being in the engineers, my company was subjected to many trying and nerve-racking experiences. However, the greater the danger grew the calmer I became. After witnessing the horrible sights and scenes that I have in France, it seems to me that a world without war would be worth living in." On the eve of the armistice, Schadel wrote a poem entitled "Made for America":

> Steady tread and glitt'ring eye,
> True model of determination,
> Helmet cocked, a rifle, too;
> His object is emancipation.
> In the stillness of the night,
> A sculptor's model, standing
> Unabashed by shrapnel's hiss,
> America's good name commanding.
> Victory at last is won;
> His mighty task with care is ended;
> O'er the foamy waves to home,
> By all the big wide world befriended.[69]

The Inhumanity of War

Although most overcame the shock of warfare, others spoke out with aggression and bitterness. Maurice B. Fischman of New Haven had been a member of the National Guard since 12 March 1914. Fischman first saw action near Chemin des Dames on 2 February 1918, prompting him to comment that "a man when going 'over the top' is temporarily insane."[70] The Germans took Fischman prisoner at Seicheprey on 20 April 1918 and did not release him until after the armistice, on 24 November 1918.

After his first night at the front (1 August 1918), Ernest E. Strong, a twenty-year-old mechanic from Salt Lake City, asserted, "I'll never forget that night as long as I live. I imagined I could hear shells flying in every direction. I was alright after I got used to it."[71] Strong enlisted on 7 May 1917 and trained at Camps Greene and Merritt in the United States, as well as at Camp de Souge in France. He sustained a shrapnel wound to the left shoulder on 11 August 1918 and died from erysipelas and pneumonia on 8 June 1919, the day before he was supposed to leave for home.

Niels A. W. Johnson of Manchester, Connecticut, saw heavy action in the war. He had volunteered on 27 March 1917 and served temporarily as a cook in the 1st Connecticut National Guard. Reflecting on his combat experiences, Johnson said, "It made me Bloodthirsty & I feared nobody, not even death. It teaches you to take no back talk from anyone. It has given me one big lesson— I shall wait to be drafted—(volunteer) never again."[72]

Virginius L. Bland, a twenty-four-year-old, unmarried Virginia farmer, said the fighting "taught me that man was an animal, that he could ignore the laws of mankind."[73] Bland engaged the Germans at Meuse-Argonne and sustained gas injuries. "I had a real desire for action, it brought out the real caliber of a man as nothing else will," said Private First Class Frank E. Murphy of Hartford. He added, "I was scared many times but tried not to show it. I had great contempt for a coward. As the war continued I was disgusted with the horror, waste, and foolishness of it all."[74]

Disgust for War

Polish-born Michael Fydenkeuez was an electrician at the Hartford Rubber Works when he enlisted in the army on 22 May 1917. The twenty-three-year-old went into action five months later in Lorraine. "Fighting is about the hardest kind of business," he concluded. "My overseas experience in the war has injured my health and I rate about twenty-five percent disability."[75]

Many soldiers expressed their abhorrence of war, its destructiveness, and the loss of life. Despite his commendations for bravery, Private John P. Dwyer expressed a "hatred of war as now I consider it both silly and inhuman and not a civilized way of settling anything." Dwyer learned "what a rotten thing war is. The first time I began to say that was when I saw three comrades about 18 years old blown to bits with a HE shell. Then I began to wonder just what it was all about."[76] Used for its blast effect and minimal fragmentation, the high-explosive (HE) shell was fired mainly by heavy guns and howitzers (short-barreled artillery with a high trajectory and low velocity). Artillery killed more soldiers than any other weapon in the First World War.[77]

First Lieutenant Robert C. Duval Jr., a Virginia lawyer, noted "the small value placed on human life. The reckless disregard on the part of the American soldiers for their safety. The great waste of material in the battlefield."[78] Connecticut native and Harvard University student Sergeant Philip W. Higgins, who went into action on 24 September 1918, described the conflict as a "needless waste of human material."[79]

"I was impressed with the enormity of affairs and unfeeling waste of human life. The value of a single life was lost in the large purposes. The spectacular part of the war I shall never forget," said First Lieutenant Douglas C. France of Charlottesville, Virginia, a twenty-four-year-old lawyer and graduate of the University of Virginia.[80]

Stephen J. Weston of Waterbury, Connecticut, was in the British Merchant Marine Service before he joined the army on 6 June 1917. When he enlisted at age seventeen (undoubtedly lying about his age), Weston had little idea what lay ahead. On 16 July 1918 he went into action at the Marne; he also participated in combat at Vesle, Toul, Saint-Mihiel, and Meuse-Argonne. Weston was awarded the Croix de Guerre on 5 August 1918 at Saint-Thibault-des-Vignes for evacuating French wounded while under heavy fire. He received another citation for bravery from General Mark Hersey, commander of the 4th Division, on 8 August 1918 for "leading a platoon of men with coolness and good judgment against a strong German position on the Vesle. This act was accomplished under terrific German shell and machine gun fire." He received a second citation from the army "for personally reconnoitering the German lines on 9 August 1918, and obtaining valuable information for the American Forces, which no doubt saved the lives of many men." Weston was also awarded the Distinguished Service Cross by General Pershing for charging and capturing a machine gun and killing its gunner at Bois-de-Brieulles on 28 September 1918. Weston refused hospital treatment after being gassed there on 15 October 1918.[81]

When asked about his combat experiences, Sergeant Weston remarked that his emotions were "perhaps the same as thousands of other young men, broken in health and spirit. Disgusted with the slaughter and shambles of the battlefields. Disgusted also with the filth and vermin that one was forced to live in." Weston enumerated his impressions of combat: "(First) the lack of proper facilities for caring of the wounded at the Front. (Second) the devastation of homes; the pitiable plight of the wounded, and the loathsome stench of decomposed bodies. (Third) the nerve-racking tension of living hour to hour with always the danger of becoming one of these decomposed bodies. (Fourth) the valor of the American troops."[82]

Greater Love for Humanity

Some soldiers responded to the violence and the brutal conditions with an increased appreciation for life and comrades. Morris Goldstein from New Haven "realized much more how dear life was. At times wondered why we should be killing fellow human beings."[83] Corporal Harry S. Campbell, born in Buenos Aires, Argentina, was not a US citizen when World War I broke out. Campbell, who worked in Latin America as a salesman for Colt's Firearms Manufacturing of Hartford, was thirty-three when he joined the National Guard on 22 August 1917. Campbell viewed combat as "a necessary evil. That there was neither honour nor glory in butchering someone you didn't know and couldn't hate. . . . It has given me a greater love for humanity and has even taught me to sympathize with my enemies. That might, without right, has neither honour, glory nor flag."[84]

For the African American doughboys, combat had a unique purpose: identity and recognition. The army established two African American infantry divisions; the 92nd (the Buffalo Soldiers) was relegated to manual labor, but the 93rd (the Blue Helmets) was assigned to the French army. Around 40,000 black doughboys saw combat, approximately half with the French army. The 92nd sustained 1,642 casualties: 176 killed in action and 1,466 wounded.[85] The 93rd suffered 3,167 casualties: 417 killed in action, 106 died of wounds, and 2,644 wounded in action.[86] Due to the oppressive racial atmosphere at home, African American doughboys' views of duty and combat differed from those of their white counterparts. Black veterans were patriotic and proud of their service, but they also saw their role in the war as an opportunity to prove themselves and to receive proper recognition in society. At the front, where the goal was to defeat the enemy, killing was power. To many black troops, killing Germans also showed that they were equal to any other doughboy.

African Americans represented 10 percent of the US population and accounted for 13 percent of men drafted.[87] Colonel William Hayward received eleven citations for bravery while leading the all-black 369th Infantry, which fought with tenacity, including heavy combat in the Champagne offensive in September and October 1918. The first American soldiers to receive the French Croix de Guerre were African Americans Henry Johnson of Albany, New York, and Needham Roberts of Trenton, New Jersey. Both men were privates in the 369th, which was part of the 15th New York National Guard. As a testament to their fighting spirit, a Prussian officer captured by the 369th supposedly declared, "We can't hold up against these men. They are devils! They smile while they kill and they won't be taken alive."[88]

The Germans feared the African American troops, equating them with the fierce colonial (Senegalese) soldiers who fought with the French; these African soldiers took no prisoners and reportedly collected enemy body parts as trophies—notably, ears. Lieutenant A. L. Clark, an American aviator from Boston, Massachusetts, described the black soldiers as "even harder, more scientific and more dangerous fighters. They . . . fought with precision . . . being dashing whirlwind fighters in attacks, or as shock troops."[89] The Germans held Clark prisoner for two months, and he reported that they often questioned him about the number of black soldiers in the AEF.

Private John S. Fields, a twenty-two-year-old African American with a grammar school education from Church Roads, Virginia, was employed as a teamster when he received his induction notice on 29 October 1917. He went into action with the 369th Infantry on 17 April 1918 at the Champagne front, where he was gassed in the trenches. Fields spoke matter-of-factly about his experiences at the front: "We knew the Huns would cut our ears off, etc., if they caught us and so we killed them whenever we could. We hardly felt like they were people but more like some wild animal and did not mind killing them." Of the French, he added, "They are grand soldiers and I don't believe they are afraid of anything. Sometimes they would tell us to capture the Huns instead of killing them but we always killed them."[90]

African American Louis Scowffield echoed his fellow Virginian, Private Fields, in his opinion of the Germans: "I knew if I didn't kill them they would kill me and from what I had seen with my own eyes, I figured they just had a killing coming to them. They were not human no how. . . . I had Germans laid out just like cutting down cornstalks."[91]

Sergeant Harry E. Curry, an African American from Hampton, Virginia, emphasized, "War like fighting is a matter of life and death. The enemy fights you to keep you from killing him and you fight him to keep him from killing you." Curry summarized, "I learned that every man was for himself."[92] Private William P. Jones, an African American laborer from Berkley, Virginia, declared, "I took part in fighting; this was great. I can tell more and even do more, for after seeing so many killed I am now preaching the Gospel." He added, "I have always been a Christian, but I am stronger."[93]

"While in battle I felt no fear; men were falling on both sides of me, and I felt like fighting, too," remarked twenty-two-year-old Corporal Thomas M. Clary, an African American farmer and blacksmith from White Plains, Virginia.[94] Clary entered action at Champagne and spent six months in the trenches in France. African American Private James P. Spencer of Petersburg, Virginia, age twenty-nine and a high school graduate, entered the infantry on 26 October 1917. Spencer's unit "held the line at Argonne Forest twice" in July 1918 and saw action throughout that summer; he suffered a machine gun wound to his hand during Château-Thierry. He reflected, "My experience at the front impressed me with the idea that blood seems to be the only atonement for man's sin, the price of all true sacrifice."[95]

An African American farmer with a year and a half of college, Private First Class Waverly L. Crawford of Dendron, Virginia, enlisted on 10 January 1917. Crawford served as a telephone and telegraph operator in the Argonne and emphasized that "no civilian could realize a soldier's position and state of mind on the front."[96]

Second Lieutenant John M. Ross, an African American field artilleryman from New Haven, reflected on the effects of combat: "A terrible horror of war, but realizing that it was simply scientific murder. That all men are of the same clay, whether black or white, and that under fire, all color, race and creed is forgotten. That fear for self can be forgotten when others are in danger."[97]

The exposure to violence altered each man in a different way, depending on his background. Every soldier either embraced or attempted to deflect the killing; violence, however, especially front-line combat, had a lasting impact.

Being Gassed

Chemical warfare was one of the most damaging aspects of World War I, and many AEF soldiers suffered the effects of gas while at the front. The Germans first used poison gas at Bolimów (near Warsaw) in January 1915 against the Russians; then on 22 April 1915 in Ypres, German soldiers opened 6,000 cylinders of chlorine gas along the Western Front. Renowned German scientist Fritz Haber developed the method of dispersing gas from cylinders and personally directed the attack at Ypres. At first, the Allied forces had no defense against this deadly weapon, but they soon developed gas masks, and the doughboys drilled in their proper use to protect themselves from the enemy's noxious chemicals. Men, horses, and dogs wore respirators, or gas masks, but these contraptions were cumbersome and difficult to wear during combat. Lieutenant Hervey Allen of the 28th Division recounted his experiences with gas at the front:

> The men had been taught to put the gas mask on and to give the alarm at the slightest indication or sniff. This, of course, was nonsense, as around the front one came into contact with and breathed more or less gas of one kind or another half the time, especially in the woods. Given a condition such as existed, however, with the men trained to believe that a light sniff might mean death, with nerves highly strung by being shelled more or less for a month or so, and the presence of not a few who really had been gassed—it is no wonder that a gas alarm went beyond all bounds. It was remarked as a joke that when someone yelled, "Gas!" everybody in France put on the mask. At any rate, the alarm often spread for miles.[98]

The Allies and the Central Powers all used gas artillery shells as the war progressed, but the Germans were the leaders in chemical warfare. They concocted a more dangerous gas called phosgene that eclipsed the lethality of chlorine in 1915. The following year, a deadlier strain of phosgene and diphosgene premiered. In 1917 blue cross and mustard gas were developed. By the last year of the war, armies fired shells containing a potent blend of all gas types. Mustard gas (dichloroethyl sulfide), however, was the deadliest and best remembered. Even after the shell burst, the threat of mustard gas could linger for weeks in the murky pools, mud, and leafy debris of the Western Front. Unsuspecting troops would cross this toxic terrain and re-release the chemical agents. When breathed in, mustard gas burned the lungs and bronchial tubes and caused large, painful blisters; blindness sometimes resulted from exposure to mustard gas as well. The Germans called it yellow cross due to the emblem inscribed on the shells; the French called it Ypertie, after Ypres, where it was first used by the Germans on 17 July 1917; and the British termed it mustard gas because of its odor.[99]

Masks could protect a soldier's lungs from the searing effects of the chemicals, but the gas could also badly burn the skin, so the doughboys carried bars of soap so they could wash it off as soon as possible. The first treatment administered in the field hospital consisted of showering to remove traces of the chemicals on the skin. Often, however, the men did not get their masks on fast enough and inhaled the noxious fumes.

Grant H. Lyman, a twenty-one-year-old student from Salt Lake City, joined the Marine Corps on 5 May 1917 and embarked for France on 17 January 1918 as part of the 2nd Division. Five months later, Lyman found himself in Belleau Wood, a densely treed area with strong German defenses about five miles northwest of Château-Thierry. The marines suffered 1,087 casualties on the first day of combat alone; overall, they sustained a 55 percent casualty rate: 1,062 killed and 3,615 wounded. Yet they held the line at Belleau Wood until the Germans pulled back on 26 June. Lyman was one of those marines—and one of the casualties. During a heavy barrage on 14 June, Lyman received devastating injuries to both legs and was gassed. He died three days later at Evacuation Hospital No. 8. Della A. McNamara, an Army Corps nurse who attended to Lyman, described the horror of chemical weapons in a letter to the marine's mother: "His worse and chief complaint was his suffering from gas. Gas penetrates the lungs and so affects the mucous membrane that it often results fatally."[100]

Nurses and Their Patients

Nurses and civilians who worked in the hospitals near the front witnessed firsthand the horrors of combat. Mary Borden was a nurse with the French army from 1914 to 1918, and her hospital unit was located in *La Zone Interdite*, which she described as "the strip of land immediately behind the zone of fire."[101] Borden called the war a "conspiracy" in which a steady stream of men flowed from the front to the hospital and back out to the front lines again:

> It is all carefully arranged. It is arranged that men should be broken and that they should be mended. Just as you send your clothes to the laundry and mend them when they come back, so we send our men to the trenches and mend them when they come back again. You send your socks and your shirts again and again to the laundry, and you sew up the tears and clip the raveled edges again and again just as many times as they will stand it. And then you throw them away. And we send our men to the war again and again, just as long as they will stand it; just until they are dead, and then we throw them back into the ground.[102]

Mabel Bettilyon of Reading, Pennsylvania, was a nurse at Evacuation Hospital No. 1 in France. In a letter home, she told of more than 800 wounded Americans brought in during a single night, 136 of whom doctors assigned to her care. Lauding their courage, Bettilyon wrote that many of the injured men refused to be sent home "until we get the Kaiser."[103]

Nurses worked long, exhausting hours administering medical attention and solace to the wounded and the dying. Twenty-nine-year-old nurse Verna M. Smith from Clifton Forge, Virginia, recalled, "There we were only three miles behind the rear trenches and very often could not sleep for the sound of the guns. I don't think I ever worked as hard and carried as much responsibility at the same time in my life . . . in the two weeks that we were there we took in and cared for over 200 wounded patients. We worked from six A.M. until 11 and 12 P.M."[104]

Ruth Clayton of Salt Lake City joined the Army Nurse Corps in 1916 and worked in a hospital tent near the front, where often the only place to sit and eat a hurried meal was a wooden coffin. Describing her wartime service as "the most important experience of her life," Clayton was part of a surgical team for the severely wounded. One of the doctors she assisted became addicted to morphine, which he took so that he could keep working day and night.[105]

Many nurses wrote letters for the injured or ill doughboys; others wrote letters to the families of the soldiers who passed away in their care. In her letter to Grant Lyman's mother, nurse Della A. McNamara included her recollection of his last moments:

> When I asked him, as I do all my soldier patients if there is anything he desired me to do for him and if he desired to see a chaplain, he said: "Will you please write a letter to my mother and tell her she is all the world to me." . . . His last hour was quiet and peaceable; he only slept. . . . I hope to have the pleasure of meeting you some day. I love my work here. There is nothing gives the nurses so much pleasure as being able to do something for our brave khaki boys. . . . Any time I can be of service to you or to any mother who suffers the greatest loss in this cruel war just let me know.[106]

Another field hospital nurse, Ellen N. LaMotte, worked with the French a few miles behind the lines in Belgium during 1915 and 1916. She described her experience: "The bad days are those when the endless roar of the guns makes the little wooden *baraques* rock and rattle and when endless processions of ambulances drive in and deliver broken, ruined men, and then drive off again, to return loaded with more wrecks. The beds in the *Salle d'Attente* where the ambulances unload, are filled with heaps under blankets. Coarse, hobnailed boots stick out from the blankets, and sometimes the heaps, which are men, moan or are silent."[107]

Twenty-one-year-old Corporal Wayne H. Castle of Salt Lake City wrote home from a hospital in France shortly after the armistice: "I have been having some busy times dodging bullets and I haven't been entirely successful. I shall probably be in the hospital for a couple of months. My next move will be for home, and the orders sending me there will surely be music to my ears."[108] On 10 November Castle had left the hospital after recovering from previous injuries and returned to the front. At 2:30 a.m. the following day, a German machine gunner hit him with several bullets in the left knee, necessitating the amputation of his leg.

Some severely wounded men managed to display grit and even a sense of humor while recovering. One such doughboy was Corporal John E. Holden of Salt Lake City, who wrote a reassuring letter to his parents from a French hospital:

> I've had three operations and all were successful. My left shoulder and right arm have been sewed up but it will be some time before I can use either arm. My jaw has healed up to some extent, my eyes give me no trouble at all and my face is getting into shape again. I have four teeth left, but I am in a ward of broken jaws and it is comical to watch each other at meal times. All of us are fed through tubes. Don't worry about me as I'll be able to do most any kind of work in a few months, although I have only one eye, and a bunch of wound scars."[109]

Holden had enlisted in the field artillery on 1 June 1916. Despite his numerous wounds, he remained cheerful and was discharged on 28 June 1919.

Hospital workers, especially those near the front, saw the devastating results of combat every day. Twenty-four-year-old civilian Bland S. Hobson of Richmond, Virginia, worked as a stenographer at Base Hospital No. 45 in Toul for six months, beginning on 7 September 1918. She observed, "As I was stationed in a hospital 8 miles back from the firing line, I saw only the result upon the wounded boys brought in for attention, and they were always cheerful and plucky except in cases of shell shock which were pitiful in the depressing effect upon the minds of the boys."[110] For the doughboys on the front lines, the reality of war was even closer. In a letter to his sister on 3 September 1918, Forest Montgomery of Heber, Utah, confided, "We don't get any rest over here. We get a little phisical rest but very little mentle rest and that is what we need more than anything else for instance we go to bed at nights and hear the ariplains fly over us and we don't know wetther they are going to drop some booms on us or not so you can emagine just how it is." Montgomery was wounded on 17 October, suffering "a slight gun shot on left foot."[111]

Coping with Combat

The relationship between soldier and combat differed, depending on each man's cultural, social, and demographic background; regardless, combat altered their perceptions and, in most cases, sobered the soldiers whose heads were filled with romantic ideals of warfare. How the doughboys coped with or made sense of their combat experiences varied from soldier to soldier, but several patterns are evident.

Comradeship and Responsibility

A number of soldiers attempted to make combat a positive experience by focusing on the completion of their mission and dedication to their fellow doughboys. "From what I saw of the fighting proves to me that the yanks stick together through thick and thin and leave nothing that is started unfinished," said Seward H. Strickland of Hartford. "These experiences," he continued, "are absolutely good. I have more initiative and self confidence and hope to become a better citizen."[112]

For the most part, soldiers' combat experiences were negative, but the men were positive about the comradeship they felt, as expressed by Percy P. Markham of Hartford, a marine private: "That it is a great sacrifice for humans to make. It made me look to myself and at the same time help my buddy. I think it has helped me in more ways than it has harmed me."[113] During combat, many soldiers developed close ties with the men they fought side by side with; they looked after one another.

At twenty-two, Private Evern E. Saville of Salt Lake City was drafted in October 1917, trained for two months, and left for France on 12 December. He participated in five offensives and one defensive encounter. In a letter dated 17 September 1918, Saville described his emotions as he drove a motorcycle across a battlefield, delivering dispatches:

> As I rode over the battlefield, many a boy would raise his hand and motion for me to help but I couldn't stop. I had to harden my heart and make myself bear all such sights. . . . It was hard to see the sights of those who were dressed in olive drab but when I saw at the wayside a man that I had known for some time and had gotten attached so to, I tell you it made me feel pretty bad. My heart ached for some time after to think of the wounded that I had seen and of the many friends that I saw dead on the battlefield.[114]

Norfolk physician First Lieutenant Raleigh A. Bagley enlisted on 6 June 1917 at age twenty-six. He spent almost two months in the trenches beginning on 25 July 1918 in the Vosges sector, and he was relieved of duty two months

Sergeant E. F. O'Leary and his artillerymen from Battery A, 102nd Field Artillery, 26th Division, in Beaumont, France, 30 April 1918. (Photograph Collection, box 150, Historical Data File, Connecticut State Library)

later when he sustained a fractured left leg. Bagley's combat experience left him with strong impressions: "I learned that every man in my command was a better man than I thought he was; and a normal, healthy man can work himself into a state of absolute savagery in case of emergency and come back from this condition apparently normal in every way."[115]

William E. Mills, a college student from Portsmouth, Virginia, was "never subjected to small arms fire" himself, but he was impressed by the bravery of his fellow soldiers: "It was marvelous, how much the human body can stand. I have hauled an ambulance full of men shot out of semblance to human beings, and not a one whimpered."[116] Sergeant Emile P. Ragna from Hartford stated, "It is surprising what a human being can put up with when he is forced to." Ragna continued, "The greatest comradeship is in battle. After I was wounded, two of my men carried me and my equipment two miles to a first aid station amid a barrage of shrapnel and gas shells."[117]

In a letter home to his wife, Corporal Thomas Anderson, a thirty-year-old volunteer from Salt Lake City, confessed, "We know that 'Old Glory' means something. The men over here and those that have fought battles are anxious to do even more than salute. No patriot can fail to honor the flag. It stands for everything he stands for. For his nation, for his nation of liberty—loving people who are fighting for the liberty of the world." After two months in France, Anderson experienced close combat and captured a German spy. "This capture," he stated, "gives me an honor, if so it be, of being the first man in this regiment to get a German." He continued, "It won't be long before we are eating our meals in Germany. If our boys keep pushing as they are we will soon be back in God's country—America."[118]

While the enlisted men did not want to let their friends down, the officers had to be concerned for all the men under their command. The responsibilities of leadership made the combat experiences of AEF officers different from those of their troops. Twenty-two-year-old Second Lieutenant Elliott M. Braxton Jr. of Newport News, Virginia, wrote to his uncle Will on 17 August 1917, expressing his concerns about leading his men of the 80th Division in combat:

On the fourteenth of this month I cease to be a candidate and become an officer. I cease to be a youth and become a man. I leave behind childish things and assume responsibility for life and property of others. The preliminaries are over; the great game is on. After aimless wanderings I have attained a definite object. . . .

I can feel how Napoleon's words at the battle of the Pyramids affected the French. A thousand years look down upon me. They are not impersonal years; they are vitally interested in how I do. They are ancestors and relations who have made good. When the crisis arose they met them. Will I do the same?

At some critical instant will I flinch or hesitate? It's a horrible thought. I don't think I fear death by sea or land, but I do fear at some point where seconds mean life or death to lose control of myself for a minute, to scream and turn, to slink in the bottom of a trench, to fail, to lack the nerve to lead my men over the parapet when the supreme need comes. These worry me more than any possible wound . . . it's the impulse of the moment; the lack of control that scares me. . . .

The notes on warfare say that a second lieutenant or any platoon commander has almost life and death power over about thirty men. I know they look to him for everything. But I can't get the feel of it. Other men will do these things, but it is not personal to me. It is like being in a glass cage when it is raining. You know it is raining and wet, but you are dry, there is only a faint barrier between you and the water, yet the moisture doesn't affect you. I can think of it, but I can't feel it. The actual life don't touch me. What will it feel like to send a man to his death? What will it be like to cause the death of several men? What will their mothers think? Will everybody point at me and say there's a man who made John die? I can't feel that such things are possible. It is not a question of just knowing. I have to have a physical sensation to understand and realize. The thing is too big for me. . . .

This sounds wild and is poorly expressed, but it mirrors my ideas. All is hazy. My duties, responsibilities, problems and successes are dim, nebulous, intangible, misty. One thing alone is clear. I want to play the game to the end without flinching. My first duty is to help mold two hundred and some odd, many very odd, men into a team, not a machine, for a machine is driven, but a team will follow me wherever I lead with absolute confidence.[119]

Braxton was killed in action on 11 October 1918 near the town of Cunel on the Meuse-Argonne front. On 15 May 1919 Brigadier General Brett cited Braxton "for meritorious services and extraordinary gallantry in action." He continued:

When the Company had been cut in two by having the artillery barrage pass thru, Lieut. Braxton collected the scattered units left and took up the attack. As he led his command over the crest of the hill which led down into Cunel, his command came under annihilating machine gun fire. While attempting to lead his men forward under this he fell, mortally wounded, dying almost instantly. Lieut. Braxton by his coolness and courage stopped his panic-stricken men, leading them forward in the advance, and filling in the gap in the attacking lines.[120]

Braxton's letter to his uncle and his bravery in his final moments encapsulate the responsibility many officers and noncommissioned officers felt toward their men and their country. Hoping to emulate and honor their ancestors, especially those from the Civil War, the doughboys wanted to be heroic, but industrialized warfare tested their convictions. When that test came, some wavered, some broke, but most endured.

Forgetting

Other soldiers had little to say and attempted to erase their battle experiences from memory. Sergeant Ralph W. Lee from Hartford said, "I do not care to speak of the fighting in France as it is as a dream."[121] Private Hyman Lipshetz of New Haven remarked, "It was as a dream to me and I did not realize my surroundings."[122] A private in an engineer unit, Francis H. Bragan of Hartford observed, "My first time at the front I did not feel any of that fear that you read about. But did not relize what I whent through till after I came back and was thinking it over."[123] Corporal Thomas E. Carey of New Britain, Connecticut, explained, "When in a battle it was impressed on my mind that if you didn't get the enemy he would get you. So I made it my business to always get him." Carey added, "All the experiences I have been through doesn't effect my mind at all. I just think of it as a dream, and forget all about it."[124] These soldiers tried to dismiss their combat experiences, relegating them to cloudy reminiscences. But like it or not, the experience changed them.

Glory

In contrast to the majority, a few doughboys relished combat. Sergeant James Lewis of Orange, Connecticut, who served with a machine gun company, remarked, "I like army life in France. I love to hear those big shells burst. I thought nothing of it for I like to use the Hotchkiss machine gun and I could use one, too, at least those Germans thought so." He recalled, "I were in battle 9 day at the Champagne front. 5 days and nights without closing my eyes. 9 day with out a swallow of water eating off of the dead." Lewis declared, "I allway said if I had a chance I would go to war for I love to handle a gun and now I am satified. I had plenty of it over there."[125]

Sergeant Fairfield H. Hodges, a twenty-year-old native of Portsmouth, Virginia, went into action on 4 October 1918 east of Verdun: "When in the lines I never felt stronger in my life. It didn't seem to have any bad effects upon my nerve, except one time, but after a shot of medicine from the doctor, I braced up and never again felt nervous or afraid. I can't explain the cause of the steadiness because I was constantly handling or seeing handled the thousands of wounded that passed through an advanced ambulance dressing station."[126]

New Haven resident Louis J. Popolizio, a corporal with the 102nd Infantry, 26th Division, said he "enlisted with intention to fight. . . . The little fighting that I experienced was sufficient proof to let anybody know when I got home there would never be any Job too big for me to tackle." He recounted, "Our Company was in the front lines in that famous battle of Seicheprey 'Toul sector' April 20th 1918 some of my guns was firing over the left of the town during the conflict. Lots of the Germans were hanging on the barbed wire in the morning."[127] Private Ephraim Poulter of Ogden, Utah, declared, "Com. M, 305 Inf killed every Boch they saw we didn't waist time on prisoners."[128] Poulter, a twenty-five-year-old insurance company district manager, was inducted on 27 June 1918. He was exposed to mustard gas while fighting in the Argonne Forest in October 1918.

Combat became a thrilling sport to some soldiers, an ultimate life-or-death game as portrayed in the war literature of their youth: fiction and reality intertwined. Evern E. Saville wrote to his mother in Utah about his first glimpse of the front on 13 July 1918: "It was here where I received my first real sights of a battlefield. It was like the big battles that I have read about in the Civil War and in the Revolutionary War. It reminded me of the big battle we saw in the movie picture of the Birth of a Nation."[129] Fellow Utahan Lorenzo D. Allcocke, whose parents had been born in England, enlisted on 6 February 1918. A blacksmith's assistant by trade, Corporal Allcocke of Salt Lake City served with the 33rd Division and participated in several engagements, where he was gassed and sustained a wound in the arm. He wrote to his sister, Emma, concerning his combat experience:

> You can feel proud of my repitation as I have been in one of the honored divisions. We took part in all the big battles of this year we were with the british on the albert ammiens front and at Verdun, arragonne, Muse, and the St. Mihiel. So you see I have been in some of the worst battles of the war. I don't know of any of the boys from home that had the chance to see the action I have it sure was great experience. . . . I was hit in the arm once but it was not bad just broke the skin and bruised it a little I also had a sniff of gas but not enough to bother I know how it feels to get it anyhow.[130]

Resignation

Leaving their destiny in the hands of fate, several soldiers were philosophical about the war. Corporal Theodore E. Whitney of Hartford commented, "In actions, my reactions and impressions were varied: Fear giving way to amazement that anyone could continue to live under such conditions. Sometimes a great rage. All reactions resolving themselves into one, usually—To reach the source of danger and eliminate it. Great Pity." Whitney concluded, "Under no circumstances are we 'Captains of our destiny.' Our lives are mapped out for us. In my own case it has been proved that no human hand can take life unless it is so 'written.'"[131] Wounded in the right leg on 4 October 1918 at the Battle of Blanc Mont Ridge on the Champagne front, marine Private Ralph M. Angell of Richmond, Virginia, reported, "I saw a considerable lot of fighting in the short while I was there and it impressed on my mind that you do not know when your time has come to pass away, it might be any minute."[132]

Eighteen-year-old C. R. Johnston of Hurricane, Utah, volunteered for service in May 1917. He wrote to his mother from France on 26 March 1918 and explained what the war meant to him: "I haven't an allusion left about war, it doesn't mean pomp and circumstance for me, or to become a hero, or get mixed up in a romance. It means something that has to be done, just as you have to water your flowers to keep them alive. I don't matter a single thread to a living soul, but you, and myself."[133]

Ethelbert T. Smith of Hartford, who served in the Army Ambulance Service, noted that he "very soon assumed a fatalistic attitude, and that ended all worry as to personal safety. Seemed to get hardened to human suffering. Could not help considering that after all, a human life was a very little thing."[134] "To tell the truth about it Praying to forget about them, and regretting that I couldn't get the next boat to the good old USA. . . . When I was in the fighting, the impression it made upon me is you would be thinking in your mind about the kind of death you would get and above all you would be thinking of your dear ones at home," remarked Private First Class James P. Sheehan of Hartford.[135] Private Robert W. Marchant, also from Hartford, believed in "hope, and kidding yourself that you would not get hit helped a lot. That man does not amount to much when a H.E. hits him."[136]

The stress of combat, coupled with the strain of living under horrible conditions, made many AEF soldiers resigned to their surroundings. Twenty-one-year-old sheep herder Forest Montgomery wrote to his father on 8 July 1918: "I am still at the front where there is plenty of excitement. . . . I have been here . . . for sometime now and am getting used to it. Don't worrie about me pa because it wont do any good one never will go until his time comes to be called on and I don't feel like my time will come in this war."[137]

Karl Spencer, a marine with the 2nd Division at Belleau Wood, survived an attack on Hill 142 in which half the men in his company were lost. He wrote to his mother on 28 June 1918, dissecting his combat experience: "I used to be ambitious. I desired a war cross and honor, but my ideas have changed. I have seen too many men with those ambitions go down riddled with bullets. . . . So I've come to the conclusion that I am of more value and credit to my country, to you and myself, as a live solder, obedient and ready for duty, than as a dead hero. No grand-standing—just good honest team work and common sense."[138]

No matter how much combat an individual soldier endured, he was changed by it. The fragility of human life was one theme pondered by many veterans, while others addressed the ability of violence to alter their subconscious. "I did not expect a picnic and it was what I looked for. The glory of war is all on canvas, but therefore do not jump to the conclusion that there are not worse evils which only war can overcome," said Captain Clarence M. Thompson.[139] He first saw action on 1 March 1918 at Chemin des Dames, in defensive fighting, followed by combat in the Toul sector, Seicheprey, Aisne-Marne, and Saint-Mihiel. On 21 April 1918 Thompson's division commander awarded him the Croix de Guerre.

Soldiers—sometimes surprised at their own reactions—described different emotions under different conditions. Sergeant Alexander J. Flynn summed up the lesson learned by the majority of soldiers: "That the United States is a pretty good country to live in and my desire for the romance and glory of war is at an end."[140] Private Brigham Reese, a twenty-six-year-old farmer from Loa, Utah, fought at the front for thirty-six days. In a letter to his wife dated 7 October 1918, Reese declared, "I have read of war, talked of war, and heard others talk of the terrible scenes of war but that is nothing to compare with the awful reality of being in the front line. I hate war! I hate the bloodshed, and shall be very thankful when it is over."[141]

Reflecting on combat, German-born Private Paul Glaser of Rockville, Connecticut, concluded that war was "exactly what Sherman said."[142] Glaser, a machine gunner who survived combat and a gas attack, went back to his old job as an office clerk after the war. Eagleville, Connecticut, native Samuel A. Morse, who saw heavy action at the Argonne, acknowledged that he was left with the "same impression as Sherman told the world."[143] Morse went back to work as a farmer when he returned home. "My impression of fighting may well be quoted in Sherman's words, 'War is Hell,'" stressed Private Prescott E. Haskell, a marine combat veteran from Mansfield, Connecticut.[144]

It is interesting to note how many men were familiar with Sherman's words yet failed to believe them prior to experiencing combat for themselves. As in any aspect of life, it is one thing to receive advice and another thing to believe it; only hindsight shows the truth. Or perhaps the doughboys did believe Sherman; they knew war would be hell but felt it was their duty to go and fight anyway. By stating that Sherman was right, they were acknowledging the truth of his maxim. "We shall never forget what we have seen and taken part in 'over here' . . . one cannot grasp the idea of the power that is let loose 'over here,' except by really seeing. Sherman, I think, were he alive, would make an apology to hell," explained Cyril B. Mosher in his last letter home on 16 June 1918, two days before he was killed in action at Belleau Wood. In a letter written six days earlier, Mosher had emphasized, "And while papers can publish, and articles be written, it won't be until her men come home that the U.S. will *really know*."[145]

6

"Would Not Take Anything for It"

"Everything in war is very simple, but the simplest thing is difficult."[1] In war, what could be simpler than returning home after enduring months of rigorous training and vicious combat? It sounds simple—go home and take up your previous life. But for the thousands of men ordered to stay in Europe, the Great War continued, and not every soldier received a warm greeting when he got home. Few doughboys could simply erase their war experiences by resuming their civilian lives. The war had changed them, altering their characters and their perceptions of the military, of combat, of Europe, and of themselves.

The majority of AEF soldiers saw their participation in the war as extraordinary journeys, with most of their diaries, journals, and memoirs expressing enthusiasm and positive outlooks. Of the 30,847 Military Service Records (MSRs) collected in Connecticut, Utah, and Virginia, the great majority of responses were upbeat: despite the horrors of combat, the doughboys believed they had become better human beings. Other returning soldiers portrayed their experiences as hellish and damaging, and the remaining few fell somewhere in between, seemingly unaffected by or indifferent to their ordeal.

The AEF lost far fewer lives than the European forces, but given the short time US soldiers engaged in combat, the cost was dear: 320,518 casualties, including 116,516 dead.[2] Statistics, however, do not do justice to the soldiers' experience; that requires a subtler approach, expressed by the veterans' thoughts. Although the doughboys did not spend as much time at the front as their Allied counterparts did (AEF units endured heavy combat for almost 200 days), the men who saw action gained a new understanding of warfare.

With their task completed, the doughboys wanted to go home. Some of the wounded had already returned to the States before the AEF's massive demobilization campaign after the armistice on 11 No-

Doughboys flock to the upper deck of the *Agamemnon* as they approach Boston harbor, 22 April 1919. (Photograph Collection, box 131, Historical Data File, Connecticut State Library)

vember 1918. When Mrs. W. K. Vanderbilt returned to New York City after aiding the wounded in Paris, she lamented society's treatment of the veteran doughboys:

> They come back here, these boys who have been so wonderful, and have fought and suffered so for us all, to a perfectly cold reception in this cheerless, gray city, that isn't even their home; nobody seems to pay any attention to them; every one looks as if nothing had happened, as if life were going on just the same. I used to say to the boys in the hospital, "Wait until you get home; you'll see how proud we all are of you!" and when they get in to New York—these boys whom the French have cheered and covered with flowers—they see nothing of the sort. They meet a stolid lot of people who are afraid even to speak to them.[3]

The majority of AEF divisions returned to the United States in the spring and summer of 1919 to ports in New York City and Boston. The second trip across the pond felt nothing like the first. Gone were the U-boats and the an-

Members of the 102nd Infantry, 26th Division, march under the Civil War Memorial Arch with their mascot, a Boston terrier named Stubby, during the welcome-home parade in Hartford, Connecticut, 1919. (Photograph Collection, box 129, Historical Data File, Connecticut State Library)

ticipation of combat. The two-week trip could not end fast enough for the American veterans. Once they disembarked from their ships, many soldiers participated in parades before returning to the training camps to be discharged. General John J. Pershing led the largest and grandest of these parades. The first one occurred on 10 September 1919, as the 1st Division marched down Fifth Avenue in New York City. A week later, on 17 September, Pershing led another parade in Washington, D.C.

Rhine Watchers

In spite of months of hardship and danger, when the armistice was declared, the soldiers of the AEF found it hard to believe that the war was over. Private John L. Barkley, 3rd Division, described his reaction when he heard the news:

> We were all fixed up, ready to load on the trucks. We were sure this time we were headed for Metz. But the final orders to move didn't come through. . . . Down the street came a soldier. He was telling everybody the armistice was signed. I said, "What's an armistice?" It sounded like

some kind of a machine to me. The other boys around there didn't know what it meant either. . . . When the official word came through that it meant peace, we couldn't believe it. . . . Finally Jesse said, "Well Kid, I guess it really does mean the war is over." I said, "I just can't believe it's true." But it was.[4]

In November 1918, however, only 26,000 of the 1,929,760 soldiers in the AEF went home.[5] A steady stream of troop transports began carrying most AEF divisions back to the United States in the spring and summer of 1919. By August, there were only 40,000 US troops left in France. The 240,000 soldiers of the newly formed Third Army remained in Germany from 11 November 1918 to 24 January 1923 as part of the occupation force.[6] General Pershing created the Third Army (later referred to as the American Army of Occupation) from ten different divisions; officially, it became the American Forces in Germany (AFG) in July 1919.

The Rhineland consisted of 12,000 square miles (about the size of Belgium) and had a population of 7 million. The Allies divided the area into four zones. The American zone contained little industry but a lot of wine—a product that made the region famous. The capital of the Rhineland, Coblenz, served as the AFG's administrative center.[7]

Veteran doughboys composed the majority of the AFG at first, and many of these men had experienced intense combat in the last year of the war during the Germans' spring offensives and the Allies' counteroffensives. American forces sustained severe casualties in battles such as the Meuse-Argonne: 26,227 killed and 95,778 wounded.[8] Understandably, these combat veterans would have preferred to go home rather than be stationed along the Rhine. Utahan Frank V. Free, a combatant at Château-Thierry and the Argonne Forest, had volunteered on 4 March 1918, served with the 4th Division, and later served in the Quartermaster Department with the AFG. Free echoed the feelings of many in a letter he wrote to his parents on 17 February 1919:

Just a word to let you know I am OK but dammed tired of this country. The 4th of next month (March) will be 1 year in the army for me. 10 months out of the year overseas and by the looks of things will be over here another year. It sure is the bunk just because you enlisted for the duration of the war, you are in the regular army and those drafted men are sent home quickly as possible. I see that the 145th Field Artillery, the outfit Lee Williams is in has gone home after spending all there time over here in Southern France. No action, or anything, only taking it easy. While a few others do it all. The only thing to do though is wait.[9]

A month later, on 8 March 1919, Free's patience was clearly strained:

I see a sailing list up to July 1st & there is not a sign of the 4th Div. going home before next Sept. or Oct. while these other divisions are going home early. Well that's what you get for being patriotic, enlisting in the regular army. I'll bet if there is ever another war I will wait and be Drafted. Here they are sending home outfits that never heard a shell break & keeping those that has been in the thick of it most of the time over here. . . . Germany is a pretty place but far behind the states in everything. . . . Give me the Good old U.S.A.[10]

Fellow Utahan John W. Barton, a twenty-two-year-old farmer from Parago-nah who had volunteered on 5 April 1917, agreed with Free: "I like Army life fine but as the war is over would sooner be home and helping on the farms. It was easy enough to stay whiel we were fighting for our country but now we want to get out of it."[11] Barton got his wish. The army discharged him on 21 May 1919. Other doughboys, such as Captain David Bellamy of the Marine Corps, focused on the positive aspects of occupation. On 10 January 1919 Bellamy noted, "Living conditions are good. Grub plentiful. People are courteous and obliging. Probably it is propaganda, but our people are taking advantage of the benefits."[12]

Most AFG officers were proud of their men as they made the transition from combatant to sentry. Officers admired the doughboys' service during the occupation: "For weeks at a time during the recent past they had lived in dugouts or in 'fox-holes,' sleeping in the mud and the muck, with lice and rats for their constant companions. For months they had been denied most of the ordinary comforts of modern life," one officer remarked, "and often they had been face to face with death, sometimes for days on end. They had witnessed violence and death in innumerable forms, and they had seen good comrades go to their Maker in the twinkling of an eye. They had been exhausted—physically, mentally and emotionally. . . . The soldier was separated by thousands of miles from the supporting and restraining influence of his home and his own country. In a strange land, among a people whose ideals and customs were different from his own and whose language he could not speak."[13]

Pershing, however, harbored doubts about how the men of the AFG would handle their new situation. In a message to the AFG, he sternly reminded his soldiers to "remember that each officer and each soldier is the representative in Europe of his people. . . . You will so bear yourself in discipline, in appearance and respect for all civil rights that you will confirm for all time the pride and love which every American feels for your uniform and for you."[14] As time progressed, however, Pershing's words had less of an effect. Some of the men became curious about what Germany had to offer, and certain soldiers discovered the vices available in the Rhineland. Some Germans complained about the doughboys' behavior: drunkenness, immorality, reckless driving, and tobacco chewing were among the most common grievances. To be sure, there were troublemakers and even a few criminals intermixed in the AFG. Altogether, doughboys committed 256 felonies, and the army held 118 trials resulting in 71 convictions, many for violent crimes or robbery. For this reason, the AFG established a prison in Coblenz, yet not all the inmates were American. During the occupation, especially in the early months, the AFG apprehended Germans committing crimes while dressed as American soldiers.[15]

The biggest issue for AFG commanders, however, was trying to stop the doughboys from consorting with German women.[16] During the occupation, there was an interesting spike in flower sales in the Rhineland, as the doughboys tried to woo the local fräuleins. Many soldiers requested permission to marry their German girlfriends, much to the frustration of AFG commanders. Other doughboys knew better. In a letter to his father, Sergeant Fidler wrote, "I am not quite such a fool as some of the fellows. Lots have married these French & German girls over here, but none of them for me."[17] Overall, improper doughboy behavior was the exception, not the rule, during the AFG's years along the Rhine.

At first, the Rhinelanders were afraid of the AFG, but the occupiers' positive behavior assuaged their fears. Karl Schramm, a German civilian from the town of Zermüllen, proclaimed, "The American troops show more consideration for the private rights of the inhabitants of the village than did the German troops."[18] Montabaur resident Hans Kalb echoed these positive feelings, declaring on 17 December 1918 that "the Americans have proved themselves very courteous and have inflicted no inconvenience on the civil population. It is evident that they do not hate us as do the French, who have been taught to hate ever since school."[19]

The main source of friction between the German residents and the American soldiers was that the AFG billeted the doughboys in German homes and other buildings. That did not last long, however; most American combat units left the Rhineland by mid-1919, after which the army assigned the men to barracks. Even during the billeting, most Germans preferred it to the alternative of having the *Spartakusbund* (the Spartacus League) or other revolutionaries in their town—Rhinelanders generally considered communism a ruthless enemy.

Food shortages outside the occupied zone led to black marketeering, rationing, and hoarding. But in the American zone, the AFG handled food distribution well and respected existing German laws unless they conflicted with the rights and security of the occupying forces. In the district of Ahrweiler, a local man interviewed by an American intelligence agent indicated that "people west of the Rhine . . . are luckier than those on the east side. . . . No American would watch even an enemy starve." Another German conceded that there were "no strikes nor disturbances and above all good food."[20] In 1920, aided by American charitable organizations, the AFG started an assistance program to help undernourished children in the Rhineland, eventually helping more than 100,000 children aged twelve and younger return to health. The AFG also employed many local citizens, thus aiding the economy; as a result, many Germans attempted to migrate to the American zone, seeking employment or even passage to the United States. American occupation was largely successful in creating a positive relationship between US troops and Rhinelanders.

This relationship contrasted sharply with that between American and French forces. General Henri Mordacq, commander of the French 30th Army Corps during the occupation of the Rhineland, found the American presence unbearable. He stated, "It was different for us, because little by little, the small American army became more German than the Germans themselves, and this made the last years in the Rhineland unbearable for our *poilus*: officers and soldiers alike."[21] Joint occupation with mutually incompatible purposes amplified the differences in American and French attitudes toward Germany. In addition, the Americans underestimated the grim task of occupying a devastated country, where the strains and disruptions of total war had created a huge burden on the economic, social, and political structure of Germany. *Stars and Stripes* pointed out this daunting mission on the eve of the Rhineland occupation:

> Those of us who are fortunate enough to have been selected for the Army of Occupation have a far more difficult task than that of merely policing a certain strip of ground. We shall be in the midst of a people who are drinking the dregs of the cup of defeat, who are seeing their lands held by an alien force to insure their own good behavior, who have been deserted by the ruler in whose defense they gave something more precious than life, a people who, to fit themselves for a place in the society of nations, must build up on the moral ruins of the past four years.
>
> We go in among them as conquerors—there is no need to conceal that fact from them or from ourselves. But we must go in among them with a humble and contrite heart. For, though we enter as conquerors, we enter also as peace-makers, "for they shall be called the children of God."
>
> The new watch on the Rhine must be a watch of courtesy, of tolerance, for a people who apparently are at last snatching from their eyes the bloody bandage of imperial illusion.[22]

. Referencing Matthew 5:9, this message conveys the formidable responsibility of creating stability in a foreign country devastated by war.

The importance of the AFG waned after 1920, and American troop strength decreased as the months turned into years. The drawdown continued, and by 15 September 1922, only 2,000 doughboys remained in the American zone. Two months later, President Warren G. Harding informed AFG commander General Henry Allen that the army would not send any more soldiers to the Rhineland. The following year, on 11 January 1923, France and Belgium occupied the Ruhr area of Germany in an attempt to force the Germans to pay war reparations. The United States did not support this move, believing that it might be an effort to restart the war. Two weeks later, the last AFG troops left the Rhineland.

Some of the American soldiers stayed in Europe to travel, believing they would not have an opportunity to visit Europe again. Others did not want to leave their beer and fräuleins. As David M. Kennedy writes, "They were, first of all, as much tourists as soldiers."[23] Except for those filled with wanderlust, the last AEF veterans were finally leaving Europe.

Returning Home

Regardless of when they arrived, most men were thrilled to return to the States. Infantryman Corporal Carl Noble, 5th Division, described his passage home: "There were nine thousand soldiers on our ship. We made the crossing in five and one-half days. It was raining when we landed, and everyone got wet; but we were very glad to reach home. I felt a thrill as my feet trod American soil. I stopped and picked up a handful of dirt. It had been trampled by millions of feet, but it was part of our country. Someone asked me what I was doing. I said I was just shaking hands with America. Several of the men reached down and felt of the ground."[24] Each man who left the army received his discharge papers, his uniform, a pair of shoes, a coat, and a $60 bonus; the army also allowed those who had served overseas to keep their helmets and gas masks.[25]

The veterans adjusted gradually as they resumed their civilian lives. The majority of doughboys slipped back into their old lives without experiencing any difficulties. Others faced challenges. Physical injuries, for example, prevented some veterans from returning to their previous occupations. Without limbs, eyesight, or hearing, their former skills were lost to them, and their futures were uncertain. Social changes also made readjustment more difficult. By the time the last of the AEF came home in 1923, there was a new president in the White House; the United States had not become a member of the League of Nations, as Woodrow Wilson had envisioned; Prohibition was in force; job availability had changed; women could vote; and the era of the Roaring Twenties was altering the social rules for both sexes.[26]

Doughboys had many different reactions when they returned home. Some men actually missed the war—or at least they missed the excitement of it. David M. Kennedy compares the Old West with World War I: both the frontier and the war fostered danger, adventure, and male comradeship, as well as an uncivilized atmosphere; some soldiers missed this feeling of peril and risk when they returned to their civilian lives.[27]

Other soldiers rejoiced that the war was over and hoped for a lasting peace. Twenty-four-year-old sheepherder Corporal Lorenzo Heaps, a native of Teasdale, Utah, had served with the 362nd Infantry, 91st Division, and fought in the Argonne Forest. While recovering from rheumatism in a convalescent camp, Heaps wrote to his father on 24 November 1918 and praised the Allied forces:

> This is a great day which has dawned upon the world. . . . Autocracy has been overcome. . . . And we need not worry anymore about war . . . we need not worry of Germany ever rising up and waging war again on the world. . . . The war is over, we all find great consolation and happiness knowing that the terrible conflict is at an end. Let us rejoice and be happy and thank God that the world is once more free. . . . Let us sympathize with those who are suffering the loss of their loved sons, and honor those who have died that the world may be safe for democracy. For we know that they have done the greatest thing in the world that they have died for others.[28]

The majority of returning soldiers attempted to resume their previous lives. The war had made them stronger and more determined, and it gave them a desire to build a better future. World War I veterans established the American Legion in an attempt to maintain a sense of comradeship and to protect soldiers' interests. On 16 September 1919 the American Legion received congressional approval through the efforts of Theodore Roosevelt III (the former president's son), one of its chief supporters. Originally an organization for those who served in the military from 6 April 1917 to 11 November 1918, the American Legion eventually expanded to include veterans from other wars. Today, it is still an advocate for veterans' benefits and a place where servicemen and -women can continue their comradeship.

Former doughboys often sought the company of their wartime friends, remarking that civilians did not understand what the war had been like for them. Lieutenant Louis F. Ranlett, 23rd Infantry, 2nd Division, observed that civilians seemed to think, "'The boys won't talk about the war.' That is not true. But it is true that the boys do not talk about the war. The reason is not because the war is something not to be thought of. The boys would talk if the questioners would listen. But the questioners do not. They at once interrupt with 'It's all too dreadful,' or 'Doesn't it seem like a terrible dream?' or, 'How can you think of it?' or, 'I can't imagine such things.' That is as bad as telling a humorist you've heard that one before. It shuts the boys up."[29] When they had a sympathetic ear, many doughboys had a lot to say about their wartime experiences.

Humbert F. Cofrancesco, inducted into the army on 3 October 1918 at age eighteen, reflected:

> My idea, or state of mind, before the war—and I feel certain I am voicing the sentiments of others who have seen service elsewhere—was very dissimilar to my actual experience. I used to think that army life was very dull and monotonous; lacking that stimulative, creative force, which we call spirit. But I found the army to be as human as—if not more so than—any other organization, institution, or association of people. By its heterogeneous character, it lacked no worldly element. It contained every variety of people—from the point of view of race, nationality, religion, political views, domestic and financial conditions, manners, thoughts, ambitions. Its diversity made it an attraction—a loveableness in itself. Its morale was high; it was enthusiastic, looking forward to some great accomplishment. This is, indeed, an amazingly novel thing to one who had a rather radically different pre-war conception of military life and experience.[30]

Before joining the army, Cofrancesco had been a Yale University student and member of the Student Army Training Corps in New Haven, Connecticut. This gave him a sense of pride in military service. "I am of the opinion," he observed, "that all former soldiers have more respect and admiration for the army and military training than ever; and if ever there was a time for introducing a light system of military training—e.g. the Swiss system—it will now meet with hearty approval on the part of a very large majority of the people; for now is the psychological moment."[31] After being discharged on 19 December 1918, Cofrancesco returned to Yale.

Others were not so happy. "Before the war I was enthused with the great adventure of it, and the great desire to see American arms successful, to see the German autocracy humiliated in defeat; but I thought little of the grimness of the actual battle, the terrible destruction of property and desolation of modern battle, all of which I now know, and I am for the League of Nations, or any other honorable means of preventing war," said First Lieutenant Herman R. Furr, 314th Machine Gun Battalion, 80th Division, a thirty-one-year-old real estate broker from Norfolk, Virginia.[32]

Artillery bugler Leo J. Hill from East Haven, Connecticut, toured France after the armistice with a troupe of entertainers that he and a friend had organized. Hill spoke about his state of mind both before and after the war: "Before the war I was satisfied with things in general. Now it seems that something is wrong and the old order of things does not fit."[33] Hill was one of those returning soldiers who had difficulty readjusting to civilian life. They seemed to feel as if something was wrong or missing in their lives, but they had trouble putting those feelings into words. Some men searched for their old identities; others, having just experienced the Western Front, found civilian life rather insignificant.

Joseph Ryan of Putnam, Connecticut, a student at the Philadelphia Textile School of the Pennsylvania Museum and School of Industrial Art, was nineteen years old when he enlisted in the Marine Corps on 9 April 1917; he was wounded by shrapnel during combat in Belgium. When asked to describe how his wartime experiences had affected his state of mind, Ryan remarked that he would "need a psychologist to answer this."[34]

Raymond A. Preston of Danielson, Connecticut, educated at Brown and Harvard Universities, was a twenty-four-year-old teacher when he enlisted on 7 June 1917. A private first class in the Army Ambulance Service, Preston had definite opinions about the military:

> That military service in time of peace is anomalous; in time of war, an unmitigated evil, though perhaps a necessary duty. That murder is a crime and a cardinal sin, and that the commission of it wholesale is only an aggravation of the offense. Demoralization, degradation, hypocritical conformity to a system that I knew to be foolish and believed to be wrong, full realization that an army cannot be a wholesome or a democratic thing, that it is inherently aristocratic, a survival of one of the worst institutions of mediaevalism. Hopelessness of justice under the present courts martial; complete recognition of the riotous wastefulness of property and human life; not only in war, but in the whole damnable military system. Compulsary military training would force some of these effects on any intelligent young man. Conscription, whether for military training or service is an unwarrantable curtailment of the human rights to liberty, equality and the pursuit of happiness.[35]

Private First Class Frank E. Murphy, a twenty-one-year-old from Hartford, felt vaguely different after the war: "I believe I returned more ambitious, less petty and less selfish. However, I am more restless and dissatisfied than formerly." Murphy added, "I do not believe in military training. It undoubtedly develops a man physically and broadens his mind—if it would end there, but it doesn't."[36] Murphy believed in preparedness but wished he had not needed to put his military training to use during the war. Leslie H. Patterson was a twenty-two-year-old resident of Bedford, Virginia, and a student at Davidson College when he entered the service on 29 September 1917. Like Murphy, Patterson, who had served with the Tank Corps, found himself to be "a little more restless and dissatisfied to live quietly and take things as I find them."[37]

William E. Steven of Hartford, a private first class in the artillery, expressed mixed emotions, saying that although he had "increased self-confidence, and satisfaction of knowing that you were 'over there' during the time of hostilities," he noticed a "tendency to be restless even after six months of civilian life again."[38] Private Herman A. Jacot from New Haven observed, "the world is more dishonest and unscrupulous than I previously thot. Had difficulty in settling down and have not yet wholly succeeded."[39] Sergeant Philip W. Higgins of Clinton, Connecticut, became a farmer after his discharge on 31 May 1919, and in August he described his state of mind: "Am now less content to stay in one place and live an ordinary and uneventful life. Am eager to be on the go, to enjoy any kind of excitement, and to move rather than to stand still."[40] Combat made these soldiers and others restless when they returned to civilian life.

Other men grasped a new and better understanding of human nature and its history of bloodshed. These men realized that war was inevitable and, in the future, the United States would have to make a choice: remain isolationist, or join an organization capable of negotiating peace instead of waging war. Manchester, Connecticut, resident Edward B. Allen, a captain in the Medical Corps, said, "The chief lesson I have learned from the war is that no nation can exist by itself alone, but that its interests are dependent upon and determined by its relations with its neighbors." Allen had enlisted on 7 January 1918 at age twenty-eight; when he left the service, he said, "I believe now that never will treaties or any league of nations ever prevent war, but that strife is bound to continue as long as human nature exists."[41] Representing those who preferred isolationism, Second Lieutenant Julius I. Twiss, a Hartford resident, described the war as "a bunch of damned foolishness with lives lost so some big head could have what his pig head wanted." Twiss warned "that the European powers will fight as long as there is material to fight with and that the U.S. had better pull in her neck and keep out of family scraps."[42]

"After the Armistice, with the loss of a definite purpose, it was much harder to maintain health, spirits and morale generally," observed Captain Anson T. McCook from Hartford. He did not see action and remarked, "I was never so fortunate." Nevertheless, he had a great deal to say about his military service. McCook listed those convictions that the war had strengthened in him:

(1) my aversion to war; (2) my indignation at the needless loss of time, money and life caused by the Administration's refusal to prepare, after war had long become inevitable; (3) my conviction that we must guard against future war—first by an international tribunal with full power to enforce its decisions, secondly, by universal training which alone provides reasonable defense without the dangers of militarism; (4) my regret that the war's lessons should so soon be forgotten and our Allies left to bear its burdens rather than the aggressors; (5) my faith in and admiration for the American soldier.[43]

After his discharge from the infantry on 11 February 1919, First Lieutenant Albert M. Simons remarked, "I am fully convinced that the millennium has not yet arrived. There will continue to be war just as long as human nature exists. Aside from the fact that it has given me an opportunity to study man under extraordinary conditions, I have learned that a man can do most anything if he makes up his mind to accomplish a certain purpose."[44]

Born in Dublin, Ireland, First Lieutenant Kieran J. Harford of Stamford, Connecticut, was twenty-five years old when he enlisted in the National Guard on 14 April 1917; he served with the AEF from 18 August 1918 until his discharge on 30 October 1919. Harford's wartime experiences "convinced me that the savage instinct is still in evidence in the human race and that it will be a great many years before wars will be looked upon as unnecessary."[45] Another soldier who believed in the inevitability of war was twenty-three-year-old Newport, Virginia, clerk Curry P. Hutchison, a corporal in the 317th Infantry, 80th Division. Following his discharge on 12 June 1919, Hutchison observed, "I like so many others before the war thought that such a thing as war only belonged in history and would never be again. Now I realize that so long as nations are as suspicious of each other as our European sisters and will not keep faith with each other there will be wars regardless of any agreement recorded on any parchment or paper."[46] These prophetic statements proved correct. As the guns fell silent on 11 November 1918, dissonant voices were already rumbling for revenge.

Farwell Knapp of Hartford, a regimental supply sergeant in the 302nd Field Artillery, was twenty-four years old when he was inducted into the army. According to Knapp, military service "made me more self-confident and independent, thereby maturing me . . . probably toughened me morally." Yet he noted little effect on his state of mind: "with one exception, very little change. The exception is that I ceased to see War with any glamour, and saw it as a sordid, disgusting, but chiefly futile business."[47] Twenty-six-year-old First Lieutenant John W. Covington, a bricklayer from Culpeper, Virginia, concurred with Knapp. Covington saw "no reason why disputes of any magnitude cannot be settled in other ways than by the sword with all its ghastly horrors."[48] Covington was cited for bravery and became deaf in his left ear after being knocked unconscious by a high-explosive (HE) shell.

Private First Class Eugene M. Kelcy of Hartford was inducted into the army on 19 August 1917 at age twenty-five. Kelcy, who served overseas in the Photographic Division of the Signal Corps from September 1917 until June 1919, said, "I often had in mind during the fighting that if our side was as well organized as the German, we would have needed only one man to four of the enemy." He concluded, "My heart has been changed like the map of the world. I love my mother worlds more than before. I am not half as selfish, my uppishness of manner has entirely disappeared. I am more a Man."[49]

For some doughboys, the war was a long, frightening ordeal. "The nurses asked me while I was laying in the hospital 'When was you scared most?' I said 'All the time.' And that's the truth," reflected Corporal Joseph Rendinell of the 6th Marines, 2nd Division. Rendinell, an Ohio native, was wounded during the counteroffensive at the Marne-Aisne front in July 1918 and was gassed at Champagne on 3 October 1918. He received three citations, the Croix de Guerre, a US Marine Good Conduct Medal, the Liberty Medal with three stars and a bar, and a sharpshooter's medal, but according to Rendinell, "the best of ALL" was "an Honorable Discharge."[50]

A second lieutenant in the 102nd Infantry, Seth A. Beeker of New Haven, Connecticut, enlisted in the National Guard on 24 June 1916 at age nineteen. He served with the AEF from September 1917 to December 1918. Beeker was wounded twice—in March and again in September 1918—and his commanding officer cited him for heroism in action. Perhaps because of his combat experiences, Beeker spoke with an insight that belied his young age. He returned from the war impressed by "the folly of life in general and the cheapness of things we value so highly here. Nothing but a good meal, and a place to lay one's head matter." Beeker added, "I think most of us that have seen hard, real service, have lost to a certain extent their sense of proportions; and one might say a certain amount of mental stability in comparison to before."[51] Another doughboy from New Haven, Private First Class Dexter A. Cargill of the 103rd Machine Gun Battalion, served overseas from October 1917 to February 1919. Cargill said the war changed him "from a boy to a man, tho only 22. I sometimes feel like thirty-five, I have seen and know so much of life (not in a drawing room) but in the army where things happened quick."[52]

Bristol, Virginia, native Private First Class Garnett D. Claman was discharged on 15 April 1919, just four months after his twenty-first birthday. Upon returning home, he stated, "Before the war I was an innocent, ignorant child, while now I feel that I could easily go insane by permitting my mind to recall and dwell upon the horrors of my experience." Claman suffered a "loss of general health" and an almost complete loss of his eyesight due to gas and shrapnel wounds; nonetheless, he returned to his previous occupation as a farmer after the war.[53]

A sergeant in the Medical Corps, twenty-year-old Edward S. Webster from Hartford enlisted in the army on 12 November 1917. He described the ill effects the war had on him: "I seem to be awfully depressed often and lonesome, the bottom seems to have dropped out of things sometimes, and life seems shorter somehow, I can't explain it."[54] Artilleryman First Sergeant Stephen J. Weston of Waterbury, Connecticut, also discussed the negative effects of the war: "My state of mind before the war was serene. After the war one sort of lacks faith with the class of people that would, without compunction, raze a nation or nations in a ruthless warfare." Before his discharge on 1 August 1919, Weston served with the AFG. His opinion of the soldiers' morale after the armistice was that "much was done in Germany to infuse in the men the zeal that was theirs upon entering the service. Baseball, football, track, and etc. But the men seemed indifferent, and I believed then that the zest for such things was sapped out of them by the war." Weston was unable to work and underwent treatment at the US Veterans' Hospital in Newington, Connecticut. He readjusted to civilian life by "reading the classics," painting, and doing "pen and ink drawings."[55]

Private Ratcliffe M. Hills of Hartford was a machine gunner in the 102nd Infantry. Though "opposed to the declaration of war against Germany," Hills "volunteered to help end the war." Upon his discharge from military service on 10 June 1919, Hills was "impressed with the utter needlessness, futility and unthinkable horror of modern warfare" and noted that he was "more against war than before the War." In spite of his strong opposition to war, Hills "still believe[d] in military preparedness for defense."[56] Hospitalized after Château-Thierry and again after the Meuse-Argonne, Hills suffered from anxiety, fatigue, and weakness and was diagnosed with neurasthenia. Somewhat akin to neurasthenia was war neurosis, also termed "shell shock." Characterized by anxiety and depression, shell shock was usually associated with prolonged exposure to artillery fire. In some ways, shell shock has become a metaphor for the war itself, which is unfortunate.[57]

"Scars Faded as Flowers"

Even before the doughboys returned home, the AEF began to see signs of what the Europeans called shell shock.[58] Doctors believed exposure to the vacuum produced by exploding shells caused the condition. It was not the vacuum but the concussive blast of the artillery shell that could cause shell shock. Doctors today would term the effects of such a blast *traumatic brain injury* (TBI), which "is defined . . . as a traumatically induced structural injury and/or physiological disruption of brain function as a result of an external force."[59] It is impossible to know how many "shell-shocked" doughboys sustained physical brain damage that resulted in TBI, and it is important to note the difference between TBI (an actual physical injury) and the self-induced mental state known as shell shock. Today, the American Psychiatric Association (APA) would designate shell shock as post-traumatic stress disorder (PTSD), which it defines as "the development of characteristic symptoms following exposure to one or more traumatic events."[60] These "events" are legion. With each new edition of the *Diagnostic and Statistical Manual of Mental Disorders* (DSM), the APA expands the symptoms and conditions associated with PTSD. Dr. Derek Summerfield notes this development: "The American Psychiatric Association widened the criteria for traumatic stressors, making it still more useful to an expansive trauma industry. Although we recognize that the medicalization of life has been a Western cultural trend gathering pace in the past century, some professional stock-taking is surely overdue."[61]

First appearing in *DSM-III* in 1980, PTSD is a sociopolitical construction that has been exploited not only in the United States but also in other countries, such as France.[62] After the Vietnam War, PTSD and war became intertwined and inseparable. As Nigel C. Hunt proclaims, "We have now almost reached the stage where we expect people to break down after a traumatic event, and there is something wrong if they do not. In a single century we have seen views go from one extreme to the other, from the view that breakdown was a capital offence to the view that not to break down is a sign of a problem."[63] Ascribing the label of PTSD has become commonplace, omnipresent, the norm. Some researchers allege that even men and women of antiquity suffered from it. For example, Daryl S. Paulson and Stanley Krippner claim that biblical "accounts of Isaac, after he was bound and nearly sacrificed by his father, Abraham . . . include an arranged marriage at the age of 40, a dispute over the ownership of local wells, and the deception by his son Jacob, who stole his brother's birthright. These incidents imply a passivity and tendency for social altercation in Isaac, which are two hallmarks of what today is called PTSD."[64] It is now in vogue to diagnose people of the past, including veterans of the Great War. Spearheaded by the Lost Generation novelists, American society labeled the doughboys as disillusioned veterans. This label endures, but it is incorrect.[65] It is unjust to view the First World War as a conflict that traumatized an entire generation.

Whether combat produces trauma depends on the individual, not the event. During the war, soldiers who exhibited emotional disturbances such as anxiety, irritability, and depression, as well as more severe symptoms such as tremors, spasms, apathy, and speech or hearing disorders, were labeled shell-shocked by themselves and their fellow doughboys. Some soldiers sensed emotional and psychological changes in themselves, and although they continued to function in daily life, they felt imbalanced and restless.

In May 1917 reserve US Army psychiatrist Major Thomas Salmon traveled to Europe and later suggested the establishment of a special center for the treatment of shell shock. The army constructed Base Hospital No. 117 near La Fauche, along the Vosges Mountains, as a war neurosis treatment center. There, doctors and staff treated patients with a combination of physical tasks such as woodcutting and road construction, occupational therapy workshops, and art therapy classes. Neurologist Sidney I. Schwabe believed these therapies helped patients "remember past experiences and thus learn to compromise with them instead of dodging them."[66] Doctors treated nearly 3,000 soldiers for shell shock at Base Hospital No. 117, with an improvement rate of 40 to 75 percent.[67]

The Western Front could leave physical and psychological scars, but most doughboys did not allow their ordeals to define them. A switchboard equipment engineer before the war, Earle T. W. Gronk was wounded in combat and became shell-shocked on 16 June 1918. When reflecting on his overseas service, he asserted, "Would not take anything for it nor give anything for it again."[68] Gronk returned to work as an engineer with a telephone company after the war. The vast majority of AEF veterans proved resilient; for them, like Henry Fleming, "Scars faded as flowers."[69]

Positive Transformations

After the armistice, the doughboys returned home; functioned as normal citizens; went back to work, most to their former occupations; and realized that, in some ways, their war experiences had changed them for the better. The government passed what Beth Linker calls "rehabilitation legislation," which ensured that doughboys, especially amputees, would receive ample support. The aim was not only to reduce or eliminate the payment of government pensions to veterans but also to enable doughboys who had lost limbs or suffered blindness or deafness to return to work and support themselves and their families.[70] In addition, according to Steven Trout, society paid a great deal of positive attention to the doughboys (however, his book ends in 1941 for a reason: with the outbreak of World War II, memorialization of the doughboys dissolved).[71] Like the collective patterns identified in the doughboys' combat experiences, each soldier's adjustment to civilian life differed, but similarities existed.

A Desire for World Peace

After surviving combat, many soldiers expressed a longing to end war and work for peace. Edwin R. Carter, a sergeant in the Medical Corps, said, "I felt that war was absolutely the last thing to be used in bringing righteousness on earth. President Wilson to my mind had done his best to keep us out of it and it was only when no other course was open to us, that we entered. Therefore, I enlisted with the one ideal in mind of fighting for a righteous and everlasting peace for the world." He also observed that his wartime experiences had changed him: "They have made me hate war more than ever. I am entirely out of sympathy with the present method of conducting our army. I agree with the Washington official who declared it was a relic of ancient Feudalism of Lord and peasant. I believe the military system breaks more men than it makes. War should be used only when all else has failed."[72]

First Lieutenant Arthur A. Grove, a thirty-four-year-old graduate of Roanoke College, remarked, "I went into the war from a sense of duty. It seemed that the war had to come and I wanted to do my duty. Did not look forward to any 'fun' and I was not disappointed. War is even worse than I had ever imagined. I believe in keeping out of war as long as we can do so honorably but I am not a peace at any price man. I believe, in fact I know, that I have been greatly benefited in every way. I could do it again if necessary but hope it will not be necessary."[73] Subsequent to his discharge on 29 May 1919, Grove returned to his home in Luray, Virginia, and resumed his occupation as a merchant. Methodist William F. Bartlett, who enlisted on 26 March 1917, agreed with Grove. Bartlett explained, "I wouldn't take anything for my experience while overseas as it surely taught me a great deal." He continued, "I only can only say that I would do the same again if I was called upon to do so."[74] An infantry corporal and a combat veteran, Bartlett returned to his home in Rockville, Connecticut, after his discharge and worked as a mill hand. The feelings expressed by Grove and Bartlett were widespread among the doughboys: war was not pleasant, and they hoped war never returned, but if it did, they were ready.

Czechoslovakian Edward G. Pobuda of South Willington, Connecticut, participated in combat for three months. "The war has taught me a great lesson, morally, socially, physically, mentally, politically, and otherwise," he wrote. "It has been a great experience. I never realized the deep seriousness of war until I got into the fray and now I pledge myself to fight again, but in a fight for a lasting World Peace."[75]

Becoming a Better Man

Once their expectations of war were shattered, many doughboys found themselves altered in ways they could not have predicted. Surviving life-and-death situations and witnessing suffering and destruction made the soldiers different men. There was a change in the way they viewed themselves and in the way they viewed the world and their own role in it.

New Haven resident Private Edwin B. J. Priest, 102nd Infantry, was one such soldier. "At first I was sorry that I had ever joined the Army, but after being through what I have gone through, and seeing what I did I am very glad that I got the chance that quite a number did not get," remarked Priest.[76] Even though he sustained severe wounds two days before the armistice, Priest would not have missed the opportunity to serve in the AEF. Many soldiers felt the same way. "I wouldn't have missed it for a million and I wouldn't want to go through it again for two million," said New Haven native Corporal Wilber S. Jewell. "I served in the intelligence section as a scout, sniper, and observer and believe it was one of the most interesting branches of the service at times it was very interesting," he reported. "I believe now as I did before the war a big army and a big navy will make other countries leave us in peace."[77] Private Leonard R. Bennett, 12th Field Artillery, of Hartford remarked, "It has made me a better man in many ways. I consider my experiences more valuable than gold."[78]

After surviving intense combat, Russian Adam P. Rubinousky reflected, "I did not seem to feel any unusual excitement but felt somewhat like you feel in a heavy thunder shower." Hospitalized in Nancy after being wounded during a battle along the Marne, Rubinousky reported no alteration in his state of mind when he returned home: "I don't notice any difference."[79] He resumed his old trade as a painter in Rockville, Connecticut. Marine private and combat veteran Prescott E. Haskell concluded, "All these experiences have broadened my mind and have given me a wide vision of life."[80] Haskell, a Connecticut native, relocated to Washington, D.C., after the war.

Like Haskell, Second Lieutenant Paul M. Atkins from New Haven spoke of attaining a more expansive vision: "It has all helped to broaden my point of view to a remarkable extent, and has given me an appreciation of the complexity of international problems that I have never had before. It has added to the number of my friends among people with whom I could never have come in contact in any other way."[81] First Lieutenant Russell Y. Moore of Hartford stressed that "the smallness and narrowness of our ordinary daily life was impressed on my mind by the bigger things that happened everyday." To Moore, his life in Connecticut "looks better and happier than it did before the war."[82] Harold J. Dougan, of Manchester, Connecticut, stated, "I feel that I have at least done a small part of what is expected of one during his life." A sergeant in the infantry, Dougan "received a higher education than one could get in another way" by serving his country during the war.[83]

A captain in the field artillery, Edgar C. Outten of Hampton, Virginia, described the changes in his state of mind after his discharge on 7 February 1919: "One is not easily worried or irritated over trivial things any longer. Our country has duties to perform and obligations to fulfil beyond her own borders and shores just as surely as we have obligations to fulfil toward our fellow-man beyond the limits of our own self interests. I shall help her willing when needed."[84] Outten was twenty-six years old, had a bachelor's degree in electrical engineering, and was employed as a clerk and private secretary when he entered the service; after the war, he became an assistant manager at an oyster packing plant in Hampton.

Wilson H. Whitehouse, born in England, observed, "There is a way to do anything no matter how hard or far away it may seem." He believed the experience of war "gives a person greater insight into big things, develops a greater will power and self-determination to succeed despite the cost."[85] New Haven infantryman Morris Goldstein commented, "I believe that the experiences of war brought out some of the finer dormant instincts i.e. sympathy, courage, unselfishness, independency."[86]

"The effect does not seem to be permanent, and it seems hard to realize that I really went over-seas and lived under the conditions I did," said Hartford resident Sergeant Sydney D. Pinney, 101st Machine Gun Battalion. "However, I think that most of us returned with a more serious idea of life in our minds than we had previous to serving over-seas."[87] Like the majority of doughboys, twenty-one-year-old Pinney, wounded in action on 23 October 1918, handled his readjustment to civilian life well.

First Lieutenant Douglas C. France of Charlottesville, Virginia, served with the Army Ambulance Service and remarked on his return, "I believe I see life from a different position, viewing its seriousness both as to myself and as to those who are to come. There appears now a duty owing by us living to those yet unborn."[88] France received his discharge papers on 6 June 1920 and found employment as a lawyer with the US Department of Justice.

Carroll B. Case, a twenty-one-year-old Trinity College student from Hartford, joined the National Guard on 15 July 1917. He stated, "I enlisted voluntarily, considering it my duty as an American citizen." Case appreciated the time he spent at the front and acknowledged that "it was an experience never to go thru again, but which I would not have missed for anything. It made me like home better. Experience has broadened my views in general."[89]

"I always did believe that the Germans aimed to whip the world, and I believe we done the right thing before and after the war, since I seen so many of our boys killed," observed infantryman Private James O. McKarney, who was discharged on 11 April 1919 and returned to farming in Washington County, Virginia.[90] "Consider myself fortunate to be among those to see, and, witness the great struggle. And to see the heads of the allied gov'ts in Paris on May 30, 1919," reflected Private Henry P. Lynch, a resident of New Haven. He added that his involvement in the war supplied "a world of experience, which has given me a better outlook on life."[91]

"I'm glad I was in, enjoyed the experience and feel quite fortunate that I was not even scratched. That I am able to earn a living today, and am happy. In an emergency, you'll find me present again," emphasized New Haven resident Captain Isadore M. Levine, 122nd Cavalry, Connecticut National Guard.[92] "I am well satisfied with what I learned in the service and am ready to answer my country's call at any time I am needed," remarked Eugene M. Lamb of Fielding, Utah.[93] Lamb, a twenty-four-year-old farmer, joined the Marine Corps on 12 June 1917. Fellow Utahan, twenty-two-year-old farm helper Leroy Newbold of Murray, volunteered on 21 March 1918. Newbold trained for only one month before shipping out to France on 26 April. He saw action with the 35th Division at Verdun and in Lorraine. Newbold declared, "I am glad and proud that I could serve my country in time of need."[94]

Thirty-four-year-old First Lieutenant William P. Nye from Radford, Virginia, was a building contractor with a high school education before serving with the 29th Division. After his discharge on 28 May 1919, Nye returned to his previous occupation with a new outlook on humanity: "There is lots of good in the worst of us. Lots of bad in the best of us. The German people are not all bad. Nor the allies all good. Room for improvement in any country, including the U.S.A."[95]

Corporal Mark N. Holmes from Manchester, Connecticut, said, "I will hereby observe Nov. 11 1918, and July 16 1919 as holidays. Nov. 11 should be observed as a holiday by all People, and as for July 16, I will observe it with a sense of FREEDOM, it being the day of my discharge. What could be sweeter?" Holmes continued, "I will say that I am not sorry for my experience. So heres thanking Uncle Sammy and the State of Conn. for all they have done for me. Amen."[96]

In spite of what they endured during the war, the doughboys extracted benefits from their experiences, returning with conviction to their civilian lives.

Moving Closer to God

Some men embraced religion to see them through their combat experience. William N. Webb, a thirty-four-year-old sheep handler from Charleston, Utah, was inducted on 28 April 1918 and discharged exactly one year later. He served with the 361st Infantry, 91st Division, and "went over the top three times and come out without a scratch." He recalled, "I have fought in three battles—was in the Orgonne Forest and up in Belgium. When we were at the front I tell you it was fierce. I did not know when I would get mine as men were falling on all sides of me and the big shells were bursting all around me. If ever a man prayed and thought of home it was I . . . I thank God I am still alive."[97] In a letter written home on 18 March 1918 from "somewhere in France," wagoner Parley O. Pratt of Salt Lake City expressed the effects of front-line warfare on his religious thinking. He emphasized, "You boys, if you ever come over here especially where you reach the trenches where I am at present, and get to know the whistles of the big H.E.'s and of shrapnel, the crackle of the machine guns and rifles and the myriad of noises that go with it, will eventually know what it means to fervently pray to your God. I never took religion very seriously until now."[98]

Sergeant William W. Parker from Norfolk, Virginia, noted a change in his attitude after serving with the AEF: "Before the war I was all for myself and the devil take the other fellow. I lived in today, let tomorrow take care of its self, these things are changed, we must work together for we need each other in this life. Our trust should be in God, so we should live as such."[99] While Parker was leading his platoon along the Vesle River near Soissons on 9 August 1918, an HE shell buried him and fractured a vertebra; he spent the next eight months at base hospitals. After being discharged on 17 April 1919, Parker was unable to find employment in Norfolk, but in August of that year he enrolled in Bowman Technical School in Lancaster, Pennsylvania.

Congregationalist Emil H. Miller, whose father had been born in Germany, stated, "It didn't seem possible at first that I should kill another person, but that soon left me as it was a case look out for yourself & get the other man before he got you." Miller continued, "I think it has brought most of us closer to our own individual religion."[100] After the war, Miller returned to his former occupation as an accountant.

As Jonathan H. Ebel explains, the doughboys "believed in the righteousness of the cause, believed in the communal and personal value of their errand, believed that in answering the call to arms they were answering the call of their faith."[101] Private David Reed, a fisherman from Chincoteague, Virginia, provided a short but clear description of the front: "Everything bad—waste—dirt—wickedness—bloodshed, all manner of evil." Reed fought at Verdun and in the Argonne Forest, where his "left hand was partly shot away." He thought it was "awful that every nation had forgotten God and resorted to the sword instead of returning to prayer."[102] For the majority of AEF soldiers, their wartime experiences brought them closer to God and strengthened their religious beliefs.

A Greater Love of Country

Returning to their former place in society posed a challenge for some doughboys. Despite their problems readjusting, the veterans overwhelmingly expressed their patriotism. "I am more contented to be in the United States after seeing foreign countries and foreigners. The world seems smaller and I feel lucky to be in," said Private Edward B. Caulfield, 11th Engineers, of Hartford. He added that he "learned to appreciate the United States more than ever before."[103]

"I have better learned to appreciate the home country and see better the enlightenment our country has reached. Believe my 'state of mind' is a bit more settled," commented Earle T. W. Gronk, an engineer from Pembroke, Virginia, after his discharge on 25 June 1919.[104] Captain Ulysses H. Brockway of Hartford declared that his wartime experience "made me a firmer and more enthusiastic believer in preparedness and strengthened my own belief in the glory of the U.S."[105] Private First Class James P. Sheehan, also of Hartford, affirmed, "I forget all about my experiences, I believe I was a better man after getting out of the Army than before I went in."[106]

"It made me appreciate the U.S.A. It has given me a pride I didn't have before," said Captain Arthur E. Westphal of Hartford. He added his recommendations for military training: "Lots to be said in favour of German efficiency and in disfavor of our own inefficiency. It has made me appreciate the need of universal military training."[107] Another call for training came from Major Stillman F. Westbrook of Hartford, who summed up his impressions of war succinctly: "As a very observing Englishman put it 'Damned dull, Damned dirty and Damned dangerous.'"[108] He felt his experiences served "to absolutely disillusion me of the romance of war," yet Westbrook also declared, "I have always been and still am in favor of some form of universal service."[109] Even doughboys who hated the war believed the United States should continue the policy of conscription, and many called for "universal military service" or "training" in the future. Scores of these same men believed that universal service would remedy the country's martial unpreparedness.

Captain Cyrus C. Washburn called himself "a firm believer in universal training" and added, "I believe that every male child who is physically qualified should receive at least one year of military training. Time spent now in training may prove a blessing in future years." Washburn, from Hartford, was most impressed by "the cheerfullness with which our men went forward to almost sure death, the amount of hardships that a man can stand without breaking."[110] A wagoner in the 101st Machine Gun Battalion, 26th Division, Earle A. Penfield of Hartford achieved "a deeper and stronger sense of duty to my fellow men and a deeper understanding of what life really is."[111]

Even the foreign-born felt closer to their adopted country. Twenty-three-year-old William G. B. Augermann of Hartford had been born in Brandenburg, Germany, enlisted in the National Guard on 23 June 1916, and served as a private with the 104th Ambulance Company, 26th Division. He stated, "It is an easy matter to forget blood-ties where once liberty is in the balance, and that is quite easy to die when one has his mind made up when death arrives." Upon his discharge on 29 April 1919, Augermann reflected, "I can now, although a foreigner, feel the pulse throb of America and I am happy in the thought that was able to help preserve the regular, healthy beat of life in America."[112]

"I feel that I have been especially privileged to have lived at a time when it was possible for me to take part in the greatest of all wars," observed twenty-eight-year-old First Lieutenant Thomas N. Williams, 3rd Regiment, Anti-Aircraft Battalion, after his discharge on 18 August 1919.[113] Previously employed as a clerk with one year of college in Berryville, Virginia, Williams found work with the US Shipping Board after the war.

John Knudson of New Haven expressed a willingness to serve again, if necessary, stating, "If the country has another good 'scrap,' don't forget to drop me a line." According to Knudson, after participating in the conflict overseas, "I began to realize what 'Home, Sweet Home,' meant." He added, "It has broadened my view of life and given me trust in myself. I realized more fully what it means to live in a 'Free Country.'"[114]

"My impressions are, that there is not a Nation in the world that can conquer the U.S. fighting as we did in the world war. My mind has been changed since we entered the war, as we stand high above any nation in the world in the manner of fighting and military training etc.," said New Haven resident Corporal Charles H. Henderling. His words reflected the pride expressed by many doughboys for their nation and the AEF. "I gained considerable in my experiences overseas," Henderling continued, "and will never forget what I have seen, and learned by the trip."[115]

Brotherhood

Other doughboys recalled the friendships they made during the grueling hours, days, and weeks spent in cold, muddy trenches. With so much uncertainty, the soldiers depended on one another for support. Lieutenant Colonel Charles W. Whittlesey, 308th Infantry, 77th Division, spoke with emotion of his comrades: "We remember them as friends . . . such men are richer to have known."[116] In the depths of the Argonne Forest, Whittlesey commanded the "Lost Battalion" for five harrowing days in October 1918. Surrounded by Germans, he marshaled a staunch defense that even withstood accidental friendly artillery fire. For his gallant leadership and his stand against overwhelming odds, he received the Medal of Honor. Whittlesey returned home a hero and resumed his law practice. Three years later, perhaps burdened by the thought that he had let too many of his men down in the Argonne, he climbed overboard while sailing to Cuba on the SS *Toloa* sometime on 27 November 1921. His body was never recovered.

Sergeant Alvin C. York, 328th Infantry, 82nd Division, a farmer from the mountains of Tennessee, remembered the friends he made:

The war brings out the worst in you. It turns you into a mad, fightin' animal, but it also brings out something else, something I jes don't know how to describe, a sort of tenderness and love for the fellows fightin' with you. . . . I had kinder got to know and sorter understand the boys around me. I knowed their weakness as well as their strength. I guess they knowed mine. If you live together for several months sharing and sharing alike, you learn a heap about each other. It was as though we could look right through each other and knowed everything without anything being hid. I'm a telling you I loved them-there boys in my squad. . . . They were my buddies. That's a word that's only understood by soldiers who have lived under the same blankets, gathered around the same chow can, and looked at death together. I never knowed I loved my brother-man so much until I was a doughboy.[117]

Pride and Hope for Equality

The black doughboys' war experience differed from that of their white counterparts: the African Americans fought not only for the United States but also for racial equality. This desire for equality is a distinctive aspect of many of the questionnaires completed by African Americans; at the very least, these men wanted to draw attention to the prejudices embedded in American culture, and they expressed the hope that attitudes in the United States would change.

Grammar school–educated African American Private Charles L. Hogue, 80th Division, returned to his home in Norfolk, Virginia, and his occupation as a freight handler with the Southern Railway after his discharge on 18 June 1919. Reflecting on his service with the AEF, Hogue commented, "If it could have been possible for me to have seen some of the consequences before I entered the army, I would sware it is impossible to endure these ordeals." He added, "If this record will be of any service to the War History Commission by me filling it out, please use it the best of our advantage. The colored boys of our beloved State of Virginia."[118] Hogue, who resided in East Pittsburgh, Pennsylvania, after his discharge, wrote a separate letter to the Virginia War History Commission in which he observed:

> I am delighted to fill out this War History blank. I know it is for the purpose of perpetuating the memory of Virginia's part in the World War. I am glad to state the fact, that Virginia sent me into the service, and I did everything in my power to gain honor for myself and the beloved state whom I represented in the greatest and most terrific conflict that ever defaced humanity. I am not saying it because I went into the service from Virginia, but I want you to know that the Black boys from Virginia was second to none. We respected the government regardless of past circumstances.[119]

As Hogue's remarks indicate, African American doughboys felt the sting of racial bigotry as they fought for their country. Hogue's words also epitomize the identity of black soldiers: they felt the same sense of duty as the white doughboys, and they served with pride for themselves, their state, and most of all their country.

Thirty-year-old Private James P. Spencer, an African American student attending Virginia Normal and Industrial Institute, had much to say about discrimination both during and after the war. Spencer, from Petersburg, Virginia, said he had been "cheated out of disability claims by prejudice on part of medical officers after discharge. Was not helped by anyone to re-enter new line of work. Change of occupation was due to injury." Spencer also cited racism on the Western Front: his African American commanding officer, Colonel Franklin A. Dennison, "an officer of rare intelligence and ability" who led his men with distinction, had been replaced with "a white colonel simply on prejudicial grounds." Spencer hoped "such information will aid in printing or recording the deeds of the Negro soldiers in the Great War for democracy." Discharged on 22 April 1919 and employed as a book agent, Spencer also voiced his opinions about war: "That most wars are fought from a selfish viewpoint, fought from an economic viewpoint; that the Great War was fought over the German's desire to exploit Ethiopia and her rich resources instead of England and other countries." He added, "Am now about to post-graduate from Virginia Normal and Industrial Institute to serve my race in my humble capacity, and to help the Old Dominion to still be great among the many states."[120]

Another characteristic shared by African American soldiers was the pride they felt in contributing to the Allied effort. African American Second Lieutenant John M. Ross of New Haven concluded that the war gave him "a greater feeling of pride in the achievements of my race, and a hope that this great country of ours will give every man in it a square deal, no matter what his race or color may be."[121]

Sergeant Harry E. Curry, an African American student from Hampton, Virginia, was not quite sixteen years old when he joined the National Guard on 23 May 1915. He was stationed at Potomac Park, Washington, D.C., until 24 December 1917, when he was called to duty with the AEF. After his discharge on 1 March 1919, Curry found employment as a laborer and reflected on his views about patriotism: "Before the war it all seemed foolish to me, but as I received training I learned each country must be protected and I was ready to go at any time. Any man living in a country under its Flag and is not willing to go to protect his Flag which he is living under I say should be killed."[122]

Private John S. Fields, an African American from Church Roads, Virginia, who served with the 369th Infantry, said this about the war: "I do not think about it if I can help it, and whenever it does come in my mind it seems like a dream and I wonder if it all really did happen. About most things in life I think just as I did before."[123] Fields, discharged on 28 February 1919, went back to his former occupation as a teamster. African American Corporal Thomas M. Clary of White Plains, Virginia, stated, "Before the war, I thought it was awful, now I feel it was just the thing to do, fight for right and liberty."[124] Clary also returned to his prewar occupation, blacksmith and farmer, after his discharge from the army on 28 February 1919. Private Moses Randolph of Farmville, Virginia, served with the 369th Infantry. An African American section hand for the Norfolk Western Railroad with an eighth-grade education, Randolph said, "I am more interested in what is going on in the world than before."[125]

Forgotten at Home

Whether he was black or white, Christian or Jew, each AEF soldier discovered (like the veterans of prior wars) that the civilians around him soon forgot about the war. Corporal Emory P. Barrow of Alberta, Virginia, who practiced law after being discharged from the Military Police on 23 July 1919, said his experiences gave him a "more intense devotion for the Stars and Stripes. The U.S. should not be the world's dumping ground. Taught me something of the greatness of our country." Barrow went on to express his dismay at the public's turnaround: "To my mind the most marvelous and irreconcilable thing about the whole war was the rapid change in public sentiment for the soldier and away from the ex-soldier. Boys it is tough luck to be so soon forgotten, but we will never forget our 'buddies' who sleep in Flanders Field."[126]

Other soldiers, such as Private William J. B. Morris of Mappsville, Virginia, also noted the change in public attitude toward veterans of the war. Morris, a twenty-four-year-old traffic manager with a business college degree when he entered the service, had much to say about his personal experiences and the welfare of his fellow veterans:

> It gave me a wider scope of vision, I view things now from a world stand point instead of from a state or National viewpoint. It has been particularly interesting to personally watch and take note of the height that public opinion did and can reach from the standpoint of Loyalty, Liberality and Devotion and then watch to what depths it can sink. When we went away there was nothing too good for us and if and when we came back we could have anything we wanted, but soon after it was over even before I returned, any thing that an ex-service man asked for was quite out of the question, even our jobs were given and kept by fellows and girls that stayed here. (mine wasn't).

Morris received his discharge papers on 10 July 1919 and asked the state of Virginia to aid its veterans:

> I am and have been very much disappointed that Va. and the Old Dominion hasn't as a state recognized the Sacrifice her men and women so nobly made in the World War and given them a bonus, not that I personally care or particularly need it, but it would set a good many of the Va. ex-service men to think that after all the sacrifice we made was appreciated, not that money could ever repay anyone, especially those of us that were fortunate enough to get into real action, for the Hell we went through. I am a member of the American Legion and as a Legionaire I plead with you above all things to take care of our sick and wounded.[127]

Corporal Wilbur L. Brownley of Norfolk, Virginia, was seventeen years old and employed as a warehouse clerk when he joined the 4th Virginia National Guard, 29th Division. After his discharge on 29 May 1919, Brownley found employment as a nautical instruments mechanic and observed that "civilians are patriotic during the time of trouble. But don't believe in it after the soldiers get home."[128]

Corporal Carl Noble, 60th Infantry, 5th Division, acknowledged the change in public sentiment toward returning soldiers:

> We were en route for Fort D. A. Russell, Wyoming. This trip was quite different from our trip from Camp Greene to Camp Merritt in the spring of 1918. I suppose the people had seen so many soldiers and troop trains during the past two years that it was an old sight; they had become

indifferent. There was little shouting, cheering or hand waving. In one town in my native state, Ohio, the train stopped for a few minutes. I got off the train and rushed across the street to buy a watermelon. I bought a melon and started to leave the store, when a gentleman spoke to me: "I beg your pardon, but I would like to know how much the lady charged you for that melon." I said I had paid seventy-five cents for it. "I thought so," he said. "I thought that was what she charged you. Those melons have been selling for twenty-five cents. Come with me and I'll see that you get your fifty cents back." The train whistle was blowing and I told him I must go. The girl who had sold me the melon could hear our conversation, and looked perturbed. As I started for the train the man who had accosted me said, "Soldier, I'm going to do my part to see that this doesn't happen again." I thought of the Y.M.C.A. chap who had made that speech when we went into the Argonne: "Men, when you get back to America and see anything you want, do not ask the price; just pick it up and walk off with it, and you will have carpets strewn with flowers to walk on!"[129]

These doughboys expressed the powerful sentiments felt by many returning veterans. Arthur G. Empey had entreated young men to join the AEF, because those who did would "have it all over" those who did not do their bit.[130] But after the war, as had happened in the past and would happen in the future, Americans soon forgot the veterans and their sacrifices. At the national level, America displayed pride in the AEF. After the government entombed the Unknown Soldier and the parades ended, however, attention at the individual level waned. And once World War II began, it vanished. The doughboys, especially those who had engaged in heavy, close combat, learned the true nature of war—it was a reality they could grasp, but they could not confer that reality on the nation. War remained distant to the public, something they only read about in newspapers or watched on newsreels in the theaters. But when the film ended, so did the lesson. Society best remembered the war through the lens constructed by Lost Generation novelists. The public found the war too brutal, too dark to remember or reexamine. Perhaps Second Lieutenant Orswald Fisher of Manchester, Connecticut, described it best: "To the citizen patriotism is often but a word. To a soldier it is a feeling."[131]

Conclusion: "If It Has to Come I Am Here"

Why was Sherman right? And why did so many young men think so only *after* they returned from the Great War? What factors cloaked the reality of the front lines—battles that were reported on and photographed extensively before the United States entered the war—and perpetuated a romantic vision of war instead?

Of the 30,847 Military Service Records (MSRs) examined for this book, 400 men wrote that "Sherman was right," "War is hell," or some combination of these powerful three-word sentences. Some doughboys went even further. "Sherman had an inadequate vocabulary," wrote one Virginian. The Civil War ended in 1865, and Sherman gave his famous speech at a veterans' reunion in Columbus, Ohio, on 11 August 1880. He stated, "There is many a boy here today who looks on war as all glory, but, boys, it is all hell. You can bear this warning voice to generations yet to come. I look upon war with horror, but if it has to come I am here." As the *Ohio State Journal* noted, "This last remark was received with long applause and a hurrah by the audience."[1]

The *Enquirer and News*, published in Battle Creek, Michigan, credits Sherman with an earlier "war is hell" speech, delivered on 19 June 1879 at the Michigan Military Academy. He opened his speech by addressing the "cadets of the graduating class," at which point the students rose and saluted. Sherman then continued, departing from his prepared remarks: "Boys, I've been where you are now and I know just how you feel. It's entirely natural that there should beat in the breast of every one of you a hope and desire that some day you can use the skill you have acquired here. Suppress it! You don't know the horrible aspects of war. I've been through two wars and I know. I've seen cities and homes in ashes. I've seen thousands of men lying on the ground, their dead faces looking up at the skies. I tell you, war is hell!"[2]

Sherman died in 1891, around the same time most of the doughboys were being born. They had not lived through the horrors of the 1860s, and Sherman's grim warnings did not discourage them from answering the call to war. Most important, it did not deter just over 300,000 men from deciding to enlist and "not wait to be called."[3] How could Americans so quickly forget the painful memories of the Civil War?

Heroic Remembrance

This fallibility of memory can be attributed to the romanticization of the Civil War and of warfare in general in the United States. The only way to justify the deaths of 752,000 soldiers—more than 2 percent of the population—during the War between the States was to glorify their sacrifice.[4] Only fifty years after the Civil War, men once again rushed off to battle with romantic notions of honor, manhood, and heroism. This romanticism was perpetuated by war memorials and statues in countless town greens across the country; it even seeped into the literature, in books the young doughboys had read in their childhoods. The children's literature of Oliver Optic and the work of Stephen Crane constructed the future doughboys' conceptions of war, combat, and heroism on the battlefield. Filled with heroic imagery, Crane's *The Red Badge of Courage* inspired young men the moment it first appeared in a serialized version in newspapers in 1894. The story reached an even greater audience a year later when it was published in book form by D. Appleton and sold for $1.50. The book was America's first best seller. Appleton made several printings in 1895 and again in 1896, and it continued to do so until the first year of the Great War.[5]

Many future doughboys felt a connection to Crane's main character, the young soldier Henry Fleming. In his first battle, Fleming flees, fearing death. He later overcomes his fear, overcomes death, fights, and becomes a man. War transforms Fleming: "He felt a quiet manhood, non-assertive but of sturdy and strong blood. He knew that he would no more quail before his guides wherever they should point. He had been to touch the great death, and found that, after all, it was but the great death. He was a man."[6] Having "rid himself of the red sickness of battle," and with his soul at peace, Fleming embraces nature and life with a newfound delight, as expressed in the last line of the novel: "Over the river a golden ray of sun came through the hosts of leaden rain clouds."[7] The future doughboys could relate to Fleming's journey and psychological transformation—in effect, they became Fleming. As John Higham argues, American males became more martial in the 1890s, and literature showcased society's interest in nature and sports.[8]

Prolific writer Oliver Optic published books and stories for children during the 1880s and 1890s. One of his most successful endeavors was the Blue and the Gray series: six historical novels set during the Civil War, written in a style reflecting the glory and romanticism of war. Optic's first Civil War novels (the

Army and Navy collection) had "received more commendatory letters from young people in regard to the books of this series than concerning those of any other," leading him to create the Blue and the Gray series.[9] He wrote his novels from the point of view of the Union, but with "ample justice" given to the Confederacy. The main character is seventeen-year-old Christy Passford, who responds as follows when he learns that his father, Captain Passford, will be joining the conflict: "'I want to go with you; and I am sure I can do my share of the duty, whatever it may be,' demanded Christy . . . who had thrown back his head as though he felt the inspiration of all the manliness in his being." He continued: "'There is to be a war for the Union, I am a Union man, or boy, as you like; and it would be as mean and cowardly for me to turn my back to the enemy as it would be for you to do so, sir' . . . his chest heaving with patriotic emotion."[10]

Optic's theme of duty and manhood continues in the second book of the series, as Christy's father agrees to let him join the Union cause: "The young man, just entering his seventeenth year, protested against being left at home, and as the captain believed that a patriotic citizen ought to be willing to give his all, even his sons, to his country, the young man went with his father. The mother was as devoted to her country as the father, and terrible as was the ordeal, she consented to part with him for such a duty."[11] The novels of Crane and Optic stirred visions of heroic battle among the future AEF soldiers.

The romanticism of the war stretched to every corner of the country, and a respect and appreciation for warfare grew. Grandeur returned to the art of combat. The success of the Spanish-American War in 1898 only augmented a belief in the heroic nature of combat among American youth of the twentieth century.[12] Images such as Theodore Roosevelt's charge up Kettle Hill further motivated young American males to seek manhood through military service and war. That allure even extended to future president Franklin D. Roosevelt, whose fifth cousin Theodore implored him in April 1917 to leave his post as assistant secretary of the navy and enlist in the AEF: "You must get into uniform at once. You must get in."[13] Franklin attempted to resign his position, but President Wilson denied his request. It did not matter whether the personal motivation came from Theodore Roosevelt or elsewhere; the average American man wanted to enlist, or he willingly answered the call to arms when drafted.

Almost fifty years after he wrote his memoirs in 1918, William L. Langer reflected: "What strikes me most, I think, is the constant reference to the eagerness of the men to get to France and above all to reach the front. One would think that, after almost four years of war, after the most detailed and realistic accounts of the murderous fighting on the Somme and around Verdun, to say nothing of the day-to-day agony of trench warfare, it would have been all but impossible to get anyone to serve without duress! But it was not so."[14]

I Missed My Chance

Men who did not see combat or never even crossed the pond illustrate this cultural and literary romanticism at work. Most men who did not see action wished they had. On 13 April 1918 Sidney R. Godfrey, a twenty-five-year-old farmer from Murray, Utah, volunteered for the Marine Corps. He was discharged on 27 January 1919, with no combat experience. Godfrey expressed his disappointment: "One regret, after 10 months of hard service that I didn't see active service & get any overseas address to my credit. . . . We were all disappointed when the War stopped. We were sore because they wouldn't ship us across. Capt. Merrill said He would like to lead us in battle. 1st because we were from the west and 2nd because we had that western health, pluck & nerve."[15]

Corporal C. Ralph Amott of Salt Lake City was a twenty-three-year-old stenographer and insurance clerk when he enlisted in the army on 18 June 1918. Amott spent seven months at the Vancouver Barracks in Washington, working on government insurance and allotments. He regretted having "no such luck" in seeing combat and commented, "The most peaceful time I ever spent was while I was in the war (army)." Amott was discharged on 23 January 1919.[16]

Thirty-year-old Jesse C. Larsen of Reno, Nevada, served with the 7th French Mortar Battery, 7th Division. He trained at Camp Lewis and shipped out on 22 August 1918, headed for Brest. In a letter to his father from Camp de Meucon, France, dated 24 November 1918, Larsen wrote: "The nearest I have been to the front is in the naborhood of 400 miles so you see I haven't saw any thing of war (luckily for me) although I would liked very much to have saw some action after so long training. We were under orders to move to the front when the armistice was signed, but any way the 'Huns' are whiped, the war is over, and we expect to be back in the states in a few months."[17] Larsen was discharged on 15 February 1919.

Much to their disappointment, the men of the 145th Field Artillery, 64th Artillery Brigade, 40th Division, did not see combat. The unit crossed the Atlantic in August 1918, arrived in Le Havre on 2 September, and trained at Camp de Souge near Bordeaux with French 75mm guns. Metz was supposed to be their first foray into action, but the armistice came first. Officers and enlisted men alike expressed their dissatisfaction with that turn of events. After the guns went silent, Lieutenant Colonel E. LeRay Bourne of the 145th wrote to his wife, "You cannot realize the disappointment we all feel in not participating in the war as combat troops. It is also inadequate consolation to know that there are hundreds of thousands of other American troops more fortunate than we. Someone has to be last, it is true, but the pity we bestow upon ourselves doesn't ameliorate our great disappointment. But we are making the best of it and are ready for the next job, be that what it may."[18] Echoing Bourne's sentiments, Private Ralph Duvall expressed his frustration in a short poem entitled "Doggerel":

> At De Souge they made us like it. We began to drill some more,
> But it wasn't any use at all, for soon they stopped the war.
> Now all we want to know is, what the Hell we soldiered for?[19]

On 27 December 1918, 1,400 men of the 145th left Bordeaux aboard the *Santa Teresa*, docked in New York on 5 January 1919, and arrived home in Ogden, Utah, on 17 January. Of their original complement, sixty-five enlisted men and five officers remained in France as part of the occupation force, serving as military police and mechanics. Thirteen men had died of influenza while training in France.

William S. Willes, a twenty-six-year-old druggist from Salt Lake City, was a married man and the father of one when he volunteered on 15 December 1917. Willes served as a private with the 145th and trained with other Utahans at Camp Kearny, California, for seven months, followed by four months at Camp de Souge, France. After his discharge on 25 January 1919, Willes echoed the disappointment of his fellow soldiers: "Haven't one Hun to my credit and very sorry I haven't a million. . . . Did not see service, unfortunately, too many ahead of us."[20] Pindar's words, written nearly 2,400 years before the doughboys entered the trenches, remained true: "War is sweet to those who have no experience of it, but the experienced man trembles exceedingly at heart on its approach."[21]

Soldiers who saw little action lamented their minimal participation in the war. One of them, thirty-one-year-old factory worker Mike Sedlak from Fairfield, Connecticut, offered these comments about combat: "Didn't mind it in the least. I just kept my eyes opened and watched every move." Sedlak, who had volunteered for service, said, "I knew what I was going for, and wanted the experience."[22]

Twenty-one-year-old George S. Crockett, a student at the Virginia Military Institute, remarked, "In our branch (Aviation) it was taken and considered as sport and we found the Germans the same true sportsmanship." The scenes between Captains Boëldieu and von Rauffenstein in Jean Renoir's film *La Grande Illusion* (1937) accurately depict the Great War pilots' chivalry and respect for one another. Crockett continued, lamenting his lack of participation in air combat: "My duty was the safe conveyance of fighting planes to the front—too bad no active fighting."[23]

Twenty-five-year-old John E. Howell, a sales clerk from Alexandria, Virginia, served as an ordnance sergeant in the Coast Artillery. Howell saw limited action and stated, "I liked the Artillery fine and in time of war would gladly return to it."[24]

Doughboys who had engaged in heavy combat were more reluctant to repeat their ordeal. Charles M. Pratt of Cedar City, Utah, had completed one year of college when he volunteered for the Marine Corps on 19 June 1917. After training, Pratt sailed to France aboard the *Von Steuben*, and by March 1918 he was engaged in his first battle in the Verdun sector. Pratt was wounded on 19 July at Soissons, receiving "machine gun bullets . . . through groin and lodged in hip"; he was decorated with a French War Cross, a sharpshooter's badge, and twenty-two regimental citations. In April 1919, when asked by a reporter for the *Iron County Record* whether he would volunteer again if the United States went to war, Pratt replied, "Well, I don't know. That would depend—upon how badly my country needed me."[25]

Alvin C. York, who killed 28 Germans, captured 35 machine guns, and, with a small group of soldiers, took 132 prisoners on 8 October 1918 in the Argonne, explained:

> I didn't want to kill a whole heap of Germans nohow. I didn't hate them. But I done it jes the same. I had to. I was cornered. It was either them or me, and I'm a-telling you I didn't and don't want to die nohow if I can live. . . . Jes the same I have tried to forget. I have never talked about it much. I have never told the story even to my own mother. For years I done refused to write about it for the newspapers, and wasn't at all pleased when others wrote about it.[26]

York's reticence was common. For example, Corporal John J. Deloughery of New Haven noted, "Do not care to talk about war."[27]

Some veterans contemplated the cost of war and who benefited from it. Twenty-four-year-old Vahow Shabazian, a Turk from Bridgeport, Connecticut, "was in the battle zone from June 7, 1918 to Nov. 10, 1918 without rest. Covered over 2000 miles of France by train and wagon roads during my stay of over 5 months." Upon returning home, he reflected, "I often wondered was the sacrifice of human beings, animals, and equipment worth the territory that was being so stubbornly fought for. I candidly believe that war benefits only the very select few, and that in a financial way."[28] Private Amillo Aiello of the 102nd Infantry, a resident of New Haven, had "the impression that too much was lost for the gain."[29] "Lives of humans are expendable when a financial goal is to be reached," stressed machine gunner Private Otis H. Culver of New Haven.[30]

Twenty-five-year-old David C. Dettor, a college-educated farmer from Bristol, Virginia, was a second lieutenant in the 317th Infantry, 80th Division. He concluded "that war is the greatest piece of false economy in the world. Sometimes necessary, perhaps war develops the animal in man more than anything else." He added, "War never was worth what it cost, but subjects of the State can't question this."[31]

Fighting for Identity

Principally, the doughboys were willing to fight the Central Powers for several reasons: manhood, patriotism, and, above all, duty. But two groups in particular fought for something more: their identities. African Americans and Italian Americans expressed more pride than their fellow doughboys in killing Germans. Where did that pride originate?

For African Americans, part of the answer lies in Germany's past and its oppression of the native peoples of eastern and southern Africa (mainly the Nama and Herero peoples of modern-day Namibia and Botswana) beginning in the nineteenth century. Leading the bigotry was German socialist August F. Bebel, who remarked in March 1904, "I have not held a speech in favor of the Hereros; I have repeatedly emphasized that they are a wild people, very low in culture."[32] From 1904 to 1907 the German army killed 50 percent of the Nama population and close to 80 percent of the Herero population. A decade later, the German army reacted with shock and insult when the French drew soldiers from their African and Indochinese colonies, especially modern-day Senegal, to form *La Coloniale*, also known as *Tirailleurs Sénégalais*.[33]

First Lieutenant Samuel Woodfill of the 60th Infantry, 5th Division, from Jefferson County, Indiana, made the following observations about the African troops serving with the French:

> The Algerian and Senegalese soldiers, the chaps who liked to bring back souvenirs as visible evidence of what they had accomplished. A lot of them were serving down here in the Vosges, and whenever the sector got too quiet they would just sneak over to some German outpost during the night, slit a sentry's throat, cut off his ears or mebbe his whole head, and carry it around with them for a few days. They would keep their souvenirs until the news got to their higher-up French officer's ears—or noses. But if the French tried to make them give up their little keepsakes, that would only make them all the more determined to sneak out for a new supply of trophies at the first chance.[34]

Private Stanley J. Herzog, 103rd Field Artillery, 26th Division, also recalled the battlefield practices of the African troops: "These Algerian soldiers, when over the top, each and every one of them, providing they kill a German, would either cut off an ear or some other part of the body, just to show or have evidence that he had killed his foe. Every Algerian soldier carries a small bag in which to place their souvenirs."[35]

In a letter dated 2 September 1917, ambulance driver Avery Royce Wolfe from Buffalo, New York, recounted what took place in the back of his ambulance between a German prisoner of war and a Malagasy soldier:

The German was huddled in one corner, absolutely scared to death. The big negro was sitting on the seat calmly, whetting a huge knife on the sole of his shoe. When I made my appearance he indicated to me that he was going to add a trophy to his necklace. It seems that it is the custom of the Madagascars to cut off the little fingers of their prisoners and wear them on a necklace, as evidence of their fighting ability. A bit shocked and almost as terrified as the poor German, I nevertheless persuaded the negro to wait until we arrived at the hospital so the doctors could witness the fun. Needless to say, when we finally arrived at the hospital the negro was dissuaded from his intention, much to the relief of the German.[36]

The Senegalese infantrymen in particular were feared and hated by the Germans, especially when France stationed Senegalese troops in the Rhineland after the war. The Nazis would later use this act, called *die schwarze Schande* (the Black Horror), to conduct an aggressive propaganda campaign to demonize black soldiers and instill fear in German troops.[37] During World War I, the Germans associated the African American doughboys with the bloodthirsty *Tirailleurs Sénégalais*, and in fact, most black doughboys served with the French African troops because the AEF segregated them in the 92nd and 93rd Divisions.[38] The four African American infantry regiments of the 93rd Division—three made up of National Guardsmen and one of draftees, including the famous 369th Infantry—served with the French and thus tapped into decades of racial tension between Germans and Africans.

The stronger African American motivation was not European history but US history—a past filled with racism. It was a racially tense time in the United States, and lynchings of blacks remained common.[39] Only one month after the United States declared war, a race riot erupted in East St. Louis, Illinois, where whites killed more than 100 African Americans. Nonetheless, black doughboys went to war to fight oppression, believing that their patriotic military service would win them equal rights, once and for all.

Even in this atmosphere of bigotry, W. E. B. Du Bois, editor of the NAACP's journal *Crisis*, called on African Americans to "forget our special grievances and close our ranks shoulder to shoulder with our own white fellow-citizens and the allied nations that are fighting for democracy. We make no ordinary sacrifice, but we make it gladly and willingly with our eyes lifted to the hills."[40] African American soldiers answered this call and entered the service to fight for equality and to prove that they, too, were Americans.

African American James P. Spencer, a twenty-nine-year-old student at the Virginia Normal and Industrial Institute, stated, "I felt that it was my patriotic duty to serve my country at the most critical hour in the Nation's history. Though my Race had not been given the proper rights."[41] Thirty-year-old African American Corporal Benjamin Skinner of Norfolk, Virginia, was a longshoreman when he joined the National Guard. He believed in fighting "for democracy" and "trusting in God that my Mother, Sister & Race should be benefited by it."[42]

Twenty-eight-year-old African American artilleryman Sergeant Jacob M. Sampson of Richmond, Virginia, expressed his views on the war: "An evil which was inevitable, and therefore should be faced gracefully. War is the most diabolically inhuman method of settling a dispute among intelligent men. I volunteered so as not to be sent like all other Negro men from my state into a service, or depot brigade, but to choose a more satisfactory branch of service."[43]

African American Christopher C. Watts had spent three years at a military school in Lawrenceville, Virginia, prior to the war. When he entered the service on 27 October 1917, he was a twenty-three-year-old farmer from Portsmouth. Upon his return from France, Watts pointed out the differences he had observed: "There are no separation of races in Europe or elsewhere except in this country. All men are the same—not jim-crowed." Watts also stressed the importance of the African American presence in the AEF, saying, "I think the Negro deserves much credit for what he has done for this country. I think if it weren't for the black fighters, the war would be going on now."[44] African American Willis B. Godwin of Smithfield, Virginia, was a twenty-two-year-old student when he entered the service on 28 October 1917. Like Watts, he reflected on his time in France and commented, "After the fighting and my return back to this country U.S. it made me wonder why can't all men be treated equally. What did we fight for? Democracy. Are we having it?" Godwin added, "After the war I realized more clearly what a man's life means to him."[45]

Despite his frightening encounter with the Malagasy soldier, ambulance driver Avery Royce Wolfe reflected on the absence of racism: "It is strange to see how the colored troops are received over in France. There seems to be absolutely no race question, such as exists in America. The negro is accepted everywhere on the same basis as a white men."[46]

"My attitude toward military service in general is against it, and especially compulsory military service. I don't believe greater injustice could be done to a man than to take him from his home against his will to fight on foreign soil," declared Waverly L. Crawford, a twenty-seven-year-old African American farmer from Dendron, Virginia. Crawford continued by commenting on the "injustice in the ranks. . . . But practically a private in the U.S.A. has no right which an officer is bound to respect; and there is no such thing as a fair decision in a Courts Martial when it comes to a Commissioned officer trying a private if it happens that he doesn't like the Private. . . . There is nothing at all of the United States army that would or could encourage me to join any part of it. Especially when the investigation by the War Dept. failed to eliminate some of the evils of the Army."[47]

Other African Americans emphasized the killing of the enemy. "Impressions were made upon me to fight for my country, and to kill as many Huns as I could for the benefit of my people at home," noted seventeen-year-old Corporal Vernon Smith of Portsmouth, Virginia.[48] Moses Randolph, an African American from Farmville, Virginia, served as a private in the 369th Infantry and remarked, "I wanted to kill as many as I could."[49]

Despite the African American troops' hope that fighting the Germans would win them equal rights at home, racial injustice and discrimination continued after the war.[50] The African American doughboys were not the first or the last to be disappointed in this way—this same belief motivated their ancestors during previous wars (e.g., the Civil War) and their descendants in future wars.

Racial prejudice in the United States was not limited to African Americans. Some Americans viewed Italians as mongrels and were unsure whether they were black or white. Italians living in the South incurred the wrath of whites because they associated with blacks as equals. From 1896 to 1915, lynch mobs murdered forty-six Italians. At least a dozen lynchings of Italians occurred across the country, including in Colorado and Florida. The worst violence took place on 14 March 1891, when whites lynched eleven Italians in New Orleans.[51] At the time of the First World War, America continued to display prejudice against Italians.

During the war, Congress passed the Espionage Act on 15 June 1917 and the Sedition Act on 16 May 1918. After the war, these two acts enabled Attorney General A. Mitchell Palmer to lead raids against foreign-born individuals and other political radicals (anarchists) suspected of terrorizing prominent citizens such as Justice Oliver Wendell Homes Jr. The Palmer raids resulted in the arrest of thousands and the deportation of hundreds of suspects. Government agents invaded homes without warrants, detained people without counsel, and deported foreigners, including many Italians, back to their native countries. In 1927 Massachusetts executed anarchists Nicola Sacco and Bartolomeo Vanzetti, who had been convicted of a 1920 murder.[52]

Like their African American counterparts, Italian doughboys were anxious to serve their country and engage in combat. Sergeant Alvin C. York served in a platoon that included soldiers from various backgrounds, including many Italians. He described their eagerness to fight:

> The trouble with our boys when we went into this quiet sector was they would want to go out on top of the trenches and start something. They

was wanting to get into it and get it over. I knowed now that the Greeks and Italians and Poles and New York Jews were fighters. Ho! ho! As right-smart fighters as the American-borned boys. They didn't want to lay around and do nothing. And they would even go on top and get the Germans out. Once one of them come up to me right there in the front line and asked me, "Where is the war?" They was always wanting to go over the top—and keep a-going. They shore were ambitious.[53]

Americus Paoletti, a truck driver from Bridgeport, Connecticut, had just turned nineteen when he enlisted in the National Army on 2 April 1917. Paoletti, whose father had been born in Italy, was "willing to fight for the country" and described himself as "one of the best fighting men of the Co."[54] "I thought it was my duty to serve for the country an to hold up its flag from falling. The impression that I got while I was in fighting I thought it was heaven," responded Italian-born Robert Deilus, who was employed as a chemical printer in South Norwalk, Connecticut, when he entered the National Army.[55]

Another Italian-born soldier, twenty-six-year-old laborer Frank Piazza from New Britain, Connecticut, said of his military service, "I enjoyed it very much." Regarding his participation in combat, he claimed, "It did not frighted me at all."[56] Born in Tusa, Sicily, laborer Giuseppe S. Peronne of New London, Connecticut, was twenty-two when he entered the service. After the war, Peronne said combat had caused him "no feeling of fear, rather a feeling of strength."[57]

"Well before I went to France I was thinking of having some of the hand to hand fight just with rifle and M.G. and artillery but when came to the real thing it was all different," stressed eighteen-year-old Salvatore Distefano, an Italian-born resident of East Hampton, Connecticut. Employed as a buffer in a bell shop, Distefano added, "It wasn't as hard as the French was tell me."[58] Twenty-two-year-old Italian American John F. Carini, a mechanic from Chester, Connecticut, explained, "I felt that it was my duty as a U.S. citizen to help defend my country. I preferred being in the Machine Gun Co. to any other service."[59]

In addition to duty, another motivation for Italian Americans was the quest for honor and status.[60] In 1870, when the *Risorgimento* (Italian unification) ended, King Vittorio Emanuele III declared, "The age of prose had replaced the age of poetry," but the Great War gave Italy a chance to return to its romantic roots—something that many citizens desired.[61] Even Italian cinema attempted to inflame the passion for combat when Giovanni Pastrone released *Cabiria* in 1914, which, according to Leo Braudy, "argued for Italy's entry into the war under the guise of an epic story of the wars between Italy and Carthage."[62] The war gave Italian Americans in the AEF a chance to prove that Italians' courage did not die with men such as Giuseppe Garibaldi; more important, it gave them a chance to avenge their countrymen who died during the disastrous battle at

Caporetto in the autumn and winter of 1917. Yet, even without Caporetto as incentive, Italians (especially northern Italians), despised Austrians, whom they had fought for their independence in the 1860s.

Italians wanted to demonstrate that they deserved to live in America, and they thought the best way to do that was on the Western Front. With this purpose in mind, as described earlier, Italian immigrant Tony Monanco stormed into his local Selective Service Office in Buffalo, New York, and declared, "In dees countra seex months. Gimme da gun."[63] These doughboys felt there was no better way to prove their prowess than going to war and killing Austrians and Germans. But ultimately, like African Americans, Italian Americans fought for equality in the United States—a status denied them for decades.

This pride demonstrated by Italian Americans and African Americans was not an anomaly—British and German soldiers both acknowledged the ferocity of Canadian troops, who strove to prove their patriotism for Britain. In a letter to his parents on 29 August 1918, Lieutenant R. C. Germain, 20th Canadian Infantry Battalion, proclaimed, "We rushed them and they had the nerve to throw up their hands and cry, 'Kamerad.' All the 'Kamerad' they got was a foot of cold steel thro them from my remaining men while I blew their brains out with my revolver without any hesitation."[64] Fellow Canadian Richard Rogerson declared, "I have got my share of Germans. I got fourteen to my credit in about two hours some I shot with my rifle more I drove bayonit into and two I killed with a milles bomb. . . . Once I killed my first German with my bayonit my blood was riled every german I could not reach with my bayonit I shot. I think no more of murdering them than I usted to think of shooting rabbits."[65] This loathing between the Canadians and the Germans parallels that between the Africans and the Germans; rumors of extreme violence and the killing of prisoners—whether imagined or real—aggrandized both groups' aversion for the other.

Regardless of race or ethnicity, men who participated in combat differed from those who did not. Men who were not on the front lines or saw only limited action were enthusiastic for a second round, whereas those who came under fire and engaged in hand-to-hand combat—regardless of whether they were wounded (by gunshot, gas, or shrapnel)—were apprehensive about going through it again. Even so, the majority of doughboys were proud to serve their country, hoped for a peaceful world, but would serve again, if necessary. This majority represented the archetypal World War I combat veteran. Representing the minority were two groups at opposite ends of the spectrum: those who enjoyed killing and combat, and those who hated every aspect of the war and the army. Unfortunately, these latter voices, made famous by the Lost Generation novelists (American and European), have defined the Great War, but it is really the archetypal combat veteran whose voice should be heard.

Reflective Return

The AEF represented an array of men and women from a variety of backgrounds, occupations, ethnicities, religions, and educational levels. For the most part, officers and enlisted men, especially those who had seen combat or sustained wounds, proposed an end to all wars and supported more peaceful means of solving the world's differences in the future. After the armistice, doughboy William L. Langer observed: "For though we have been through hell together and know that many times in the years to come we shall miss the comradeship of the buddies and friends of our army days, we are, after all, essentially a peaceful lot, quite ready to forget the shot and shell, the gas and flame, and return to win our future laurels in the fields of peace."[66] Decades later, in his 1977 autobiography, Langer wrote: "When the American soldiers returned from abroad, they were cured of the yearning for danger and conflict. . . . Most returning soldiers felt that they had seen enough, and that no such cataclysm should be permitted to occur again, if humanly possible."[67]

Robert C. Duval Jr., a thirty-year-old attorney from Richmond, Virginia, was a first lieutenant in the 318th Infantry. Wounded in the left thigh on 5 October 1918 during an attack near the Meuse River, he reflected on his war experience almost two years later: "It makes one feel older and more mature in every way. Apparently most of us have forgotten that there was a war, and have gone back to the old way of thinking and living, but I don't think this is entirely the case, certainly not with the men who saw action."[68] First Lieutenant Herman R. Furr, a thirty-one-year-old real estate broker from Norfolk, Virginia, stated, the war "has aged me, made me more serious, and to some extent has modified my belief in the 'Glory of War.'"[69] Furr's father had been a Confederate soldier during the Civil War.

Participation in the war sobered the attitudes of many doughboys; men who were still young in years returned from combat with a seriousness of purpose they had previously not possessed. "It has been a great education all in itself. Things that once interested me no longer make the same appeal. I have become much more serious in my ways, and perhaps may say that I believe I get a much better view of life and living in general," commented twenty-two-year-old John R. Castleman of Berrysville, Virginia. His experiences, he said, "left me in the most restless sort of condition, the excitement which had keyed me to a high pitch when taken away I did not want to do anything but dream and wander over the country."[70]

Thomas G. Hardy, a captain in the Medical Reserve Corps, was called to active service on 15 August 1917 and immediately sent to the front. The twenty-seven-year-old physician from Farmville, Virginia, summarized his experience: "My part was only to mend those torn by the fighting, and my impression was that war is a bloody, horrible, useless game."[71] Battalion Sergeant Major Frederick W. Rowe, 102nd Infantry, of Waterbury, Connecticut, stressed, "Before the war I pictured men going 'over the top' with colors flying and bugles blowing and the band playing Yankee Doodle, but there is no glory in it. Its just a dirty, filthy game."[72]

Men and women who spent extended amounts of time (several months or more) in active war sectors sometimes succumbed to fatigue.[73] For one exhausted French soldier, even going to a small shop was an uplifting experience: "The crowd, the lights, the rustling of the silk, the colors of the merchandise—all was a delight to the eyes, a contrast after the misery of our trenches."[74] But unlike the Allied armies that fought for the first three years of the war, most doughboys did not have to endure such lengthy periods of intense combat. As Langer reflects, "Fortunately for us, we were spared the ordeal of the French, British, Germans, Russians, and Italians. Our term of service under fire was short. We got just enough of blood, sweat, and tears to satisfy our craving for adventure. And then, we were lucky enough to be on the winning side."[75] For the AEF, the cost of being on the winning side—with only one year at the front (beginning with Cambrai on 20 November 1917)—was 116,516 deaths, or an average of 327 men a day. By contrast, the French army lost 1,397,000 in four years—an average of 897 French soldiers each day.[76] Fortunately for the AEF, in 1918 the war once again became one of movement, and as Frederic C. Bartlett states, "it is easier and requires less courage to attack than to withstand fire without retaliation, and extreme possession by unpleasant thoughts is apt to be peculiarly intense during much of the disagreeable routine of trench-fighting."[77] It is important to note that the short duration of the conflict for America may have colored the doughboys' reactions, skewing them in a more positive direction. Americans did not endure four years of war, as did their French and British allies. Nonetheless, the AEF saw heavy action for eight months, and thousands of doughboys remained at the front line for months at a time.

Those AEF soldiers who stated they suffered shell shock during the war had often endured prolonged periods of combat; more often, the reason for their shell shock was an artillery shell that threw them or knocked them unconscious. Eighteen-year-old Corporal Charles T. Clement of Salt Lake City volunteered on 15 October 1917 and served with the 4th Balloon Squadron. Sent overseas on 30 June 1918, Clement saw action from 10 August until the armistice. In a letter to his mother dated 20 November 1918, Clement described how combat had affected him: "One time when they were shelling our . . . position, I happened to get to close to an 'Austrian 88' as it exploded, and believe me I had a wonderful headache for days. At times I thought Old Liberty Bell was ringing in my ears. All the other machinery was working at once and my head was in an uproar. In other words I was slightly shell-shocked." Clement continued, "I try to write letters but it is almost impossible. . . . I don't know what is the matter, but it is the hardest thing for me to do now. At one time I could write all day but now I can't stay in one place long enough to write a letter. . . . Since the Big Guns have ceased firing it don't seem natural. Everything seems so mono-tamous. I suppose it is because we have been in one place to long."[78] Clement received his discharge on 21 May 1919.

Some veterans sensed a lack of compassion among the public when they returned home, but they continued to function in daily life. Lieutenant Frank A. Holden of the 328th Infantry, 82nd Division, reflected, "We felt on our re-turn 'let down' and disappointed over something. What that something is, I do not know. I wish I did. We criticize no one for it."[79]

Alvin C. York tried to explain how he felt after his return from the war: "But I knowed, though, that I had done changed. I knowed I wasn't like I used to be. The big outside world I had been in and the things I had fought through had teched me up inside a most powerful lot. The old life I had lived seemed a long, long way behind me. It seemed to be a sort of other life in another world. I knowed I had changed. I was sort of restless and full of dreams and wanting to be doing something; and I didn't understand. So I sat out on the hillside try-ing to puzzle it out."[80]

Nineteen-year-old Hugh H. Bishop, a silk weaver with an eighth-grade ed-ucation from Marion, Ohio, participated in heavy combat and was shot in the left leg below the knee on 16 September 1918; his battery was cited for brav-ery in action under heavy fire at Boncourt. After his discharge, Bishop described his condition as "not very good. I have a lot of nervous disorders now. A kind of shell-shock and nervousness. I give a jump now when a fuse blows out in a street car, which I never took notice of before I went to France. . . . In other words I do not feel as good now as I did when I went over."[81] Hartford private Edward F. Plumridge's war experiences left him "with a broader mind, but shat-tered my nerves."[82]

Twenty-nine-year-old farmer Frank A. Starr from Easton, Connecticut, a wagoner in the 56th Artillery, saw a great deal of action. He emphasized, "The experience is very hard to explain as I saw thirty men in my own Battery fall one night and shells were bursting all around us for two days and nights. But it was our duty to face them to bring us liberty so we all did it." Starr also noted a change in himself: "Before the war my mind was free and clear. And since I returned to civil life I am more or less nervous all the time."[83]

Twenty-five-year-old Lawrence T. Hager, an actor and vaudeville performer from Danbury, Connecticut, was wounded by shrapnel—"had my forehead and part of my chin blown off"—at the Argonne on 15 October 1918. When he re-turned from France, Hager remarked, "Wouldn't want to take a million for my experiences, or go through it again. I have had lots of trouble with my head and my mind so bad. And I am very nervous."[84]

Before the war, Syrian-born Samuel George, age twenty-three, worked in a fur factory and resided in Danbury, Connecticut. He was gassed at Verdun on

14 October 1918 and spent the next two months at base hospitals in France. George described the aftereffects: "I am nervous for the rest of my life and never expect to enjoy the health before I went across." He went on to explain his change in occupation after being discharged on 30 January 1919: "On account of being gassed I am nervous and could not handle a machine in the factory I used to work in before I went in the army. So I have a little fruit stand, from which I think to earn my living, but I hardly can earn the most necessary thing."[85] "The experience I had in the fighting is very hard to explain because it is always before my eyes and I still think about it while I sleep," stressed thirty-year-old Private Patrick Wynne of Bridgeport, Connecticut, an Irish-born street-car conductor.[86]

Sergeant Harry B. L. Marvin, an infantryman cited for gallantry during the Argonne offensive, concluded, "The impressions made upon me was the wonderful morale of the American soldier and the spirit of self-sacrifice of the men, not alone in their willingness to die but in every way. One is left with an uneasy feeling when first returning to civil life this however wears off and leaves one with a feeling of great satisfaction for having done his bit."[87] Marvin returned to his previous occupation as an insurance agent. The war affected every combat veteran—it overcame some, but the majority endured. To affix a blanket label to the doughboys as shell-shocked and disillusioned is completely inaccurate. They were not a Lost Generation. If the men and women of the AEF were "lost," it is only in the sense that society forgot and misremembered them. The majority of the doughboys overcame the horrors of the war. These men returned to their lives, some of them more stoic or serious, but all of them proud of what they had accomplished in France. Two weeks after the armistice, combat veteran Walter H. Anderson of Toquerville, Utah, concluded, "We all feel good about seeing that this awful hell is ended."[88]

Veterans of the AEF testified about their inadequate training for industrialized warfare. The Western Front spawned a level of brutality the American soldiers did not anticipate. Their immediate memories, recorded shortly after the war's conclusion, provide a glimpse into their state of mind. It is these memories that best describe the doughboys' ordeal.

Memories are delicate and impressionable—they change and fade with time. Moreover, shifts in sociocultural perceptions can alter and reduce the precision of memory, and as decades pass, memories weaken and even confabulate. As Elizabeth Loftus and Katherine Ketcham write, "Memories don't sit in one place, waiting patiently to be retrieved; they drift through the brain, more like clouds or vapor than something we can put our hands around."[89] The truth lies within the moment of the event; as time passes, so does the truth. The MSRs used for this study provide new and unique voices because they were compiled almost immediately after the war—a sort of exit interview for American soldiers. Nothing similar is available in any other country. Veterans filled out these MSRs when their memories were still vivid and before they could be influenced by any future social, cultural, or political biases.

As noted in the introduction, the case of Great War veteran Maurice Genevoix illustrates the elusiveness of memory. With every retelling of his war story, Genevoix added and subtracted details. Affected by social and cultural norms, Genevoix's memories changed to fit the propriety of the time: in 1914 it was a great achievement to shoot Germans; in the twilight of his life it was not. By repressing or confabulating his memories, Genevoix muddled the facts, and in the end, even he did not know the truth anymore.

Unlike Genevoix, William L. Langer did know the truth. He wrote *Gas and Flame* in 1918, but the publisher printed only 400 copies for distribution to the officers and men of Company E, 1st Gas Regiment, as they were discharged. When Knopf republished the book in 1965, Langer wrote a new preface but left the text unchanged. He observed, "As I reread this simple narrative after a lifetime spent in the teaching and writing of history, I find its immediacy rather appealing. It has nothing of the sophisticated rationalization that invariably creeps into reminiscences recorded long after the event."[90]

The young men of 1917 did not want to believe that Sherman was right; they just wanted to cross the Atlantic as soon as possible. To the doughboys, especially those from the South, Sherman represented the polar opposite of romantic warfare: a modern Black Prince whose *chevauchée* style of combat diminished war to a vulgar, dishonorable horror.[91] What did Sherman know of war? In their minds, Sherman's most notable achievement had left swaths of Georgia and the Carolinas in ruins.[92]

But as the doughboys eventually learned, Sherman was right—war is hell. For the doughboys, however, the most telling part of Sherman's famous speech was not "war is hell" but the line that followed: "I look upon war with horror, but if it has to come I am here."[93] The doughboys echoed that vow. War was a horror, but if it returned, they would be ready. Imbibing a potent elixir of romanticism, the doughboys went to war. But more powerful than any elixir was the sense of duty shared by every officer, enlistee, and conscript. Indeed, the doughboys dressed in their best and were prepared to go down like gentlemen.

Appendix A: Unpacking the Source

The Military Service Records (MSRs) are an invaluable historical resource, but why did only Connecticut, Minnesota, Utah, and Virginia distribute them? What entity issued them? And why is so little known about them? To answer these important questions, one must start from the beginning—when Congress created the Council of National Defense on 29 August 1916. Established by section 2 of the Army Appropriation Act, the council coordinated industry and resources for the security of the United States.[1] It was the first emergency government agency designed to aid in the production of war materials, and it spawned other commissions dealing with specific war-related issues. When the United States actively entered World War I, historians in every state immediately took steps to preserve materials and information they considered vital to the nation's chronological records. This movement began with historians in Washington, D.C., who formed the National Board for Historical Service in April 1917. This nonofficial group sought "to place historical scholarship at the service of the government by adapting educational and research efforts to war needs throughout the country."[2]

The National Board for Historical Service corresponded with state libraries, historical commissions, and defense councils, urging them to collect war records and other items related to the role of American servicemen and -women during the war. This group of historians provided the impetus for the establishment of a national agency as well as state agencies to collect and preserve World War I memorabilia and official records. Although the National Board for Historical Service was short-lived (owing to the lack of archival data, it is unclear why the board disbanded), its work continued under the auspices of the National Association of State War History Organizations, established in 1919.

Each state formed a committee designed to document its citizens' participation in the war. Connecticut and Virginia were at the forefront of collecting data about their respective soldiers. After the United States declared war on 6 April 1917, the Connecticut General Assembly and Governor Marcus H. Holcomb approved legislation to establish a Department of Historical Records to preserve war-related materials. In March 1919 this department became known as the Department of War Records (a subsidiary of the Connecticut State Council of Defense), and state librarian George S. Godard was appointed its administrator. Supported by an appropriation of $20,000 from the state legislature, Godard's department began collecting and recording war data in early 1919.[3] In fact, Connecticut devised and circulated its MSR before the first meeting of the National Association of State War History Organizations. These MSRs were to be "filed, as a permanent memorial of the deeds of Connecticut soldiers and sailors in the service of federal, state and allied governments during American participation in the World War."[4] In Virginia, Governor Westmoreland Davis created the War History Commission in January 1919 and named Professor Arthur Kyle Davis (no relation) of Southern College in Petersburg as its chairman.

Representatives from sixteen states met in Washington, D.C., on 9–10 September 1919 and drafted a proposal for the creation of the National Association of State War History Organizations to coordinate the collection of war records.[5] Among those attending were James Sullivan, state historian of New York; Arthur Kyle Davis of the Virginia War History Commission; and Franklin Holbrook of Minnesota's War Records Commission. For an annual membership fee of $200, states could participate in the exchange of war-related publications, information, records, and memorabilia. Adjutant generals and historical commissioners from every state were invited to join the national association. Newton D. Mereness acted as the director of research for the group and compiled a report outlining the activities of each state's organization.[6]

After 1920, as the interest in war information declined, it became more difficult for commissions to obtain funds to continue their research and data collection. As a result, historical commissions grew more dependent on voluntary information provided by concerned citizens or civic groups. States collected all types of material and information for their archives; this most commonly consisted of war service records, but the data took many forms. Table A.1 shows that only Connecticut and Virginia asked the vital subjective questions that allowed veterans to expand on their answers. Minnesota's questionnaire was similar in presentation but lacked subjective questions. Utah's questionnaire solicited less information than the MSRs of Connecticut, Virginia, and Minnesota; it contained no subjective questions but did include a "Remarks" sections that urged the veterans to provide details of their experiences. Finally, Vermont prepared a questionnaire comparable in style to those of Connecticut, Minnesota,

Table A.1. Method of Data Collection by State

State	Type	Format
Virginia	Questionnaire	Four pages, six subjective questions
Connecticut	Questionnaire	Four pages, five subjective questions
Minnesota, Utah	Questionnaire	Four pages, no subjective questions
Vermont (never issued)	Questionnaire	Eight pages, no subjective questions
Missouri, New Mexico, Wyoming	Vital statistics	One page, no subjective questions
Delaware, Florida, Georgia, Kentucky, Maine, Mississippi, Nebraska, Nevada, New York, North Carolina, Oregon, Rhode Island, South Carolina, Tennessee, Washington, Wisconsin	Vital statistics	Two-sided card, no subjective questions

and Virginia (minus the subjective questions), but it was never sent to veterans. Nineteen other states sent out either simple sheets or small cards.

Discovering an Untapped Resource

By chance, I discovered Connecticut's MSRs for the Great War in 2000, while working as an archival assistant in the Connecticut State Archives. At first, it seemed impossible that no historian had ever used this detailed source, but in all the scholarship I read or referenced, not one mentioned the Connecticut records or anything similar to them. This seemed improbable. Consulting the latest publications and scouring the Internet for primary sources provided no new insight.[7] For instance, Christina K. Schaefer's guide supplies excellent details on the service records of Great War veterans, and she even provides a state-by-state listing of sources in the appendix, but the book does not mention the questionnaires anywhere.[8] This seemed even more improbable. But Connecticut state archivist Mark Jones confirmed that, with the exception of a few genealogists over the years, no one had ever used these records for serious historical research.

This led to other questions: How many other states issued questionnaires? Who created these records? How did they go about it, and why? The next step seemed simple enough: contact or visit every state and significant government agency. I assumed that this vast search would produce an overabundance of information and supply all the answers. It did not. However, after a series of informative but ultimately fruitless discussions with state archivists, librarians, and military officers, I found the answer to one of my questions: Virginia was the only other state that had issued a questionnaire like Connecticut's, as confirmed by the Library of Virginia. Otherwise, state after state responded with answers such as "We are unaware of any such forms being sent out by this state" or "We do not have any records relating to World War I questionnaires in our archives."[9]

Some answers seemed plain wrong. Vermont responded, "The State Archives does not have records relating to a Service Questionnaire sent out after WWI."[10] Yet the Connecticut State Library contains an eight-page questionnaire from Vermont dating from 1919.[11] This indicates one of two possibilities. Either Vermont's MSRs and all the information pertaining to them disappeared—perhaps lost forever or buried deep within some random vault in a derelict municipal building—or the questionnaire in Connecticut's archive was a proposed sample copy and Vermont did not have the funding to pursue the project. What is striking is the resemblance between the two questionnaires. Both seem to have been molded from the same template.

Most states responded like Vermont did, and it began to make sense why scholars had never used these records. Besides Connecticut and Virginia, few states know the questionnaires even existed. Moreover, each of the four states that issued questionnaires (Connecticut, Minnesota, Utah, and Virginia) believed its survey was unique; no state had knowledge of any other state sending MSRs to veterans. In addition, no state archives contained any information concerning the origin of the questionnaire.

The responses of government agencies were also discouraging: "You may wish to use an Internet search engine or visit a local library" or "I'm afraid you will have to contact individual state historical departments."[12] The Indiana State Archives responded, "There is nothing like this in our State Council of Defense Collection, you might check with the State Library."[13] The response from the Indiana State Library: "We do not have any records of this kind; another agency who may have these records is the State Archives."[14]

Replies from other agencies ranged from helpful to redundant. The best piece of information came from Mitchell Yockelson of the National Archives, who recommended a search of the Selective Service System (SSS) records. According to the SSS's national headquarters, "The Selective Service System was not established until September 16, 1940."[15] This was contradicted by the SSS's website, which states that it inducted 2,810,296 men during World War I.[16] Further research conducted at the National Archives proved that although the SSS did draft men and place them in training camps, it did not play any part in the questionnaires.

Many states suggested that I contact the state Adjutant General's Office (AGO), so I did, but none of them knew anything about a questionnaire. Even the AGO of the United States in Washington, D.C., had no knowledge of any such records and later confirmed that the AGO had nothing to do with the questionnaires.[17] The Library of Congress was immensely helpful, combing every key file index for information regarding a questionnaire, but every search produced the same answer: "In a review of the index for that file I did not identify any headings that seemed relevant to your topic."[18]

Despite the seemingly fruitless search, many helpful individuals provided enough information to confirm which states issued a questionnaire and which did not. In addition, I found a definite connection between the creation of World War I historical committees and the distribution of questionnaires. The proof lies in the papers of Godard and Davis. The former handled all inquiries from Connecticut veterans concerning the questionnaires and issued the promised certificates of service when the state library received the completed questionnaires. The latter, in a newsletter issued in Virginia, wrote about his duties as head of the commission, one of which was to collect the questionnaires.[19]

In his report concerning the activities of the Connecticut State Library from 30 June 1920 to 30 June 1922, Godard expressed his disappointment in the rate of return of the MSRs:

> It is to be regretted that so many of the Connecticut boys who saw service in the World War, do not appreciate the opportunity given by our Department of War Records to record, in their own words and in their own way, on special uniform blanks furnished for this purpose—for the benefit of those who shall come after them—something of the services which they were able to render; and for the benefit of the state and country, a statement of their observations and recommendations.[20]

It is obvious that Godard recognized the questionnaires' historical significance and conscientiously exercised his duties and responsibilities as head of the Connecticut Department of War Records. However, he never revealed the origin of the MSR or how he decided which questions to include on the form.

Connecticut and Virginia issued their questionnaires around the same time, in the late winter or early spring of 1919. With the exception of one question— Virginia asks about the war's effect on the soldiers' religious beliefs—these two questionnaires are almost exact duplicates. This suggests that some government agency created a template for the states to follow. But only Minnesota and Utah issued questionnaires with a parallel style (Minnesota's was an abridged version), and, of these, only Minnesota included the state seal in the top left corner of the first page, as did Connecticut and Virginia. Minnesota and Utah also requested that the veterans include photographs and any additional information that would help detail their wartime experiences.[21]

Rather than a questionnaire or a service card (issued by sixteen states), Missouri, New Mexico, and Wyoming issued a sheet of vital statistics, which resembled a service card except for its size (either eight and a half by eleven inches or eight and a half by fourteen inches). Though useful for statistical purposes, these service cards and sheets did not allow veterans to write about their wartime experiences, and none of these other states' records were as comprehensive as those of Connecticut, Minnesota, Utah, and Virginia.

State Historical Commissions

In conjunction with compiling war records, many states formed historical commissions or committees. Each state gave its group a different title, but each committee's goal was the same: to preserve and collect everything of historical importance regarding the state's participation in the war. States created most of these committees in early 1919, based on the need for a single unit to collect historical war data. The question remains: given that more than half the states created historical commissions, why did only four states create a questionnaire?

The formation of these state historical committees was a major initiative that required both money and coordination. Although there was a federal recommendation to establish historical commissions, there were no mandatory guidelines for states to follow. Left to their own devices, states relied on one another for direction. For instance, Davis from Virginia corresponded with his counterpart in Wyoming and asked "what methods you employed to secure official citations and authentic information."[22] Table A.2 illustrates each state's level of commitment to creating a historical commission and compiling service records.

Other correspondence between state archivists revealed some of the problems involved in establishing these historical commissions. Thomas M. Owen, director of the Alabama Department of Archives and History, wrote to Eunice G. Anderson, the state historian of Wyoming: "In many states the regularly established Historical Departments, Commissions or Societies have for months been collecting such data, while in other states historians of State Councils of Defense, or of Committees of Public Safety, have been appointed, with carefully selected historians of County Councils of Defense."[23]

Additional correspondence from Anderson in Wyoming disclosed that inadequate financial support was hindering the committee's performance: "Owing to lack of sufficient funds and a staff large enough to compile such statistics, Wyoming's Historical Department has not as yet gathered as much data regarding our service men as we hope ultimately to do."[24] A year earlier, Anderson had congratulated the Virginia War History Commission for its "splendid" work in collecting material but lamented her own state's inability to match Virginia's efforts: "We of this Department were very disappointed to not suc-

Table A.2. Creation of State Historical Committees and Distribution of MSRs

State	Date Committee Established	Type of MSR Issued	Date Sent
Alabama	1919	None	NA
Alaska	NA	None	NA
Arizona	NA	None	NA
Arkansas	NA	None	NA
California	NA	None	NA
Colorado	NA	None	NA
Connecticut	March 1919	Four-page questionnaire	Early 1919
Delaware	1919	Service card	Late 1919
Florida	1919	Service card	Mid 1919
Georgia	1919	Service card	Mid 1919
Hawaii	NA	None	NA
Idaho	NA	None	NA
Illinois	NA	None	NA
Indiana	NA	None	NA
Iowa	1919	None	NA
Kansas	NA	None	NA
Kentucky	15 March 1918	Service card	1919
Louisiana	NA	None	NA
Maine	1919	Service card	Late 1919
Maryland	NA	None	NA
Massachusetts	NA	None	NA
Michigan	NA	None	NA
Minnesota	April 1919	Four-page questionnaire	Late 1919
Mississippi	1919	Service card	Early 1920
Missouri	August 1919	Service sheet	Late 1919
Montana	NA	None	NA
Nebraska	1919	Service card	Mid 1919
Nevada	1919	Service card	Mid 1919
New Hampshire	NA	None	NA
New Jersey	31 March 1919	None	NA
New Mexico	1919	Service sheet	Late 1919
New York	1919	Service card	Early 1919
North Carolina	1919	Service card	Mid 1919
North Dakota	NA	None	NA
Ohio	1919	None	NA
Oklahoma	NA	None	NA
Oregon	28 April 1917	Service card	Mid 1919
Pennsylvania	22 September 1919	None	NA
Rhode Island	1919	Service card	1919

(continued on next page)

Table A.2. *Continued*

State	Date Committee Established	Type of MSR Issued	Date Sent
South Carolina	11 July 1919	Service card	Early 1920
South Dakota	NA	None	NA
Tennessee	24 January 1919	Service card	Early 1919
Texas	NA	None	NA
Utah	1 April 1919	Four-page questionnaire	Early 1919
Vermont	1919	Eight-page questionnaire (never issued)	NA
Virginia	7 January 1919	Four-page questionnaire	Early 1919
Washington	NA	Service card	1919
West Virginia	NA	None	NA
Wisconsin	1919	Service card	1919
Wyoming	25 February 1919	Service sheet	Early 1919

NA, not applicable.

ceed in obtaining a special appropriation for the carrying on of this division of History in the State of Wyoming."[25] These committees depended on non-governmental funding and volunteers to maintain their agencies.

Committees collected any material dealing with their state's participation in the war, including diaries, memoirs, newspaper clippings, soldiers' souvenirs, and every type of war memorabilia possible. Connecticut's collection includes many of these items as well as dozens of photographs taken by the US Signal Corps and memorial parade programs from individual towns. Collecting the questionnaires, service cards, or service sheets issued to all returning veterans was also one of the committees' duties. In many states, only a small percentage of veterans returned their forms, and those that were received were often only partially filled out. The more questions a form asked, the fewer returns it generated. Table A.3 shows MSR return rates for the four key states. About the same percentage of veterans returned their surveys in each state, except for Minnesota, which did not ask any subjective questions and got a much higher return rate. For a point of comparison, Table A.4 lists the casualties the four key states suffered during the war.

In Tennessee on 24 January 1919, "the state legislature resolved that a committee of 25 be appointed, to be known as the Tennessee State Historical Committee, part of whose duties was to 'collect, compile, index and arrange all data and information of every kind and character relating to the part Tennessee has

Table A.3. MSR Return Rates by State

State	Number of Soldiers in Service	Number of MSRs Returned	Percentage Returned	Number of MSRs Fully Completed	Percentage Fully Completed
Connecticut	67,000	12,947	19	798	6
Minnesota	120,000	80,000	71	NA	NA
Utah	21,000	3,000	14	NA	NA
Virginia	100,000	14,900	15	394	3

NA, not applicable.

played in the Great War.'"[26] Tennessee Senate Joint Resolution 12 read, "Resolved, that this committee shall serve without compensation, and that the Governor be requested to direct the sympathetic help of every department of the state government to assist in their undertaking."[27] Tennessee's World War I veterans' questionnaire resembled an index card.

Virginia established the same type of committee: "On 7 January 1919, Governor Davis created the Virginia War History Commission whose goal was 'to complete an accurate and complete history of Virginia's military, economic and political participation in the World War.'"[28]

New York also formed a committee and compiled records: "These records were procured in 1920, by the Bureau of War Records, from the federal government pursuant to Chapter 75 of the Laws of 1919, which directed the Adjutant General, through the Bureau, to compile, collect, and preserve the 'records and relics . . . relating to the wars in which the state participated.'"[29]

Table A.4. Casualty Statistics for States Distributing MSRs

State	Killed in Action	Died of Wounds	Died of Disease	Died from Accident	Total Deaths*
Connecticut	572	234	230	67	1,103
Minnesota	885	379	744	95	2,103
Utah	168	51	414	32	665
Virginia	659	307	517	89	1,572

Source: Based on data in W. M. Haulsee, F. G. Howe, and A. C. Doyle, comps., *Soldiers of the Great War*, 3 vols. (Washington, DC: Soldiers Record Publishing Association, 1920), 1:169–173, 2:115–122, 3:307–308, 353–359.

*The total for the four key states is 5,433, which equals 4.7 percent of the total casualties suffered by the United States (116,516 deaths). Anne Leland, *American War and Military Operations Casualties: Lists and Statistics* (Washington, DC: Congressional Research Service, 2012), 3.

Unfortunately, a fire in 1973 destroyed many of New York's World War I records. A similar fate could have befallen other states' First World War data.

At least twenty states verified the existence of a historical committee or some sort of World War I veterans' records, but the difficulty lies in discovering the origin of these documents and committees. Virtually every state responded with the same answer: they have no information about the origins of the questionnaires or the historical committees. Many of the state historical commissions created in 1919 were disbanded in the early 1920s due to a lack of funding or a lack of interest among state officials. Tennessee abolished its committee in 1923, and Utah shut down its committee in 1920.

Explaining the Similarities

There is no evidence that the federal government participated in the creation of the MSRs. Each state apparently acted on its own initiative, yet the strong similarities among the states suggest a common influence in the creation and organization of historical commissions and war records departments. A prime example is Connecticut:

> In 1919, the General Assembly created the Department of War Records in the State Library "whose purpose and duty it shall be to collect, classify, index and install in the library all available material relating to Connecticut participation, public or private, in the world war and thus to establish a permanent and accessible record of its extent and character, such record to be as complete and comprehensive as possible and to cover not only the activities of the state, its subdivisions and agencies but also of Connecticut agencies of the federal government, organizations of private persons and of those individuals who were direct participants in the great struggle, whether as soldiers, sailors, aviators or otherwise."[30]

This same phrasing is found in the records of each state that formed a similar committee. In Utah, the questionnaire "was the result of a request by Governor Bamberger to the State Council of Defense that a War History of the State be compiled."[31]

When I first began this project, it seemed likely that each state had received a template or a set of guidelines from the federal government. But after conducting research at the National Archives (and state archives), it is apparent that the federal government was not involved with the MSRs. There is not a single mention of the questionnaires in the entire War Records collection in the National Archives. After the United States entered the war, the AGO created casualty cards to keep a record of the death of each AEF soldier, and "it would appear that the casualty file established in February of 1918 was the forerunner of the idea of furnishing statement of service cards to the several States."[32] However, these service cards were concerned with veterans' benefits, not with historical preservation, which was the clearly stated purpose of the Connecticut and Virginia MSRs. Since there was no federal initiative for the creation of questionnaires, the similarities can only be attributed to a personal relationship between the states that issued them.

The Connecticut-Virginia Connection

Among the three states with similar questionnaires, the strongest connection is between Connecticut and Virginia.[33] In a letter dated 27 January 1919, Colonel C. R. Keiley, the federal field secretary for the Council of Defense, wrote to Arthur Kyle Davis about the "submission of questionnaires."[34] Keiley stated that he wanted the war history of Virginia to be even more extensive than previously planned by Governor Davis and the Virginia Council of Defense. Keiley asked Davis to submit a questionnaire at a meeting to be held on 4 February 1919. Prior to this, Virginia's MSRs had consisted of index cards (the format used by the majority of states). In a letter to Arthur Kyle Davis dated 15 January 1919, Governor Westmoreland Davis referred to these cards used by the Virginia War History Commission, which included vital statistics as well as military service dates and locations but did not ask about the veterans' beliefs and impressions of the war, as the questionnaire did.

A reference to Connecticut's questionnaire is found in the minutes of a conference attended by both Arthur Kyle Davis and George Godard of Connecticut's Department of War Records. On 9–10 September 1919, at the conference of representatives of state war historical agencies held in Washington, D.C., Godard reported, "To further the filling of questionnaires, certificates of service are given to every man answering the questions."[35] Davis made no mention of questionnaires in his report from this same conference. Was this because the MSR was not Davis's invention but Godard's? Connecticut was already sending out its forms in March 1919, and Virginia sent out its questionnaires in the spring and summer of that year, indicating that Davis implemented Godard's project.

The Questionnaires' Content

There are only four minor differences in the questionnaires from Connecticut and Virginia. The first two differences occur on page 1. The wording of the paragraph below each state's seal differs, and Virginia has blanks for College Fraternities and Education. The other two differences occur on page 4. Virginia drops the second part of question 3, which asks about overseas experiences, and adds a sixth question concerning the war's effect on the veteran's religious beliefs. Other than these slight variations, the two questionnaires are identical.

D. H. R.—Form 1
State Library

State of Connecticut

MILITARY SERVICE RECORD

Compiled by the Department of Historical Records of the Connecticut State Council of Defense, State Library, Hartford, where it will be filed, as a permanent memorial of the deeds of Connecticut soldiers and sailors in the service of the federal, state and allied governments during American participation in the World War.

Name in full...
          (family name)   (first name)   (middle names)

Date of birth..
          (month)   (day)   (year)

Place of birth...
          (town)   (county)   (state)   (country)

Name of father.. Birthplace..
                                              (country)

Maiden name of mother... Birthplace...
                                              (country)

Are you White, Colored, Indian or Mongolian?...

Citizen................ Voter................ Church..
    (yes or no)   (yes or no)   (denomination)

Married...1........at...

To.. Born................1........at......................................
          (maiden name)

Children... Born................1........at......................................
          (name)

.... Born................1........at......................................

.... Born................1........at......................................

Fraternal Orders...

Previous military service or training...

....

....

....

Occupation before entry into the service...

....

....; employer..

Residence before entry into the service...
                                (street number)   (town)   (county)

Present home address..
          (street number)   (town)   (county)   (state)

Page one of Connecticut's MSR. (Box 168, War Records Department, Historical Data File, Connecticut State Library)

WAR RECORD

Inducted into service or enlisted on........................, at........................
..........(date).......... ....(place)..........

...., as a..........................
..........(rank)..........

in the..section of
..........(infantry, artillery, aviation, etc.)..........

the..
(regular Army, National Guard, Home Guard, National Army, Navy, Naval Reserve, or Marine Corps)

....Identification number....................

Assigned originally to..
..........(company).......... ....(regiment).......... ....(division)..........

(or)..at..................................
..........(ship).......... ....(place)..........

Trained or stationed before going to Europe: —

School, camp, station, ship	From (date)	to (date)

Transferred to: —

Company	Regiment	Division	Ship	Date	New Location

Promoted: —

From (rank)	to (rank)	Date

Embarked from..on..
..........(port).......... ....(ship)..........

..........................and arrived at..
..........(date).......... ....(foreign port).......... ....(date)..........

Proceeded from..to..................................
..........(date)..........

From ....to..................................
..........(date)..........

From ....to..................................
..........(date)..........

Trained or stationed abroad: —

Country	Place	From (date)	to (date)

NOTE: — Should form or space in any case prove inadequate for recording the desired information, please state facts on separate sheet of paper and enclose with this record.

Page two of Connecticut's MSR. (Box 168, War Records Department, Historical Data File, Connecticut State Library)

WAR RECORD

First went into action..
                               (date)   (place)

Participated in the following engagements..

Cited, decorated, or otherwise honored for distinguished services (give circumstantial accounts of exploits, including dates and places where performed, also by whom and in what manner the honors were bestowed):

Killed in action, killed by accident, died of wounds, died of disease, wounded, gassed, shell-shocked, taken prisoner:

Nature of casualty	Place	Date

Under medical care: —

Name of hospital	Location	From (date)	to (date)

Permanently disabled (through loss of limb, eyesight, etc.)..
                                                          (specify disability)

Arrived at..on..
         (American port)   (ship)   (date)   (from)

Discharged from service at..
                         (place)   (date)

as a..
            (rank)

RETURN TO CIVIL LIFE

Occupation after the war..

If a change of occupation was occasioned by reason of disability acquired in the service, describe the process of re-education and readjustment, and indicate the agencies or individuals chiefly instrumental in furnishing the new occupations:

NOTE: — Should form or space in any case prove inadequate for recording the desired information, please state facts on separate sheet of paper and enclose with this record.

Page three of Connecticut's MSR. (Box 168, War Records Department, Historical Data File, Connecticut State Library)

ADDITIONAL INFORMATION

What was your attitude toward military service in general and toward your call in particular?..............................

What were the effects of camp experiences in the United States upon yourself — mental and physical?

What were the effects upon yourself of your overseas experience, either in the army or navy or in camp in France or in England?

If you took part in the fighting, what impressions were made upon you by this experience?

What has been the effect of all these experiences as contrasted with your state of mind before the war?

Photographs — If possible enclose one taken before entering the service and one taken afterwards in uniform, both signed and dated.

Additional data..........................

Signed at.......................... on.......................... 1..........
         (place)   (date)

....
   (full name)   (rank)   (branch of service)

The information contained in this record, unless otherwise indicated, was obtained from the following persons or sources:

Page four of Connecticut's MSR. (Box 168, War Records Department, Historical Data File, Connecticut State Library)

WAR HISTORY COMMISSION
State of Virginia
MILITARY SERVICE RECORD

Compiled by the Virginia War History Commission for a permanent record in the State Library, where it will be filed, as a memorial of the deeds of Virginia soldiers and sailors in the service of the federal, state and allied governments during American participation in the World War.

Name in full ....
(family name)   (first name)   (middle name)

Date of birth ....
(month)   (day)   (year)

Place of birth ....
(town)   (county)   (state)   (country)

Name of father .... Birthplace ....
(country)

Maiden name of mother .... Birthplace ....
(country)

Are you White, Colored, Indian or Mongolian? ....

Citizen .... Voter .... Church ....
(yes or no)   (yes or no)   (denomination)

Married ...., 1........ at ....

To .... Born .... 1 .... at ....
(maiden name)

Children .... Born .... 1 .... at ....
(name)

.... Born .... 1 .... at ....

.... Born .... 1 .... at ....

Fraternal Orders ....

College Fraternities ....

Previous military service or training...

....

Education (Preparatory) .... (College) ....

(University) .... (Degrees) ....

Occupation before entry into the service...

..................................; employer ....

Residence before entry into the service...
(street number)   (town)   (county)

Present home address ....
(street number)   (town)   (country)   (state)

Page one of Virginia's MSR. (Box 188, War History Commission, series XI: Office Files, 1917–1927, subseries E: Forms, Library of Virginia)

WAR RECORD

Inducted into service or enlisted on ...., at ....
 (date) (place)
...., as a ....
 (rank)
in the .... section of
 (infantry, artillery, aviation, etc.)
the ....
 (Regular Army, National Guard, Home Guard, National Army, Navy, Naval Reserve, or Marine Corps)
....Identification number ....

Assigned originally to ....
 (company) (regiment) (division)
(or) ....at ....
 (ship) (place)

Trained or stationed before going to Europe:—

School, camp, station, ship	From (date)	to (date)

Transferred to:—

Company	Regiment	Division	Ship	Date	New Location

Promoted:—

From (rank)	to (rank)	Date

Embarked from ....on ....
 (port) (ship)
....and arrived at...
 (date) (foreign port) (date)
Proceeded from ....to ....
 (date)
From ....to ....
 (date)
From ....to ....
 (date)

Trained or stationed abroad:—

Country	Place	From (date)	to (date)

NOTE:—Should form or space in any case prove inadequate for recording the desired information, please state facts on separate sheet of paper and enclose with this record.

Page two of Virginia's MSR. (Box 188, Library of Virginia)

WAR RECORD

First went into action _____
                              (date)   (place)

Participated in the following engagements_____

_____

_____

_____

Cited, decorated, or otherwise honored for distinguished services (give circumstantial accounts of exploits, including dates and places where performed, also by whom and in what manner the honors were bestowed) :

_____

_____

_____

Killed in action, killed by accident, died of wounds, died of disease, wounded, gassed, shell-shocked, taken prisoner:

Nature of casualty	Place	Date

Under medical care :—

Name of hospital	Location	From (date)	to (date)

Permanently disabled (through loss of limb, eyesight, etc.) _____
                                                                              (specify disability)

Arrived at _____ on _____
              (American port)   (ship)   (date)   (from)

Discharged from service at _____
                                         (place)   (date)

as a _____
          (rank)

RETURN TO CIVIL LIFE

Occupation after the war _____

If a change of occupation was occasioned by reason of disability acquired in the service, describe the process of re-education and readjustment, and indicate the agencies or individuals chiefly instrumental in furnishing the new occupations:

_____

_____

NOTE:—Should form or space in any case prove inadequate for recording the desired information, please state facts on separate sheet of paper and enclose with this record.

Page three of Virginia's MSR. (Box 188, Library of Virginia)

ADDITIONAL INFORMATION

What was your attitude toward military service in general and toward your call in particular?

What were the effects of camp experiences in the United States upon yourself—mental and physical?

What were the effects upon yourself of your overseas experience?

What effect, if any, did your experience have on your religious belief?

If you took part in the fighting, what impressions were made upon you by this experience?

What has been the effect of all these experiences as contrasted with your state of mind before the war?

Photographs—If possible enclose one taken before entering the service and one taken afterwards in uniform, both signed and dated.

Additional data

Signed at .... on .... 1..........
 (Place) (date)

....
 (full name) (rank) (branch of service)

The information contained in this record, unless otherwise indicated, was obtained from the following persons or sources:

Page four of Virginia's MSR. (Box 188, Library of Virginia)

With no records of a federal initiative to create such a questionnaire, the only explanation for the two states issuing nearly identical questionnaires is that one state copied the other. Based on the Latin adage *lectio difficilior potior* (the more difficult reading is the stronger), one might conclude that Virginia's questionnaire, which included information on education and religion, came first—but maybe not. Virginia used a shortened version of question 3 concerning overseas experience, and Virginia's archives contain a copy of Connecticut's questionnaire, three photographs of War Department holdings at the Connecticut State Library, and correspondence between George Godard and Arthur Kyle Davis. Did Godard send Davis a copy of Connecticut's questionnaire, which the latter then used to create Virginia's questionnaire? A personal connection existed between the two men, but how influential was it? Did they exchange ideas during 1917 or 1918 to create the questionnaire, or did one man share his idea with the other?

The answer, I believe, lies in Minnesota's archives, which also contain a copy of Connecticut's questionnaire. Thus, both Minnesota and Virginia have a copy of Connecticut's MSR, but Connecticut has neither of the other two states' MSRs. In addition, Minnesota's archives do not contain a copy of Virginia's MSR, nor do Virginia's archives contain a copy of Minnesota's MSR. The most logical conclusion is that Godard, or one of his associates, created the MSR and shared it with Minnesota and Virginia, both of which quickly drafted their own designs and mailed them off to returning veterans. Perhaps, hidden somewhere, there are some long-forgotten answers to the origin of the questionnaires, or even more questionnaires. In any case, gentlemen such as Godard and Davis realized that the doughboys' impressions of their war service would be of historical importance to future generations.

STATE OF MINNESOTA

MILITARY SERVICE RECORD

Compiled by the Minnesota War Records Commission as a permanent memorial of the deeds of Minnesota soldiers and sailors in the service of the federal and state governments during American participation in the World War.

Name in full..
              (surname)   (Christian name)   (middle name)

Date of birth..
              (month)   (day)   (year)

Place of birth..
             (town)   (county)   (state)   (country)

White, colored, Indian, or Mongolian?...

Birthplace of father..; of mother...
                (country)   (country)

Nearest relatives

Name	Residence	Relationship
		father
		mother
		wife

Previous military service or training..

....

Occupation before entry into the service...

....; employer..

Residence before entry into the service..

....
       (street number)   (town)   (county)

Page one of Minnesota's MSR. (Minnesota War Records Commission Collection, 1917–1921, Minnesota Historical Society, St. Paul)

Military Record

Inducted into the service on.., at...
(date) (place)

...., as a..
(rank)

in the.. section of
(infantry, artillery, aviation, etc.)

the..
(Regular Army, National Guard, Home Guard, National Army, Navy, Naval Reserve, or Marine Corps)

.... Identification number..

Assigned originally to..................................., ..., ...
(company) (regiment) (division)

(or)..at..
(ship) (place)

Trained or stationed before going to Europe

School, camp, station, ship	From (date)	to (date)

Transferred to

Company	Regiment	Division	Ship	Date	New Location

Promoted

From (rank)	to (rank)	Date

Embarked from...on...,
(American port) (ship)

..............................., and arrived at...
(date) (foreign port)

....
(date)

Note. Should form or space in any case prove inadequate for recording the desired information, please state facts on separate sheet of paper and enclose with this record.

Page two of Minnesota's MSR. (Minnesota War Records Commission Collection, 1917–1921, Minnesota Historical Society, St. Paul)

Military Record

Trained or stationed abroad

Country	Place	From (date)	to (date)

First went into action...
                                        (date)   (place)

Participated in the following battles :...
....

Cited, decorated, or otherwise honored for distinguished services (give circumstantial accounts of exploits, including dates and places where performed, also by whom and in what manner the honors were bestowed):

....

....

....

Killed in action, killed by accident, died of wounds, died of disease, wounded, gassed, shell-shocked, taken prisoner:

Nature of casualty	Place	Date

Under medical care

Name of hospital	Location	From (date)	to (date)

Permanently disabled (through loss of limb, eyesight, etc.)...

Arrived at..., ...
                              (American port)   (date)

Discharged from service at.., ...
                                                    (place)   (date)

as a..
                    (rank)

Note. Should form or space in any case prove inadequate for recording the desired information, please state facts on separate sheet of paper and enclose with this record.

Page three of Minnesota's MSR. (Minnesota War Records Commission Collection, 1917–1921, Minnesota Historical Society, St. Paul)

Return to Civil Life

Resumed former activities in civil life under much the same conditions as before?..
(yes or no)

If not, what changes occurred with respect to occupation, employer, etc. and why?..

....

....

If a change of occupation was occasioned by reason of disability acquired in the service, describe the process of re-education and readjustment, and indicate the agencies or individuals chiefly instrumental in furnishing the new start:

....

....

....

Home address..

          (street number)   (town)   (county)   (state)

....

The information contained in this record (except as otherwise indicated) was obtained from the following persons or sources:

....

....

    Note. The value of this record will be greatly increased if there is filed with it a photograph of the subject, preferably in uniform, together with letters or copies of letters written by him, a specially written account of his experiences, and other things connected with his life in the service.

(This space reserved for file references)

Page four of Minnesota's MSR. (Minnesota War Records Commission Collection, 1917–1921, Minnesota Historical Society, St. Paul)

Appendix B: Biographies

Anderson, James W. Anderson trained at Camp Gordon from 10 August 1917 to 6 May 1918, sailed aboard the *Persia* out of New York on 6 May 1918, and arrived in London on 21 May 1918. When Anderson entered the service at age twenty-two, he had a medical degree from the Atlanta Medical College. He engaged in action at the Somme, Saint-Mihiel, Argonne, and Toul.

Andreozzi, Nicola. The Italian-born Andreozzi enlisted on 25 April 1918 and trained at Camp Devens before leaving for France. He entered combat on 2 August 1918 at the Marne and served with the Army of Occupation. He was discharged on 19 May 1919.

Angell, Ralph M. A high school–educated clerical worker, Angell entered the Marine Corps at age twenty-four. He trained at Parris Island, South Carolina, from 13 May to 2 July 1918 and at Quantico, Virginia, from 3 July to 4 August 1918. He left Philadelphia aboard the *Henderson* on 12 August 1918, arrived in Brest on 27 August, and went into action on 11 September in the Toul sector. Angell spent five months at base hospitals in France after he was wounded.

Augermann, William G. B. The German-born Augermann enlisted in the National Guard on 23 June 1916. During his tour of duty he engaged in combat at Toul, Saint-Mihiel, Verdun, and Meuse-Argonne. He was wounded in action on 20 April 1918.

Bagley, Ralcigh A. Bagley trained at Camp Roanoke, Virginia, and in Alabama before sailing from Hoboken, New Jersey, aboard the *Finland* on 15 June 1918. He arrived in Saint-Nazaire, France, on 27 June 1918; he received no additional training abroad.

Barnes, John E. Barnes joined the Norfolk Light Artillery Blues on 20 June 1916 "when the President called for volunteers in regard to the Mexican situation." A private in B Battery, 11th Field Artillery, 29th Division, Barnes trained at Camp Stuart, Virginia. He arrived in Liverpool on 11 July 1918 and attended motor school in Lyon, France, from 26 August to 23 September 1918. Barnes fought at Meuse-Argonne and served with the Army of Occupation from 20 November 1918 to 2 July 1919.

Barrow, Emory P. After being inducted on 10 May 1918, Barrow trained at Camp Wadsworth, South Carolina, from 19 May to 30 June and at Camp Mills from 2 to 7 July 1918. He served with Company D, 1st Army Military Police Battalion. He sailed from New York aboard the *Deana Belfast* on 7 July 1918 and arrived in France on 27 July. Barrow received gas school training at Châtillon-sur-Seine from 15 to 22 August. He saw combat on 1 September 1918 in the Vosges sector and at Meuse-Argonne on 30 September.

Bell, Alden. Bell served as a private first class in the 116th Infantry, 29th Division. He trained at Camp McClellan, Alabama; embarked from Hoboken, New Jersey; and arrived in Saint-Nazaire in May 1918. Bell "was blinded for 4 months by a bursting German gas shell, Argonne Forest," and he saw action from July to November 1918. After being discharged on 14 April 1919, Bell resumed his law practice. After the war, Bell lectured on "The Patriotism of the American Soldier" in the United States, Rome, and Paris.

Bishop, Hugh H. Private Bishop served with Battery B, 3rd Field Artillery. He sailed out of New York aboard the *Caronia* and arrived in Liverpool on 2 September 1917. Bishop trained at camps in France from 8 September 1917 to 23 February 1918; he entered action on 27 February 1918 at Boncourt, where his battery was cited for bravery in action under heavy shell fire. He was wounded on 16 September 1918, shot in the left leg. After being discharged on 29 February 1920, Bishop worked as a shoe salesperson.

Bonham, James F. Bonham enlisted on 4 August 1917 and then trained at Kelly Field, Texas, and Fort Sill, Oklahoma. He embarked for Liverpool aboard the *Cedric* out of New York, arriving on 18 March 1918. Bonham was cited for expert marksmanship with a Colt .45 pistol.

Bowen, Joseph B. Bowen was commissioned as a second lieutenant in the Air Service on 19 February 1918; he was a member of the 148th Aero Squadron on active duty with the 32nd British Aero Squadron. Bowen was killed in action on 7 September 1918.

Brown, Hugh E. Brown began his training with the 1st Balloon Company at Omaha, Nebraska, on 13 May 1917. He embarked from Newport News, Virginia, aboard the *America* on 4 June 1918 and arrived in Brest on 18 June. He served as a corporal with the 166th Aero Squadron Balloon Service in France and as a member of the Army of Occupation in Germany beginning on 15 November 1918.

Brownley, Wilbur T. Brownley trained at Camp McClellan, Alabama, from 3 September 1917 to 13 June 1918. He embarked on 15 June 1918 from Hoboken, New Jersey, aboard the *DeKalb*; arrived in Brest on 27 June; and entered action on 28 July. He was gassed at Bois de Consenvoye on 19 October 1918.

Callahan, Harvey G. Callahan was a second lieutenant in the field artillery and trained in Alexandria, Virginia, from May to December 1917. He left New York on the *Olympic* on 11 January 1918 and arrived in Liverpool on 19 January. Callahan entered action on 20 March 1918 at Verdun; he was discharged on 23 August 1919.

Campbell, Harry S. Campbell trained at Camp Niantic, Connecticut, from 22 August to 9 October 1917; left Montreal aboard the *Megantic* on 10 October; and arrived at Neufchâteau, France, on 1 November 1917. On 11 February 1918 Campbell saw action at Chemin des Dames; he also participated in engagements at Toul, Aisne-Marne, Saint-Mihiel, and Meuse-Argonne. Campbell was promoted to private first class and then to corporal on 21 September 1918. After the war, Campbell returned to his position as a traveling salesperson for Colt's Firearms.

Carini, John F. Carini entered the service on 19 September 1917 and served in Company C, 120th Machine Gun Battalion, 32nd Division; he trained at Camp Devens from 19 September 1917 to 7 July 1918. He then shipped out from Boston on 8 July 1918 and arrived in England on 22 July. Carini saw action at the Aisne and in the Meuse-Argonne offensive. After being discharged on 23 May 1919, he resumed employment as a mechanic.

Case, Carroll B. Case, a Trinity College student, trained at Goodwin Park in Hartford, Connecticut, for a week in July 1917 and then at Camp Yale from 23 July to 15 September 1917. He went into action at Chemin des Dames on 8 February 1918 and participated in engagements at Seicheprey (where he was gassed on 20 April 1918), the second Battle of the Marne, Saint-Mihiel, Marcheville, and Meuse-Argonne. He was discharged on 29 April 1919.

Castle, Wayne H. Castle volunteered on 12 June 1917 and served with the 18th Company, 5th Regiment, of the Marine Corps. He trained in San Diego and Mare Island, California, before shipping out on 26 May 1918. His commanding officer cited Castle for bravery on the Champagne front for taking a machine gun nest.

Castleman, John R. Castleman trained at Fort Myer, Virginia, from 14 May to 4 July 1917 and then at Wilbur Wright Aviation School at the Ohio State University and in Dayton, Ohio, from 4 July to 25 October 1917. He embarked on 2 November 1917, went into action on 18 August 1918 as a first lieutenant with the Army Air Service, and received a Distinguished Service Cross.

Catlin, Albertus W. Catlin was born in Gowanda, New York, on 1 December 1868. He graduated from Annapolis in 1890, served during the Spanish-American War, graduated from the National War College in May 1917, and led the attack on Belleau Wood on 6 June 1918, where he was wounded by a bullet through the right lung.

Chenault, James E. Nineteen-year-old Chenault, who worked at the Standard Paper Company in Richmond, Virginia, enlisted the day after the United States declared war; he was a private in the 116th Company, 29th Division. He trained at Camp McClellan, Alabama, from 19 April 1917 to 10 June 1918. Chenault boarded the *Finland* out of Hoboken, New Jersey, on 16 June 1918 and arrived in Saint-Nazaire on 28 June; he entered combat on 23 July 1918.

Claman, Garnett D. Claman, a farmer by trade, entered service on 28 July 1917; trained at Camp Sevier in Greenville, South Carolina; and arrived in France in June 1918. Claman first saw action on 17 July 1918 at Ypres. During the battle he was gassed and wounded by shrapnel, which caused the almost total loss of his eyesight.

Clary, Thomas M. Clary enlisted in the army on 30 October 1917 and served as a corporal with the 15th Company, 369th Regiment. A blacksmith by trade, Clary spent four months at Camp Lee, Virginia, before setting sail on the *Pocahontas* out of New Jersey in March 1918. He arrived in Brest and spent six months in combat.

Cofrancesco, Humbert F. Cofrancesco was inducted into the National Army on 3 October 1918; he was a student at Yale University and trained there until his discharge on 19 December 1918. He returned to his studies at Yale after the war.

Cooke, Joseph R. Cooke was a captain in the infantry, 82nd Division. He trained at Camp Gordon, Georgia, from 29 August 1917 to 11 April 1918 and embarked on the *Khyber* out of Hoboken, New Jersey, on 6 May 1918. Cooke first engaged in combat on 26 June 1918 in the Toul sector; he was wounded by an enemy hand grenade on 29 July 1918 and returned to the front line at Meuse-Argonne from 6 October to 1 November 1918.

Cooke, Wylie R. Cooke was a first lieutenant with Company D, 314th Infantry, 80th Division, and had been a member of the Mexican Border Service for six months prior to the war. He attended the Second Reserve Officers Training Camp at Fort Myer, Virginia, and trained at Camp Lee, Virginia, from 15 December 1917 to 25 May 1918. Cooke left from Newport News, Virginia, aboard the *Mercury* on 26 May 1918 and arrived in Bordeaux on 8 June; he saw action during the Meuse-Argonne offensive. Following his discharge he found employment as a chemist.

Covington, John W. Covington enlisted in the National Army on 10 September 1917 and trained at Camp Funston, Kansas, from 15 December 1917 to 25 May 1918, where he was also an instructor. He first saw action on the front lines on 12 September 1918 and was cited for bravery in the Argonne Forest. During an intense firefight, Covington regrouped an unorganized cluster of men and destroyed two German machine gun nests. Later, he was knocked unconscious by an HE shell, causing deafness in his left ear.

Crawford, Waverly L. Crawford entered the army on 10 January 1918 and trained at Camp Sherman, Ohio, with the 325th Field Signal Battalion of the National Army until 10 June 1918. Nine days later he embarked out of Hoboken, New Jersey. He served as a telephone and telegraph operator in the Vosges and during the Meuse-Argonne offensive. After being discharged on 31 March 1919 Crawford became a public school teacher.

Curry, Harry E. Curry served with the National Guard at Potomac Park, Washington, D.C., until 24 December 1917; he then trained at Camp Stuart until 30 March 1918, when he sailed on the *Susquehanna* out of Newport News, Virginia. He arrived in Saint-Nazaire on 14 April. Curry participated in combat at Champagne from 26 September to 14 October 1918. He stated, "At a rough calculation about 250 killed, 75 wounded, 150 gassed, 30 shell-shocked, no prisoners" during that battle. Sergeant Curry's unit—the 372nd Regiment, 37th Infantry— was "cited for bravery under heavy shell fire and captured 10 Germans." After being discharged on 1 March 1919, Curry returned to work as a laborer.

Daniel, Channing W. Daniel served with the 16th Field Artillery, 4th Division, and entered Reserve Officers Training Camp on 28 August 1917. He received his commission three months later; the army then sent him to Camp Greene, North Carolina, for another five months. He left New York on 21 May 1918 aboard the *Northern Pacific*. On 1 August 1918 he took part in the battle for the Marne salient and fought at Aisne-Marne and Saint-Mihiel and in the Meuse-Argonne defensive sector. Daniel was gassed and then wounded in the Argonne on 29 September and 2 October 1918.

Davis, Curtis R. Davis trained at Camp Mills, Long Island, from August to October 1917. He left Hoboken, New Jersey, aboard the *Covington* on 18 October 1917 and arrived in Saint-Nazaire on 1 November. Davis entered combat on 20 February 1918; he fought at Champagne-Marne, Saint-Mihiel, and Meuse-Argonne and served with the Army of Occupation.

Day, Arlie I. Private First Class Day served with the 318th Regiment, 80th Division; he trained at Camp Lee, Virginia, from 24 October 1917 to 1 May 1918. He left on the *Vaterland* out of New Jersey on 21 May 1918 and arrived in Brest on 30 May. Day entered action on 4 July 1918 at Verdun; he was gassed in the Argonne on 5 October 1918. Day wanted to "kill every darn German that I could." He added, "I think I got some of them."

Deilus, Robert. Italian-born Deilus was a private first class in Company B, 305th Regiment, 77th Division. He trained at Camp Devens, Massachusetts, and participated in action at Alsace-Lorraine, in the Argonne Forest, and along the Meuse River. After his discharge, Deilus worked at a hat factory.

Dettor, David C. Dettor entered the service on 22 September 1917 and trained at Camp Lee, Virginia, until 26 May 1918, when he sailed aboard the *Mongolia* out of Newport News, Virginia. Dettor arrived in Brest on 8 June 1918 and almost immediately entered combat, participating in action at the Somme from 18 June to 1 July and at Meuse-Argonne from 26 September to 8 October 1918. After his discharge, he returned to farming and worked as a sales clerk.

Dickerson, John N. Dickerson entered the National Army on 19 September 1917 at age twenty-eight. He served with the 302nd Field Artillery and trained at Camp Devens before going overseas; he trained at Camp No. 2 in France from 6 August to 16 September 1918.

Distefano, Salvatore. Distefano, a private first class in the Regular Army, entered the service on 21 July 1917 and trained in Syracuse, New York. He embarked on 7 September 1917 and arrived in Saint-Nazaire on 21 September. He saw action beginning on 17 March 1918 and fought at Soissons, Saint-Mihiel, and Meuse-Argonne.

Du Trienille, Hamilton, Jr. Du Trienille enlisted in the National Guard on 10 September 1917 and trained at the Springfield Armory and at Camp Bartlett, Massachusetts, until 22 November 1917. He then trained at Camp Greene, North Carolina, from 24 November to 10 December 1917 and at Camp Stuart, Virginia, from 11 December 1917 to 30 March 1918. He embarked from Newport News, Virginia, aboard the *Susquehanna* on 30 March 1918 and arrived in Saint-Nazaire on 14 April. He saw action in Champagne from 28 September to 7 October 1918. After his discharge from the infantry, Du Trienille returned to his occupation as a letter carrier.

Dunn, Samuel. The army assigned Russian-born Dunn to the Ordnance Corps, and he trained from 18 June to 24 July 1918 at Camp Hancock, Georgia. He boarded the *America*, sailing out of Newport News, Virginia, on 31 July 1918 and landed at Brest on 12 August.

Duval, Robert C., Jr. After spending ninety days at the First Training Camp for Officers at Fort Myer, Virginia, Duval received his commission as a first lieutenant in Company A, 318th Infantry, 80th Division, on 14 August 1917. He was stationed at Camp Lee, Virginia, for the next nine months and did not sail for France until May 1918. Duval fought at Saint-Mihiel and Meuse-Argonne from 25 September to 5 October 1918, when he was wounded in the left thigh by a piece of HE shell in an attack on Bois de Forêt. He remained at base hospitals until 29 December 1918 and was discharged on 27 January 1919. Back home, Duval returned to his law practice.

Dwyer, John P. Dwyer trained at Camp Yale in New Haven from June until September 1917. He shipped out aboard the transport *Lenake* in September, but the ship broke down only two days out of port. Upon returning to shore, he spent the next three weeks at Fort Totten. In October, Dwyer and a number of other Connecticut soldiers left aboard the *Adriatic* and arrived in Europe in November 1917. The army promoted Dwyer to sergeant in October 1918. He was discharged on 17 November 1919 after serving with the 204th Military Police in Paris from January to July 1919.

Edwards, Daniel R. Edwards served in the 26th Infantry, 1st Division, as a sergeant. He embarked on 12 June 1917 from Hoboken, New Jersey, aboard the *San Jacinto* and arrived in Saint-Nazaire on 26 June—among the first American soldiers to arrive in France. Edwards won the Distinguished Service Cross and the Congressional Medal of Honor. Despite being severely wounded, Edwards killed four German soldiers and captured four others in a German trench.

Elmore, Theodore. Elmore trained at Parris Island, South Carolina, from 30

June 1916 to 13 January 1917; he served aboard the USS *Maine* from 26 January to 9 March 1917 and in Cuba from 10 March to 25 May 1917. Elmore embarked from Philadelphia aboard the *Henderson* on 8 June 1917, arrived in Saint-Nazaire on 27 June, and entered his "first real battle" on 6 June 1918 at Belleau Wood. Corporal Elmore also participated at Château-Thierry, Saint-Mihiel, and Meuse-Argonne, and he later served with the Army of Occupation. Elmore "received citation certificate and Croix de Guerre for carrying important messages through heavy barrages and machine gun fire in Belleau Woods June 1918 by French government."

Fields, John S. Fields, a Baptist from Dinwiddie, Virginia, served with the 369th Infantry and trained at Camp Lee, Virginia, from 29 October 1917 (the date he was drafted) to 2 March 1918 and then at Camp Merritt, New Jersey, from 2 to 14 March 1918. He then embarked on the *Pocahontas* from Hoboken and arrived in France on 27 March 1918. Fields felt that God "had brought him home safe again."

Fischman, Maurice B. Fischman embarked for France aboard the *Arcadia* from Halifax, Nova Scotia, and arrived on 26 September 1917. He spent two months in the base hospital in Langue, France. When he was discharged on 26 March 1919, Fischman returned to his wife and young son and resumed his occupation as a printer in New Haven.

Flynn, Alexander J. Flynn was almost twenty-two years old when he became a private in the Medical Corps, 102nd Field Hospital, 101st Sanitation Train, 26th Division. On 3 October 1917 Flynn left the United States aboard the *Cedric*, bound for Liverpool; from there, he proceeded to France. Flynn engaged in combat for the first time on 10 February 1918 at Chemin des Dames and participated in the fighting at Toul, where he was promoted to corporal. He also saw action at Aisne-Marne, Saint-Mihiel, and Meuse-Argonne and was promoted to the rank of sergeant in October 1918. Upon his discharge on 29 April 1919, Flynn returned to his position as a clerk in New Haven.

Furr, Herman R. Furr enlisted in the National Army on 15 May 1917; he trained at Camp Lee, Virginia, from 15 August 1917 to 24 May 1918. He sailed aboard the *Mercury* from Newport News, Virginia, on 24 May 1918 and arrived in Bordeaux, France, on 9 June. Furr served in the trenches with the British until the end of August 1918; he then went into action northeast of Verdun on 25 September 1918; he also saw combat at Béthincourt, Cunel, the Somme, and the Meuse-Argonne. Furr wrote a brief history of his battalion, made up largely of Virginians, at the request of his major, and he offered a copy to the Virginia War History Commission.

Fydenkeuez, Michael. Fydenkeuez was assigned to Battery B, 7th Field Artillery, 1st Division, and trained at Camp Sam Houston in San Antonio, Texas, from 1 June to 15 July 1917. He sailed across the Atlantic aboard the *Pastores* out of Hoboken, New Jersey, and arrived in Saint-Nazaire, France, where he trained from 23 August to 1 October 1917. Fydenkeuez participated in engagements at Lunéville, Aisne-Marne, Saint-Mihiel, and Meuse-Argonne. Wounded by shell fire and gassed on 2 August 1918, he spent the next two weeks at a field hospital; he was then transferred to Base Hospital No. 66, where he remained for one week before returning to active duty, even though his eyesight and hearing were impaired. On 30 July 1919 he was awarded the Victory Medal with four battle clasps, and on 30 September 1919 he was discharged at the rank of private first class and returned home.

George, Samuel. Syrian-born George served as a private in Company B, 315th Infantry of the National Army. He trained at Camp Meade, embarked from Hoboken on 7 July 1918, and arrived in Brest on 17 July; he entered action on 26 September 1918 and participated in the Meuse-Argonne offensive.

Goddard, Charles R. Goddard was inducted into the National Army on 19 September 1917. He served in Company B, 303rd Machine Gun Battalion, 76th Division, and trained at Camp Devens from 20 September 1917 to 6 February 1918 and at Camp Greene from 9 February to 6 April 1918. He embarked from Hoboken, New Jersey, aboard the *Czar* on 16 April 1918 and arrived in Brest on 28 April; he received training at Camp Pontanezen, Couvignon, and Liézey in France. Goddard entered action on 20 June 1918 in the Vosges; he was gassed during the Meuse-Argonne offensive in October 1918 and suffered partial loss of eyesight. Discharged on 6 August 1919, Goddard returned to his occupation as an attorney.

Godwin, Willis B. Godwin served as a sergeant in Company K, 370th Infantry, 93rd Division; he began his training at Camp Lee, Virginia, on 28 October 1917 and left Hoboken, New Jersey, aboard the *President Grant*. Godwin arrived in Brest on 12 May 1918 and went into action on 11 June 1918. He fought at Soissons, Saint-Mihiel, and Meuse-Argonne; according to Godwin, his regiment won numerous medals, was cited for bravery, and "fought the last battle of the war with 20% casualties." After being discharged on 27 February 1919, Godwin became an instructor in agriculture.

Gronk, Earle T. W. Gronk, a Lutheran from South Carolina, trained at Camp Grant in Rockford, Illinois, from 10 October to 16 December 1917 and at Camp Merritt from 19 to 26 December 1917. He embarked aboard the *President Grant* from Hoboken, New Jersey, on 26 December and arrived at Brest on 10 January 1918; mumps delayed him from entering the front lines with his regiment. He was wounded and survived heavy combat.

Grove, Arthur A. Grove entered the service on 25 March 1917; served as a first lieutenant in the 115th Infantry, 29th Division; trained at Camp McClellan, Alabama; and sailed from Hoboken aboard the *Finland* on 15 June 1918. He attended the Second Corps Machine Gun School at Châtillon-sur-Seine from 13 July to 13 August 1918 and entered action on 20 August 1918 at Balschwiller, France (then part of Germany). Grove returned to his occupation as a merchant following his discharge on 29 May 1919.

Hager, Lawrence T. Hager entered the service on 29 March 1918 and served as a private in the Depot Brigade, Company A, 320th Machine Gun Battalion, 82nd Division. He trained at Camp Devens and Camp Upton from 30 March to 24 April 1918, left aboard the *Caronia* on 24 April, and arrived in Liverpool on 7 May. Hager entered action on 16 July 1918 in the Toul sector and participated at Saint-Mihiel and in the Argonne Forest. After being wounded, he underwent surgery to graft an eyebrow from a dead soldier over his right eye and to insert silver plates in his head and chin; he spent three months in Base Hospital No. 46 in France. Hager received his discharge papers on 3 June 1919 and returned to his profession as an actor.

Haislip, Walter B. Haislip, a Baptist from Virginia, was a high school principal before the war. He entered the National Army on 18 September 1917; trained at Camp Lee, Virginia, from 19 September to 20 May 1918; and served in the 80th Division. He embarked on the *Leviathan* out of New York on 21 May 1918 and arrived in Brest on 30 May but never saw combat.

Hardy, Thomas G. Hardy, a Methodist, had recently graduated from the Medical College of Virginia in Richmond when the army called him into active service from the reserves on 5 August 1917. Hardy received no camp training in the United States before being sent to England and then on to Ypres, Belgium, on 20 November 1917, where he attended to the troops in action there. He returned to Virginia on 9 February 1919 to practice medicine.

Hills, Ratcliffe M. Hills enlisted in the National Guard on 5 June 1917 and trained at Camp Yale before leaving for France in September 1917. He was twenty-one years old when he entered combat in February 1918. He also fought in the Aisne-Marne and Meuse-Argonne offensives.

Hodges, Fairfield H. Hodges, a Methodist, spent three months in camp at the armory in Norfolk, Virginia, and received additional training at Camp McClellan, Alabama; he arrived in Liverpool aboard the *Aquitania* on 11 July 1918. Fairfield was gassed on 15 October 1918.

Hogue, Charles L. Hogue entered the National Army on 27 October 1917; trained at Camp Lee, Virginia, from 29 October 1917 to 18 March 1918; embarked from Hoboken aboard the *Martha Washington*; and arrived in Bordeaux, France, on 4 April 1918. General John J. Pershing and French officials honored Hogue and his unit for their work in constructing a railway stop in Montierchaume.

Howell, John E. Howell, a Presbyterian and a salesman by trade, trained at Camp Merritt and Camp Meade from 24 October 1917 to 22 February 1918. He embarked on the *Agamemnon* from Hoboken, New Jersey, on 7 April 1918 and arrived in Brest on 15 April. He saw action on 27 July 1918 at La Ferté-sous-Jouarre. After the war, Howell worked as a real estate salesman.

Hutchison, Curry P. Hutchison, a Methodist, did not finish his senior year in high school. He served with the 317th Infantry, 80th Division, and trained at Camp Lee, Virginia, from 10 October 1917 to 25 May 1918. He arrived in Brest on 8 June 1918 and entered action on 1 August 1918 in the Artois sector; he also engaged in combat during the Meuse-Argonne offensive.

Isleib, Henry A. The army inducted Isleib on 29 March 1918. After training at Camp Devens and Camp Upton in New York, Isleib was assigned to Company C, 325th Regiment, 82nd Division. He arrived in France in May 1918 and first saw action on 27 June 1918; he also fought in the Saint-Mihiel and Meuse-Argonne offensives.

Jacobs, John M. Born in Philadelphia, Jacobs (whose mother came from Ireland) was a second lieutenant in the 50th Infantry; he trained at Camp Greene, North Carolina, and embarked from Hoboken, New Jersey, on 16 April 1918. Jacobs went into action in June 1918 and was wounded on 11 October by machine gun fire during the Meuse-Argonne offensive; he suffered a head wound and disfigurement and spent twenty-one months in numerous hospitals. He was discharged on 10 June 1920 and became a student.

Jarman, Miletus B. Jarman trained at the Second Officers Training Camp in Fort Myer, Virginia; Camp Meade, Maryland; and Camp Wadsworth, South Carolina. He belonged to the 1st Pioneer Infantry and sailed to Brest aboard the *Mt. Vernon* out of Hoboken, New Jersey, on 8 July 1918. Seventeen days later, he participated in the second Battle of the Marne. After the war, in January 1919, the army assigned Jarman to the "general supervision of the U.S. Army

Post Schools in city of Coblenz and some of the surrounding villages. These schools employed 50 teachers and enrolled more than 2,000 American soldiers." Jarman remained there until the army disbanded the schools in May 1919; he was discharged on 31 July 1919 and found employment with Standard Oil Company.

Johnson, Niels A. W. Johnson sailed from Montreal and arrived in Liverpool on 10 October 1917. A week later, Johnson and his fellow soldiers were in Neufchâteau, France, for training. Johnson first saw action in February 1918 and later fought in several battles, including Château-Thierry, Saint-Mihiel, and Meuse-Argonne. When he was discharged on 23 June 1919, Johnson was nine days away from his twenty-fourth birthday.

Kimberly, Clarke O. Kimberly, an Episcopalian, attended both Yale University and the Virginia Military Institute. He participated in the First Officers Training Camp at Fort Myer, Virginia, from 15 May to 15 August 1917. He sailed on the *Olympic* from Hoboken, New Jersey, on 11 January 1918; was gassed at Soissons on 23 July 1918; and received the Croix de Guerre on 10 October 1918 at Blanc Mont Ridge.

Kinzer, John D. Kinzer, a farmer by trade, was a private first class with the Military Police; he trained at Fort Thomas, Kentucky, and Camp Wadsworth, South Carolina, from 11 May to 30 June 1918. He embarked aboard the *Deana Belfast* out of Hoboken, New Jersey, on 7 July 1918 and arrived in France on 25 July. Kinzer entered action on 7 September 1918 and fought in the Meuse-Argonne offensive from 2 to 11 November 1918.

Langer, William L. A Boston-born Harvard graduate, Langer taught modern languages at a boarding school in New England when he enlisted in the army in November 1917. He served with the 1st Gas Regiment of the Chemical Warfare Service. After the war, Langer distinguished himself as a writer and historian.

Lawson, Charles T. Lawson was a graduate of the Virginia Polytechnic Institute and State University (Virginia Tech), with a degree in engineering. He enlisted in the Marine Corps on 24 May 1917 and attended Officers Training Schools at Parris Island, South Carolina, from 12 June to 18 July 1917 and at Quantico, Virginia, from 20 July to 21 October 1917. Captain Lawson sailed for France on 22 October 1917 aboard the *Von Steuben* out of Philadelphia and arrived in Brest on 13 November. He first saw combat on 14 March 1918.

Lofland, Hezekiah E. Lofland trained on the rifle range at Camp Humphreys for six weeks and served as a private first class in Company A, 540th Regiment, Engineers Medical Detachment. He embarked from Hoboken, New Jersey, on the *Leviathan* on 24 October 1918 and spent four months in camp at Abinsville after arriving in Southampton. Lofland did not see action, as he was assigned to care for influenza patients; he contracted the flu himself and left the service "with weak eyes and a weak back." After his discharge on 17 June 1919, Lofland worked as a waiter and a reporter.

Lyons, Harold T. Lyons enlisted in the Regular Army on 24 October 1917 and spent only two months training at Fort Myer, Virginia. He embarked for Liverpool aboard the *Olympic* on 9 January 1918 and spent two months at Le Havre, France, before entering combat on 24 March 1918 as a private in the 12th Field Artillery, 2nd Division.

May, Herbert D. May was a captain in C Company, 116th Infantry, 29th Division. He attended the Infantry School of Arms at Fort Sill, Oklahoma, in 1917 and then became an instructor at Camp McClellan, Alabama. He left Hoboken aboard the *Finland* on 11 June 1918 and arrived in France on 27 June. He graduated from the Army Intelligence School at Langres, France, in 1918.

McDermott, Thomas B. McDermott trained at Plattsburgh, New York, from 15 May to 15 August 1917 and at Camp Mills, New York, from 30 August to 29 September 1917. He served as a captain in the 165th Infantry and left Hoboken aboard the *America* on 29 September 1917. McDermott went into action on 20 February 1918 and fought in engagements at Château-Thierry, Saint-Mihiel, and Meuse-Argonne, among others. McDermott was cited for "conspicuous and exceptionally meritorious services and gallantry" by General Pershing on 16 July 1918 and 19 April 1919. Discharged on 7 May 1919, McDermott returned to work at the Rossia Insurance Company.

McKarney, James O. Born in Tennessee, McKarney, a Baptist and a farmer by trade, trained at Camp Lee, Virginia, with Company B, 318th Regiment, 80th Division. He embarked on 22 May 1918 from Hoboken aboard the *Northland* and reached Brest on 30 May. He entered action on 20 June 1918 and sustained a shrapnel wound to his left leg on 5 October 1918.

Morris, William J. B. Morris, a Baptist, trained at Camp Wadsworth, South Carolina, from 17 May to 28 June 1918. He arrived in France on 26 July 1918 and went into action on 1 September in the Vosges; he also participated in combat in Alsace-Lorraine and Meuse-Argonne.

Mosher, Cyril B. Mosher, of Providence, Rhode Island, was a student at Yale

University when he enlisted in the regular ranks on 23 May 1917 because he was underage for officer training. Mosher was a sergeant with Battery D, 12th Field Artillery, 2nd Division; he trained at Fort Myer, Virginia, and embarked for France in early spring 1918.

Nye, William P. Nye, a Lutheran, enlisted in the National Guard on 20 February 1914 and later served with Company M, 116th Regiment, 29th Division. He trained at Brownsville, Texas, from July 1916 to February 1917 and at Camp McClellan, Alabama, until June 1918. He embarked aboard the *Finland* out of Hoboken, New Jersey, on 15 June 1918, arrived at Saint-Nazaire on 28 June, and entered action on 12 August. Nye spent fifty-six days in the trenches in Haute-Alsace and twenty-one days in the trenches on the east bank of the Meuse, north of Verdun, from 8 to 29 October 1918.

Outten, Edgar C. Outten, an Episcopalian, was a graduate of the Virginia Military Institute with a BS in electrical engineering. He was a sergeant in the National Guard Field Artillery when the United States declared war. He attended Fort Myer Reserve Officers Training Camp from 31 May to 15 August 1917 and was commissioned as a first lieutenant. He embarked for France on 7 September 1917 aboard the *Pocahontas* and then trained at École d'application de l'artillerie in Fontainebleau from 24 September to 30 November 1917. Outten received his captain's commission and entered action on 16 March 1918. He was discharged on 7 February 1919 and found employment at an oyster packing plant in Hampton, Virginia.

Overton, Nelson C. Born in Baltimore, Overton became an officer after spending three months at the First Officers Training Camp at Fort McPherson, Georgia. After instructing troops at Camp Gordon from 1 September 1917 to 11 April 1918, Overton sailed from New York on the *Carmela*, arriving in Liverpool on 5 May 1918. After three months of combat in the Toul sector, Overton was "sent back to the US to act as an instructor with some knowledge of actual warfare for the army of the new draft."

Paoletti, Americus. Paoletti served as a private first class in the National Army's 119th Field Artillery. He trained at Fort Terry, New York, from 29 January to 26 March 1918 and then embarked aboard the *Olympic*, bound for Brest. Paoletti participated in action at Château-Thierry and the Meuse-Argonne. After being discharged on 15 May 1919, he went to work as a truck driver.

Parker, William W. Parker, a Baptist, enlisted on 9 June 1917 and trained at Camp Syracuse, New York, from 21 June to 10 September 1917 and at Camp Greene, North Carolina, from 12 September 1917 to 11 March 1918. He embarked from Halifax, Nova Scotia, on board the *Corsican* on 24 March 1918 and entered action on 1 June at Château-Thierry. He helped hold the line during the Germans' last spring offensive. Parker was later wounded while leading an advance; he was buried by an HE shell and suffered a fractured tenth thoracic vertebra.

Patterson, Leslie H. Born in Nebraska, Patterson, a Presbyterian and a student at Davidson College, entered the service on 29 September 1917. He trained at Camp Lee, Virginia, for five months and arrived in England aboard the *Olympic* on 5 April 1918. At King's College in London, Patterson, a sergeant in the Tank Corps of the 301st Battalion, instructed other soldiers "how to protect themselves from the enemy's poison gas."

Pemburn, Charles S., Jr. Pemburn served as a private in Company E, 11th Engineers; he trained at Camp Devens from 30 October 1917 to January 1918, embarked from Hoboken on the *America* on 26 February 1918, and arrived in Brest on 10 March. Pemburn entered action in March 1918 and fought at Château-Thierry and Saint-Mihiel; he was gassed and suffered a concussion from an HE shell and spent several months at base hospitals in France. Pemburn was discharged on 25 January 1919.

Peronne, Giuseppe S. Peronne served as a private in Company E, 59th Infantry; he trained for a short time at Camp Mills on Long Island, New York, and embarked for Liverpool on 6 May 1918. Peronne entered action on 18 July 1918 and engaged in combat at Aisne-Marne, Saint-Mihiel, and Meuse-Argonne. He was discharged on 6 August 1919 and returned to employment as a laborer.

Piazza, Frank. Piazza enlisted in the Regular Army on 16 July 1917 and served as a private in Company E, 9th Infantry. He was in camp in Syracuse, New York, for forty-five days and then shipped out in September 1917; he participated in combat at Château-Thierry, Saint-Mihiel, and Meuse-Argonne. Piazza received his discharge papers on 13 August 1919.

Porter, Ernest C. Porter trained at Fort Myer, Virginia, from 14 May to 25 August 1917, left New York aboard the *Adriatic* on 6 September 1917, and arrived in Liverpool on 22 September 1917. He was a captain with the field artillery at the time of his discharge.

Preston, Raymond A. Preston trained at Camp Crane in Allentown, Pennsylvania, from 21 June 1917 to 12 June 1918. He embarked on 13 June 1918, then arrived on the Western Front on 30 August, and entered action on 12 September.

Queenin, Raymond J. Queenin trained at Camp Yale and at Fort Totten, New York, and received additional training in France before entering combat on 8 February 1918 with the 26th Division. At Château-Thierry on 23 July 1918 he inhaled a dose of mustard gas and became "exhausted" from combat after an HE shell "wrenched" his back and threw him into a trench at Verdun on 24 October. After the war, Queenin returned to his former occupation as a salesperson.

Randolph, Moses. Randolph, a Baptist, worked as a section hand before the war. He trained at Camp Lee, Virginia, from 27 October 1917 to 29 April 1918 and then embarked from Newport News, Virginia. He landed in Bordeaux on 13 May 1918; arrived at the front on 23 May; engaged in combat near Mount Kemmel, Hill 44; and remained under shell fire from 10 June until late October 1918, when he was shot in the right leg and hospitalized in Paris. According to Randolph, he "was in an engagement at Rattlesnake Hill and my regiment received a flag from the French—a silver rattlesnake on a black field. We all received a device similar to it to wear on the left shoulder." Randolph received his discharge papers on 27 February 1919 and returned to employment as a section hand.

Ryan, Joseph. Ryan trained in Maryland from April to July 1917; in Mineola, Long Island, New York, from July to September 1917; and in Miami, Florida, from September to December 1917, when he embarked for France.

Sampson, Jacob M. Sampson, a Baptist, received his AB degree from Columbia University in New York and taught at Virginia Union University in Richmond prior to his enlistment in the National Army on 25 March 1918. He trained at Camp Meade, Maryland, from 25 March to 18 June 1918; embarked for Brest from Hoboken, New Jersey, aboard the *Great Northern* on 19 June 1918; and arrived in France seven days later. Sampson was discharged on 6 March 1919 and returned to his previous job.

Sanford, Nora B. Sanford started working at the Camp Jackson Base Hospital on 1 May 1918; she sailed from Hoboken on 23 August 1918 and proceeded to her assignment at Hospital Nos. 45 and 87 in France.

Schadel, Joseph R. Schadel was inducted into the National Army on 28 March 1918 and received no military training in the United States. He left aboard the *Metagama*, bound for Liverpool, on 18 May 1918; arrived in England on 31 May; and reached Bellebrune, France, on 7 June. After a brief period of training in France, Schadel went into action on 28 June and fought in several engagements, including Saint-Mihiel and Meuse-Argonne. On 18 August 1918 he was gassed at Le Charmel. After his discharge on 2 August 1919, Schadel returned to Hartford, where he worked as a bank clerk.

Sedlak, Mike. Sedlak was a private in Company K, 64th Infantry, 7th Division. He trained at Fort Bliss, Texas, from 25 May 1917 to 8 August 1918; arrived in Brest on 26 August; and entered action on 10 October 1918. After his discharge, he returned to employment as a laborer and factory worker.

Shabazian, Vahow. Shabazian was a private in the 147th Light Field Artillery, 32nd Division. He trained at Camp Mills and Camp Merritt from 11 November 1917 to 11 January 1918, embarked out of Hoboken aboard the *Olympic* on 11 January 1918, and arrived in Liverpool on 23 January. Shabazian entered action on 10 June 1918 and fought in the Aisne-Marne and Meuse-Argonne offensives. Discharged on 22 May 1919, Shabazian resumed employment as a laborer.

Simons, Albert M. Simons was wounded twice during the conflicts at Château-Thierry and Saint-Mihiel, and his regiment received the Croix de Guerre for its service at Apremont Forest in April 1918, when the 116 men of H Company, 104th Regiment, 26th Division, fought bravely and held their line against the Germans. Simons spent a month in Base Hospital No. 25 in Allerey, France, recovering from his wounds. After his discharge on 11 February 1919, he returned to his position as city assessor in Hartford.

Skinner, Benjamin. Skinner worked as a longshoreman before the war and trained at Camp Lee, Virginia, from October 1917 to March 1918. He sailed for Saint-Nazaire aboard the *Pocahontas* out of Hoboken and entered action on 12 April 1918. After his discharge, Skinner returned to his occupation as a dockworker.

Smith, Verna M. Smith left New York on 25 March 1918 and arrived at Le Havre on 6 April. After the armistice, she served in the Army of Occupation. Smith returned to the United States on 20 June 1919 due to sickness; when she recovered, she worked at Walter Reed Hospital.

Smith, Vernon. Smith, a Baptist, worked as a ship fitter's helper before the war and entered the infantry on 19 May 1917 in New York City. He trained at Camp Merritt and embarked for Brest aboard the *George Washington* on 3 December 1917. He entered action on 15 March 1918 and received a citation for distinguished service at Champagne from Marshal Ferdinand Foch. Upon his discharge on 12 February 1919, Smith returned to his former occupation.

Spencer, James P. Born in Charlotte, Virginia, in 1888, Spencer, a Baptist, enlisted in the infantry on 26 October 1917 and trained at Camp Lee, Virginia, until 29 April 1918. He embarked for France aboard the *Finland* on 30 April and arrived in Saint-Nazaire on 12 May. Spencer went into combat in July 1918 and fought in the Aisne-Marne offensive; he sustained a machine gun wound to his hand on 18 September 1918. After his discharge on 22 April 1919, Spencer worked as a book agent prior to enrolling at the Virginia Normal and Industrial Institute.

Spencer, Walter T. A bookkeeper before the war, Spencer served in the Border Service from 16 October 1913 to 4 April 1918, when he shipped out for France. Spencer was a supply sergeant; his commanding officer cited him for bravery at Château-Thierry on 15 July 1918. While operating a machine gun, Spencer and another doughboy forced the retreat of a large group of German soldiers. He lost his hearing during that engagement.

Starr, Frank A. Starr trained at Fort Terry from 20 December 1917 to 27 March 1918, sailed from New York on the *Olympic* on 28 March 1918, and arrived in Brest on 4 April. He entered action on 20 August 1918 and fought in the Meuse-Argonne offensive from 26 September to 11 November 1918. Starr was discharged on 28 January 1919 and returned to farming.

Stevenson, William Y. Stevenson attended a six-week training course at the Technical School for American Officers in Meaux, France, during September and October 1917 and was commissioned as a lieutenant. He received the Croix de Guerre.

Taliaferro, Thomas B. Taliaferro, a Catholic, trained at Fort Myer, Virginia, from 13 May to 15 August 1917 and at Camp Lee, Virginia, from 27 August 1917 to 26 May 1918. He embarked from Newport News, Virginia, aboard the *Mercury* on 26 May 1918 and arrived in Bordeaux on 9 June. In France he attended the Infantry and Small Arms School at Langres from 1 July to 1 August 1918. Taliaferro saw action with the British; he was wounded by machine gun fire at Saint-Juvin on 1 November 1918 and was hospitalized until 7 February 1919. He was discharged on 2 May 1919 and found employment as a merchant of fish and oysters.

Thompson, Clarence M. Thompson was born 18 August 1881 and was employed as a secretary and agent of the Connecticut Prison Association when he joined the National Guard on 26 March 1917. Before embarking for Europe, Thompson was stationed in Hartford and New Haven. He sailed from Montreal aboard the *Canada* on 16 September 1917, bound for Liverpool, and arrived in Neufchâteau, France, on 6 October 1917. On 1 August 1918 the army promoted him to major. Discharged from the service on 4 June 1919, Thompson returned home and worked in the insurance industry.

Voight, Albert S. Born in Baltimore, Voight, a Baptist, trained at Camp Wheeler, Georgia. He served as a private with the 112th Machine Gun Company and embarked from New Jersey on 14 June 1918 aboard the *Orduna*, arriving in Liverpool on 28 June. On his first day of combat, 26 July 1918, Voight "tried to take prisoner who yelled 'Kamerad!' and afterward shot me in left leg with a pistol." Voight was also "partly shell-shocked from explosion of our M.G. team nested in stone quarry when my two buddies were shattered." Discharged on 20 January 1919, Voight found employment as a swimming instructor.

Waters, Nelson F. Waters enlisted in the National Guard on 19 June 1916 and served with the Border Service. In France, he saw action at Seicheprey, where he sustained hand and leg wounds on 20 April 1918. Waters was a prisoner of war from 28 April to 8 December 1918, when the Germans released him. During his time as a prisoner, he contracted typhoid fever and influenza. Waters received his discharge on 12 February 1919 and returned to his occupation as a sales clerk.

Watts, Christopher C. Watts, a Baptist, served as a sergeant in the 369th Infantry. After training at Camp Lee, Virginia, he embarked for France on board the *Pocahontas* out of Hoboken on 12 March 1918 and arrived at Saint-Nazaire on 26 March. Watts went into action on 1 April 1918 and participated in two drives at the Champagne front; he was gassed three times during the Meuse-Argonne offensive. Discharged on 12 March 1919, Watts found employment as a laborer.

Weston, Stephen J. As a private in the infantry, Weston trained at the Fair Grounds in Syracuse, New York, from June to October 1917. He was promoted to corporal on 9 October 1917. Weston embarked from New York on the *Caserta* on 13 May 1918 and arrived with Company I, 47th Regiment, 4th Division, in Rosoy-en-Multien on 14 June. At the time of his discharge on 1 August 1919, after serving eight months with the Army of Occupation, Weston had been promoted to first sergeant.

Whitehouse, Wilson H. Whitehouse worked as a toolmaker for R. Wallace and Sons Manufacturing Company of Wallingford, Connecticut, and served with the National Guard. After training at Camp Yale, he sailed from Montreal on 16 September 1917. Whitehouse was gassed on 17 March 1918 and again on 25 October. He received his discharge on 29 April 1919.

Williams, Thomas N. Williams, an Episcopalian, entered the service on 14 May

1917, received his commission as a first lieutenant in the infantry on 15 August 1917, and underwent further training at Camp Lee, Virginia, Camp Wadsworth, South Carolina, and Camp Stewart, Georgia, from 29 August 1917 to 14 August 1918. He embarked from Newport News, Virginia, aboard the *Martha Washington* on 14 August 1918 and arrived in France on 23 August. He entered action at the Meuse-Argonne on 1 November 1918. Williams was discharged on 18 August 1919 and found employment with the US Shipping Board.

Wollman, Solomon. Wollman, born in Hartford on 29 September 1895, was a printer at Case, Lockwood and Brainard Company for six years before he enlisted. Wollman's parents were Russian-born Jews, and he attended a synagogue in Hartford. On 28 July 1917 Wollman became an infantry private in the National Guard, 26th Division. After training at Camp Yale, Wollman's company left for England on 15 September 1917. On 5 October 1917 Wollman began training in France.

Wynne, Patrick. Wynne served in the 316th Infantry, 79th Division; he trained at Camp Meade, Maryland, from 27 June to 7 July 1918. He sailed on the *Agamemnon* on 9 July 1918 and arrived in Brest on 19 July. Wynne first saw combat on 26 September 1918 and sustained gunshot wounds just three days later; he was hospitalized from 2 October 1918 to 5 February 1919 and underwent surgery twice. Wynne received his discharge papers on 8 March 1919, at which time he was "waiting to hear from the government" regarding civilian employment.

Wysocki, Paul T. Born in Pennsylvania to Polish parents, Wysocki, a Catholic, trained at Camp Lee, Virginia, from 22 September 1917 to 20 May 1918. He embarked on the *Leviathan* out of Jersey City and arrived in Brest on 30 May 1918, entered action on 12 August 1918, and fought in the Meuse-Argonne offensive. Wysocki returned to work in the navy yard after his discharge on 27 May 1919.

Yaffo, Samuel B. Yaffo was born in Russia in 1890. He worked as a salesclerk at G. Fox and Company, a Hartford department store. Yaffo enlisted in the Regular Army on 13 December 1917 and trained at Camp Jackson, South Carolina, and Camp Hancock, Georgia, until 15 May 1918. He embarked on the *Cedric* out of Hoboken, New Jersey, on 26 May 1918 and arrived in Liverpool on 6 June. He went into action on 3 September 1918 and later fought in the Meuse-Argonne offensive, where he remained until Armistice Day. Yaffo then served with the Army of Occupation. Following his discharge on 8 July 1919, he returned to his previous job.

Yancey, William B. Yancey, a Methodist, entered service on 15 April 1917, trained at Cedar Bluff, Virginia, from 20 April to 20 May 1917, and served as a first lieutenant in the 6th Division's machine gun company. He sailed from Hoboken aboard the *Cedric* on 6 July 1918, arrived in Liverpool on 20 July, and entered action on 27 August. He sustained a gunshot wound to his right foot (causing the bone to protrude through the skin) on 15 September and was a patient at Walter Reed Hospital at the time of his discharge on 15 February 1919. Yancey returned to Virginia and became a lawyer.

York, Alvin C. York trained at Camp Gordon, Georgia, from 17 November 1917 to 19 April 1918, embarked from Boston on 1 May 1918, and arrived in Liverpool on 16 May. York served with Company G, 328th Infantry, 82nd Division, known as the All-American Division because it was made up of "boys from every state in the Union." He received several medals, including the Medal of Honor and the Ordre national de la Légion d'honneur (Legion of Honor).

Notes

Abbreviations

CSL	Connecticut State Library, Hartford
LVA	Library of Virginia, Richmond
MHI	United States Army Military History Institute, Carlisle, PA
NARA II	National Archives and Records Administration II, College Park, MD
USA	Utah State Historical Society and Archives, Salt Lake City
WSA	Wyoming State Archives, Cheyenne

Introduction

1. The term *doughboy* has an uncertain origin, but one popular theory from the US Army's newspaper *Stars and Stripes* states: "The word 'doughboy' originated in the Philippines. After a long march over extremely dusty roads the Infantrymen came into camp covered with dust. The long hikes brought out the perspiration, and the perspiration mixed with the dust formed a substance resembling dough; therefore, their lucky brothers, the mounted soldiers, called them 'doughboys.'" *Stars and Stripes*, 25 April 1919, 4. At least two different soldiers, however, used the term *doughboy* to describe American troops during the Mexican-American War (1846–1848). Regardless of its origin, *doughboy* became the most popular name for American soldiers during the Great War, until *GI* replaced it during the Second World War.

2. "Guggenheim, Dying, Sent Wife Message," *New York Times*, 20 April 1912. See also Irwin Unger and Debi Unger, *The Guggenheims: A Family History* (New York: Harper-Collins, 2005), 65–66, and Mary V. Dearborn, *Mistress of Modernism: The Life of Peggy Guggenheim* (New York: Houghton Mifflin, 2004), 23.

3. "Guggenheim, Dying, Sent Wife Message." This message and the one cited at note 2 appear in many studies of the *Titanic* disaster.

4. Percentages calculated from Lord Mersey, *The Loss of the* Titanic, *1912* (London: Stationery Office, 1999), 110–111, and Daniel Allen Butler, *"Unsinkable": The Full Story of the RMS* Titanic (Cambridge, MA: Da Capo Press, 2012), 258–259. For a study of male heroism, see Steven Biel, *Down with the Old Canoe: A Cultural History of the* Titanic *Disaster* (New York: Norton, 2012), especially 23–58.

5. Other scholars have examined the battles of World War I in many excellent books, including Edward G. Lengel's *To Conquer Hell: The Meuse-Argonne, 1918* (New York: Holt, 2008). Others focus on the national or strategic level, such as Justus D. Doenecke's *Nothing Less than War: A New History of America's Entry into World War I* (Lexington: University Press of Kentucky, 2011), or on the operational or tactical level, such as Mitchell A. Yockelson's *Borrowed Soldiers: Americans under British Command, 1918* (Norman: University of Oklahoma Press, 2008).

6. Denis Winter, *Death's Men: Soldiers of the Great War* (London: Penguin Books, 1979), 13.

7. Stephen G. Fritz, *Frontsoldaten: The German Soldier in World War II* (Lexington: University Press of Kentucky, 1995), 1–10.

8. Peter Englund, *The Beauty and the Sorrow: An Intimate History of the First World War* (New York: Knopf, 2011), xi. Englund follows twenty people throughout the war, including two Americans: a Polish aristocrat's wife and an army field surgeon.

9. Although some Civil War books mention World War I, none of them focus on how the heroic legacy of the Civil War affected the prewar motivations and emotions of the young men growing up in the 1890s and 1900s. See David Blight, *Race and Reunion: The Civil War in American Memory* (Cambridge, MA: Belknap Press of Harvard University Press, 2001); Drew Gilpin Faust, *This Republic of Suffering: Death and the American Civil War* (New York: Knopf, 2008).

10. The percentage is calculated from the 2,086,000 men sent overseas and the 1,390,000 who fought in France, drawn from figures in Leonard P. Ayres, *The War with Germany: A Statistical Summary*, 2nd ed. (Washington, DC: Government Printing Office, 1919), 11. Although dated, Ayres's book still provides an approximation for statistical purposes.

11. Veterans from Connecticut and Virginia included all branches of the service, as well as nurses and stenographers. Minnesota's questionnaire was also called the Military Service Record, but it deviated from the template used by Connecticut and Virginia. Utah deviated even further; its War Service Questionnaire was four pages long, but its dimensions measured half the size of the others. For a closer look at each form, see appendix A.

12. The figure 27,847 combines the total number of questionnaires returned by veterans from Connecticut and Virginia; if Minnesota and Utah are included, the total is 110,847.

13. Leonard V. Smith, *The Embattled Self: French Soldiers' Testimony of the Great War* (Ithaca, NY: Cornell University Press, 2007), 97.

14. Ibid., 99.

15. William L. Langer, *Gas and Flame in World War I* (New York: Knopf, 1965), xvii. See Langer's biography in appendix B.

16. Richard Rubin, *The Last of the Doughboys: The Forgotten Generation and Their Forgotten World War* (Boston: Houghton Mifflin Harcourt, 2013), 123.

17. Ibid., 71–85.

18. Robert J. Clark, 1st Division, World War I Veterans Survey, MHI. When quoting veterans, I do so verbatim and with the original spelling.

19. For an in-depth, classic study of memory, see Frederic C. Bartlett, *Remembering: A Study in Experimental and Social Psychology* (Cambridge: Cambridge University Press, 1932), especially chapter 5, which discusses his famous experiment called the "War of the Ghosts." In this experiment, Bartlett told a Native American story to a test group and asked the participants to recount the tale minutes, days, and even years later. As time progressed, their recollection of the story became cloudier.

20. Christopher M. Sterba, *Good Americans: Italian and Jewish Immigrants during the First World War* (New York: Oxford University Press, 2003). Sterba used the same few MSRs for an article focusing on Italian machine gunners; see Christopher M. Sterba, "'Your Country Wants You': New Haven's Italian Machine Gun Company Enters World War I," *New England Quarterly* 74, 2 (June 2001): 179–209.

21. See Chad L. Williams, *Torchbearers of Democracy: African American Soldiers in the World War I Era* (Chapel Hill: University of North Carolina Press, 2010).

22. Jonathan H. Ebel, *Faith in the Fight: Religion and the American Soldier in the Great War* (Princeton, NJ: Princeton University Press, 2010).

23. Aaron Coplin, 29th Division, World War I Veterans Survey, MHI.

24. Paul J. McMahon, 29th Division, World War I Veterans Survey, MHI.

25. Louis C. Ciccone, 29th Division, World War I Veterans Survey, MHI.

26. Around 40 of the 5,800 respondents to the MHI questionnaires wrote "War is hell" or a close variation. First Sergeant Karl W. Fritz of the 6th Infantry concluded, "Sherman was right 'War is hell.'" Karl W. Fritz, 5th Division, World War I Veterans Survey, MHI.

27. Lloyd Lewis, *Sherman: Fighting Prophet* (Lincoln: University of Nebraska Press, 1993), 637.

28. Finlan D. Cuddy, 3 July 1919, box 30, Military Service Questionnaires, 1920–1930, War Records Department, Record Group 12, State Archives, CSL. The date after the veteran's name indicates when he or she filled out the form; if no date is given, it means the veteran left the "Signed at" section blank.

29. Egbert B. Inman, 7 August 1919, box 9, CSL.

30. William W. Ward, box 8, World War I History Commission, series I, Individual Service Records (Questionnaires), 1919–1924, LVA.

31. Bernard C. Paggett, 28 May 1919, box 2, LVA.

32. Charles Johnston, 22 June 1922, box 22, series II, LVA.

33. Roy D. Hitchcock, 20 September 1921, box 8, CSL.

34. John B. Vaninetty, November 1931, box 20, CSL.

35. Jerry M. Davis, 8 September 1919, box 7, CSL.

36. Jack F. Molloy, 18 July 1919, box 34, CSL.

37. Edgar H. Dowson, 22 December 1920, box 31, CSL.

38. Edward M. Coffman, *The War to End All Wars: The American Military Experience in World War I* (Lexington: University Press of Kentucky, 1998), 54.

39. Primo Levi, *The Drowned and the Saved*, trans. Raymond Rosenthal (New York: Vintage International, 1989), 84.

40. For a close examination of the two Russian campaigns, see Carl J. Richard, *When the United States Invaded Russia: Woodrow Wilson's Siberian Disaster* (Lanham, MD: Row-

man and Littlefield, 2013), and Robert L. Willett, *Russian Sideshow: America's Undeclared War, 1918–1920* (Washington, DC: Brassey's, 2003).

41. Calculated from American Battle Monuments Commission, *American Armies and Battlefields in Europe: A History, Guide and Reference Book* (Washington, DC: Government Printing Office, 1995), 515 (table).

42. Calculated from Ayres, *War with Germany*, 114 (table).

43. The 5th Marine Brigade served in France but acted as a replacement unit. At the armistice on 11 November 1918, there were 73,000 marines, of which 24,555 were in France. See George B. Clark, *Devil Dogs: Fighting Marines of World War I* (New York: Presidio Press, 1999), 18.

44. E. B. Sledge, *With the Old Breed: At Peleliu and Okinawa* (Annapolis, MD: Naval Institute Press, 1996), 315.

45. Frederick Downs, *The Killing Zone: My Life in the Vietnam War* (New York: Norton, 2007), 265. A Bouncing Betty is an antipersonnel mine first used in World War II. When tripped, the mine launches into the air and explodes at waist height, sending shrapnel in a horizontal blast pattern.

46. Chris Kyle, *American Sniper: The Autobiography of the Most Lethal Sniper in U.S. Military History* (New York: William Morrow, 2012), 378.

Chapter 1. The Great Adventure

1. The concept of universal European excitement and whether government coercion or citizen consent led to war remain contentious topics. See Christopher M. Clark, *The Sleepwalkers: How Europe Went to War in 1914* (New York: Harper, 2013), and Michael S. Neiberg, *Dance of the Furies: Europe and the Outbreak of World War I* (Cambridge, MA: Belknap Press of Harvard University Press, 2011). For a concise overview of the topic, see Jay Winter, ed., *The Legacy of the Great War: Ninety Years On* (Columbia: University of Missouri Press, 2009), chap. 3.

2. James Marten, *Sing Not War: The Lives of Union and Confederate Veterans in Gilded Age America* (Chapel Hill: University of North Carolina Press, 2011), 284.

3. Stuart McConnell, *Glorious Contentment: The Grand Army of the Republic, 1865–1900* (Chapel Hill: University of North Carolina Press, 1992), 168.

4. Quoted in Nina Silber, *The Romance of Reunion: Northerners and the South, 1865–1900* (Chapel Hill: University of North Carolina Press, 1993), 168–169.

5. Quoted in Gerald Linderman, *Embattled Courage: The Experience of Combat in the American Civil War* (New York: Free Press, 1987), 284.

6. Silber, *Romance of Reunion*, 169.

7. James M. McPherson, *For Cause and Comrades: Why Men Fought in the Civil War* (Oxford: Oxford University Press, 1996), 26.

8. John William De Forest, *A Volunteer's Adventures: A Union Captain's Record of the Civil War*, ed. James H. Croushore (Baton Rouge: Louisiana State University Press, 1996), 123–124.

9. Thomas J. Brown, ed., *The Public Art of Civil War Commemoration: A Brief History with Documents* (Boston: Bedford / St. Martin's, 2004), 20–21.

10. Bell Irvin Wiley, *The Life of Billy Yank: The Common Soldier of the Union*, 2nd ed. (Baton Rouge: Louisiana State University Press, 2008), 15.

11. Quoted in ibid., 335–336.

12. Bell Irvin Wiley, *The Life of Johnny Reb: The Common Soldier of the Confederacy*, 2nd ed. (Baton Rouge: Louisiana State University Press, 2008), 149–150.

13. Alice Fahs, "Remembering the Civil War in Children's Literature of the 1880s and 1890s," in *The Memory of the Civil War in American Culture*, ed. Alice Fahs and Joan Waugh (Chapel Hill: University of North Carolina Press, 2004), 91.

14. Stephen Crane, *The Red Badge of Courage: A Norton Critical Edition*, 4th ed., ed. Donald Pizer and Eric Carl Link (New York: Norton, 2008), 76.

15. Ibid., 103.

16. The introductory essays from the newest editions of the Oxford and Penguin volumes of *The Red Badge of Courage* both argue that Crane's novel is an ironic and antiwar diatribe. See Anthony Mellors and Fiona Robertson, eds., *The Red Badge of Courage and Other Stories* (Oxford: Oxford University Press, 2005), vii–xxvi, and Gary Scharnhorst, ed., *The Red Badge of Courage and Other Stories* (New York: Penguin Books, 2005), vii–xlviii.

17. Crane structured the battle on the Southern victory at Chancellorsville, fought 30 April to 6 May 1863.

18. Michael C. C. Adams, *The Great Adventure: Male Desire and the Coming of World War I* (Bloomington: Indiana University Press, 1990), 48.

19. Corwin K. Linson, *My Stephen Crane*, ed. Edwin H. Cady (Syracuse, NY: Syracuse University Press, 1958), 37.

20. R. W. Stallman and Lillian Gilkes, eds., *Stephen Crane: Letters* (New York: New York University Press, 1960), 109.

21. Ibid., 158.

22. Linda H. Davis, *Badge of Courage: The Life of Stephen Crane* (Boston: Houghton Mifflin, 1998), 205.

23. Ibid., 263.

24. Crane, *Red Badge of Courage and Other Stories*, ed. Mellors and Robertson, 121–122.

25. Marten, *Sing Not War*, 281.

26. Davis, *Badge of Courage*, 267.

27. Elliott J. Gorn, *The Manly Art: Bare-Knuckle Prize Fighting in America*, 2nd ed. (Ithaca, NY: Cornell University Press, 2010), 188.

28. Between 15 and 40 percent of American men were involved in fraternal organizations and secret societies at the turn of the nineteenth century. Mark C. Carnes, *Secret Ritual and Manhood in Victorian America* (New Haven, CT: Yale University Press, 1989), 2.

29. The United States Sedition Act of 1918, section 3.

30. "It's Duty Boy," *Four Minute Men News*, 22 May 1917.

31. Plutarch, *Moralia*, 241. Also translated as "Either this or upon this" in *Sayings of Spartan Women*, Loeb Classical Library ed., trans. Frank Cole Babbitt (Cambridge, MA: Harvard University Press, 1931), 465; see also 455–469.

32. *New York Times*, 22 July 1915.

33. Billy Sunday, *Watchman Examiner*, 18 April 1918, 503.

34. Garnett D. Claman, 6 August 1921, box 11, LVA. See Claman's biography in appendix B.

35. Henry A. Isleib, 27 September 1919, box 19, CSL. See Isleib's biography in appendix B.

36. Joseph J. O'Connell, 26 September 1919, box 17, CSL.

37. James P. Spencer, 25 April 1921, box 3, LVA. See Spencer's biography in appendix B.

38. Niels A. W. Johnson, 15 August 1919, box 16, CSL. See Johnson's biography in appendix B.

39. Harold J. Dougan, 9 August 1919, box 15, CSL.

40. James O. McKarney, box 11, LVA. See McKarney's biography in appendix B.

41. Thomas M. Clary, box 2, LVA. See Clary's biography in appendix B.

42. Paul T. Wysocki, 25 August 1919, box 8, LVA. See Wysocki's biography in appendix B.

43. Arthur F. Lundin, 26 September 1920, box 38, CSL.

44. William W. Parker, 22 August 1919, box 22, series II, LVA. See Parker's biography in appendix B.

45. John S. Fields, 8 December 1919, box 4, LVA. See Fields's biography in appendix B.

46. Arthur A. Grove, 18 November 1920, box 9, LVA. See Grove's biography in appendix B.

47. Donald Day, ed., *Woodrow Wilson's Own Story* (Boston: Little, Brown, 1952), 247.

48. Emory P. Barrow, 11 November 1921, box 2, LVA. See Barrow's biography in appendix B.

49. Theodore Elmore, 15 March 1922, box 21, series II, LVA. See Elmore's biography in appendix B.

50. Edgar C. Outten, 8 November 1919, box 4, LVA. See Outten's biography in appendix B.

51. Hew Strachan, *The First World War* (New York: Viking, 2003), 192. This number varies from source to source, as does the total number of casualties (57,470), which includes British soldiers wounded, captured, or missing at the end of the first day.

52. At the national level, however, American interests during this period led to involvement in Latin America and Asia and to global naval treaties. See Christopher McKnight Nichols, *Promise and Peril: America at the Dawn of a Global Age* (Cambridge, MA: Harvard University Press, 2011).

53. George Washington, *Writings*, ed. John Rhodehamel (New York: Library of America, 1997), 974–976.

54. Harlow Giles Unger, *The Last Founding Father: James Monroe and a Nation's Call to Greatness* (Philadelphia: Da Capo Press, 2009), 350–351. The Monroe Doctrine was part of the president's seventh annual message to Congress.

55. Gary Mead, *The Doughboys: America and the First World War* (Woodstock, NY: Overlook Press, 2000), 19–20. The "rape of Belgium," the first atrocity to emerge from

the war, is examined in John Horne and Alan Kramer, *German Atrocities 1914: A History of Denial* (New Haven, CT: Yale University Press, 2001). The authors argue that it began when Germany violated Belgian neutrality in its quest to invade France—a flagrant disregard of The Hague and Geneva conventions. The Germans used the tactic of *Schrecklichkeit* (terror) to force the Belgians and French to submit to their will. Several historians point to *Schrecklichkeit* as a precursor of Nazi atrocities during the Second World War, such as Annette Becker, *Les Cicatrices Rouges 14–18: France et Belgique Occupées* (Paris: Fayard, 2010).

56. Jay M. Winter, "Propaganda and the Mobilization of Consent," in *The Oxford Illustrated History of the First World War*, ed. Hew Strachan (Oxford: Oxford University Press, 1998), 216.

57. Celia M. Kingsbury explores this development in detail in her book *For Home and Country: World War I Propaganda on the Home Front* (Lincoln: University of Nebraska Press, 2010).

58. Frank Trommler, "The *Lusitania* Effect: America's Mobilization against Germany in World War I," *German Studies Review* 32, 2 (May 2009): 241. See also David Ramsay, *Lusitania: Saga and Myth* (New York: Norton, 2002), and Diana Preston, *Lusitania: An Epic Tragedy* (New York: Walker Publishing, 2002).

59. Friedrich Katz, *The Life and Times of Pancho Villa* (Stanford, CA: Stanford University Press, 1998), 546, 566.

60. Woodrow Wilson, *War Messages*, 65th Congress, 1st Session, Senate Doc. No. 5, Serial No. 7264 (Washington, DC, 1917), 3–8.

61. Day, *Wilson's Own Story*, 248.

62. Mark Ethan Grotelueschen stresses the Punitive Expedition's effect on the army's artillery branch, which closed its School for Fire at Fort Sill, Oklahoma, and shut down the Field Artillery Board. Mark Ethan Grotelueschen, *The AEF Way of War: The American Army and Combat in World War I* (Cambridge: Cambridge University Press, 2007), 24–25.

63. James J. Hudson, *Hostile Skies: A Combat History of the American Air Service in World War I* (Syracuse, NY: Syracuse University Press, 1968), 2–3. By 1915, the airplane had become a necessity on the Western Front, mostly for reconnaissance and artillery spotting. In a short time, Europe realized the true power of the airplane, and the modern military role of the fighter and bomber materialized. As in many other areas of wartime supply, the AEF depended on the Allies to provide airplanes. American ace Eddie Rickenbacker and every other American pilot flew French and British airplanes, predominantly the French SPAD 13 and Nieuport 28. Besides being short on planes, the army had only twenty-six pilots. See Roger G. Miller, *A Preliminary to War: The 1st Aero Squadron and the Mexican Punitive Expedition of 1916* (Honolulu: University Press of the Pacific, 2005), 53, and Herbert A. Johnson, *Wingless Eagle: U.S. Army Aviation through World War I* (Chapel Hill: University of North Carolina Press, 2001), 157–216.

64. Tami Davis Biddle, *Rhetoric and Reality in Air Warfare: The Evolution of British and American Ideas about Strategic Bombing, 1914–1945* (Princeton, NJ: Princeton University Press, 2002), 49.

65. Ibid., 319.

66. John P. Finnegan, *Against the Specter of a Dragon* (Westport, CT: Greenwood Press, 1974), 189.

67. Johnson Hagood, *The Services of Supply: A Memoir of the Great War* (Boston: Houghton Mifflin, 1927), 22–23, 27.

68. George W. Cheney, 10 July 1919, box 15, CSL.

69. Marcel W. Rice, 21 July 1919, box 35, CSL.

70. John M. Ross, 6 October 1919, box 35, CSL.

71. Francis P. Duffy, *Father Duffy's Story* (New York: George H. Doran, 1919), 18.

72. Ibid.

73. Albertus W. Catlin, *With the Help of God and a Few Marines* (New York: Doubleday, Page, 1919), 15. See Catlin's biography in appendix B.

74. Harold Elk Straubing, ed., *The Last Magnificent War: Rare Journalistic and Eyewitness Accounts of World War I* (New York: Paragon House, 1989), 198.

75. Wilbur T. Brownley, 18 August 1919, box 13, LVA.

76. Kerry William Bate, "Kanarraville Fights World War I," *Utah Historical Quarterly* 63, 1 (Winter 1995): 32.

77. Herman R. Furr, 14 October 1919, box 21, series II, LVA. See Furr's biography in appendix B.

78. Edward G. Pobuda, 22 May 1919, box 64, CSL.

79. Joseph Ryan, 30 November 1919, box 58, CSL. See Ryan's biography in appendix B.

80. Stephen J. Weston, 8 November 1933, box 39, CSL. See Weston's biography in appendix B.

81. Douglas C. France, 16 November 1920, box 12, LVA.

82. Millard C. Life, 7 January 1920, box 9, LVA.

83. Theodore E. Whitney, 16 February 1927, box 14, CSL.

84. Thomas B. McDermott, 24 March 1920, box 11, CSL. See McDermott's biography in appendix B. At the time of the First World War, Plattsburgh was spelled without the *h* at the end. For purposes of consistency, it is spelled Plattsburgh throughout this book.

85. Alvin C. York, *Sergeant York: His Own Life Story and War Diary*, ed. Tom Skeyhill (Garden City, NY: Doubleday, Doran, 1928), 154. See York's biography in appendix B.

86. Martin J. Hogan, *The Shamrock Battalion of the Rainbow* (New York: D. Appleton, 1919), 8.

87. Rudyard Kipling, *Complete Verse: Definitive Edition* (New York: Anchor Press, 1989), 328–329.

88. David M. Kennedy, *Over Here: The First World War and American Society*, 2nd ed. (Oxford: Oxford University Press, 2004), 179. Kennedy stresses the upper class's strong support of the war as a way to reinvigorate male honor.

89. George H. Nettleton, ed., *Yale in the World War*, 2 vols. (New Haven, CT: Yale University Press, 1925), 1:ix.

90. Catlin, *With the Help of God*, 19–20.

91. William B. Yancey, 9 October 1919, box 12, LVA. See Yancey's biography in appendix B.

92. Joseph B. Bowen quoted in Nettleton, *Yale in the World War*, 1:274. See Bowen's biography in appendix B.

93. Horace's (65–8 BC) famous line is from his *Odes*, book III, 2.13. British soldier Wilfred Owen (1893–1918) mocked the phrase in his poem "Dulce et Decorum est," calling it "The old Lie." Kennedy, *Over Here*, 179.

94. John Dos Passos, *One Man's Initiation: 1917* (Ithaca, NY: Cornell University Press, 1969), 4–5.

95. Alan Seeger, *Letters and Diary of Alan Seeger* (New York: Charles Scribner's Sons, 1917), 154.

96. Ibid., 126. See also Seeger's thoughts on chivalry (100–101) and death in combat (108–109).

97. Duffy, *Father Duffy's Story*, 16. Kilmer served as a sergeant in HQ Company of the Fighting 69th and died in battle on 30 July 1918.

98. Arthur G. Empey, *First Call* (New York: G. P. Putnam's Sons, 1918), 279–280.

99. Ibid., 319–320. After the war, not all civilians considered the veterans' sacrifice worthwhile; see the end of chapter 6, especially Carl Noble's story.

100. Jack Morris Wright, *A Poet of the Air: Letters of Jack Morris Wright First Lieutenant of the American Aviation in France April, 1917–January, 1918* (Boston: Houghton Mifflin, 1918), 167–168.

101. Richard C. Cabot, *Mademoiselle Miss* (Boston: W. A. Butterfield, 1916), 68.

102. Miriam B. Murphy, "'If Only I Have the Right Stuff': Utah Women in World War I," *Utah Historical Quarterly* 58, 4 (Autumn 1990): 338.

103. *Salt Lake Tribune*, 10 April 1918.

104. Miletus B. Jarman, 7 January 1920, box 9, LVA. See Jarman's biography in appendix B.

105. John W. Covington, 24 September 1920, box 20, series II, LVA. See Covington's biography in appendix B.

106. Empey, *First Call*, 4.

107. Curry P. Hutchison, 15 December 1919, box 5, LVA. See Hutchison's biography in appendix B.

108. William P. Nye, 14 February 1921, box 22, series II, LVA. See Nye's biography in appendix B.

109. John Whiteclay Chambers II, *To Raise an Army: The Draft Comes to Modern America* (New York: Free Press, 1987), 213–214.

110. Raleigh A. Bagley, 1 September 1919, box 13, LVA. See Bagley's biography in appendix B.

111. Fairfield H. Hodges, 25 February 1920, box 15, LVA. See Hodges's biography in appendix B.

112. Channing W. Daniel, 10 March 1921, box 16, LVA. See Daniel's biography in appendix B.

113. Hugh E. Brown, box 13, LVA. See Brown's biography in appendix B.

114. James F. Bonham, 26 September 1920, box 10, LVA. See Bonham's biography in appendix B.

115. Duffy, *Father Duffy's Story*, 20.

Chapter 2. "Gimme da Gun"

1. According to Gertrude Stein, a French mechanic told her that the soldiers of the Great War were *une génération perdue* (a lost generation). Stein agreed and passed the idea on to Ernest Hemingway. James R. Mellow, *Charmed Circle: Gertrude Stein and Company* (New York: Owl Books, 2003), 273–274.

2. Henri Barbusse, *Under Fire* (New York: Penguin, 2004), 237. Although antiwar at its core, Barbusse's book ends with a glimmer of hope as a feeble ray of sunlight peaks through foreboding clouds. This parallels Stephen Crane's imagery in the last lines of *The Red Badge of Courage*.

3. William March, *Company K* (Tuscaloosa: University of Alabama Press, 1989), 14. March's novel, perhaps the most violent and extreme of America's Lost Generation, was originally published in 1933, a year after a group of World War I veterans, dubbed the Bonus Army, marched on Washington, D.C., to appeal to the government for a monetary service bonus. For an in-depth study of the Bonus Army, see Stephen R. Ortiz, *Beyond the Bonus March and GI Bill: How Veteran Politics Shaped the New Deal Era* (New York: New York University Press, 2010), and Jennifer D. Keene, *Doughboys, the Great War and the Remaking of America* (Baltimore: Johns Hopkins University Press, 2001).

4. March, *Company K*, 182.

5. Thomas Boyd, *Through the Wheat* (Lincoln: University of Nebraska Press, 2000), 210–211, 266.

6. Erich Maria Remarque's novel *Im Westen nichts Neues* (published in English as *All Quiet on the Western Front* in 1929) and the American film adaptation by Lewis Milestone (released on 21 April 1930) also played a significant role in shaping society's interpretation of the war. Milestone won Academy Awards for Best Director and Best Picture (called Outstanding Production in 1930). James Whale later made Remarque's 1931 sequel, *Der Weg zurück* (The Road Back), into a film (released on 1 June 1937). See Leslie Midkiff DeBauche, "The United States' Film Industry and World War One," in *The First World War and Popular Cinema: 1914 to the Present*, ed. Michael Paris (New Brunswick, NJ: Rutgers University Press, 2000), 138–161, and Andrew Kelly, *Filming* All Quiet on the Western Front: *"Brutal Cutting, Stupid Censors, Bigoted Politicos"* (London: I. B. Tauris, 1998).

7. Keith Gandal, *The Gun and the Pen: Hemingway, Fitzgerald, Faulkner and the Fiction of Mobilization* (New York: Oxford University Press, 2008), 219.

8. F. Scott Fitzgerald, *The Great Gatsby* (Oxford: Oxford University Press, 2008), 96.

9. Faulkner's Civil War novel *The Unvanquished* (1938) illustrates the impact of Colonel Falkner's heroic legacy on his great-grandson, as does the use of the shadow motif in *The Sound and the Fury* (1929). In that novel, Quentin Compson (representing Faulkner), a member of the dysfunctional Compson family, strives to honor and equal his ancestors but ultimately fails to achieve greatness. Overwhelmed, Quentin commits suicide by diving into the water, where his shadow awaits him.

10. Ernest Hemingway, *A Farewell to Arms* (New York: Scribner, 2012), 161. See also "Soldier's Home," which features a man named Harold Krebs who returns from the war disillusioned and aloof. Ernest Hemingway, *The Complete Short Stories of Ernest Hemingway* (New York: Scribner, 1998), 109–116. Krebs's condition parallels that of war vet-

eran Nicholas Adams (representing Hemingway). See Ernest Memingway, *The Nick Adams Stories* (New York: Scribner, 1972).

11. Quoted in Stanley Cooperman, *World War I and the American Novel* (Baltimore: Johns Hopkins Press, 1967), 195.

12. Quoted in ibid., 196–197.

13. Coningsby Dawson, "Insulting the Army," *New York Times*, 2 October 1921.

14. The AEF contained immigrants from forty-six countries worldwide. Nancy Gentile Ford, *Americans All! Foreign-born Soldiers in World War I* (College Station: Texas A&M University Press, 2001), 3.

15. William L. Langer, *Gas and Flame in World War I* (New York: Knopf, 1965), xviii.

16. Quoted in George H. Nettleton, ed., *Yale in the World War*, 2 vols. (New Haven, CT: Yale University Press, 1925), 1:45.

17. Quoted in Johnson Hagood, *The Services of Supply: A Memoir of the Great War* (Boston: Houghton Mifflin, 1927), ix.

18. William Y. Stevenson, *From "Poilu" to Yank* (Boston: Houghton Mifflin, 1918), 12. See Stevenson's biography in appendix B.

19. Pictorial section, *New York Times*, 20 September and 22 November 1914.

20. Ibid., 31 January 1915.

21. Donald Smythe, *Pershing: General of the Armies* (Bloomington: Indiana University Press, 1986), 8.

22. Lowell Thomas, *This Side of Hell, Dan Edwards, Adventurer* (New York: P. F. Collier and Son, 1932), 73. See Edwards's biography in appendix B.

23. Harvey G. Callahan, 23 September 1920, box 12, LVA. See Callahan's biography in appendix B.

24. David M. Kennedy, *Over Here: The First World War and American Society*, 2nd ed. (Oxford: Oxford University Press, 2004), 149–150.

25. Edward M. Coffman, *The War to End All Wars: The American Military Experience in World War I* (Lexington: University Press of Kentucky, 1998), 28.

26. Leonard P. Ayres, *The War with Germany: A Statistical Summary*, 2nd ed. (Washington, DC: Government Printing Office, 1919), 17–19. According to SSS records, the board drafted 2,810,296 men from September 1917 to November 1918 (516,212 in 1917 and 2,294,084 in 1918); see http://www.sss.gov/induct.htm.

27. Frank P. Sibley, *With the Yankee Division in France* (Boston: Little, Brown, 1919), 16.

28. Quoted in Daniel W. Strickland, *Connecticut Fights: The Story of the 102nd Regiment* (New Haven, CT: Quinnipiac Press, 1930), 54.

29. Richard C. Roberts, "The Utah National Guard in the Great War, 1917–1918," *Utah Historical Quarterly* 58, 4 (Autumn 1990): 318.

30. Quoted in Daniel J. Sweeney, ed., *History of Buffalo and Erie County 1914–1919* (Buffalo, NY: Committee of One Hundred, 1919), 76.

31. Robert H. Zieger, *America's Great War: World War I and the American Experience* (Lanham, MD: Rowman and Littlefield, 2000), 87.

32. Christopher M. Sterba, *Good Americans: Italian and Jewish Immigrants during the First World War* (New York: Oxford University Press, 2003), 57.

33. David Laskin, *The Long Way Home: An American Journey from Ellis Island to the Great War* (New York: HarperCollins, 2010), 128.

34. Ibid., 141.

35. William Mitchell, *Memoirs of World War I: From Start to Finish of Our Greatest War* (New York: Random House, 1960), 294.

36. Joseph R. Cooke, 10 June 1922, box 15, LVA. See Cooke's biography in appendix B.

37. James W. Anderson, box 12, LVA. See Anderson's biography in appendix B.

38. Nicola Andreozzi, box 29, CSL. See Andreozzi's biography in appendix B. I thank Antonio DiRubba for his help in translating Andreozzi's dialectal Italian response.

39. Alvin C. York, *Sergeant York: His Own Life Story and War Diary*, ed. Tom Skeyhill (Garden City, NY: Doubleday, Doran, 1928), 180.

40. Ibid., 184–185.

41. Frederick M. Wise, *A Marine Tells It to You* (New York: J. H. Sears, 1929), 282. George ruined the pâté, which had been sent by Wise's wife, by frying it. Wise became a second lieutenant in the Marine Corps in 1899 and retired as a colonel in 1926. He first commanded the 5th Marine Regiment, 2nd Division, but in late August 1918 he assumed command of the 59th Infantry of the 8th Brigade, 4th Division. See George B. Clark, *Devil Dogs: Fighting Marines of World War I* (New York: Presidio Press, 1999), 408.

42. Ford, *Americans All*, 3; see also Ford's footnote on 147–148.

43. York, *Sergeant York*, 175–176.

44. *Iron County Record*, 30 November 1917.

45. Arlie I. Day, 14 January 1920, box 9, LVA. See Day's biography in appendix B.

46. Moses Randolph, 17 July 1919, box 4, LVA. See Randolph's biography in appendix B.

47. Wylie R. Cooke, 21 August 1919, box 13, LVA. See Cooke's biography in appendix B.

48. Robert W. Marshall, 8 July 1919, box 34, CSL.

49. Zoil A. Beaudoin, 9 April 1919, box 38, CSL.

50. Alden Bell, 15 September 1920, box 3, LVA. See Bell's biography in appendix B.

51. Byron Farwell, *Over There: The United States in the Great War, 1917–1918* (New York: Norton, 1999), 51.

52. James J. Marooney, 17 July 1919, box 34, CSL.

53. Charles S. Pemburn Jr., box 51, CSL. See Pemburn's biography in appendix B.

54. Ensworth M. Godard, 10 July 1919, box 8, CSL.

55. Jewell W. Godard, 9 June 1919, box 8, CSL.

56. Albert S. Voight, 21 August 1920, box 14, LVA. See Voight's biography in appendix B.

57. Joseph R. Cooke, 10 June 1922, box 15, LVA.

58. "Incident connected with the draft of Goochland," box 5, LVA.

59. Drew Gilpin Faust, *This Republic of Suffering: Death and the American Civil War* (New York: Knopf, 2008), 268.

60. Eric T. Dean Jr., *Shook over Hell: Post-Traumatic Stress, Vietnam and the Civil War* (Cambridge, MA: Harvard University Press, 1997), 213.

61. Francis P. Duffy, *Father Duffy's Story* (New York: George H. Doran, 1919), viii.

62. Curtis R. Davis, 5 September 1921, box 20, series II, LVA. See Davis's biography in appendix B.

63. Walter C. Sage, 23 June 1919, box 13, CSL.

64. Seward H. Strickland, 5 September 1919, box 13, CSL.

65. Nelson C. Overton, 7 November 1919, box 13, LVA. See Overton's biography in appendix B.

66. Raymond J. Queenin, 26 August 1919, box 20, CSL. See Queenin's biography in appendix B.

67. Joseph R. Schadel, 2 August 1919, box 13, CSL. See Schadel's biography in appendix B.

68. Albert M. Simons, 8 August 1919, box 13, CSL. See Simons's biography in appendix B.

69. Alexander J. Flynn, 10 August 1919, box 31, CSL. See Flynn's biography in appendix B.

70. Frederick J. Burke, 14 July 1919, box 30, CSL.

71. Arthur L. Cartier, 17 July 1919, box 30, CSL.

72. John M. Jacobs, box 13, LVA. See Jacobs's biography in appendix B.

73. Joseph Cosenzo, 14 May 1935, box 30, CSL.

74. John D. Kinzer, 12 July 1920, box 2, LVA. See Kinzer's biography in appendix B.

75. Dale M. Hoyt, reel 25, USA.

76. Edward H. Roesch, reel 19, USA.

77. Thomas B. Taliaferro, 26 September 1922, box 4, LVA. See Taliaferro's biography in appendix B.

78. Raymond E. Landmesser, 29 May 1919, box 10, CSL.

79. Byron P. Graff, 22 November 1920, box 8, CSL.

80. Thomas N. Williams, 3 October 1919, box 3, LVA. See Williams's biography in appendix B.

81. Harry E. Curry, box 4, LVA. See Curry's biography in appendix B.

82. African Americans represented less than 3 percent of the National Guard. Most served with the 8th Illinois or the 15th New York, and companies of a hundred men came from Massachusetts, Maryland, Ohio, Tennessee, and Washington, D.C. See Michael Lee Lanning, *The African-American Soldier: From Crispus Attucks to Colin Powell*, 2nd ed. (New York: Citadel Press, 2004), 102, and Chad L. Williams, *Torchbearers of Democracy: African American Soldiers in the World War I Era* (Chapel Hill: University of North Carolina Press, 2010), 68.

83. Williams, *Torchbearers of Democracy*, 5–6. Adriane Lentz-Smith's figures for black troops differ slightly from Williams's. According to Lentz-Smith, almost 400,000 African Americans served, 200,000 black doughboys went to France, and 42,000 saw combat. Adriane Lentz-Smith, *Freedom Struggles: African Americans and World War I* (Cambridge, MA: Harvard University Press, 2009), 4, 111.

84. Clifford R. Haskins, 13 November 1919, box 8, CSL.

85. Hugh H. Bishop, 19 March 1921, box 16, LVA. See Bishop's biography in appendix B.

86. Willis B. Godwin, 27 February 1929, box 4, LVA. See Godwin's biography in appendix B.

87. George L. Ayotte, 4 April 1923, box 39, CSL.

88. Nelson F. Waters, 15 July 1919, box 37, CSL. See Waters's biography in appendix B.

89. Louis J. Popolizio, 8 May 1919, box 35, CSL.

90. Hezekiah E. Lofland, box 1, LVA. See Lofland's biography in appendix B.

91. The title of Owen's poem quotes a line from the Roman poet Horace: "Dulce et Decorum est Pro patria mori" (it is sweet and glorious to die for one's country). Owen calls this "The old Lie."

92. Albert W. Stone, reel 17, USA.

93. James E. Chenault, 26 May 1919, box 16, LVA. See Chenault's biography in appendix B.

Chapter 3. Wooden Weapons

1. Frank M. McMurry, *The Geography of the Great War* (New York: Macmillan, 1919), 26–27, provides an excellent map of the United States that shows the layout of every camp.

2. Richard S. Faulkner, *The School of Hard Knocks: Combat Leadership in the American Expeditionary Forces* (College Station: Texas A&M University Press, 2012), 107.

3. Charles T. Holtzman Jr., 25 June 1921, box 8, LVA. The French army issued the first automatic rifle, the 8mm M1915 CSRG (Chauchat), called the "Show-Show" by doughboys. Holtzman might be referring to the Chauchat or to the .30-caliber M1918 Browning Automatic Rifle (BAR), which did not appear on the battlefield until September 1918. By that time, the war was nearly over, but the army made extensive use of the BAR until the late 1960s.

4. Quoted in Harold Elk Straubing, ed., *The Last Magnificent War: Rare Journalistic and Eyewitness Accounts of World War I* (New York: Paragon House, 1989), 221.

5. Philip W. Higgins, box 60, CSL.

6. Jacklin M. Holmes, 17 July 1920, box 4, LVA.

7. Richard H. Baker Jr., 15 September 1919, box 20, series II, LVA.

8. Emory P. Barrow, 11 November 1921, box 2, LVA.

9. Arlie I. Day, 14 January 1920, box 9, LVA.

10. Samuel L. Alexander, 27 April 1918, reel 1, USA.

11. Donald Smythe, *Pershing: General of the Armies* (Bloomington: Indiana University Press, 1986), 8.

12. Ralph P. Howard, box 57, CSL.

13. Harold T. Lyons, box 59, CSL. See Lyons's biography in appendix B.

14. Brack M. Osborne, 27 February 1922, box 6, LVA.

15. David M. Kennedy, *Over Here: The First World War and American Society*, 2nd ed. (Oxford: Oxford University Press, 2004), 198–199.

16. Faulkner, *School of Hard Knocks*, 327.

17. Ensworth M. Godard, 10 July 1919, box 8, CSL.

18. Jewell W. Godard, 9 June 1919, box 8, CSL.

19. Albert M. Simons, 8 August 1919, box 13, CSL.

20. Afanariy Boyko, 15 July 1919, box 29, CSL.

21. John W. Covington, 24 September 1920, box 20, LVA.

22. Thomas J. Bannigan, box 5, CSL.

23. Max Climon, 30 June 1919, box 6, CSL.

24. Stanley W. Elovetsky, 2 August 1920, box 38, CSL.

25. Curry P. Hutchison, 15 December 1919, box 5, LVA.

26. Albert J. Engelberg, 3 November 1919, box 4, LVA.

27. Marcia Black and Robert S. McPherson, "Soldiers, Savers, Slackers, and Spies: Southeastern Utah's Response to World War I," *Utah Historical Quarterly* 63, 1 (Winter 1995): 21.

28. Bert Swindlehurst, reel 22, USA.

29. Roger Batchelder, *Camp Devens* (Boston: Small, Maynard, 1917), 8–9. The lumber figure is calculated from 40 million board feet (40 million board feet × 0.083 = cubic feet).

30. Batchelder, *Camp Devens*, 10.

31. Daniel W. Strickland, *Connecticut Fights: The Story of the 102nd Regiment* (New Haven, CT: Quinnipiac Press, 1930), 60.

32. Charles R. Goddard, 28 August 1919, box 8, CSL. See Goddard's biography in appendix B.

33. Hamilton Du Trienille Jr., 10 September 1919, box 31, CSL. See Du Trienille's biography in appendix B.

34. Dennis F. Flynn, 15 July 1919, box 31, CSL.

35. Thomas Myers, 14 April 1919, reel 16, USA.

36. Mifflin T. Gibbs, 8 August 1919, box 32, CSL.

37. Howard J. Dunn, 6 July 1919, box 31, CSL.

38. Miletus B. Jarman, 7 January 1920, box 9, LVA.

39. Charles L. Hogue, box 15, LVA. See Hogue's biography in appendix B.

40. Leo J. Hill, 29 September 1919, box 32, CSL.

41. Ulysses S. G. Mayo, box 4, LVA.

42. Byron P. Graff, 22 November 1920, box 8, CSL.

43. Seward H. Strickland, 5 September 1919, box 13, CSL.

44. Frederick J. Burke, 14 July 1919, box 30, CSL.

45. Nelson F. Waters, 15 July 1919, box 37, CSL.

46. James O. McKarney, box 11, LVA.

47. Harry E. Curry, box 4, LVA.

48. James R. Miller, 30 April 1919, box 11, CSL.

49. Jack M. Bowen, 23 August 1919, box 13, LVA.

50. Marshall W. Butt, 24 August 1919, box 15, LVA.

51. Frederick E. Benjamin, box 29, CSL.

52. Edward M. Coffman, *The War to End All Wars: The American Military Experience in World War I* (Lexington: University Press of Kentucky, 1998), 35.

53. Dryden L. Phelps, 9 October 1919, box 35, CSL.

54. Wilson H. Whitehouse, 7 June 1920, box 38, CSL. See Whitehouse's biography in appendix B.

55. Francis P. Pallotti, 1 March 1920, box 12, CSL.

56. This number of calories is not much more than what today's recruits receive during basic training. The Military Dietary Reference Intake (MDRI) for men involved in heavy activity is 3,950 calories a day; for those involved in exceptionally heavy activity, it is 4,600 calories a day. See table 2-1, Army Regulation 40-25 (Washington, DC, 15 June 2001), 5.

57. Coffman, *War to End All Wars*, 65.

58. Harvey E. Braxton, 19 December 1922, box 1, LVA.

59. Humbert F. Cofrancesco, 23 July 1919, box 30, CSL. See Cofrancesco's biography in appendix B.

60. Carol R. Byerly, *Fever of War: The Influenza Epidemic in the U.S. Army during World War I* (New York: New York University Press, 2005), 8.

61. Nora B. Sanford, box 9, LVA. See Sanford's biography in appendix B.

62. William A. Bergen, 20 May 1931, box 39, CSL.

63. Robert S. McPherson, "The Influenza Epidemic of 1918: A Cultural Response," *Utah Historical Quarterly* 58, 2 (Spring 1990): 184. See also Byerly, *Fever of War*, 6, and John M. Barry, *The Great Influenza: The Epic Story of the Deadliest Plague in History* (New York: Penguin, 2005), 98.

64. Byron Farwell, *Over There: The United States in the Great War, 1917–1918* (New York: Norton, 1999), 233.

65. Patrick Zylberman, "A Holocaust in a Holocaust: The Great War and the 1918 Spanish Influenza Epidemic in France," in *The Spanish Influenza Pandemic of 1918–19: New Perspectives*, ed. Howard Phillips and David Killingray (London: Routledge, 2003), 192.

66. Jeffrey K. Taubenberger, "Genetic Characterization of the 1918 'Spanish' Influenza Virus," in Phillips and Killingray, *Spanish Influenza*, 41, figure 2.2. Since the Spanish flu may have originated in America (i.e., Fort Riley, Kansas), the mortality rate was higher in the United States than in western Europe. Mark Osborne Humphries, however, argues that the pandemic originated in China; see his article "Paths of Infection: The First World War and the Origins of the 1918 Influenza Pandemic," *War in History* 21, 1 (January 2014): 55–81.

67. Leonard P. Ayres, *The War with Germany: A Statistical Summary*, 2nd ed. (Washington, DC: Government Printing Office, 1919), 126.

68. Leonard J. Arrington, "The Influenza Epidemic of 1918–19 in Utah," *Utah Historical Quarterly* 58, 2 (Spring 1990): 166.

69. Coffman, *War to End All Wars*, 84.

70. Richard C. Roberts, "The Utah National Guard in the Great War, 1917–1918," *Utah Historical Quarterly* 58, 4 (Autumn 1990): 333.

71. Batchelder, *Camp Devens*, 58.

72. Lisa Grunwald and Stephen J. Adler, eds., *Letters of the Century: America 1900–1999* (New York: Dial Press, 1999), 132–133.

73. David Fransen, 12 August 1919, box 7, CSL.

74. Frederick E. Benjamin, box 29, CSL.

75. Donald L. Jacobno, 11 November 1919, box 33, CSL.

76. William J. B. Morris, box 1, LVA. See Morris's biography in appendix B.

77. Charles A. Cormier, 12 September 1919, box 30, CSL.

78. Donald L. Jacobno, 11 November 1919, box 33, CSL.

79. Frank Costello Jr., box 30, CSL.

80. War Service Records, World War I, 1914–1919, Ruth Wyllys Chapter, Daughters of the American Revolution, Connecticut Chapter, No. 3, box 132, Historical Data File, CSL. On 14 May 1917 the army appointed Brown to the Reserve Officers' Training Camp at Fort Myer, Virginia, and later transferred him to Camp Lee, Virginia.

81. Edgar O. Shirley, box 13, CSL.

82. Julian C. Warner, box 14, CSL.

83. Clarence Anderson, reel 1, USA.

84. Harry Keyes, reel 13, USA.

85. John P. Dwyer, 19 December 1921, box 39, CSL. See Dwyer's biography in appendix B.

Chapter 4. Across the Pond

1. Johnson Hagood, *The Services of Supply: A Memoir of the Great War* (Boston: Houghton Mifflin, 1927), 32.

2. Kerry William Bate, "Kanarraville Fights World War I," *Utah Historical Quarterly* 63, 1 (Winter 1995): 33.

3. George B. Clark, ed., *Devil Dogs Chronicle: Voices of the 4th Marine Brigade in World War I* (Lawrence: University Press of Kansas, 2013), 81.

4. Louis M. Lindsay, reel 14, USA.

5. Hagood, *Services of Supply*, 183.

6. Walter H. Anderson, reel 1, USA.

7. Daniel W. Strickland, *Connecticut Fights: The Story of the 102nd Regiment* (New Haven, CT: Quinnipiac Press, 1930), 72.

8. Stanley J. Herzog, *The Fightin' Yanks* (Stamford, CT: Cunningham Print, 1922), 32.

9. Clark, *Devil Dogs Chronicle*, 76–77.

10. Joseph J. O'Connell, 26 September 1919, box 17, CSL.

11. George S. Crockett, 3 April 1923, box 1, LVA.

12. Maurice M. Condon, 29 September 1919, box 6, CSL.

13. Miletus B. Jarman, 7 January 1920, box 9, LVA.

14. Edgar C. Outten, 8 November 1919, box 4, LVA.

15. Matthew M. Quinn, 27 May 1919, box 35, CSL.

16. Charles H. Henderling, 27 June 1919, box 32, CSL.

17. Arthur A. Grove, 18 November 1920, box 9, LVA.

18. Leslie A. Tracy, 10 November 1919, box 14, CSL.

19. Paul T. Wysocki, 25 August 1919, box 8, LVA.

20. Thomas B. McDermott, 24 March 1920, box 11, CSL.

21. John E. Barnes, 10 September 1919, box 13, LVA. See Barnes's biography in appendix B.

22. Leslie H. Patterson, 23 September 1920, box 2, LVA. See Patterson's biography in appendix B.

23. Jack Morris Wright, *A Poet of the Air: Letters of Jack Morris Wright First Lieutenant of the American Aviation in France April, 1917–January, 1918* (Boston: Houghton Mifflin, 1918), 203.

24. Neufchâteau was about thirty-three miles northeast of General Pershing's headquarters in Chaumont, France.

25. Strickland, *Connecticut Fights*, 74.

26. Virginius L. Bland, box 6, LVA.

27. During World War I, the army's most famous newspaper, *Stars and Stripes*, was published from 8 February 1918 to 13 June 1919. The eight-page paper, which came out every Friday, was intended to improve troop morale; it contained jokes, illustrations, advertisements, and articles written by doughboys of various ranks.

28. Jimmy Murrin, "Not a Single One," *Stars and Stripes*, 29 November 1918, 4. Murrin also included his own ode to the cootie in the letter.

29. A. P. Bowen, "If I Were a Cootie," *Stars and Stripes*, 1 November 1918, 4.

30. George C. Pierce, reel 18, USA.

31. "Whole Cootie Clan Rapidly Dying Off," *Stars and Stripes*, 4 April 1919, 3. In the spring of 1919, out of the 454,703 troops examined, only 8,820 had lice.

32. Walter T. Spencer, 1 December 1923, box 7, LVA. See Spencer's biography in appendix B.

33. Strickland, *Connecticut Fights*, 74–75.

34. Russel Muir, reel 16, USA.

35. Frank P. Sibley, *With the Yankee Division in France* (Boston: Little, Brown, 1919), 49.

36. Albertus W. Catlin, *With the Help of God and a Few Marines* (New York: Doubleday, Page, 1919), 24.

37. Frederick M. Wise, *A Marine Tells It to You* (New York: J. H. Sears, 1929), 164.

38. Rob Engen, "Steel against Fire: The Bayonet in the First World War," *Journal of Military and Strategic Studies* 8, 3 (Spring 2006): 14.

39. Wise, *A Marine Tells It*, 35.

40. Harold T. Lyons, box 59, CSL.

41. Fairfield H. Hodges, 25 February 1920, box 15, LVA.

42. Theodore E. Whitney, 16 February 1927, box 14, CSL.

43. Hugh E. Brown, box 13, LVA.

44. Nelson C. Overton, 7 November 1919, box 13, LVA.

45. Philip W. Higgins, box 60, CSL.

46. Eugene M. Kelcy, 11 August 1919, box 9, CSL.

47. John M. Ross, 6 October 1919, box 35, CSL.

48. Abraham Miskin, 5 November 1919, box 11, CSL.

49. Leo J. Hill, 29 September 1919, box 32, CSL.

50. Jacob Salovitz, 20 May 1919, box 36, CSL.

51. George W. Cheney, 10 July 1919, box 15, CSL.

52. Joseph Cosenzo, 14 May 1935, box 30, CSL.

53. Henry Evanier, 3 August 1919, box 11, CSL.

54. John D. Kinzer, 12 July 1920, box 2, LVA.

55. Frank E. Murphy, 11 April 1920, box 11, CSL.

56. Thomas G. Hardy, 5 April 1920, box 9, LVA. See Hardy's biography in appendix B.

57. Albert M. Simons, 8 August 1919, box 13, CSL.

58. John N. Dickerson, 9 July 1919, box 31, CSL. See Dickerson's biography in appendix B.

59. Horton J. Dorkendorff, 4 September 1919, box 31, CSL.

60. Thomas M. Clary, box 2, LVA.

61. Channing W. Daniel, 10 March 1921, box 16, LVA.

62. William G. B. Augermann, 29 August 1919, box 5, CSL. See Augermann's biography in appendix B.

63. Lawrence W. Porter, 5 July 1919, box 35, CSL.

64. John R. Castleman, 15 May 1922, box 19, LVA. See Castleman's biography in appendix B.

65. Robert C. Duval Jr., 23 July 1920, box 16, LVA. See Duval's biography in appendix B.

66. William J. B. Morris, 13 January 1923, box 1, LVA.

67. Anson T. McCook, 27 March 1920, box 11, CSL.

68. Quoted in Richard Pritchett, "Lassies and Doughboys," *Hartford Magazine*, 11 November 1979, 12.

69. Quoted in Daniel J. Sweeney, ed., *History of Buffalo and Erie County 1914–1919* (Buffalo, NY: Committee of One Hundred, 1919), 182. During the war, American soldiers were sometimes called Sammies (after Uncle Sam), but doughboys soon became the most popular moniker. *Stars and Stripes* referred to American troops as doughboys and sometimes as Yankees or Yanks.

70. "Mrs. W. K. Vanderbilt Discusses the Doughboy," *New York Times*, 19 January 1919.

71. Fred W. Chitty, 3 July 1919, box 30, CSL.

72. Samuel Dunn, 31 July 1919, box 7, CSL. See Dunn's biography in appendix B.

73. Charles R. Goddard, 28 August 1919, box 8, CSL.

74. Postcard from Carl C. Senkbeil to John Knoll, box 132, Historical Data File, CSL.

75. Julius I. Twiss, 2 August 1919, box 14, CSL.

76. Solomon Wollman, 11 June 1920 (killed in action; MSR filled out by his mother), box 14, CSL. See Wollman's biography in appendix B.

77. Alvin C. York, *Sergeant York: His Own Life Story and War Diary*, ed. Tom Skeyhill (Garden City, NY: Doubleday, Doran, 1928), 190.

78. Solomon Wollman, box 14, CSL.

79. Fred W. Chitty, 3 July 1919, box 30, CSL.

80. Louis J. Popolizio, 9 May 1919, box 35, CSL.

81. Charles T. Lawson, 26 February 1920, box 6, LVA. See Lawson's biography in appendix B.

82. Clarence H. Brinkley, box 11, LVA.

83. James F. Bonham, 20 September 1920, box 10, LVA.

84. Wylie R. Cooke, 21 August 1919, box 13, LVA.

85. Herman R. White, 3 July 1919, box 37, CSL.

86. Walter B. Haislip, 31 August 1920, box 9, LVA. See Haislip's biography in appendix B.

87. Max L. Cohen, 16 September 1919, box 37, CSL.

88. Harlin Blair, 15 September 1918, reel 2, USA.

89. Ralph L. Goodrich, reel 9, USA.

90. Emory P. Barrow, 11 November 1921, box 2, LVA.

Chapter 5. The Supreme Test

1. Vera Brittain, *Testament of Youth* (New York: Penguin, 2005), 420–421.

2. Frank P. Sibley, *With the Yankee Division in France* (Boston: Little, Brown, 1919), 92.

3. Lloyd Lewis, *Sherman: Fighting Prophet* (Lincoln: University of Nebraska Press, 1993), 637.

4. Casualty figures include army, navy, marines, and air service. If battle death figures are broken down between the Western Front and the Russian campaigns, then 53,265 men were killed in action on the Western Front and 137 men died in combat during the Russian expeditions. For total AEF casualties, see Anne Leland, *American War and Military Operations Casualties: Lists and Statistics* (Washington, DC: Congressional Research Service, 2012), 3.

5. George B. Clark, *Devil Dogs: Fighting Marines of World War I* (New York: Presidio Press, 1999), 94.

6. Floyd P. Gibbons, *"And They Thought We Wouldn't Fight"* (New York: Doran, 1918), 304.

7. During the war, Belleau Wood lay about a quarter of a mile directly south of the town of Belleau.

8. John Keegan, *The First World War* (New York: Knopf, 1999), 411. Another prime example is Niall Ferguson's treatment of the AEF. After dismissing the AEF's combat effectiveness, Ferguson concludes, "It was the *idea* of ever-increasing American reinforcements rather than their actual presence which contributed to the collapse of German morale." Niall Ferguson, *The Pity of War* (New York: Basic Books, 1999), 312–313, 386–387.

9. Robert L. Bullard, *American Soldiers also Fought* (New York: Longmans, Green, 1936), 39.

10. Erich Ludendorff, *Ludendorff's Own Story: August 1914–November 1918*, 2 vols. (New York: Harper, 1919), 2:276.

11. Clarence M. Thompson, 26 April 1921, box 14, CSL. See Thompson's biography in appendix B.

12. Edgar Halyburton, *Shoot and Be Damned* (New York: Covici, Friede, 1932), 33. Duckboards are wooden slats laid over water and mud to form a walkway. Armies on all sides used duckboards during the war to aid in troop movement, especially in trenches. Doughboys dubbed General Smedley D. Butler "General Duckboard" for his use of 80,000 sections of slats at Camp Pontanezen in Brest, France. See Clark, *Devil Dogs*, 402, and Hans Schmidt, *Maverick Marine: General Smedley D. Butler and the Contradictions of American Military History* (Lexington: University Press of Kentucky, 1987), 96–109.

13. Halyburton, *Shoot and Be Damned*, 35.

14. William Mitchell, *Memoirs of World War I: From Start to Finish of Our Greatest War* (New York: Random House, 1960), 290.

15. Albertus W. Catlin, *With the Help of God and a Few Marines* (New York: Double-day, Page, 1919), 171.

16. Byron P. Graff, 22 November 1920, box 8, CSL.

17. Carl J. Schultze, 2 September 1919, box 13, CSL.

18. Robert E. Livingston, reel 14, USA.

19. Leonard R. Bennett, 18 August 1919, box 5, CSL.

20. Emory P. Barrow, 11 November 1921, box 2, LVA.

21. Marcel W. Rice, 21 July 1919, box 35, CSL.

22. James B. Moody Jr., 1 May 1919, box 11, CSL.

23. Walter T. Spencer, 1 December 1923, box 7, LVA.

24. John McDaniel, reel 15, USA.

25. Alexander J. Flynn, 10 August 1919, box 31, CSL.

26. Garnett D. Claman, 6 August 1921, box 11, LVA.

27. Miletus B. Jarman, 7 January 1920, box 9, LVA.

28. George A. Fordham, reel 9, USA.

29. All Europe froze and starved in the winter of 1917–1918. C. Paul Vincent, *The Politics of Hunger: The Allied Blockade of Germany, 1915–1919* (Athens: Ohio University Press, 1985), 160–161, quotes a report predicting that the malnutrition of infants born in Germany between 1916 and 1919 would produce a generation of stunted adults.

30. James T. Duane, *Dear Old "K"* (Boston: n.p., 1922), 23–24.

31. Mitchell, *Memoirs of World War I*, 172.

32. John J. Sullivan, box 13, CSL.

33. Joseph J. O'Connell, 26 September 1919, box 17, CSL.

34. Bert Swindlehurst, reel 22, USA.

35. Raymond S. Jackson, reel 12, USA.

36. Evern E. Saville, reel 20, USA.

37. Frederick M. Wise, *A Marine Tells It to You* (New York: J. H. Sears, 1929), 183.

38. Wilson H. Whitehouse, 7 June 1920, box 38, CSL.

39. Samuel B. Yaffo, 8 November 1919, box 15, CSL. See Yaffo's biography in appendix B.

40. John A. Rosner, 23 July 1919, box 12, CSL.

41. James O. McKarney, box 11, LVA.

42. Edward F. Plumridge, 28 June 1923, box 12, CSL.

43. Catlin, *With the Help of God*, 31.

44. Leo J. Hill, 29 September 1919, box 32, CSL.

45. Richard C. Roberts, "The Utah National Guard in the Great War, 1917–1918," *Utah Historical Quarterly* 58, 4 (Autumn 1990): 327.

46. John J. Eckels, 18 May 1925, box 7, CSL.

47. Samuel C. McDaniel, 19 June 1920, box 8, LVA.

48. John R. Castleman, 15 May 1927, box 19, LVA.

49. Albert M. Simons, 8 August 1919, box 13, CSL.

50. Edward Wilson, 29 July 1919, box 19, CSL.

51. John E. Howell, 30 August 1920, box 12, LVA. See Howell's biography in appendix B.

52. Ray Van Cott Madsen, reel 15, USA.

53. Ernest C. Porter, 24 August 1919, box 14, LVA. See Porter's biography in appendix B.

54. Kerry William Bate, "Kanarraville Fights World War I," *Utah Historical Quarterly* 63, 1 (Winter 1995): 33–35. A local newspaper, the *Iron County Record*, published Stapley's diary on 18 April 1919 under the title "War Experiences from Iron County Soldier's Diary."

55. Henry A. Isleib, 27 September 1919, box 19, CSL.

56. Mark N. Holmes, 22 July 1919, box 16, CSL.

57. Thomas B. McDermott, 24 March 1920, box 11, CSL.

58. Channing W. Daniel, 10 March 1921, box 16, LVA.

59. The Allies dubbed the five heavily fortified defensive positions on the Western Front the Hindenburg Line (called *Stellungen* by the Germans). The Siegfried Line (*Siegfriedstellung*) was the oldest and most elaborate of the five, which defended the terrain from Arras to Soissons.

60. LeRoy H. Cox, reel 6, USA.

61. Clarke O. Kimberly, 10 May 1920, box 22, LVA. See Kimberly's biography in appendix B.

62. Fred Lindbeck, reel 14, USA.

63. Herbert D. May, 26 September 1921, box 3, LVA. See May's biography in appendix B.

64. John A. Holt, reel 11, USA.

65. Walter H. Anderson, reel 1, USA.

66. Millard C. Life, 7 January 1920, box 9, LVA.

67. John P. Dwyer, 19 December 1921, box 39, CSL.

68. Earle T. W. Gronk, 9 December 1919, box 5, LVA. See Gronk's biography in appendix B.

69. Joseph R. Schadel, 2 August 1919, box 13, CSL.

70. Maurice B. Fischman, 6 October 1919, box 31, CSL. See Fischman's biography in appendix B.

71. Ernest E. Strong, reel 22, USA.

72. Niels A. W. Johnson, 15 August 1919, box 16, CSL.

73. Virginius L. Bland, box 6, LVA.

74. Frank E. Murphy, 11 April 1920, box 11, CSL.

75. Michael Fydenkeuez, 11 December 1920, box 7, CSL. See Fydenkeuez's biography in appendix B.

76. John P. Dwyer, 19 December 1921, box 39, CSL.

77. David T. Zabecki, *Steel Wind: Colonel Georg Brüchmuller and the Birth of Modern Artillery* (Westport, CT: Praeger, 1994), 8. See also J. B. A. Bailey, *Field Artillery and Firepower*, 2nd ed. (Annapolis, MD: Naval Institute Press, 2004), 240–270, and Bruce I. Gudmundsson, *On Artillery* (Westport, CT: Praeger, 1993).

78. Robert C. Duval Jr., 23 July 1920, box 16, LVA.

79. Philip W. Higgins, 30 August 1919, box 60, CSL.

80. Douglas C. France, 16 November 1920, box 12, LVA.

81. Stephen J. Weston, 8 November 1933, box 39, CSL.

82. Ibid.

83. Morris Goldstein, 1919, box 32, CSL.

84. Harry S. Campbell, 30 April 1919, box 6, CSL. See Campbell's biography in appendix B.

85. George B. Clark, *The American Expeditionary Force in World War I: A Statistical History, 1917–1919* (Jefferson, NC: McFarland, 2013), 249.

86. Frank E. Roberts, *The American Foreign Legion: Black Soldiers of the 93rd in World War I* (Annapolis, MD: Naval Institute Press, 2004), 203–204.

87. David M. Kennedy, *Over Here: The First World War and American Society*, 2nd ed. (Oxford: Oxford University Press, 2004), 162.

88. Quoted in Emmett J. Scott, *The American Negro in the World War* (New York: Arno Press, 1969), 208.

89. Ibid., 276–277.

90. John S. Fields, 8 December 1919, box 4, LVA.

91. Louis Scowffield, box 4, LVA.

92. Harry E. Curry, box 4, LVA.

93. William P. Jones, 6 May 1920, box 8, LVA.

94. Thomas M. Clary, box 2, LVA.

95. James P. Spencer, 20 April 1921, box 7, LVA.

96. Waverly L. Crawford, 25 November 1919, box 11, LVA. See Crawford's biography in appendix B.

97. John M. Ross, 6 October 1919, box 35, CSL.

98. Hervey Allen, *Toward the Flame* (Lincoln, NE: Bison Books, 2003), 91.

99. By the end of the war, poison gas represented 20 to 40 percent of all artillery shells in each belligerent's army. The AEF's gas shell ratio was 20 percent, with a planned 5 percent increase for 1919. See Tim Cook, *No Place to Run: The Canadian Corps and Gas Warfare in the First World War* (Vancouver: UBC Press, 1999), 214–216. Mark Ethan Grotelueschen, *The AEF Way of War: The American Army and Combat in World War I* (Cambridge: Cambridge University Press, 2007), 52, states that the AEF did not "make adequate use" of chemical weapons during the war.

100. Grant H. Lyman, reel 14, USA.

101. Mary Borden, *The Forbidden Zone* (Garden City, NY: Doubleday, Doran, 1929), i. Although her book was not published until 1929, Borden recorded her impressions (which she calls sketches) during the four years she worked with the French hospital unit.

102. Ibid., 124.

103. Quoted in Miriam B. Murphy, "'If Only I Have the Right Stuff': Utah Women in World War I," *Utah Historical Quarterly* 58, 4 (Autumn 1990): 343–344.

104. Letter from Verna M. Smith to Mrs. Farrar, 8 February 1920, box 12, LVA. See Smith's biography in appendix B.

105. Quoted in Murphy, "'If Only I Have the Right Stuff,'" 345.

106. Grant H. Lyman, reel 14, USA.

107. Ellen N. LaMotte, *The Backwash of War* (New York: G. P. Putnam's Sons, 1934), 89–90. LaMotte first published her book in the autumn of 1916, but it was banned in England and France because its images were considered too damaging to the troops' morale; the book was sold in the United States until America entered the war. LaMotte republished her work in 1934.

108. Wayne H. Castle, reel 2, USA. See Castle's biography in appendix B.

109. Quoted in Noble Warrum, *Utah in the World War: The Men behind the Guns and the Men and Women behind the Men behind the Guns* (Salt Lake City, UT: Arrow Press, 1924), 71.

110. Bland S. Hobson, 16 July 1920, box 17, LVA.

111. Forest Montgomery, reel 16, USA.

112. Seward H. Strickland, 5 September 1919, box 13, CSL.

113. Percy P. Markham, 28 November 1919, box 10, CSL.

114. Evern E. Saville, reel 20, USA.

115. Raleigh A. Bagley, 31 May 1919, box 13, LVA.

116. William E. Mills, 28 December 1921, box 15, LVA.

117. Emile P. Ragna, 31 May 1919, box 12, CSL.

118. Thomas Anderson, reel 1, USA.

119. Elliott M. Braxton Jr., box 20, LVA.

120. Ibid.

121. Ralph W. Lee, 9 September 1921, box 33, CSL.

122. Hyman Lipshetz, 1 October 1919, box 33, CSL.

123. Francis H. Bragan, 28 July 1919, box 5, CSL.

124. Thomas E. Carey, 13 May 1919, box 19, CSL.

125. James Lewis, 19 December 1919, box 37, CSL.

126. Fairfield H. Hodges, 25 February 1920, box 15, LVA.

127. Louis J. Popolizio, 9 May 1919, box 35, CSL.

128. Ephriam Poulter, reel 18, USA.

129. Evern E. Saville, reel 20, USA. The 1915 silent film *The Birth of a Nation*, directed by D. W. Griffith, is the saga of a southern family, the Camerons, during and after the Civil War. Although the movie is strewn with racism, the depiction of the soldiers' bravery on the battlefield captivated theatergoers. As Gary W. Gallagher states, the "sustained courage" of the Confederate soldiers personifies "devotion to duty uncompromised by eventual defeat." This valor enthralled audiences throughout the country. Gary W. Gallagher, *Causes Won, Lost, and Forgotten: How Hollywood and Popular Art Shape What We Know about the Civil War* (Chapel Hill: University of North Carolina Press, 2008), 43. *The Birth of a Nation* grossed over $10 million in 1915. Brad Chadwick, *The Reel Civil War: Mythmaking in American Film* (New York: Knopf, 2001), 132.

130. Lorenzo D. Allcocke, reel 1, USA.

131. Theodore E. Whitney, 16 February 1927, box 14, CSL.

132. Ralph M. Angell, 14 March 1921, box 16, LVA. See Angell's biography in appendix B.

133. C. R. Johnston, reel 12, USA.

134. Ethelbert T. Smith, 8 November 1919, box 13, CSL.

135. James P. Sheehan, 2 November 1920, box 13, CSL.

136. Robert W. Marchant, 17 October 1919, box 10, CSL.

137. Forest Montgomery, reel 16, USA.

138. Quoted in Lisa Grunwald and Stephen J. Adler, eds., *Letters of the Century: America 1900–1999* (New York: Dial Press, 1999), 123–124.

139. Clarence M. Thompson, 28 October 1919, box 14, CSL.

140. Alexander J. Flynn, 10 August 1919, box 31, CSL.

141. Brigham Reese, reel 19, USA.

142. Paul Glaser, box 63, CSL.

143. Samuel A. Morse, 9 October 1919, box 63, CSL.

144. Prescott E. Haskell, 23 September 1920, box 63, CSL.

145. Quoted in George H. Nettleton, ed., *Yale in the World War*, 2 vols. (New Haven, CT: Yale University Press, 1925), 1:333–334. See Mosher's biography in appendix B.

Chapter 6. "Would Not Take Anything for It"

1. Carl von Clausewitz, *On War*, trans. and ed. Michael Howard and Peter Paret (Princeton, NJ: Princeton University Press, 1984), 119.

2. Anne Leland, *American War and Military Operations Casualties: Lists and Statistics* (Washington, DC: Congressional Research Service, 2012), 3. A casualty is defined as a combatant lost to the military, which includes dead, wounded, missing, captured, ill, and status unknown. Around 4,500 Americans became prisoners of war. The number of deaths, 116,516, includes all deaths: killed in action and died from wounds, diseases, and accidents. As a point of comparison, the total deaths for other major belligerents were as follows: Germany, 2,037,000; Russia, 1,811,000; France (including colonies), 1,398,000; Austria-Hungary, 1,100,000; British Empire, 921,000; Ottoman Turkey, 804,000; Italy, 578,000. Niall Ferguson, *The Pity of War* (New York: Basic Books, 1999), 295. Casualty figures from the First World War vary from source to source; many are only best estimates, since solid data does not exist.

3. "Vanderbilt," *New York Times*, 19 January 1919.

4. John Lewis Barkley, *Scarlet Fields: The Combat Memoir of a World War I Medal of Honor Hero* (Lawrence: University Press of Kansas, 2012), 214–215.

5. US Army, *Order of Battle of the United States Land Forces in the World War: American Expeditionary Forces*, 3 vols. (Washington, DC: Center of Military History, 1988), 1:8.

6. Mark Meigs, *Optimism at Armageddon: Voices of American Participants in World War One* (New York: New York University Press, 1997), 69.

7. Since 1926, Germany has spelled the name of the city "Koblenz."

8. Leland, *American War and Military Operations Casualties*, 2.

9. Frank V. Free, reel 9, USA.

10. Ibid.

11. John W. Barton, reel 2, USA.

12. George B. Clark, ed., *Devil Dogs Chronicle: Voices of the 4th Marine Brigade in World War I* (Lawrence: University Press of Kansas, 2013), 355–356.

13. Philip Haxall Bagby, ed., *American Representation in Occupied Germany, 1920–1921*, 2 vols. (Coblenz: American Sources in Germany, 1921), 2:264–265.

14. Quoted in Alexander Barnes, *In a Strange Land: The American Occupation of Germany, 1918–1923* (Atglen, PA: Schiffer Publishing, 2011), 20.

15. Ibid., 178.

16. Erika Kuhlman explores the relationship between German women and the AEF soldiers who remained in Germany until 1923 in her article "American Doughboys and German *Fräuleins*: Sexuality, Patriarchy and Privilege in the American-Occupied Rhineland, 1918–23," *Journal of Military History* 71, 4 (October 2007): 1077–1106.

17. Quoted in Barnes, *In a Strange Land*, 233.

18. Ibid., 52.

19. Ibid., 72.

20. Ibid., 115.

21. Henri Mordacq, *La mentalité allemande: cinq ans de commandement sur le Rhin* (Paris: Plon, 1926), 76. General Mordacq, the former chief of Prime Minister Georges Clemenceau's military cabinet, wrote extensively on military problems during the latter part of the war. Mordacq disliked doughboys marrying German women, and he noted that AFG commander General Henry Allen complained about the issue as well (ibid., 75–76). Mordacq refers to French soldiers as *poilus* (hairy ones), which is the most popular moniker for French soldiers during World War I.

22. "Die Wacht Am Rhein," *Stars and Stripes*, 22 November 1918, 4.

23. David M. Kennedy, *Over Here: The First World War and American Society*, 2nd ed. (Oxford: Oxford University Press, 2004), 205.

24. Carl Noble, *Jugheads behind the Lines* (Caldwell, ID: Caxton Printers, 1938), 204.

25. Edward M. Coffman, *The War to End All Wars: The American Military Experience in World War I* (Lexington: University Press of Kentucky, 1998), 357.

26. Congress passed the Nineteenth Amendment, which gave women the right to vote, on 4 June 1919 and ratified it on 18 August 1920.

27. Kennedy, *Over Here*, 217.

28. Lorenzo Heaps, reel 11, USA.

29. Louis F. Ranlett, *Let's Go! The Story of A.S. No. 2448602* (Boston: Houghton Mifflin, 1927), vii.

30. Humbert F. Cofrancesco, 23 July 1919, box 30, CSL.

31. Ibid.

32. Herman R. Furr, 14 October 1919, box 21, series II, LVA.

33. Leo J. Hill, 29 September 1919, box 32, CSL.

34. Joseph Ryan, 30 November 1919, box 58, CSL.

35. Raymond A. Preston, 1 September 1919, box 58, CSL. See Preston's biography in appendix B.

36. Frank E. Murphy, 11 April 1920, box 11, CSL.

37. Leslie H. Patterson, 23 September 1920, box 2, LVA.

38. William E. Steven, 7 November 1919, box 13, CSL.

39. Herman A. Jacot, 9 September 1919, box 33, CSL.

40. Philip W. Higgins, 30 August 1919, box 60, CSL.

41. Edward B. Allen, 11 August 1919, box 15, CSL.

42. Julius I. Twiss, 2 August 1919, box 14, CSL.

43. Anson T. McCook, 27 March 1920, box 11, CSL.

44. Albert M. Simons, 8 August 1919, box 13, CSL.

45. Kieran J. Harford, 5 February 1921, box 32, CSL.

46. Curry P. Hutchison, 15 December 1919, box 5, LVA.

47. Farwell Knapp, 18 February 1922, box 9, CSL.

48. John W. Covington, 14 September 1920, box 20, LVA.

49. Eugene M. Kelcy, 11 August 1919, box 9, CSL.

50. Joseph E. Rendinell and George Pattullo, *One Man's War: The Diary of a Leatherneck* (New York: J. H. Sears, 1928), 177.

51. Seth A. Beeker, 1919, box 29, CSL.

52. Dexter A. Cargill, 30 November 1920, box 30, CSL.

53. Garnett D. Claman, 6 August 1921, box 11, LVA.

54. Edward S. Webster, box 14, CSL.

55. Stephen J. Weston, 8 November 1933, box 39, CSL.

56. Ratcliffe M. Hills, 1 October 1935, box 8, CSL. See Hills's biography in appendix B.

57. For an analysis of shell shock as a metaphor, see Jay Winter, "Shell-shock and the Cultural History of the Great War," *Journal of Contemporary History* 35, 1 (January 2000): 7–11. The entire issue, edited by Winter, is devoted to shell shock and includes eight essays by experts in the field.

58. The term *shell shock* varied in different languages, but the core meaning remained the same. The French called it *hystérie de guerre* (war hysteria). See Marc Roudebush, "A Battle of Nerves: Hysteria and Its Treatments in France during World War I," in *Traumatic Pasts: History, Psychiatry and Trauma in the Modern Age, 1870–1930*, ed. Mark S. Micale and Paul Lerner (Cambridge: Cambridge University Press, 2001): 253–279, and Laurent Tatu and Julien Bogousslavsky, *La folie au front: La grande bataille des névroses de guerre (1914–1918)* (Paris: Imago, 2012). Germany used the term *Kriegszitterer* (war quiverers), and German veterans said they experienced *seelische Ershütterung* (shaking of the soul). See Jason Crouthamel, *The Great War and German Memory: Society, Politics and Psychological Trauma, 1914–1945* (Exeter, UK: University of Exeter Press, 2009), 221, 4.

59. Jean A. Langlois Orman, Jess F. Kraus, Eduard Zaloshnja, and Ted Miller, "Epidemiology," in *Textbook of Traumatic Brain Injury*, 2nd ed., ed. Jonathan M. Silver, Thomas W. McAllister, and Stuart C. Yudofsky (Washington, DC: American Psychiatric Publishing, 2011), 3.

60. American Psychiatric Association, *Diagnostic and Statistical Manual of Mental Disorders*, 5th ed. (Washington, DC: American Psychiatric Publishing, 2013), 274.

61. Derek Summerfield, "Post-traumatic Stress Disorder in Doctors Involved in the Omagh Bombing," *British Medical Journal* 320, 7244 (May 2000): 1276. Summerfield has written a great deal about PTSD. For a synopsis of his findings, see Derek Summerfield, "The Invention of Posttraumatic Stress Disorder and the Social Usefulness of a Psychiatric Category," *British Medical Journal* 322, 7278 (January 2001): 95–98.

62. See the pioneering work of Didier Fassin and Richard Rechtman, *The Empire of*

Trauma: An Inquiry into the Condition of Victimhood, trans. Rachel Gomme (Princeton, NJ: Princeton University Press, 2009). Fassin and Rechtman conclude that the victim is now a celebrity in society; as a result, the PTSD label is applied to almost any stressful event, with the goal of "social recognition and financial compensation," and "ultimately, it defines the empirical way in which contemporary societies problematize the meaning of their moral responsibility in relation to the distress of the world" (ibid., 280, 284). For a taut analysis of trauma and the modern role of the victim in society, see Richard Rechtman, "Enquête sur la condition de victime," *Étvdes: revue de culture contemporaine* (February 2011): 175–186.

63. Nigel C. Hunt, *Memory, War and Trauma* (Cambridge: Cambridge University Press, 2010), 123.

64. Daryl S. Paulson and Stanley Krippner, *Haunted by Combat: Understanding PTSD in War Veterans Including Women, Reservists, and Those Coming Back from Iraq* (Westport, CT: Praeger Security International, 2007), 8. For Isaac's life, see Genesis 20–28.

65. One example that perpetuates the myth of the shell-shocked, disillusioned doughboy is the popular HBO series *Boardwalk Empire*. It takes place during the Prohibition era and features two veterans: James Darmody (a former Princeton University student) and Richard Harrow. Both men return from the war "traumatized," with physical and mental scars, and find solace as violent gangsters. The show also depicts the notorious Al Capone, who claims he served with the "Lost Battalion" and received his facial scars in battle. But Al's brother, James, is the only Capone who was actually a doughboy (and he served with distinction). Laurence Bergreen, *Capone: The Man and the Era* (New York: Simon and Schuster, 1994), 41–42.

66. Sidney I. Schwabe, "The Experiment in Occupational Therapy at Base Hospital 117, AEF," *Mental Hygiene* 3 (1919): 590.

67. Edgar Jones and Simon Wessely, *Shell Shock to PTSD: Military Psychiatry from 1900 to the Gulf War* (Hove, UK: Psychology Press, 2005), 32–33.

68. Earle T. W. Gronk, 9 December 1919, box 5, LVA.

69. Stephen Crane, *The Red Badge of Courage: A Norton Critical Edition*, 4th ed., ed. Donald Pizer and Eric Carl Link (New York: Norton, 2008), 104.

70. Beth Linker, *War's Waste: Rehabilitation in World War I* (Chicago: University of Chicago Press, 2011), 2–6. The laws establishing rehabilitation programs for veterans led to the creation of the Veteran's Bureau in 1921, later renamed the Veterans Administration and today called the Department of Veterans Affairs. Ibid., 188.

71. See Steven Trout, *On the Battlefield of Memory: The First World War and American Remembrance, 1919–1941* (Birmingham: University of Alabama Press, 2010).

72. Edwin R. Carter, 29 July 1919, box 6, CSL.

73. Arthur A. Grove, 18 November 1920, box 9, LVA.

74. William F. Bartlett, 21 October 1919, box 63, CSL.

75. Edward G. Pobuda, 22 May 1919, box 64, CSL.

76. Edwin B. J. Priest, box 35, CSL.

77. Wilber S. Jewell, 16 September 1919, box 33, CSL.

78. Leonard R. Bennett, 18 August 1919, box 5, CSL.

79. Adam P. Rubinousky, 18 June 1926, box 63, CSL.

80. Prescott E. Haskell, 23 September 1920, box 63, CSL.

81. Paul M. Atkins, 20 October 1919, box 29, CSL.

82. Russell Y. Moore, 9 May 1919, box 11, CSL.

83. Harold J. Dougan, 9 August 1919, box 15, CSL.

84. Edgar C. Outten, 8 November 1919, box 4, LVA.

85. Wilson H. Whitehouse, 7 June 1920, box 38, CSL.

86. Morris Goldstein, 1919, box 32, CSL.

87. Sydney D. Pinney, 21 August 1920, box 12, CSL.

88. Douglas C. France, 16 November 1920, box 12, LVA.

89. Carroll B. Case, 6 September 1919, box 6, CSL. See Case's biography in appendix B.

90. James O. McKarney, box 11, LVA.

91. Henry P. Lynch, 5 September 1919, box 33, CSL.

92. Isadore M. Levine, 7 December 1919, box 33, CSL.

93. Eugene M. Lamb, reel 13, USA.

94. Leroy Newbold, reel 17, USA.

95. William P. Nye, 14 February 1921, box 22, LVA.

96. Mark N. Holmes, 22 July 1919, box 16, CSL.

97. William N. Webb, reel 23, USA.

98. Parley O. Pratt, reel 18, USA.

99. William W. Parker, 22 August 1919, box 22, LVA.

100. Emil H. Miller, November 1919, box 63, LVA.

101. Jonathan H. Ebel, *Faith in the Fight: Religion and the American Soldier in the Great War* (Princeton, NJ: Princeton University Press, 2010), 2.

102. David Reed, box 1, LVA.

103. Edward B. Caulfield, 11 December 1919, box 6, CSL.

104. Earle T. W. Gronk, 9 December 1919, box 5, LVA.

105. Ulysses H. Brockway, 10 May 1920, box 5, CSL.

106. James P. Sheehan, 5 November 1920, box 13, CSL.

107. Arthur E. Westphal, 4 April 1920, box 14, CSL.

108. Stillman F. Westbrook, 26 June 1919, box 14, CSL. Westbrook references John Masefield, *The War and the Future* (New York: Macmillan, 1918), 73–74. Masefield himself quoted an unnamed British officer and then explained why the Western Front was so dull, dirty, and dangerous.

109. Stillman F. Westbrook, 26 June 1919, box 14, CSL.

110. Cyrus C. Washburn, 2 May 1919, box 14, CSL.

111. Earle A. Penfield, 16 July 1919, box 12, CSL.

112. William G. B. Augermann, 29 August 1919, box 5, CSL.

113. Thomas N. Williams, 3 October 1919, box 3, LVA.

114. John Knudson, 22 July 1919, box 33, CSL.

115. Charles H. Henderling, 27 June 1919, box 32, CSL.

116. Quoted in Joseph P. Demaree, *History of Company A (308th Infantry) of the Lost Battalion* (New York: George U. Harvey, 1920), 7–8.

117. Alvin C. York, *Sergeant York: His Own Life Story and War Diary*, ed. Tom Skeyhill

(Garden City, NY: Doubleday, Doran, 1928), 212–213.

118. Charles L. Hogue, 1 August 1919, box 15, LVA.

119. Ibid.

120. James P. Spencer, 26 April 1921, box 3, LVA.

121. John M. Ross, 6 October 1919, box 35, CSL.

122. Harry E. Curry, box 4, LVA.

123. John S. Fields, 8 December 1919, box 4, LVA.

124. Thomas M. Clary, box 2, LVA.

125. Moses Randolph, 17 July 1919, box 4, LVA.

126. Emory P. Barrow, 11 November 1921, box 2, LVA.

127. William J. B. Morris, 13 January 1923, box 1, LVA.

128. Wilbur T. Brownley, 18 August 1919, box 13, LVA. See Brownley's biography in appendix B.

129. Noble, *Jugheads*, 204–205.

130. Arthur G. Empey, *First Call* (New York: G. P. Putnam's Sons, 1918), 319–320.

131. Orswald Fisher, 12 August 1919, box 16, CSL.

Conclusion

1. Quoted in Lloyd Lewis, *Sherman: Fighting Prophet* (Lincoln: University of Nebraska Press, 1993), 637.

2. *Enquirer and News* (Battle Creek, MI), 18 November 1933. Charles O. Brown sat next to Sherman on the day he gave this speech and transcribed the general's words. Most of Sherman's biographers do not mention this speech but do discuss the 1880 "war is hell" one. See James M. Merrill, *William Tecumseh Sherman* (Chicago: Rand McNally, 1971), 379–380. John F. Marszalek claims that Sherman said "war is hell" many times throughout his life—before, during, and after the Civil War. John F. Marszalek, *Sherman: A Soldier's Passion for Order* (New York: Vintage Books, 1994), 476–477. See also Michael Fellman, *Citizen Sherman: A Life of William Tecumseh Sherman* (New York: Random House, 1995), 306.

3. John Whiteclay Chambers II, *To Raise an Army: The Draft Comes to Modern America* (New York: Free Press, 1987), 186.

4. Drew Gilpin Faust, *This Republic of Suffering: Death and the American Civil War* (New York: Knopf, 2008), 266. This reaction can occur when a country loses a catastrophic proportion of its population to war; for example, Britain and Germany reached back to the Middle Ages and connected the noble sacrifices of 1914–1918 with the warrior culture and knights of old. For an in-depth study of this phenomenon, see Stefan Goebel, *The Great War and Medieval Memory: War, Remembrance and Medievalism in Britain and Germany, 1914–1940* (Cambridge: Cambridge University Press, 2007), and George L. Mosse, *Fallen Soldiers: Reshaping the Memory of the World Wars* (New York: Oxford University Press, 1990). Mosse argues that the "Myth of the War Experience" enabled the Nazis to justify war and convince German citizens of their ideological war aims; in particular, see 159–181. For the number of Civil War dead, see J. David Hacker, "A Census-Based Count of the Civil War," *Civil War History* 57, 4 (De cember 2011): 307–348.

5. Stanley Wertheim, *The Crane Log: A Documentary Life of Stephen Crane, 1871–1900* (New York: G. K. Hall, 1994), 141.

6. Stephen Crane, *The Red Badge of Courage: A Norton Critical Edition*, 4th ed., ed. Donald Pizer and Eric Carl Link (New York: Norton, 2008), 103.

7. Ibid., 104.

8. John Higham, "The Reorientation of American Culture in the 1890s," in ibid., 139–151.

9. Oliver Optic, *Taken by the Enemy* (Lake Wales, FL: Lost Classics Book Company, 1998), 9.

10. Ibid., 41.

11. Oliver Optic, *Within the Enemy's Lines* (Lake Wales, FL: Lost Classics Book Company, 1998), 22.

12. For a closer inspection of the effects of the Spanish-American War, see Kristin L. Hoganson, *Fighting for American Manhood: How Gender Politics Provoked the Spanish-American and Philippine-American Wars* (New Haven, CT: Yale University Press, 1998).

13. Joseph E. Persico, "FDR Sees the Elephant," *Quarterly Journal of Military History* 20, 4 (Summer 2008): 28.

14. William L. Langer, *Gas and Flame in World War I* (New York: Knopf, 1965), xviii.

15. Sidney R. Godfrey, reel 9, USA.

16. C. Ralph Amott, reel 1, USA.

17. Jesse C. Larsen, reel 13, USA.

18. Quoted in Richard C. Roberts, "The Utah National Guard in the Great War, 1917–1918," *Utah Historical Quarterly* 58, 4 (Autumn 1990): 329.

19. Ibid.

20. William S. Willes, reel 24, USA.

21. Pindar, *The Odes and Selected Fragments*, trans. Richard Stoneman (London: Everyman Library, 1997), 377, fragment 110.

22. Mike Sedlak, 25 July 1919, box 53, CSL. See Sedlak's biography in appendix B.

23. George S. Crockett, 3 April 1923, box 1, LVA.

24. John E. Howell, 30 August 1920, box 12, LVA.

25. Charles M. Pratt, reel 18, USA.

26. Alvin C. York, *Sergeant York: His Own Life Story and War Diary*, ed. Tom Skeyhill (Garden City, NY: Doubleday, Doran, 1928), 236. York published his diary and wrote his autobiography ten years after the war to raise funds to build a school in his hometown of Pall Mall, Tennessee.

27. John J. Deloughery, 14 July 1919, box 31, CSL.

28. Vahow Shabazian, 20 July 1919, box 53, CSL. See Shabazian's biography in appendix B.

29. Amillo Aiello, 1 May 1919, box 29, CSL.

30. Otis H. Culver, 5 July 1919, box 30, CSL.

31. David C. Dettor, 16 September 1921, box 11, LVA. See Dettor's biography in appendix B.

32. Helmut Walser Smith, "The Talk of Genocide, the Rhetoric of Miscegenation:

Notes on Debates in the German Reichstag concerning Southwest Africa, 1904–1914," in *The Imperialist Imagination: German Colonialism and Its Legacy*, ed. Sara Friedrichsmeyer, Sara Lennox, and Susanne Zantop (Ann Arbor: University of Michigan Press, 1998), 107–109. Also see Isabel V. Hull, *Absolute Destruction: Military Culture and the Practices of War in Imperial Germany* (Ithaca, NY: Cornell University Press, 2005), 5–90.

33. About 200,000 colonial troops served for France. It drew these colonial troops from West Africa, Equatorial Africa, Madagascar, and Indochina. Three excellent studies on the *Tirailleurs Sénégalais* are Richard S. Fogarty, *Race and War in France: Colonial Subjects in the French Army, 1914–1918* (Baltimore: Johns Hopkins University Press, 2008); Marc Michel, *Les Africains et la Grande Guerre: l'appel à l'Afrique, 1914–1918* (Paris: Karthala, 2003); and Myron Echenberg, *Colonial Conscripts: The Tirailleurs Sénégalais in French West Africa, 1857–1960* (Portsmouth, NH: Heinemann, 1991).

34. Lowell Thomas, *Woodfill of the Regulars* (London: William Heinemann, 1930), 238.

35. Stanley J. Herzog, *The Fightin' Yanks* (Stamford, CT: Cunningham Print, 1922), 55.

36. William C. Harvey and Eric T. Harvey, eds., *Letters from Verdun: Frontline Experiences of an American Volunteer in World War I France* (Philadelphia: Casemate, 2009), 53–54.

37. The German army murdered 1,500 to 3,000 African soldiers in the summer of 1940 and took no black prisoners. See Raffael Scheck, *Hitler's African Victims: The German Army Massacres of Black French Soldiers in 1940* (Cambridge: Cambridge University Press, 2006), 165; for a detailed look at the murders, see ibid., 54–57, "Table 1. List of Recorded Killings, May–June 1940." For a superb text that goes beyond military matters, see Clarence Lusane, *Hitler's Black Victims: The Historical Experiences of Afro-Germans, European Blacks, Africans and African Americans in the Nazi Era* (New York: Routledge, 2002).

38. The AEF deployed 200,000 African Americans to France, 40,000 of whom participated in combat. See Michael Lee Lanning, *The African-American Soldier: From Crispus Attucks to Colin Powell*, 2nd ed. (New York: Citadel Press, 2004), 133.

39. For a comprehensive examination of lynching during this time, see Amy Louise Wood, *Lynching and Spectacle: Witnessing Racial Violence in America, 1890–1940* (Chapel Hill: University of North Carolina Press, 2009).

40. W. E. B. Du Bois, "Close Ranks," *Crisis* 16, 3 (July 1918): 111. A year later, Du Bois wrote a retraction, lamenting that the United States had not changed: "It lynches. . . . It disfranchises its own citizens. . . . It encourages ignorance. . . . It steals from us. . . . It insults us." *Crisis* 18, 1 (May 1919): 13.

41. James T. Spencer, 25 April 1921, box 3, LVA.

42. Benjamin Skinner, 20 August 1919, box 14, LVA. See Skinner's biography in appendix B.

43. Jacob M. Sampson, 6 April 1921, box 19, LVA. See Sampson's biography in appendix B.

44. Christopher C. Watts, 3 February 1920, box 15, LVA. See Watts's biography in appendix B.

45. Willis B. Godwin, 27 February 1920, box 4, LVA.

46. Harvey and Harvey, *Letters from Verdun*, 54.

47. Waverly L. Crawford, 25 November 1919, box 11, LVA.

48. Vernon Smith, 19 May 1919, box 8, LVA. See Smith's biography in appendix B.

49. Moses Randolph, 17 July 1919, box 4, LVA.

50. Shortly after the armistice, new race riots broke out in Arkansas, Illinois, South Carolina, Texas, and Washington, D.C. In addition, forced labor of blacks became rampant. The most famous case of forced labor involved John S. Williams, who murdered or aided in the murder of eleven African Americans on his farm in 1921. See Douglas A. Blackmon, *Slavery by Another Name: The Re-enslavement of Black People in America from the Civil War to World War II* (New York: Doubleday, 2008), 360, 363. For a comprehensive study of the Williams murders, see Gregory A. Freeman, *Lay This Body Down: The 1921 Murders of Eleven Plantation Slaves* (Chicago: Chicago Review Press, 1999).

51. Peter Vellon, "'Between White Men and Negroes': The Perception of Southern Italian Immigrants through the Lens of Italian Lynchings," in *Anti-Italianism: Essays on a Prejudice*, ed. William J. Connell and Fred L. Gardaphé (New York: Palgrave Macmillan, 2010), 25.

52. Anthony V. Riccio, *The Italian American Experience in New Haven* (Albany: State University of New York Press, 2006), 61.

53. York, *Sergeant York*, 202–203.

54. Americus Paoletti, box 51, CSL. See Paoletti's biography in appendix B.

55. Robert Deilus, 7 August 1920, box 56, CSL. See Deilus's biography in appendix B.

56. Frank Piazza, 14 August 1919, box 20, CSL. See Piazza's biography in appendix B.

57. Giuseppe S. Peronne, 15 July 1920, box 42, CSL. See Peronne's biography in appendix B.

58. Salvatore Distefano, 7 January 1920, box 61, CSL. See Distefano's biography in appendix B.

59. John F. Carini, 26 August 1919, box 60, CSL. See Carini's biography in appendix B.

60. For a detailed study of Italian military decline, see Gregory Hanlon, *The Twilight of a Military Tradition: Italian Aristocrats and European Conflicts, 1560–1800* (New York: Holmes and Meier, 1998).

61. John A. Thayer, *Italy and the Great War: Politics and Culture, 1870–1915* (Madison: University of Wisconsin Press, 1964), vii.

62. Leo Braudy, *From Chivalry to Terrorism: War and the Changing Nature of Masculinity* (New York: Knopf, 2003), 378.

63. Quoted in Daniel J. Sweeney, ed., *History of Buffalo and Erie County 1914–1919* (Buffalo, NY: Committee of One Hundred, 1919), 76.

64. Quoted in Tim Cook, "The Politics of Surrender: Canadian Soldiers and the Killing of Prisoners in the Great War," *Journal of Military History* 70, 3 (July 2006): 638.

65. Ibid., 650.

66. Langer, *Gas and Flame*, 121. Langer was teaching modern languages at a New England boarding school in November 1917 when he volunteered to help the 23rd Engineers translate French and German. Instead, he found himself in the "Gas and Flame" 30th Engineers, where he served as a sergeant.

67. William L. Langer, *In and Out of the Ivory Tower: The Autobiography of William L. Langer* (New York: Neale Watson Academic Publications, 1977), 98.

68. Robert C. Duval Jr., 23 July 1920, box 16, LVA.

69. Herman R. Furr, 14 October 1919, box 21, LVA.

70. John R. Castleman, 15 May 1922, box 19, LVA.

71. Thomas G. Hardy, 5 April 1920, box 9, LVA.

72. Frederick W. Rowe, 28 April 1919, box 39, CSL.

73. In 1946 psychologists Roy L. Swank and Walter E. Marchand published their study on combat fatigue, based on the 1944 Normandy campaign. They claimed that a soldier reached maximum combat efficiency in about three weeks, but at two months, he reached the stage of emotional exhaustion. Roy L. Swank and Walter E. Marchand, "Combat Neuroses: The Development of Combat Exhaustion," *Archives of Neurology and Psychiatry* 55 (1946): 236–247.

74. Bruno Cabanes, *La Victoire Endeuillée: La sortie de guerre des soldats français, 1918–1920* (Paris: Seuil, 2004), 501.

75. Langer, *Gas and Flame*, xix.

76. American figures calculated from Anne Leland, *American War and Military Operations Casualties: Lists and Statistics* (Washington, DC: Congressional Research Service, 2012), 3. French figures calculated from Jean-Baptiste Duroselle, *La Grande Guerre des Français: L'incompréhensible* (Paris: Perrin, 1994), 7; Duroselle, however, uses 1,560 days and rounds down to 890 deaths per day. My formulas are as follows: for America—116,516 deaths ÷ 356 days (20 November 1917 to 11 November 1918) = 327 deaths per day; for France—1,397,000 deaths ÷ 1,557 days (7 August 1914 to 11 November 1918) = 897 deaths per day.

77. Frederic C. Bartlett, *Psychology and the Soldier* (Cambridge: Cambridge University Press, 1927), 175. See 174–179 for Bartlett's discussion of the progression of the soldier's psyche.

78. Charles T. Clement, reel 25, USA.

79. Frank A. Holden, *War Memories* (Athens, GA: Athens, 1922), 12–13.

80. York, *Sergeant York*, 304.

81. Hugh H. Bishop, box 16, LVA.

82. Edward F. Plumridge, 28 June 1923, box 12, CSL.

83. Frank A. Starr, 6 May 1919, box 55, CSL. See Starr's biography in appendix B.

84. Lawrence T. Hager, 6 May 1921, box 55, CSL. See Hager's biography in appendix B.

85. Samuel George, 24 June 1919, box 55, CSL. See George's biography in appendix B.

86. Patrick Wynne, 21 July 1919, box 54, CSL. See Wynne's biography in appendix B.

87. Harry B. L. Marvin, 18 April 1919, box 62, CSL.

88. Walter H. Anderson, reel 1, USA.

89. Elizabeth Loftus and Katherine Ketcham, *The Myth of Repressed Memory: False Memories and Allegations of Sexual Abuse* (New York: St. Martin's Press, 1994), 4.

90. Langer, *Gas and Flame*, xvii.

91. Mark Grimsley connects Sherman's marches to the *chevauchée* in *The Hard Hand of War* (Cambridge: Cambridge University Press, 1995), 190–191, 214.

92. For an extensive examination of Sherman's legacy from 1865 to the present, see

Edward Caudill and Paul Ashdown, *Sherman's March in Myth and Memory* (Lanham, MD: Rowman and Littlefield, 2008).

93. Lewis, *Sherman*, 637.

Appendix A

1. Council of National Defense minutes, microfilm, NARA II.

2. Lester J. Cappon, "The Collection of World War I Materials in the States," *American Historical Review* 48, 4 (July 1943): 734.

3. Connecticut Public Acts, January session 1919, chapter 126, senate bill 53, CSL.

4. Connecticut Military Service Record, box 168, War Records Department, Historical Data File, CSL.

5. The sixteen states were California, Connecticut, Delaware, Georgia, Illinois, Indiana, Iowa, Kentucky, Maryland, Minnesota, New Jersey, New York, North Carolina, Pennsylvania, Texas, and Virginia.

6. For a detailed look at the report, see Waldo G. Leland and Newton D. Mereness, eds., *Introduction to the American Official Sources for the Economic and Social History of the World War* (New Haven, CT: Yale University Press, 1926).

7. Six years later, a second major Internet search provided a great deal of information. Success in this second round was due to better search engines, more detailed state websites, and more aggressive and superior tactics on my part. Further searches and research in recent years have uncovered no new data on the MSRs.

8. Christina K. Schaefer, *The Great War: A Guide to the Service Records of All the World's Fighting Men and Volunteers* (Baltimore: Genealogical Publishing, 1998), 141–155. Schaefer's exhaustive guide compiles all World War I primary sources for each state. Since my original search in 2000, three other invaluable guides to AEF sources have been published: James T. Controvich, *The United States in World War I: A Bibliographic Guide* (Lanham, MD: Scarecrow Press, 2012); David R. Woodward, *America and World War I: A Selected Annotated Bibliography of English-Language Sources* (New York: Routledge, 2007); and Edward G. Lengel, *World War I Memories and Annotated Bibliography of Personal Accounts Published in English since 1919* (Lanham, MD: Scarecrow Press, 2004).

9. Texas State Archives, e-mail message to author, 20 January 2006; Massachusetts State Archives, 8 February 2006.

10. Vermont State Archives, e-mail message to author, 23 February 2006.

11. Vermont eight-page questionnaire, box 135, Historical Data File, CSL.

12. Federal government, e-mail message to author, 26 January 2006; Department of the Army, United States Army Heritage and Education Center, MHI, e-mail message to author, 14 February 2006.

13. Indiana State Archives, e-mail message to author, 23 February 2006.

14. Indiana State Library, e-mail message to author, 3 March 2006.

15. National Headquarters, Selective Service System, e-mail message to author, 3 February 2006.

16. The Selective Service System drafted 516,212 men in 1917 and 2,294,084 men in 1918, for a total of 2,810,296 men drafted during World War I. See http://www.sss.gov/induct.htm.

17. Joint Force Headquarters, District of Columbia National Guard, e-mail message to author, 17 February 2006.

18. Library of Congress, e-mail message to author, 15 February 2006.

19. *War History Commission News Letter* 3 (October 1919), War Historical Commission Records, box 168, LVA.

20. George S. Godard, *Report of State Librarian for the Two Years Ended June 30, 1922* (Hartford: State Archives, Connecticut State Library, 1922), 90.

21. Vermont's questionnaire (never issued) also had its state seal on the first page and requested additional information on the last page, similar to those of Minnesota and Utah.

22. Arthur Kyle Davis, Virginia, to Department of Archives and History, Wyoming, 30 June 1922, Records of State Historian File, 1916–1924, WSA.

23. Thomas M. Owen, Alabama, to Eunice G. Anderson, Wyoming, 12 October 1918, WSA.

24. Eunice G. Anderson, Wyoming, to Arthur Kyle Davis, Virginia, 15 July 1922, WSA.

25. Eunice G. Anderson, Wyoming, to Arthur Kyle Davis, Virginia, 30 June 1921, WSA.

26. Tennessee World War I Veterans' Questionnaires, Tennessee State Library and Archives, http://www.tennessee.gov/tsla/history/military/ww1quest.htm.

27. Tennessee, Senate Joint Resolution 12, 1919, Records of Tennessee Senate, 1919, Tennessee State Library and Archives.

28. Virginia World War I History Commission Questionnaires Collection, LVA, http://www.lva.lib.va.us/whatwehave/mil/wwiqabout.htm.

29. New York State Archive, *A Spirit of Sacrifice: New York's Response to the Great War: A Guide to Records Relating to World War I* (New York: New York State Archives, 1993), 8.

30. WWI Veterans Database, CSL, http://www.cslib.org/ww1.asp.

31. World War I service questionnaires, 1914–1918, series 85298, USA, http://historyresearch.utah.gov/inventories/85298.html.

32. Lewis B. Hershey, *History of Furnishing Statement of Service Cards to the States, 1792–1948* (Washington, DC: Government Printing Office, 1949), 6.

33. Although Utah was one of the four key states to issue MSRs, its form bears little resemblance to those of Connecticut, Minnesota, and Virginia.

34. Col. C. R. Keiley to Arthur Kyle Davis, 27 January 1919, War Historical Commission Records, box 153, LVA.

35. Summary of Conference of Representatives of State War Historical Agencies, 9–10 September 1919, Record Group 62, Records of the Council of National Defense, box 913, NARA II.

Bibliography

Archival Sources

Connecticut State Library, State Archives, Hartford, CT
  George Goddard Papers
  Historical Data File, War Records Department, Record Group 12
  Map File, World War I, 1917–1920, War Records Department, Record Group 12
  Military Service Questionnaires, 1920–1930, War Records Department, Record Group 12
Library of Congress, Washington, DC
  John J. Pershing Papers
Library of Virginia, Richmond, VA
  War History Commission Records, 19 Series, Record Group 112
      Series I, Individual Service Records (Questionnaires)
      Series II, Virginians of Distinguished Service
      Series III, Virginia Military Organizations
      Series IV, Virginia's Camps and Cantonments
      Series V, Virginia Schools and Colleges
      Series VI, County Source Material
      Series VII, City Source Material
      Series VIII, Selective Service and Volunteers
      Series IX, Virginia War Diaries and Incidents
      Series X, Scrapbooks
      Series XI, Office Files
      Series XII, First Virginia Council of Defense
      Series XIII, Virginia Agricultural Council of Safety
      Series XIV, Second Virginia Council of Defense
      Series XV, Margaret Ethel Kelley Kern Papers
      Series XVI, H. R. McIlwaine Papers
      Series XVII, Miscellaneous Records
      Series XVIII, Lynchburg City Committee Records
      Series XIX, Prince Edward County Committee Records

Minnesota Historical Society, St. Paul, MN
    Casualty Lists and Related Materials, 1918–1920
    Edward Karow Scrapbooks
    Gold Star Roll, 1918–1921
    Loren W. Collins and Family Papers
    Minnesota War Records Commission Collection, 1917–1921
    Rollo Lester Mudge Papers
    William K. Fraser Papers
    World War I Bonus Files and Index, 1919–1943
    World War I Disallowed Bonus Files, 1919–1941
    World War I Military Service Lists, ca. 1917–1920s
    World War I Military Service Records, 1918–1920
National Archives, Washington, DC, and College Park, MD
    Records of the American Expeditionary Forces, 1917–1923, Record Group 120
    Records of the Council of National Defense, Record Group 62
New York State Archives, New York, NY
    Military Service Records, Adjutant General's Office
Tennessee State Library and Archives, Nashville, TN
    Records of Tennessee Senate, 1919
US Army Military History Institute, US Army War College, Carlisle Barracks, PA
    Don Rickey Jr. Papers
    Report of the Superior Board, Chaumont, France, 1919
    US Army, American Expeditionary Forces, Superior Board on Organization and Tac-
    tics, World War I Veterans Survey
Utah State Historical Society and Archives, Salt Lake City, UT
    Adjutant General's Records, 1895–1965
    Military Service Cards, 1898–1975
    145th Field Artillery Scrapbook, 1917–1918
    World War Military Listings, 1917–1951
    World War I Draft Board Registers, 1917–1918
    World War I Records, 1917–1923
    World War I Service Questionnaires, 1914–1918
    World War I Service Records, 1914–1925
Wyoming State Archives, Cheyenne, WY
    Records of State Historian File, 1916–1924

Published Sources

Aaron, Norman. *The Great Air War.* New York: Macmillan, 1968.
Adams, Michael C. C. *The Great Adventure: Male Desire and the Coming of World War I.*
    Bloomington: Indiana University Press, 1990.
Alexander, Jeffrey C. *Trauma: A Social Theory.* Cambridge: Polity Press, 2012.
Alexander, Joseph, and Edwin H. Simmons. *Through the Wheat: The U.S. Marine Corps in
    World War I.* Annapolis, MD: Naval Institute Press, 2008.
Allen, Henry T. *My Rhineland Journal.* Boston: Houghton Mifflin, 1923.

Allen, Hervey. *Toward the Flame*. Lincoln, NE: Bison Books, 2003.

American Battle Monuments Commission. *American Armies and Battlefields in Europe: A History, Guide and Reference Book*. Washington, DC: Government Printing Office, 1995.

American Psychiatric Association. *Diagnostic and Statistical Manual of Mental Disorders*. 4th ed. Arlington, VA: American Psychiatric Association, 2000.

———. *Diagnostic and Statistical Manual of Mental Disorders*. 5th ed. Washington, DC: American Psychiatric Publishing, 2013.

Ames, Eric, Marcia Klotz, and Lora Wildenthal, eds. *Germany's Colonial Pasts*. Lincoln: University of Nebraska Press, 2005.

Anderson, Warren D. "Homer and Stephen Crane." *Nineteenth-Century Fiction* 19, 1 (June 1964): 77–86.

Archambault, Alan H. *Fort Lewis*. Charleston, SC: Arcadia, 2002.

Arrington, Leonard J. "The Influenza Epidemic of 1918–19 in Utah." *Utah Historical Quarterly* 58, 2 (Spring 1990): 165–182.

Asprey, Robert B. *At Belleau Wood*. Denton: University of North Texas Press, 1996.

Audoin-Rouzeau, Stéphane. *Men at War 1914–1918: National Sentiment and Trench Journalism in France during the First World War*. Providence, RI: Berg, 1992.

Audoin-Rouzeau, Stéphane, and Annette Becker. *14–18: Understanding the Great War*, trans. Catherine Temerson. New York: Hill and Wang, 2002.

Axelrod, Alan. *Miracle at Belleau Wood: The Birth of the Modern U.S. Marine Corps*. Guildford, CT: Lyons Press, 2007.

———. *Selling the Great War. The Making of American Propaganda*. New York: Palgrave Macmillan, 2009.

Ayres, Leonard P. *The War with Germany: A Statistical Summary*. 2nd ed. Washington, DC: Government Printing Office, 1919.

Bachman, William E. *The Delta of the Triple Elevens*. Hazleton, PA: Standard-Sentinel Print, 1920.

Bagby, Philip Haxall, ed. *American Representation in Occupied Germany, 1920–1921*. 2 vols. Coblenz: American Sources in Germany, 1921.

Bailey, J. B. A. *Field Artillery and Firepower*. 2nd ed. Annapolis, MD: Naval Institute Press, 2004.

Baker, Carlos. *Hemingway: The Writer as Artist*. 4th ed. Princeton, NJ: Princeton University Press, 1972.

Baker, Chester E. *Doughboy's Diary*. Shippensburg, PA: Burd Street Press, 1998.

Baker, Horace L. *Argonne Days in World War I*. Columbia: University of Missouri Press, 2007.

Banks, Arthur. *A Military Atlas of the First World War*. South Yorkshire: Pen and Sword, 2004.

Barbeau, Arthur E., and Florette Henri. *The Unknown Soldiers: African-American Troops in World War I*. New York: Da Capo Press, 1996.

Barbusse, Henri. *Under Fire*. New York: Penguin, 2004.

Barczewski, Stephanie. *Titanic: A Night Remembered*. London: Continuum, 2011.

Barham, Peter. *Forgotten Lunatics of the Great War*. New Haven, CT: Yale University Press, 2004.

Barkley, John Lewis. *Scarlet Fields: The Combat Memoir of a World War I Medal of Honor Hero*. Lawrence: University Press of Kansas, 2012.

Barnes, Alexander. *In a Strange Land: The American Occupation of Germany, 1918–1923*. Atglen, PA: Schiffer Publishing, 2011.

Barnes, Harper. *Never Been a Time: The 1917 Race Riot that Sparked the Civil Rights Movement*. New York: Macmillan, 2008.

Barrett, James R., and David Roediger. "Inbetween Peoples: Race, Nationality and the 'New Immigrant' Working Class." *Journal of American Ethnic History* 16, 3 (1997): 3–44.

Barry, John M. *The Great Influenza: The Epic Story of the Deadliest Plague in History*. New York: Penguin, 2005.

Barry, John W. *The Midwest Goes to War: The 32nd Division in the Great War*. Lanham, MD: Scarecrow Press, 2007.

Bartlett, Frederic C. *Psychology and the Soldier*. Cambridge: Cambridge University Press, 1927.

———. *Remembering: A Study in Experimental and Social Psychology*. Cambridge: Cambridge University Press, 1932.

Barton, Michael, and Larry M. Logue, eds. *The Civil War Soldier: A Historical Reader*. New York: New York University Press, 2002.

Basso, Matthew, Laura McCall, and Dee Garceau, eds. *Across the Great Divide: Cultures of Manhood in the American West*. London: Routledge, 2001.

Batchelder, Roger. *Camp Devens*. Boston: Small, Maynard, 1917.

Bate, Kerry William. "Kanarraville Fights World War I." *Utah Historical Quarterly* 63, 1 (Winter 1995): 24–49.

The Bayonet: Remembrance Book of Camp Lee, Virginia. Camp Lee, VA: Thompson Illustragraph Co., 1918.

Becker, Annette. *Les Cicatrices Rouges 14–18: France et Belgique Occupées*. Paris: Fayard, 2010.

———. *Oubliés de la Grande Guerre: Humanitaire et Culture de Guerre*. Paris: Hachette Littératures, 1998.

Beckett, Ian. *The Great War*. 2nd ed. Harlow, UK: Pearson Longman, 2007.

Bederman, Gail. *Manliness and Civilization: A Cultural History of Gender and Race in the United States, 1880–1917*. Chicago: University of Chicago Press, 1995.

Belleiles, Michael A., ed. *Lethal Imagination: Violence and Brutality in American History*. New York: New York University Press, 1999.

Benwell, Harry A. *History of the Yankee Division*. Boston: Cornhill Company, 1919.

Berg, A. Scott. *Wilson*. New York: Putnam, 2013.

Bergreen, Laurence. *Capone: The Man and the Era*. New York: Simon and Schuster, 1994.

Berry, Henry. *Make the Kaiser Dance: Living Memories of the Doughboy*. New York: Priam Books, 1978.

Biddle, Tami Davis. *Rhetoric and Reality in Air Warfare: The Evolution of British and American Ideas about Strategic Bombing, 1914–1945*. Princeton, NJ: Princeton University Press, 2002.

Biel, Steven. *Down with the Old Canoe: A Cultural History of the* Titanic *Disaster*. New York: Norton, 2012.

Bingham, Hiram. *An Explorer in the Air Service*. New Haven, CT: Yale University Press, 1920.

Birdwell, Michael E. *Celluloid Soldiers: Warner Bros.'s Campaign against Nazism*. New York: New York University Press, 1999.

Black, Dora, Martin Newman, Jean Harris-Hendriks, and Gillian Mezey, eds. *Psychological Trauma: A Developmental Approach*. London: Gaskell, 1997.

Black, Marcia, and Robert S. McPherson. "Soldiers, Savers, Slackers, and Spies: Southeastern Utah's Response to World War I." *Utah Historical Quarterly* 63, 1 (Winter 1995): 4–23.

Blackmon, Douglas A. *Slavery by Another Name: The Re-enslavement of Black People in America from the Civil War to World War II*. New York: Doubleday, 2008.

Blair, William. *Cities of the Dead: Contesting the Memory of the Civil War in the South, 1865–1914*. Chapel Hill: University of North Carolina Press, 2004.

Blight, David W. *Race and Reunion: The Civil War in American Memory*. Cambridge, MA: Belknap Press of Harvard University Press, 2001.

Blom, Philipp. *The Vertigo Years: Europe, 1900–1914*. New York: Basic Books, 2008.

Bobbitt, Philip. *The Shield of Achilles: War, Peace and the Course of History*. New York: Knopf, 2002.

Bodnar, John. *The Transplanted: A History of Immigrants in Urban America*. Bloomington: Indiana University Press, 1985.

Bogacz, Ted. "War Neuroses and Cultural Change in England, 1914–1922: The Work of the War Office Committee of Enquiry into Shell Shock." *Journal of Contemporary History* 24, 2 (April 1989): 229.

Boghardt, Thomas. *The Zimmermann Telegram: Intelligence, Diplomacy, and America's Entry into World War I*. Annapolis, MD: Naval Institute Press, 2012.

Bond, Earl D. *Thomas W. Salmon, Psychiatrist*. New York: Norton, 1950.

Borden, Mary. *The Forbidden Zone*. Garden City, NY: Doubleday, Doran, 1929.

Bourke, Joanna. "The Body in Modern Warfare: Myth and Meaning, 1914–1945." In *What History Tells: George L. Mosse and the Culture of Modern Europe*, ed. Stanley G. Payne, David J. Sorkin, and John S. Tortorice. Madison: University of Wisconsin Press, 2004.

———. *Dismembering the Male: Men's Bodies, Britain and the Great War*. Chicago: University of Chicago Press, 1996.

———. *An Intimate History of Killing: Face-to-Face Killing in Twentieth Century Warfare*. New York: Basic Books, 1999.

Boyd, Thomas. *Through the Wheat*. Lincoln: University of Nebraska Press, 2000.

Braim, Paul F. *The Test of Battle: The American Expeditionary Forces in the Meuse-Argonne Campaign*. Newark: University of Delaware Press, 1987.

Braken, Patrick J., and Celia Petty, eds. *Rethinking the Trauma of War*. London: Free Association Books, 1998.

Brandt, Dennis W. *Pathway to Hell: A Tragedy of the American Civil War*. Lincoln: University of Nebraska Press, 2010.

Brannen, Carl Andrew. *Over There: A Marine in the Great War*. College Station: Texas A&M University Press, 1996.

Braudy, Leo. *From Chivalry to Terrorism: War and the Changing Nature of Masculinity*. New York: Knopf, 2003.

Brewer, Susan A. *Why America Fights: Patriotism and War Propaganda from the Philippines to Iraq*. Oxford: Oxford University Press, 2009.

Bridgland, Tony. *Sea Killers in Disguise: Q Ships and Decoy Raiders of World War I*. Annapolis, MD: Naval Institute Press, 1999.

Bristow, Nancy K. *American Pandemic: The Lost Worlds of the 1918 Influenza Epidemic*. Oxford: Oxford University Press, 2012.

Brittain, Vera. *Testament of Youth*. New York: Penguin, 2005.

Britten, Thomas A. *American Indians in World War I*. Albuquerque: University of New Mexico Press, 1997.

Brose, Eric Dorn. *A History of the Great War: World War One and the International Crisis of the Early Twentieth Century*. New York: Oxford University Press, 2010.

Brown, Carrie. *Rosie's Mom: Forgotten Women Workers of the First World War*. Boston: Northeastern University Press, 2002.

Brown, Thomas J., ed. *The Public Art of Civil War Commemoration: A Brief History with Documents*. Boston: Bedford/St. Martin's, 2004.

Brown, Walt, Jr., ed. *An American for Lafayette: The Diaries of E. C. C. Genet*. Charlottesville: University Press of Virginia, 1981.

Browne, George. *An American Soldier in World War I*. Lincoln: University of Nebraska Press, 2006.

Bruccoli, Matthew J. *Some Sort of Epic Grandeur: The Life of F. Scott Fitzgerald*. 2nd ed. Columbia: University of South Carolina Press, 2002.

Bruce, Brian. *Thomas Boyd: Lost Author of the Lost Generation*. Akron, OH: University of Akron Press, 2006.

Bruce, Robert B. *A Fraternity of Arms: America and France in the Great War*. Lawrence: University Press of Kansas, 2003.

Buckley, Harold. *Squadron 95: An Intimate History of the 95th Squadron, First American Flying Squadron to Go to the Front in the War of 1914–1918*. Paris: Obelisk Press, 1933.

Budreau, Lisa M. *Bodies of War: World War I and the Politics of Commemoration in America, 1919–1933*. New York: New York University Press, 2010.

Bullard, Robert L. *American Soldiers also Fought*. New York: Longmans, Green, 1936.

Butler, Daniel Allen. *"Unsinkable": The Full Story of the RMS Titanic*. Cambridge, MA: Da Capo Press, 2012.

Buxton, G. Edward, Jr. *Official History of 82nd Division American Expeditionary Forces "All American Division."* Indianapolis: Bobbs-Merrill, 1919.

Byerly, Carol R. *Fever of War: The Influenza Epidemic in the U.S. Army during World War I*. New York: New York University Press, 2005.

Cabanes, Bruno. *La Victoire Endeuillée: La sortie de guerre des soldats français, 1918–1920*. Paris: Seuil, 2004.

Cabot, Richard C. *Mademoiselle Miss*. Boston: W. A. Butterfield, 1916.

Campbell, Craig W. *Reel America and World War I: A Comprehensive Filmography and History of Motion Pictures in the United States, 1914–1920*. Jefferson, NC: McFarland, 1985.

Capdevila, Luc, and Danièle Voldman. *War Dead: Western Societies and the Casualties of War*, trans. Richard Veasey. Edinburgh: Edinburgh University Press, 2006.

Capozzola, Christopher. "The Only Badge Needed Is Your Patriotic Fervor: Vigilance, Coercion, and the Law in World War I America." *Journal of American History* 88, 4 (March 2002): 1354–1382.

———. *Uncle Sam Wants You: World War I and the Making of the Modern American Citizen.* New York: Oxford University Press, 2008.

Cappon, Lester J. "The Collection of World War I Materials in the States." *American Historical Review* 48, 4 (July 1943): 733–745.

Carey, Neil G., ed. *Fighting the Bolsheviks: The Russian War Memoir of Private First Class Donald E. Carey, U.S. Army, 1918–1919.* Novato, CA: Presidio, 1997.

Carnes, Mark C. *Secret Ritual and Manhood in Victorian America.* New Haven, CT: Yale University Press, 1989.

Carr, Virginia Spencer. *Dos Passos: A Life.* Evanston, IL: Northwestern University Press, 2004.

Carrington, Charles E. *Soldier from the Wars Returning.* New York: David McKay, 1965.

Caruth, Cathy, ed. *Trauma: Explorations in Memory.* Baltimore: Johns Hopkins University Press, 1995.

Cashman, Sean Dennis. *America in the Age of the Titans: The Progressive Era and World War I.* New York: New York University Press, 1988.

Catlin, Albertus W. *With the Help of God and a Few Marines.* New York: Doubleday, Page, 1919.

Caudill, Edward, and Paul Ashdown. *Sherman's March in Myth and Memory.* Lanham, MD: Rowman and Littlefield, 2008.

Chadwick, Brad. *The Reel Civil War: Mythmaking in American Film.* New York: Knopf, 2001.

Chambers, John Whiteclay, II. *To Raise an Army: The Draft Comes to Modern America.* New York: Free Press, 1987.

———. *The Tyranny of Change: America in the Progressive Era, 1890–1920.* 2nd ed. New Brunswick, NJ: Rutgers University Press, 2000.

Chickering, Roger. *Imperial Germany and the Great War, 1914–1918.* 2nd ed. Cambridge: Cambridge University Press, 2004.

Chickering, Roger, and Stig Förster, eds. *Great War, Total War: Combat and Mobilization on the Western Front, 1914–1918.* Cambridge: Cambridge University Press, 2000.

Chrislock, Carl H. *Watchdog of Loyalty: The Minnesota Commission of Public Safety during World War I.* St. Paul: Minnesota Historical Society Press, 1991.

Cimbala, Paul A. *Soldiers North and South: The Everyday Experiences of the Men Who Fought America's Civil War.* New York: Fordham University Press, 2010.

Clark, Christopher M. *The Sleepwalkers: How Europe Went to War in 1914.* New York: Harper, 2013.

Clark, George B. *The American Expeditionary Force in World War I: A Statistical History, 1917–1919.* Jefferson, NC: McFarland, 2013.

———. *Devil Dogs: Fighting Marines of World War I.* New York: Presidio Press, 1999.

———. *The Second Infantry Division in World War I: A History of the American Expeditionary Force Regulars, 1917–1919*. Jefferson, NC: McFarland, 2007.

———, ed. *Devil Dogs Chronicle: Voices of the 4th Marine Brigade in World War I*. Lawrence: University Press of Kansas, 2013.

Clausewitz, Carl von. *On War*, trans. and ed. Michael Howard and Peter Paret. Princeton, NJ: Princeton University Press, 1984.

Clodfelter, Michael. *The Lost Battalion and the Meuse-Argonne 1918: America's Deadliest Battle*. Jefferson, NC: McFarland, 2007.

Coffman, Edward M. *The War to End All Wars: The American Military Experience in World War I*. Lexington: University Press of Kentucky, 1998.

Cohen, Deborah. *The War Come Home: Disabled Veterans in Britain and Germany, 1914–1939*. Berkeley: University of California Press, 2001.

Coker, Christopher. *The Warrior Ethos: Military Culture and the War on Terror*. London: Routledge, 2007.

Connell, William J., and Fred L. Gardaphé, eds. *Anti-Italianism: Essays on a Prejudice*. New York: Palgrave Macmillan, 2010.

Controvich, James T. *The United States in World War I: A Bibliographic Guide*. Lanham, MD: Scarecrow Press, 2012.

Cook, Tim. *No Place to Run: The Canadian Corps and Gas Warfare in the First World War*. Vancouver: UBC Press, 1999.

———. "The Politics of Surrender: Canadian Soldiers and the Killing of Prisoners in the Great War." *Journal of Military History* 70, 3 (July 2006): 637–665.

Cooke, James J. *The All-Americans at War: The 82nd Division in the Great War, 1917–1918*. Westport, CT: Praeger, 1999.

———. *Pershing and His Generals: Command and Staff in the AEF*. Westport, CT: Praeger, 1997.

———. *The Rainbow Division in the Great War, 1917–1919*. Westport, CT: Praeger, 1994.

———. *The U.S. Air Service in the Great War, 1917–1919*. Westport, CT: Praeger, 1996.

Cooper, John Milton, Jr. *The Warrior and the Priest: Woodrow Wilson and Theodore Roosevelt*. Cambridge, MA: Belknap Press of Harvard University Press, 1983.

———. *Woodrow Wilson: A Biography*. New York: Knopf, 2009.

Cooperman, Stanley. *World War I and the American Novel*. Baltimore: Johns Hopkins Press, 1967.

Cornebise, Alfred E. *The Amaroc News: The Daily Newspaper of the American Forces in Germany, 1919–1923*. Carbondale: Southern Illinois University Press, 1981.

———. *War as Advertised: The Four Minute Men and America's Crusade, 1917–1918*. Philadelphia: American Philosophical Society, 1984.

Cowan, Sam K. *Sergeant York and His People*. New York: Grosset and Dunlap, 1922.

Cowley, Robert, ed. *The Great War: Perspectives on the First World War*. New York: Random House, 2004.

Craig, William J. *Fort Devens*. Charleston, SC: Arcadia, 2004.

Crane, Stephen. *The Portable Stephen Crane*, ed. Joseph Katz. New York: Penguin Books, 1977.

―――. *The Red Badge of Courage: An Episode of the American Civil War*, ed. Henry Binder. New York: Norton, 1999.

―――. *The Red Badge of Courage: A Norton Critical Edition*. 4th ed., ed. Donald Pizer and Eric Carl Link. New York: Norton, 2008.

―――. *The Red Badge of Courage and Other Stories*, ed. Anthony Mellors and Fiona Robertson. Oxford: Oxford University Press, 2005.

―――. *The Red Badge of Courage and Other Stories*, ed. Gary Scharnhorst. New York: Penguin Books, 2005.

Creel, George. *How We Advertised America: The First Telling of the Amazing Story of the Committee on Public Information that Carried the Gospel of Americanism to Every Corner of the Globe*. New York: Harper and Brothers, 1920.

Crocq, Louis. *Les traumatismes psychiques de guerre*. Paris: Odile Jacob, 1999.

Crosby, Alfred W. *America's Forgotten Pandemic: The Influenza of 1918*. Cambridge: Cambridge University Press, 1989.

Crouthamel, Jason. *The Great War and German Memory: Society, Politics and Psychological Trauma, 1914–1945*. Exeter, UK: University of Exeter Press, 2009.

Crowell, Benedict, and Robert F. Wilson. *How America Went to War*. 6 vols. New Haven, CT: Yale University Press, 1921.

Crownover, Roger. *The United States Intervention in North Russia, 1918, 1919: The Polar Bear Odyssey*. Lewiston, NY: Edwin Mellen Press, 2001.

Cullen, Jim. *The Civil War in Popular Culture: A Reusable Past*. Washington, DC: Smithsonian Institution Press, 1995.

Cummings, E. E. *The Enormous Room*. New York: Liveright, 1978.

Dalessandro, Robert J., and Rebecca S. Dalessandro. *American Lions: The 332 Infantry Regiment in Italy in World War I*. Atglen, PA: Schiffer Publishing, 2010.

Dallas, Gregor. *1918: War and Peace*. New York: Overlook Press, 2000.

Dancocks, Daniel G. *Spearhead to Victory: Canada and the Great War*. Edmonton, Canada: Hurtig, 1987.

Davis, Belinda J. *Home Fires Burning: Food, Politics, and Everyday Life in World War I Berlin*. Chapel Hill: University of North Carolina Press, 2000.

Davis, Linda H. *Badge of Courage: The Life of Stephen Crane*. Boston: Houghton Mifflin, 1998.

Day, Donald, ed. *Woodrow Wilson's Own Story*. Boston: Little, Brown, 1952.

Dean, Eric T., Jr. *Shook over Hell: Post-Traumatic Stress, Vietnam and the Civil War*. Cambridge, MA: Harvard University Press, 1997.

Dearborn, Mary V. *Mistress of Modernism: The Life of Peggy Guggenheim*. New York: Houghton Mifflin, 2004.

DeBauche, Leslie Midkiff. *Reel Patriotism: The Movies and World War I*. Madison: University of Wisconsin Press, 1997.

DeBona, Guerric. "Masculinity on the Front: John Huston's 'The Red Badge of Courage' (1951) Revisited." *Cinema Journal* 42, 2 (Winter 2003): 57–80.

De Forest, John William. *A Volunteer's Adventures: A Union Captain's Record of the Civil War*, ed. James H. Croushore. Baton Rouge: Louisiana State University Press, 1996.

Demaree, Joseph P. *History of Company A (308th Infantry) of the Lost Battalion*. New York: George U. Harvey, 1920.

Demitrack, Mark A., and Susan E. Abbey, eds. *Chronic Fatigue Syndrome: An Integrative Approach to Evaluation and Treatment*. New York: Guilford Press, 1996.

DeRosa, Christopher. *Political Indoctrination in the U.S. Army from World War II to the Vietnam War*. Lincoln: University of Nebraska Press, 2006.

Dibbets, Karel, and Bert Hogenkamp, eds. *Film and the First World War*. Amsterdam: Amsterdam University Press, 1995.

Doenecke, Justus D. *Nothing Less than War: A New History of America's Entry into World War I*. Lexington: University Press of Kentucky, 2011.

Dolden, A. Stuart. *Cannon Fodder: An Infantryman's Life on the Western Front 1914–18*. Dorset, UK: Blandford Press, 1980.

Donaldson, Scott, ed. *New Essays on* A Farewell to Arms. Cambridge: Cambridge University Press, 1990.

Dos Passos, John. *One Man's Initiation: 1917*. Ithaca, NY: Cornell University Press, 1969.
———. *Three Soldiers*. New York: Penguin, 1997.

Doughty, Robert A. *Pyrrhic Victory: French Strategy and Operations in the Great War*. Cambridge, MA: Belknap Press, 2005.

Downs, Frederick. *The Killing Zone: My Life in the Vietnam War*. New York: Norton, 2007.

Duane, James T. *Dear Old "K."* Boston: n.p., 1922.

Dudley, John. "'Subtle Brotherhood' in Stephen Crane's 'Tales of Adventure': Alienation, Anxiety, and the Rites of Manhood." *American Literary Realism* 34, 2 (Winter 2002): 95–118.

Duffy, Francis P. *Father Duffy's Story*. New York: George H. Doran, 1919.

Duroselle, Jean-Baptiste. *La Grande Guerre des Français: L'incompréhensible*. Paris: Perrin, 1994.

Dusenbery, Robert. "The Homeric Mood in the 'Red Badge of Courage.'" *Pacific Coast Philology* 3 (April 1968): 31–37.

Ebbert, Jean, and Marie-Beth Hall. *The First, the Few, the Forgotten: Navy and Marine Corps Women in World War I*. Annapolis, MD: Naval Institute Press, 2002.

Ebel, Jonathan H. *Faith in the Fight: Religion and the American Soldier in the Great War*. Princeton, NJ: Princeton University Press, 2010.

Echenberg, Myron. *Colonial Conscripts: The Tirailleurs Sénégalais in French West Africa, 1857–1960*. Portsmouth, NH: Heinemann, 1991.

Eighmey, Rae Katherine. *Food Will Win the War: Minnesota Crops, Cooks, and Conservation during World War I*. St. Paul: Minnesota Historical Society Press, 2010.

Eisenhower, John S. D. *Yanks: The Epic Story of the American Army in World War I*. New York: Free Press, 2001.

Eksteins, Modris. *Rites of Spring: The Great War and the Birth of the Modern Age*. New York: Houghton Mifflin, 1989.

Ellis, John, and Michael Cox. *The World War I Databook*. London: Aurum Press, 2001.

Ellis, Mark. *Race, War, and Surveillance: African Americans and the United States Government during World War I*. Bloomington: Indiana University Press, 2001.

Emberton, Carole. *Beyond Redemption: Race, Violence, and the American South after the Civil War*. Chicago: University of Chicago Press, 2013.

Emmerson, Charles. *1913: In Search of the World before the Great War*. New York: Public Affairs, 2013.

Empey, Arthur G. *First Call*. New York: G. P. Putnam's Sons, 1918.

———. *Over the Top*. New York: Putnam, 1917.

Engen, Rob. "Steel against Fire: The Bayonet in the First World War." *Journal of Military and Strategic Studies* 8, 3 (Spring 2006): 1–23.

English, George H., Jr. *History of the 89th Division, U.S.A.* Denver, CO: War Society of the 89th Division, 1920.

Englund, Peter. *The Beauty and the Sorrow: An Intimate History of the First World War*. New York: Knopf, 2011.

Ettinger, Albert M., and A. Churchill Ettinger. *A Doughboy with the Fighting Sixty-Ninth: A Remembrance of World War I*. Shippensburg, PA: White Mane Publishing, 1992.

Evans, Martin Marix, ed. *American Voices of World War I: Primary Source Documents, 1917–1920*. London: Fitzroy Dearborn Publishers, 2001.

Evans, Michael, and Alan Ryan, eds. *The Human Face of Warfare: Killing, Fear and Chaos in Battle*. St. Leonards, Australia: Allen and Unwin, 2000.

Evans, Suzanne. *Mothers of Heroes, Mothers of Martyrs: World War I and the Politics of Grief*. Montréal: McGill-Queen's University Press, 2007.

Fahs, Alice, and Joan Waugh, eds. *The Memory of the Civil War in American Culture*. Chapel Hill: University of North Carolina Press, 2004.

Farwell, Byron. *Over There: The United States in the Great War, 1917–1918*. New York: Norton, 1999.

Fassin, Didier, and Richard Rechtman. *The Empire of Trauma: An Inquiry into the Condition of Victimhood*, trans. Rachel Gomme. Princeton, NJ: Princeton University Press, 2009.

Faulkner, Richard S. *The School of Hard Knocks: Combat Leadership in the American Expeditionary Forces*. College Station: Texas A&M University Press, 2012.

Faulkner, William. *Soldiers' Pay*. New York: Liveright, 2011.

———. *The Sound and the Fury: A Norton Critical Edition*. 3rd ed., ed. Michael Gorra. New York: Norton, 2014.

———. *The Unvanquished*. New York: Vintage International, 1991.

Faust, Drew Gilpin. *This Republic of Suffering: Death and the American Civil War*. New York: Knopf, 2008.

Fay, Sidney B. *The Origins of the World War*. 2nd ed. 2 vols. New York: Free Press, 1966.

Feliciano, David V., Kenneth L. Mattox, and Ernest Eugene Moore, eds. *Trauma*. 7th ed. New York: McGraw-Hill Medical, 2012.

Fellman, Michael. *Citizen Sherman: A Life of William Tecumseh Sherman*. New York: Random House, 1995.

Ferguson, Niall. *The Pity of War*. New York: Basic Books, 1999.

Ferrell, Robert H. *America's Deadliest Battle: Meuse-Argonne, 1918*. Lawrence: University Press of Kansas, 2007.

———. *Collapse at Meuse-Argonne: The Failure of the Missouri-Kansas Division*. Columbia: University of Missouri Press, 2004.

———. *Five Days in October: The Lost Battalion of World War I*. Columbia: University of Missouri Press, 2005.

———. *Unjustly Dishonored: An African American Division in World War I*. Columbia: University of Missouri Press, 2011.

Figley, Charles R., and William P. Nash, eds. *Combat Stress Injury: Theory, Research and Management*. New York: Routledge, 2007.

Finley, Erin P. *Fields of Combat: Understanding PTSD among Veterans of Iraq and Afghanistan*. Ithaca, NY: Cornell University Press, 2011.

Finnegan, John P. *Against the Specter of a Dragon*. Westport, CT: Greenwood Press, 1974.

Fitzgerald, F. Scott. *The Great Gatsby*. Oxford: Oxford University Press, 2008.

Flammer, Philip M. *The Vivid Air: The Lafayette Escadrille*. Athens: University of Georgia Press, 1981.

Fleming, Thomas. *The Illusion of Victory: America in World War I*. New York: Basic Books, 2003.

Fogarty, Richard S. *Race and War in France: Colonial Subjects in the French Army, 1914–1918*. Baltimore: Johns Hopkins University Press, 2008.

Foglesong, David S. *America's Secret War against Bolshevism: U.S. Intervention in the Russian Civil War, 1917–1920*. Chapel Hill: University of North Carolina Press, 1995.

Foley, Robert T. *German Strategy and the Path to Verdun: Erich von Falkenhayn and the Development of Attrition, 1870–1916*. Cambridge: Cambridge University Press, 2005.

Foote, Lorien. *The Gentlemen and the Roughs: Violence, Honor, and Manhood in the Union Army*. New York: New York University Press, 2010.

Ford, Nancy Gentile. *Americans All! Foreign-born Soldiers in World War I*. College Station: Texas A&M University Press, 2001.

———. *The Great War and America: Civil-Military Relations during World War I*. Westport, CT: Praeger, 2008.

Foster, Gaines M. *Ghosts of the Confederacy: Defeat, the Lost Cause, and the Emergence of the New South*. New York: Oxford University Press, 1987.

Fraenkel, Ernst. *Military Occupation and the Rule of Law: Occupation Government in the Rhineland, 1918–1923*. New York: Oxford University Press, 1944.

Frandsen, Bert. *Hat in the Ring: The Birth of American Air Power in the Great War*. Washington, DC: Smithsonian Books, 2003.

Franks, Norman L. R. *Dog-Fight: Aerial Tactics of the Aces of World War I*. London: Greenhill, 2003.

Franks, Norman L. R., and Frank W. Bailey. *Over the Front: A Complete Record of the Fighter Aces and Units of the United States and French Air Services, 1914–1918*. London: Grub Street, 1992.

Franks, Norman L. R., Frank W. Bailey, and Rick Duiven. *Casualties of the German Air Service, 1914–1920*. London: Grub Street, 1999.

Frantzen, Allen J. *Bloody Good: Chivalry, Sacrifice, and the Great War*. Chicago: University of Chicago Press, 2004.

Fraser, Bruce. "Yankees at War." Ph.D. diss., Columbia University, 1976.

Freeman, Gregory A. *Lay This Body Down: The 1921 Murders of Eleven Plantation Slaves.* Chicago: Chicago Review Press, 1999.

Freidel, Frank. *Over There: The Story of America's First Great Overseas Crusade.* Philadelphia: Temple University Press, 1990.

French, Shannon E. *The Code of the Warrior: Exploring Warrior Values Past and Present.* Lanham, MD: Rowman and Littlefield, 2003.

Friedrichsmeyer, Sara, Sara Lennox, and Susanne Zantop, eds. *The Imperialist Imagination: German Colonialism and Its Legacy.* Ann Arbor: University of Michigan Press, 1998.

Fritz, Stephen G. *Frontsoldaten: The German Soldier in World War II.* Lexington: University Press of Kentucky, 1995.

Fromkin, David. *Europe's Last Summer: Who Started the Great War in 1914?* New York: Vintage, 2004.

Fussell, Paul. *The Great War and Modern Memory.* Oxford: Oxford University Press, 2013.

———. *Wartime: Understanding and Behavior in the Second World War.* New York: Oxford University Press, 1989.

Gaff, Alan D. *Blood in the Argonne: The Lost Battalion of World War I.* Norman: University of Oklahoma Press, 2005.

Gallagher, Gary W. *Causes Won, Lost, and Forgotten: How Hollywood and Popular Art Shape What We Know about the Civil War.* Chapel Hill: University of North Carolina Press, 2008.

———. *Lee and His Generals in War and Memory.* Baton Rouge: Louisiana State University Press, 1998.

Gallagher, Gary W., and Alan T. Nolan, eds. *The Myth of the Lost Cause and Civil War History.* Bloomington: Indiana University Press, 2000.

Gandal, Keith. *The Gun and the Pen: Hemingway, Fitzgerald, Faulkner and the Fiction of Mobilization.* New York: Oxford University Press, 2008.

Gavin, Lettie. *American Women in World War I: They Also Served.* Niwot: University Press of Colorado, 1997.

Genthe, Charles V. *American War Narratives 1917–1918.* New York: David Lewis, 1969.

George, Albert E., and Edwin H. Cooper. *Pictorial History of the Twenty-Sixth Division United States Army.* Boston: Ball Publishing, 1920.

Gibbons, Floyd P. *"And They Thought We Wouldn't Fight."* New York: Doran, 1918.

Gilbert, Eugene. *The 28th Division in France.* Nancy, France: Berger-Levrault, 1919.

Gilbert, James L. *World War I and the Origins of U.S. Military Intelligence.* Plymouth, UK: Scarecrow Press, 2012.

Gilbert, Martin. *The First World War: A Complete History.* 2nd ed. New York: Holt, 2004.

Godard, George S. *Report of State Librarian for the Two Years Ended June 30, 1922.* Hartford: State Archives, Connecticut State Library, 1922.

Goebel, Stefan. *The Great War and Medieval Memory: War, Remembrance and Medievalism in Britain and Germany, 1914–1940.* Cambridge: Cambridge University Press, 2007.

Goldstein, Donald M., and Harry J. Maihafer. *America in World War I: The Story and Photographs.* Washington, DC: Brassey's, 2004.

Goldstein, Joshua S. *War and Gender: How Gender Shapes the War System and Vice Versa.* Cambridge: Cambridge University Press, 2001.

Gorn, Elliott J. *The Manly Art: Bare-Knuckle Prize Fighting in America.* 2nd ed. Ithaca, NY: Cornell University Press, 2010.

Gow, Kenneth. *Letters of a Soldier.* New York: H. B. Covert, 1920.

Graham, John W. *The Gold Star Mother Pilgrimages of the 1930s.* Jefferson, NC: McFarland, 2005.

Granacher, Robert P. *Traumatic Brain Injury: Methods for Clinical and Forensic Neuropsychiatric Assessment.* 2nd ed. Boca Raton, FL: CRC Press, 2008.

Graves, Robert. *Good-Bye to All That.* New York: Anchor Books, 1998.

Gray, Edwyn A. *The Killing Time: The U-Boat War, 1914–1918.* New York: Scribner, 1972.

Gray, J. Glenn. *The Warriors: Reflections on Men in Battle.* Lincoln: University of Nebraska Press, 1998.

Green, Melissa. "'Escape' in 'The Red Badge of Courage': A Jungian Analysis." *American Literary Realism, 1870–1910* 28, 1 (Autumn 1995): 80–91.

Greenfield, Nathan. *Baptism of Fire: The Second Battle of Ypres and the Forging of Canada, April 1915.* Toronto: HarperCollins, 2007.

Greenhalgh, Elizabeth. *Victory through Coalition: Britain and France during the First World War.* Cambridge: Cambridge University Press, 2005.

Greenwood, Paul. *The Second Battle of the Marne.* Shrewsbury, UK: Airlife, 1998.

Greer, Thomas H. "Air Army Doctrinal Roots, 1917–1918." *Military Affairs* 20, 4 (Winter 1956): 202–216.

Griess, Thomas E., ed. *West Point Atlas for the Great War.* Garden City Park, NY: Square One Publishers, 2003.

Griffith, Paddy. *Battle Tactics of the Western Front: The British Army's Art of Attack, 1916–18.* New Haven, CT: Yale University Press, 1994.

Grimsley, Mark. *The Hard Hand of War.* Cambridge: Cambridge University Press, 1995.

Gross, Charles J. "George Owen Squier and the Origins of American Military Aviation." *Journal of Military History* 54, 3 (July 1990): 281–306.

Grotelueschen, Mark Ethan. *The AEF Way of War: The American Army and Combat in World War I.* Cambridge: Cambridge University Press, 2007.

Grunwald, Lisa, and Stephen J. Adler, eds. *Letters of the Century: America 1900–1999.* New York: Dial Press, 1999.

Gudmundsson, Bruce I. *On Artillery.* Westport, CT: Praeger, 1993.

———. *Stormtroop Tactics: Innovation in the German Army, 1914–1918.* New York: Praeger, 1989.

Guglielmo, Thomas A. *White on Arrival: Italians, Race, Color, and Power in Chicago, 1890–1945.* Oxford: Oxford University Press, 2003.

Haber, L. F. *The Poisonous Cloud: Chemical Warfare in the First World War.* Oxford: Oxford University Press, 1986.

Hagood, Johnson. *The Services of Supply: A Memoir of the Great War.* Boston: Houghton Mifflin, 1927.

Hall, Bert, and John J. Niles. *One Man's War: The Story of the Lafayette Escadrille.* New York: H. Holt, 1929.

Hall, James N., and Charles B. Nordhoff, eds. *The Lafayette Flying Corps.* 2 vols. Port Washington, NY: Kennikat Press, 1920.

Hall, Norman S. *The Balloon Buster: Frank Luke of Arizona.* New York: Arno Press, 1972.

Hallas, James H. *Squandered Victory: The American First Army at St. Mihiel.* Westport, CT: Praeger, 1995.

———, ed. *Doughboy War: The American Expeditionary Force in World War I.* London: Lynne Rienner, 2000.

Hallett, Christine E. *Containing Trauma: Nursing Work in the First World War.* Manchester, UK: Manchester University Press, 2009.

Halyburton, Edgar. *Shoot and Be Damned.* New York: Covici, Friede, 1932.

Hamm, Elizabeth C. *In White Armor.* New York: Knickerbocker Press, 1919.

Hanlon, Gregory. *The Twilight of a Military Tradition: Italian Aristocrats and European Conflicts, 1560–1800.* New York: Holmes and Meier, 1998.

Hanson, Neil. *Unknown Soldiers: The Story of the Missing of the First World War.* New York: Knopf, 2006.

Harbord, James G. *The American Army in France, 1917–1919.* Boston: Little, Brown, 1936.

Harris, Stephen L. *Duffy's War: Father Francis Duffy, Wild Bill Donovan and the Irish Fighting 69th in World War I.* Washington, DC: Brassey's, 2006.

———. *Duty, Honor, Privilege: New York's Silk Stocking Regiment and the Breaking of the Hindenburg Line.* Washington, DC: Brassey's, 2001.

———. *Harlem's Hell Fighters: The African-American 369th Infantry in World War I.* Washington, DC: Brassey's, 2003.

Harvey, William C., and Eric T. Harvey, eds. *Letters from Verdun: Frontline Experiences of an American Volunteer in World War I France.* Philadelphia: Casemate, 2009.

Hastings, Max. *Catastrophe 1914: Europe Goes to War.* New York: Knopf, 2013.

Haterius, Carl E. *Reminiscences of the 137th U.S. Infantry.* Topeka, KS: Crane, 1919.

Haulsee, W. M., F. G. Howe, and A. C. Doyle, comps. *Soldiers of the Great War.* 3 vols. Washington, DC: Soldiers Record Publishing Association, 1920.

Hayes, Geoffrey, Andrew Iarocci, and Mike Bechthold. *Vimy Ridge: A Canadian Reassessment.* Waterloo, ON: LCMSDS Press/Wilfrid Laurier University Press, 2007.

Hayward, James. *Myths and Legends of the First World War.* Stroud, UK: Sutton, 2002.

Hemingway, Ernest. *The Complete Short Stories of Ernest Hemingway.* New York: Scribner, 1998.

———. *A Farewell to Arms.* New York: Scribner, 2012.

———. *The Nick Adams Stories.* New York: Scribner, 1972.

———. *The Sun Also Rises.* New York: Scribner, 2014.

Hershey, Lewis B. *History of Furnishing Statement of Service Cards to the States, 1792–1948.* Washington, DC: Government Printing Office, 1949.

Herwig, Holger H. *The First World War: Germany and Austria-Hungary, 1914–1918.* New York: St. Martin's Press, 1997.

———. "Industry, Empire and the First World War." In *Modern Germany Reconsidered, 1870–1945*, ed. Gordon Martel. London: Routledge, 1992.

Herzog, Stanley J. *The Fightin' Yanks.* Stamford, CT: Cunningham Print, 1922.

Higham, John. *Strangers in the Land: Patterns of American Nativism, 1860–1925.* New Brunswick, NJ: Rutgers University Press, 1988.

Hirshson, Stanley P. *The White Tecumseh: A Biography of General William T. Sherman.* New York: Wiley, 1997.

The History Committee. *The Four Minute Men of Chicago.* Chicago: History Committee of the Four Minute Men of Chicago, 1919.

Hoehling, Adolph A. *The Fierce Lambs.* Boston: Little, Brown, 1960.

Hogan, Martin J. *Shamrock Battalion in the Great War.* Columbia: University of Missouri Press, 2007.

———. *The Shamrock Battalion of the Rainbow.* New York: D. Appleton, 1919.

Hoganson, Kristin L. *Fighting for American Manhood: How Gender Politics Provoked the Spanish-American and Philippine-American Wars.* New Haven, CT: Yale University Press, 1998.

Holbrook, Franklin F. "The Collection of State War Service Records." *American Historical Review* 25, 1 (October 1919): 72–78.

Holden, Frank A. *War Memories.* Athens, GA: Athens, 1922.

Holley, I. B., Jr. *Ideas and Weapons: Exploitation of the Aerial Weapon by the United States during World War I.* Hamden, CT: Archon Books, 1971.

Holmes, Richard. *Acts of War: The Behavior of Men in Battle.* New York: Free Press, 1985.

Hopkins, J. Castell. *Canada at War 1914–1918: A Record of Heroism and Achievement.* New York: George H. Doran, 1919.

Horne, John, ed. *A Companion to World War I.* Malden, MA: Wiley-Blackwell, 2010.

Horne, John, and Alan Kramer. *German Atrocities 1914: A History of Denial.* New Haven, CT: Yale University Press, 2001.

Hoschschild, Adam. *To End All Wars: A Story of Loyalty and Rebellion, 1914–1918.* Boston: Houghton Mifflin Harcourt, 2011.

Housman, Laurence, ed. *War Letters of Fallen Englishmen.* Philadelphia: Pine St. Books, 2002.

Howells, Richard. *The Myth of the* Titanic: *Centenary Edition.* New York: Palgrave Macmillan, 2012.

Huber, Elbert L. "War Department Records in the National Archives." *Military Affairs* 6, 4 (Winter 1942): 247–254.

Hudson, James J. *Hostile Skies: A Combat History of the American Air Service in World War I.* Syracuse, NY: Syracuse University Press, 1968.

———. *In Clouds of Glory: American Airmen Who Flew with the British during the Great War.* Fayetteville: University of Arkansas Press, 1990.

Huidekoper, Frederic Louis. *The Military Unpreparedness of the United States: A History of American Land Forces from Colonial Times until June 1, 1915.* New York: Macmillan, 1916.

Hull, Isabel V. *Absolute Destruction: Military Culture and the Practices of War in Imperial Germany.* Ithaca, NY: Cornell University Press, 2005.

Humphries, Mark Osborne. "Paths of Infection: The First World War and the Origins of the 1918 Influenza Pandemic." *War in History* 21, 1 (January 2014): 55–81.

Hungerford, Harold R. "'That Was at Chancellorsville': The Factual Framework of *The Red Badge of Courage.*" *American Literature* 34, 4 (January 1963): 520–531.

Hunt, Nigel C. *Memory, War and Trauma.* Cambridge: Cambridge University Press, 2010.

Hunton, Addie W., and Kathryn M. Johnson. *Two Colored Women with the American Expeditionary Forces*. New York: G. K. Hall, 1997.

Isenberg, Michael T. *War on Film: The American Cinema and World War I, 1914–1941*. Rutherford, NJ: Fairleigh Dickinson University Press, 1981.

Jackson, Robert. *The Prisoners, 1914–18*. London: Routledge, 1989.

Jackson, Warren R. *His Time in Hell: A Texas Marine in France*. New York: Presidio Press, 2001.

James, Pearl. *The New Death: American Modernism and World War I*. Charlottesville: University of Virginia Press, 2013.

———, ed. *Picture This: World War I Posters and Visual Culture*. Lincoln: University of Nebraska Press, 2009.

Janney, Caroline E. *Remembering the Civil War: Reunion and the Limits of Reconciliation*. Chapel Hill: University of North Carolina Press, 2013.

Jefferson, John Mahon. *New York's Fighting Sixty-Ninth: A Regimental History of Service in the Civil War's Irish Brigade and the Great War's Rainbow Division*. Jefferson, NC: McFarland, 2004.

Jensen, Kimberly. *Mobilizing Minerva: American Women in the First World War*. Urbana: University of Illinois Press, 2008.

Johanningsmeier, Charles. "The 1894 Syndicated Newspaper Appearances of 'The Red Badge of Courage.'" *American Literary Realism* 40, 3 (Spring 2008): 226–247.

Johnson, David E. *Fast Tanks and Heavy Bombers: Innovation in the U.S. Army, 1917–1945*. Ithaca, NY: Cornell University Press, 1998.

Johnson, Douglas V., and Rolfe L. Hillman. *Soissons 1918*. College Station: Texas A&M University Press, 1999.

Johnson, Herbert A. *Wingless Eagle: U.S. Army Aviation through World War I*. Chapel Hill: University of North Carolina Press, 2001.

Johnson, Ray N. *Heaven, Hell or Hoboken*. Cleveland, OH: O. S. Hubbell Printing Co., 1919.

Johnson, Thomas M., and Fletcher Pratt. *The Lost Battalion*. Lincoln: University of Nebraska Press, 2000.

Joll, James, and Gordon Martel. *The Origins of the First World War*. 3rd ed. Harlow, UK: Pearson Longman, 2007.

Jones, Edgar. "Doctors and Trauma in the First World War: The Response of British Military Psychiatrists." In *The Memory of Catastrophe*, ed. Peter Gray and Kendrick Oliver. Manchester, UK: Manchester University Press, 2004.

Jones, Edgar, and Simon Wessely. *Shell Shock to PTSD: Military Psychiatry from 1900 to the Gulf War*. Hove, UK: Psychology Press, 2005.

Jones, Heather. *Violence against Prisoners of War in the First World War: Britain, France and Germany, 1914–1920*. Cambridge: Cambridge University Press, 2011.

Judy, Will. *A Soldier's Diary*. Chicago: Judy Publishing, 1931.

Karl, Frederick R. *William Faulkner: American Writer*. New York: Weidenfeld and Nicolson, 1989.

Katz, Friedrich. *The Life and Times of Pancho Villa*. Stanford, CA: Stanford University Press, 1998.

Keegan, John. *The Face of Battle.* New York: Penguin Books, 1978.

———. *The First World War.* New York: Knopf, 1999.

Keene, Jennifer D. *Doughboys, the Great War and the Remaking of America.* Baltimore: Johns Hopkins University Press, 2001.

———. "French and American Racial Stereotype during the First World War." In *National Stereotypes in Perspective: Americans in France, Frenchmen in America,* ed. William L. Chew. Atlanta: Rodopi, 2001.

———. "Uneasy Alliances: French Military Intelligence and the American Army during the First World War." In *Knowing Your Friends: Intelligence inside Alliances and Coalitions from 1914 to the Cold War,* ed. Martin S. Alexander. London: Frank Cass, 1998.

———. *The United States and the First World War.* New York: Longman, 2000.

———. *World War I.* Westport, CT: Greenwood Press, 2006.

Keith, Jeanette. *Rich Man's War, Poor Man's Fight: Race, Class, and Power in the Rural South during the First World War.* Chapel Hill: University of North Carolina Press, 2004.

Kelly, Andrew. *Cinema and the Great War.* London: Routledge, 1997.

———. *Filming* All Quiet on the Western Front: *"Brutal Cutting, Stupid Censors, Bigoted Politicos."* London: I. B. Tauris, 1998.

Kennedy, Carrie H., and Eric A. Zillmer, eds. *Military Psychology: Clinical and Operational Applications.* New York: Guilford Press, 2006.

Kennedy, David M. *Over Here: The First World War and American Society.* 2nd ed. Oxford: Oxford University Press, 2004.

Kennedy, Kathleen. *Disloyal Mothers and Scurrilous Citizens: Women and Subversion during World War I.* Bloomington: Indiana University Press, 1999.

Kennedy, Richard S. *Dreams in the Mirror: A Biography of E. E. Cummings.* 2nd ed. New York: Liveright, 1994.

Kennett, Lee. *The First Air War, 1914–1918.* New York: Free Press, 1991.

———. *Sherman: A Soldier's Life.* New York: HarperCollins, 2001.

Kimmel, Michael. *Manhood in America: A Cultural History.* 3rd ed. Oxford: Oxford University Press, 2011.

Kindsvatter, Peter S. *American Soldiers: Ground Combat in the World Wars, Korea, and Vietnam.* Lawrence: University Press of Kansas, 2003.

Kingsbury, Celia M. *For Home and Country: World War I Propaganda on the Home Front.* Lincoln: University of Nebraska Press, 2010.

Kipling, Rudyard. *Complete Verse: Definitive Edition.* New York: Anchor Press, 1989.

Kitchen, Martin. *The German Offensives of 1918.* Gloucestershire, UK: Tempus, 2001.

Kleber, Rolf J., Charles R. Figley, and Berthold P. R. Gersons, eds. *Beyond Trauma: Cultural and Societal Dynamics.* New York: Plenum Press, 1995.

Kornweibel, Theodore, Jr. *Investigate Everything: Federal Efforts to Compel Black Loyalty during World War I.* Bloomington: Indiana University Press, 2002.

Kramer, Alan. *Dynamic of Destruction: Culture and Mass Killing in the First World War.* Oxford: Oxford University Press, 2007.

Krass, Peter. *Portrait of War: The U.S. Army's First Combat Artists and the Doughboys' Experience in WWI.* Hoboken, NJ: Wiley, 2007.

Krouse, Susan Applegate. *North American Indians in the Great War*. Lincoln: University of Nebraska Press, 2007.

Kuhlman, Erika. "American Doughboys and German *Fräuleins*: Sexuality, Patriarchy and Privilege in the American-Occupied Rhineland, 1918–23." *Journal of Military History* 71, 4 (October 2007): 1077–1106.

Kyle, Chris. *American Sniper: The Autobiography of the Most Lethal Sniper in U.S. Military History*. New York: William Morrow, 2012.

LaCapra, Dominick. *Writing History, Writing Trauma*. Baltimore: Johns Hopkins University Press, 2001.

LaMotte, Ellen N. *The Backwash of War*. New York: G. P. Putnam's Sons, 1934.

Langer, William L. *Gas and Flame in World War I*. New York: Knopf, 1965.

———. *In and Out of the Ivory Tower: The Autobiography of William L. Langer*. New York: Neale Watson Academic Publications, 1977.

Lanning, Michael Lee. *The African-American Soldier: From Crispus Attucks to Colin Powell*. 2nd ed. New York: Citadel Press, 2004.

Larner, Melissa, James Peto, and Nadine Monem, eds. *War and Medicine*. London: Black Dog Publishing, 2008.

Laskin, David. *The Long Way Home: An American Journey from Ellis Island to the Great War*. New York: HarperCollins, 2010.

Laurie, Clayton D. "'The Chanting of Crusaders': Captain Heber Blankenhorn and AEF Combat Propaganda in World War I." *Journal of Military History* 59, 3 (July 1995): 457–481.

Lebow, Eileen F. *A Grandstand Seat: The American Balloon Service in World War I*. Westport, CT: Praeger, 1998.

Lee, A. Robert. "Inside the Box: Stephen Crane's *The Red Badge of Courage*." *Atlantis* 5, 1–2 (June–November 1983): 97–110.

Lee, David D. *Sergeant York: An American Hero*. Lexington: University Press of Kentucky, 2002.

Leed, Eric J. *No Man's Land: Combat and Identity in World War I*. Cambridge: Cambridge University Press, 1979.

Leese, Peter. *Shell Shock: Traumatic Neurosis and the British Soldiers of the First World War*. Houndmills, UK: Palgrave Macmillan, 2008.

LeFew-Blake, Penelope A. *Fort Des Moines*. Charleston, SC: Arcadia, 2006.

Leland, Anne. *American War and Military Operations Casualties: Lists and Statistics*. Washington, DC: Congressional Research Service, 2012.

Leland, Waldo G., and Newton D. Mereness, eds. *Introduction to the American Official Sources for the Economic and Social History of the World War*. New Haven, CT: Yale University Press, 1926.

Lembcke, Jerry. *PTSD: Diagnosis and Identity in Post-Empire America*. Lanham, MD: Lexington Books, 2013.

Lengel, Edward G. *To Conquer Hell: The Meuse-Argonne, 1918*. New York: Holt, 2008.

———. *World War I Memories: An Annotated Bibliography of Personal Accounts Published in English since 1919*. Lanham, MD: Scarecrow Press, 2004.

Lentz, Perry. *Private Fleming at Chancellorsville:* The Red Badge of Courage *and the Civil War*. Columbia: University of Missouri Press, 2006.

Lentz-Smith, Adriane. *Freedom Struggles: African Americans and World War I*. Cambridge, MA: Harvard University Press, 2009.

Lerner, Paul. *Hysterical Men: War, Psychiatry, and the Politics of Trauma in Germany, 1890–1930*. Ithaca, NY: Cornell University Press, 2003.

Levi, Margaret. *Consent, Dissent and Patriotism*. Cambridge: Cambridge University Press, 1997.

Levi, Primo. *The Drowned and the Saved*, trans. Raymond Rosenthal. New York: Vintage International, 1989.

Levin, N. Gordon, Jr. *Woodrow Wilson and World Politics: America's Response to War and Revolution*. London: Oxford University Press, 1968.

Lewis, Edward Davis, ed. *Dear Bert: An American Pilot Flying in World War I Italy*. Trento, Italy: LoGisma, 2002.

Lewis, Lloyd. *Sherman: Fighting Prophet*. Lincoln: University of Nebraska Press, 1993.

Leys, Ruth. *Trauma: A Genealogy*. Chicago: University of Chicago Press, 2000.

Lezak, Muriel Detsch, Diane B. Howieson, Erin D. Bigler, and Daniel Tranel, eds. *Neuropsychological Assessment*. 5th ed. Oxford: Oxford University Press, 2012.

Liddell Hart, B. H. *Sherman: Soldier, Realist, American*. New York: Da Capo Press, 1993.

Linderman, Gerald. *Embattled Courage: The Experience of Combat in the American Civil War*. New York: Free Press, 1987.

———. *The Mirror of War: American Society and the Spanish-America War*. Ann Arbor: University of Michigan Press, 1974.

Linker, Beth. *War's Waste: Rehabilitation in World War I*. Chicago: University of Chicago Press, 2011.

Linn, Brian McAllister. *The Philippine War, 1899–1902*. Lawrence: University Press of Kansas, 2000.

Linson, Corwin K. *My Stephen Crane*, ed. Edwin H. Cady. Syracuse, NY: Syracuse University Press, 1958.

Lipkes, Jeff. *Rehearsals: The German Army in Belgium, August 1914*. Leuven, Belgium: Leuven University Press, 2007.

Little, Arthur W. *From Harlem to the Rhine: The Story of New York's Colored Volunteers*. New York: Covici, Friede, 1936.

Lloyd, David W. *Battlefield Tourism: Pilgrimage and the Commemoration of the Great War in Britain, Australia and Canada, 1919–1939*. Oxford: Berg, 1998.

Loftus, Elizabeth, and Katherine Ketcham. *The Myth of Repressed Memory: False Memories and Allegations of Sexual Abuse*. New York: St. Martin's Press, 1994.

Logue, Larry M., and Michael Barton, eds. *The Civil War Veteran: A Historical Reader*. New York: New York University Press, 2007.

Long, E. B. *The Saints and the Union: Utah Territory during the Civil War*. Urbana: University of Illinois Press, 1981.

Longstreet, Stephen. *The Canvas Falcons: The Story of the Men and the Planes of World War I*. New York: World Publishing, 1970.

Lord, Walter. *The Night Lives On.* London: Penguin, 1998.

———. *A Night to Remember.* London: Penguin, 2012.

Ludendorff, Erich. *Ludendorff's Own Story: August 1914–November 1918.* 2 vols. New York: Harper, 1919.

Ludington, Townsend. *John Dos Passos: A Twentieth-Century Odyssey.* New York: Dutton, 1980.

Lunn, Joseph. *Memoirs of the Maelstrom: A Senegalese Oral History of the First World War.* Portsmouth, NH: Heinemann, 1999.

Lusane, Clarence. *Hitler's Black Victims: The Historical Experiences of Afro-Germans, European Blacks, Africans, and African Americans in the Nazi Era.* New York: Routledge, 2002.

Lynn, Kenneth S. *Hemingway.* New York: Simon and Schuster, 1987.

MacKenzie, David, ed. *Canada and the First World War: Essays in Honour of Robert Craig Brown.* Toronto: University of Toronto Press, 2005.

Mackin, Elton E. *Suddenly We Didn't Want to Die.* New York: Presidio Press, 1993.

MacMillan, Margaret. *Paris 1919: Six Months that Changed the World.* New York: Random House, 2002.

———. *The War that Ended Peace: The Road to 1914.* New York: Random House, 2013.

Mailloux, Steven. "'The Red Badge of Courage' and Interpretive Conventions: Critical Response to a Maimed Text." *Studies in the Novel* 10, 1 (Spring 1978): 48–63.

Mann, Gregory. *Native Sons: West African Veterans and France in the Twentieth Century.* Durham, NC: Duke University Press, 2006.

March, William. *Company K.* Tuscaloosa: University of Alabama Press, 1989.

Marcus, Mordecai, and Erin Marcus. "Animal Imagery in *The Red Badge of Courage.*" *Modern Language Notes* 74, 2 (February 1959): 108–111.

Marshall, George C. *Memoirs of My Services in the World War, 1917–1918.* Boston: Houghton Mifflin, 1976.

Marshall, R. Jackson, III. *Memories of World War I: North Carolina Doughboys on the Western Front.* Raleigh, NC: Division of Archives and History, 1998.

Marszalek, John F. *Sherman: A Soldier's Passion for Order.* New York: Vintage Books, 1994.

Marten, James. *Sing Not War: The Lives of Union and Confederate Veterans in Gilded Age America.* Chapel Hill: University of North Carolina Press, 2011.

Martin, Edward. *The Twenty-Eighth Division: Pennsylvania Guard in the World War.* 5 vols. Pittsburgh: 28th Division Publishing Co., 1924.

Masefield, John. *The War and the Future.* New York: Macmillan, 1918.

Mason, Herbert Molloy, Jr. *The Lafayette Escadrille.* New York: Random House, 1964.

Mastriano, Douglas V. *Alvin York: A New Biography of the Hero of the Argonne.* Lexington: University Press of Kentucky, 2014.

Maurer, Maurer, ed. *The U.S. Air Service in World War I.* 4 vols. Washington, DC: Government Printing Office, 1978.

Mayhew, Emily. *Wounded: A New History of the Western Front in World War I.* Oxford: Oxford University Press, 2014.

McColly, William. "Teaching 'The Red Badge of Courage.'" *English Journal* 50, 8 (November 1961): 534–538.

McConnell, Stuart. *Glorious Contentment: The Grand Army of the Republic, 1865–1900.* Chapel Hill: University of North Carolina Press, 1992.

McCrae, John. *In Flanders Fields and Other Poems.* New York: G. P. Putnam's Sons, 1919.

McDermott, John J. "Symbolism and Psychological Realism in *The Red Badge of Courage*." *Nineteenth-Century Fiction* 23, 3 (December 1968): 324–331.

McKee, Alexander. *The Battle of Vimy Ridge.* New York: Stein and Day, 1966.

McMahan, Jeff. *Killing in War.* Oxford: Oxford University Press, 2009.

McMaster, John B. *The United States in the World War, 1914–1918.* 2 vols. New York: Appleton, 1929.

McMeekin, Sean. *July 1914: Countdown to War.* New York: Basic Books, 2013.

McMurry, Frank M. *The Geography of the Great War.* New York: Macmillan, 1919.

McPhail, Helen. *The Long Silence: Civilian Life under the German Occupation of Northern France, 1914–1918.* London: I. B. Tauris, 1999.

McPherson, James M. *Drawn with the Sword: Reflections on the American Civil War.* New York: Oxford University Press, 1996.

———. *For Cause and Comrades: Why Men Fought in the Civil War.* Oxford: Oxford University Press, 1996.

———. *What They Fought for 1861–1865.* Baton Rouge: Louisiana State University Press, 1994.

McPherson, Robert S. "The Influenza Epidemic of 1918: A Cultural Response." *Utah Historical Quarterly* 58, 2 (Spring 1990): 183–200.

Mead, Gary. *The Doughboys: America and the First World War.* Woodstock, NY: Overlook Press, 2000.

Meigs, Mark. *Optimism at Armageddon: Voices of American Participants in World War One.* New York: New York University Press, 1997.

Meilinger, Phillip S. "The Historiography of Airpower: Theory and Doctrine." *Journal of Military History* 64, 2 (April 2000): 467–501.

Mellow, James R. *Charmed Circle: Gertrude Stein and Company.* New York: Owl Books, 2003.

———. *Hemingway: A Life without Consequences.* Boston: Houghton Mifflin, 1992.

Merrill, James M. *William Tecumseh Sherman.* Chicago: Rand McNally, 1971.

Mersey, Lord. *The Loss of the* Titanic, *1912.* London: Stationery Office, 1999.

Messinger, Gary S. *British Propaganda and the State in the First World War.* Manchester, UK: Manchester University Press, 1992.

Meyer, Jessica. *Men of War: Masculinity and the First World War in Britain.* Houndmills, UK: Palgrave Macmillan, 2008.

Micale, Mark S., and Paul Lerner, eds. *Traumatic Pasts: History, Psychiatry and Trauma in the Modern Age, 1870–1930.* Cambridge: Cambridge University Press, 2001.

Michael, Moina. *The Miracle Flower: The Story of the Flanders Fields Memorial Poppy.* Philadelphia: Dorrance, 1941.

Michel, Marc. *Les Africains et la Grande Guerre: l'appel à l'Afrique, 1914–1918.* Paris: Karthala, 2003.

Miller, Kelly. *War for Human Rights.* New York: Negro Universities Press, 1969.

Miller, Roger G. *A Preliminary to War: The 1st Aero Squadron and the Mexican Punitive Expedition of 1916.* Honolulu: University Press of the Pacific, 2005.

Millett, Allan R. *Well Planned, Splendidly Executed: The Battle of Cantigny May 28–31, 1918.* Chicago: Cantigny First Division Foundation, 2010.

Millett, Allan R., and Peter Maslowski. *For the Common Defense: A Military History of the United States of America from 1607–2012.* 3rd ed. New York: Free Press, 2012.

Mitchell, William. *Memoirs of World War I: From Start to Finish of Our Greatest War.* New York: Random House, 1960.

Mjagkij, Nina. *Loyalty in the Time of Trial: The African American Experience during World War I.* Lanham, MD: Rowman and Littlefield, 2011.

Moran, Lord. *The Anatomy of Courage.* New York: Carroll and Graf, 2007.

Mordacq, Henri. *La mentalité allemande: cinq ans de commandement sur le Rhin.* Paris: Plon, 1926.

Morrow, John H., Jr. *German Air Power in World War I.* Lincoln: University of Nebraska Press, 1982.

———. *The Great War in the Air: Military Aviation from 1909 to 1921.* Washington, DC: Smithsonian Institution Press, 1993.

Morrow, John H., Jr., and Earl R. Lawrence, eds. *A Yankee Ace in the RAF: The World War I Letters of Captain Bogart Rogers.* Lawrence: University Press of Kansas, 1996.

Mosier, John. *The Myth of the Great War.* New York: HarperCollins, 2001.

Mosse, George L. *Fallen Soldiers: Reshaping the Memory of the World Wars.* New York: Oxford University Press, 1990.

———. "Two World Wars and the Myth of the War Experience." *Journal of Contemporary History* 21, 4 (October 1986): 491–513.

Mulligan, William. *The Origins of the First World War.* Cambridge: Cambridge University Press, 2010.

Murphy, Miriam B. "'If Only I Have the Right Stuff': Utah Women in World War I." *Utah Historical Quarterly* 58, 4 (Autumn 1990): 334–350.

Murphy, Paul L. "War and Modernization: The National Promise Achieved or Corrupted?" *Reviews in American History* 9, 2 (June 1981): 233–238.

Murrin, James A. *With the 112th in France.* Philadelphia: J. B. Lippincott, 1919.

Myers, Jeffrey. *Hemingway: A Biography.* New York: Harper, 1985.

Nalty, Bernard C., ed. *Winged Shield, Winged Sword: A History of the United States Air Force.* 2 vols. Washington, DC: Government Printing Office, 1997.

Nasler, Nathan D., Douglas I. Katz, and Ross D. Zafonte. *Brain Injury Medicine: Principles and Practice.* 2nd ed. New York: Demos Medical Publishing, 2013.

Neff, John R. *Honoring the Civil War Dead: Commemoration and the Problem of Reconciliation.* Lawrence: University Press of Kansas, 2005.

Neiberg, Michael S. *Dance of the Furies: Europe and the Outbreak of World War I.* Cambridge, MA: Belknap Press of Harvard University Press, 2011.

———. *Fighting the Great War: A Global History.* Cambridge, MA: Harvard University Press, 2005.

———. *The Second Battle of the Marne.* Bloomington: Indiana University Press, 2008.

Nell, John W. *The Lost Battalion: A Private's Story*. San Antonio, TX: Historical Pub Network, 2001.

Nelson, James C. *The Remains of Company D: A Story of the Great War*. New York: St. Martin's Griffin, 2009.

———. *Five Lieutenants: The Heartbreaking Story of Five Harvard Men Who Led America to Victory in World War I*. New York: St. Martin's Press, 2012.

Nelson, Keith L. *Victors Divided: America and the Allies in Germany, 1918–1923*. Berkeley: University of California Press, 1975.

Nelson, Peter N. *A More Unbending Battle: The Harlem Hellfighters' Struggle for Freedom in WWI and Equality at Home*. New York: Basic Civitas Books, 2009.

Nelson, Robert L. *German Soldier Newspapers of the First World War*. Cambridge: Cambridge University Press, 2011.

Nettleton, George H., ed. *Yale in the World War*. 2 vols. New Haven, CT: Yale University Press, 1925.

New York State Archives. *A Spirit of Sacrifice: New York's Response to the Great War: A Guide to Records Relating to World War I*. New York: New York State Archives, 1993.

Nichols, Christopher McKnight. *Promise and Peril: America at the Dawn of a Global Age*. Cambridge, MA: Harvard University Press, 2011.

Nicholson, G. W. L. *The Fighting Newfoundlander: A History of the Royal Newfoundland Regiment*. Montréal: McGill-Queen's University Press, 2006.

Noble, Carl. *Jugheads behind the Lines*. Caldwell, ID: Caxton Printers, 1938.

Nudelman, Franny. *John Brown's Body: Slavery, Violence, and the Culture of War*. Chapel Hill: University of North Carolina Press, 2004.

Office of the Adjutant General. *Service Records Connecticut: Men and Women in the Armed Forces of the United States during World War I 1917–1920*. 3 vols. New Haven, CT: United Printing Services, 1941.

O'Gorman, Tim, and Steve Anders. *Fort Lee*. Charleston, SC: Arcadia, 2003.

Oliver, John W. "War History Records." *American Political Science Review* 14, 1 (February 1920): 115–116.

Optic, Oliver. *Fighting for the Right*. Lake Wales, FL: Lost Classics Book Company, 2005.

———. *On the Blockade*. Lake Wales, FL: Lost Classics Book Company, 1999.

———. *Stand by the Union*. Lake Wales, FL: Lost Classics Book Company, 2001.

———. *Taken by the Enemy*. Lake Wales, FL: Lost Classics Book Company, 1998.

———. *A Victorious Union*. Lake Wales, FL: Lost Classics Book Company, 2005.

———. *Within the Enemy's Lines*. Lake Wales, FL: Lost Classics Book Company, 1998.

Ortiz, Stephen R. *Beyond the Bonus March and GI Bill: How Veteran Politics Shaped the New Deal Era*. New York: New York University Press, 2010.

Osborn, Eric W. *Britain's Economic Blockade of Germany, 1914–1919*. London: Frank Cass, 2004.

Owen, Peter F. *To the Limit of Endurance: A Battalion of Marines in the Great War*. College Station: Texas A&M University Press, 2007.

Paddock, Troy R. E., ed. *A Call to Arms: Propaganda, Public Opinion and Newspapers in the Great War*. Westport, CT: Praeger, 2004.

Palazzo, Albert. *Seeking Victory on the Western Front: The British Army and Chemical Warfare in World War I*. Lincoln: University of Nebraska Press, 2000.

Palmer, Alan W. *Victory, 1918*. New York: Atlantic Monthly Press, 2000.

Palmer, Frederick. *Our Greatest Battle (the Meuse-Argonne)*. New York: Dodd, Mead, 1919.

Paris, Michael, ed. *The First World War and Popular Cinema: 1914 to the Present*. New Brunswick, NJ: Rutgers University Press, 2000.

Parsons, Edwin C. *The Great Adventure: The Story of the Lafayette Escadrille*. Garden City, NY: Doubleday, 1937.

Paschall, Rod. *The Defeat of Imperial Germany, 1917–1918*. Chapel Hill, NC: Algonquin Books, 1989.

Passingham, Ian. *All the Kaiser's Men: The Life and Death of the German Army on the Western Front, 1914–1918*. Stroud, UK: Sutton, 2003.

Paulson, Daryl S., and Stanley Krippner. *Haunted by Combat: Understanding PTSD in War Veterans Including Women, Reservists, and Those Coming Back from Iraq*. Westport, CT: Praeger Security International, 2007.

Pellissier, Robert. *A Good Idea of Hell: Letters from a Chasseur à Pied*, ed. Joshua Brown. College Station: Texas A&M University Press, 2003.

Perry, John. *Sgt. York: His Life, Legend & Legacy*. Nashville, TN: Broadman and Holman, 1997.

Persico, Joseph E. "FDR Sees the Elephant." *Quarterly Journal of Military History* 20, 4 (Summer 2008): 28–35.

Petrone, Karen. *The Great War in Russian Memory*. Bloomington: Indiana University Press, 2011.

Pettegrew, John. *Brutes in Suits: Male Sensibility in America, 1890–1920*. Baltimore: Johns Hopkins University Press, 2007.

Phillips, Howard, and David Killingray, eds. *The Spanish Influenza Pandemic of 1918–19: New Perspectives*. London: Routledge, 2003.

Piehler, G. Kurt. *Remembering War the American Way*. Washington, DC: Smithsonian Institution Press, 1995.

Pindar. *The Odes and Selected Fragments*, trans. Richard Stoneman. London: Everyman Library, 1997.

Pitt, Barrie. *1918: The Last Act*. Barnsley, UK: Pen and Sword, 2003.

Pizer, Donald. *Toward a Modernist Style: John Dos Passos*. New York: Bloomsbury Academic, 2013.

Plutarch. *Moralia*, trans. Frank Cole Babbitt. Cambridge, MA: Harvard University Press, 1931.

Preston, Diana. *Lusitania: An Epic Tragedy*. New York: Walker Publishing, 2002.

Prior, Robin, and Trevor Wilson. *The First World War*. London: Cassell, 1999.

———. *The Somme*. New Haven, CT: Yale University Press, 2005.

Proctor, H. G. *The Iron Division: National Guard of Pennsylvania in the World War*. Philadelphia: John C. Winston, 1919.

Quarstein, John V. *World War I on the Virginia Peninsula*. Charleston, SC: Arcadia, 1998.

Rachamimov, Alon. *POWs and the Great War: Captivity on the Eastern Front*. Oxford: Berg, 2002.

Ramírez, José A. *To the Line of Fire! Mexican Texans and World War I*. College Station: Texas A&M University Press, 2009.

Ramsay, David. Lusitania: *Saga and Myth*. New York: Norton, 2002.

Ranlett, Louis F. *Let's Go! The Story of A.S. No. 2448602*. Boston: Houghton Mifflin, 1927.

Reardon, Carol. *Pickett's Charge in History and Memory*. Chapel Hill: University of North Carolina Press, 1997.

Rechnitz, Robert M. "Depersonalization and the Dream in 'The Red Badge of Courage.'" *Studies in the Novel* 6, 1 (Spring 1974): 76–87.

Rechtman, Richard. "Enquête sur la condition de victim." *Étvdes: revue de culture contemporaine* (February 2011): 175–186.

Reid, Fiona. *Broken Men: Shell Shock, Treatment and Recovery in Britain 1914–30*. London: Continuum, 2010.

Remarque, Erich Maria. *All Quiet on the Western Front*, trans. A. W. Wheen. New York: Fawcett Crest, 1975.

———. *The Road Back*, trans. A. W. Wheen. New York: Random House, 2013.

Rendinell, Joseph E., and George Pattullo. *One Man's War: The Diary of a Leatherneck*. New York: J. H. Sears, 1928.

Rhodes, Benjamin D. *The Anglo-American Winter War with Russia, 1918–1919: A Diplomatic and Military Tragicomedy*. New York: Greenwood Press, 1988.

Riccio, Anthony V. *The Italian American Experience in New Haven*. Albany: State University of New York Press, 2006.

Richard, Carl J. *When the United States Invaded Russia: Woodrow Wilson's Siberian Disaster*. Lanham, MD: Rowman and Littlefield, 2013.

Richards, J. Stuart. *Pennsylvanian Voices of the Great War: Letters, Stories and Oral Histories of World War I*. Jefferson, NC: McFarland, 2007.

Richardson, Frank. *Fighting Spirit: A Study of Psychological Factors in War*. London: Leo Cooper, 1978.

Richter, Donald. *Chemical Soldiers: British Gas Warfare in World War I*. Lawrence: University Press of Kansas, 1992.

Rickenbacker, Edward V. *Fighting the Flying Circus*. Chicago: Lakeside Press, 1997.

Roberts, Frank E. *The American Foreign Legion: Black Soldiers of the 93rd in World War I*. Annapolis, MD: Naval Institute Press, 2004.

Roberts, Richard C. "The Utah National Guard in the Great War, 1917–1918." *Utah Historical Quarterly* 58, 4 (Autumn 1990): 312–333.

Robertson, Linda R. *The Dream of Civilized Warfare: World War I Flying Aces and the American Imagination*. Minneapolis: University of Minnesota Press, 2003.

Robinson, Paul. *Military Honour and the Conduct of War: From Ancient Greece to Iraq*. London: Routledge, 2006.

Robinson, William J. *Forging the Sword: The Story of Camp Devens, New England's Army Cantonment*. Concord, NH: Rumford Press, 1920.

———. *My Fourteen Months at the Front: An American Boy's Baptism of Fire*. Boston: Little, Brown, 1916.

Rockwell, Paul A. *American Fighters in the Foreign Legion, 1914–1918*. Boston: Houghton Mifflin, 1930.

Roediger, David R. *The Wages of Whiteness: Race and the Making of the American Working Class.* 2nd ed. London: Verso, 2007.

———. *Working toward Whiteness: How America's Immigrants Became White.* New York: Basic Books, 2005.

Rollins, Peter C., and John E. O'Connor, eds. *Hollywood's World War I: Motion Picture Images.* Bowling Green, OH: Bowling Green State University Popular Press, 1997.

Rosen, Gerald, ed. *Posttraumatic Stress Disorder: Issues and Controversies.* Chichester, UK: Wiley, 2004.

Rotundo, E. Anthony. *American Manhood: Transformations in Masculinity from the Revolution to the Modern Era.* New York: Basic Books, 1993.

Rubin, Richard. *The Last of the Doughboys: The Forgotten Generation and Their Forgotten World War.* Boston: Houghton Mifflin Harcourt, 2013.

Ryan, Garry D. "Disposition of AEF Records of World War I." *Military Affairs* 30, 4 (Winter 1966–1967): 212–219.

Ryan, Garry D., and Timothy K. Nenninger, eds. *Soldiers and Civilians: The U.S. Army and the American People.* Washington, DC: National Archives and Records Administration, 1987.

Salmon, Thomas W. *The Care and Treatment of Mental Diseases and War Neuroses ("Shell Shock") in the British Army.* New York: War Work Committee of the National Committee for Mental Hygiene, 1917.

Savage, Kirk. *Standing Soldiers, Kneeling Slaves: Race, War and Monument in Nineteenth-Century America.* Princeton, NJ: Princeton University Press, 1997.

Schacter, Daniel L. *The Seven Sins of Memory: How the Mind Forgets and Remembers.* Boston: Houghton Mifflin, 2001.

———, ed. *Memory Distortion: How Minds, Brains, and Societies Reconstruct the Past.* Cambridge, MA: Harvard University Press, 1997.

Schaefer, Christina K. *The Great War: A Guide to the Service Records of All the World's Fighting Men and Volunteers.* Baltimore: Genealogical Publishing, 1998.

Schaffer, Ronald. *America in the Great War: The Rise of the War Welfare State.* New York: Oxford University Press, 1991.

Schantz, Mark S. *Awaiting the Heavenly Country: The Civil War and America's Culture of Death.* Ithaca, NY: Cornell University Press, 2008.

Scheck, Raffael. *Hitler's African Victims: The German Army Massacres of Black French Soldiers in 1940.* Cambridge: Cambridge University Press, 2006.

Schindler, John R. *Isonzo: The Forgotten Sacrifice of the Great War.* Westport, CT: Praeger, 2001.

Schlereth, Thomas J. *Victorian America: Transformations in Everyday Life, 1876–1915.* New York: HarperCollins, 1991.

Schmidt, Hans. *Maverick Marine: General Smedley D. Butler and the Contradictions of American Military History.* Lexington: University Press of Kentucky, 1987.

Schneider, Dorothy, and Carl J. Schneider. *Into the Breach: American Women Overseas in World War I.* New York: Viking, 1991.

Schneider, Michael. "Monomyth Structure in 'The Red Badge of Courage.'" *American Literary Realism, 1870–1910* 20, 1 (Autumn 1987): 45–55.

Schreiber, Shane B. *Shock Army of the British Empire: The Canadian Corps in the Last 100 Days of the Great War.* Westport, CT: Praeger, 1997.

Schwabe, Sidney I. "The Experiment in Occupational Therapy at Base Hospital 117, AEF." *Mental Hygiene* 3 (1919): 590.

Schwartz, Barry. *Abraham Lincoln and the Forge of National Memory.* Chicago: University of Chicago Press, 2000.

Schweitzer, Richard. *The Cross and the Trenches: Religious Faith and Doubt among British and American Great War Soldiers.* Westport, CT: Praeger, 2003.

Scott, Emmett J. *The American Negro in the World War.* New York: Arno Press, 1969.

Scudder, Robert A. *My Experience in the World War.* Dover, NJ: Robert A. Scudder, 1921.

Secretary of the State. *Connecticut State Register and Manual.* Hartford: Secretary of the State, 2003.

Seeger, Alan. *Letters and Diary of Alan Seeger.* New York: Charles Scribner's Sons, 1917.

Shaw, Mary Neff. "Henry Fleming's Heroics in 'The Red Badge of Courage': A Satiric Search for a 'Kinder, Gentler' Heroism." *Studies in the Novel* 22, 4 (Winter 1990): 418–428.

Shay, Michael E. *The Yankee Division in the First World War.* College Station: Texas A&M University Press, 2008.

Sheely, Lawrence D., ed. *Sailor of the Air: The 1917–1919 Letters and Diary of SUN CMM/A Irving Edward Sheely.* Tuscaloosa: University of Alabama Press, 1993.

Sheldon, Jack. *The German Army at Passchendaele.* South Yorkshire, UK: Pen and Sword, 2007.

———. *The German Army on the Somme, 1914–1916.* South Yorkshire, UK: Pen and Sword, 2005.

Shephard, Ben. *A War of Nerves: Soldiers and Psychiatrists in the Twentieth Century.* Cambridge, MA: Harvard University Press, 2001.

Sherman, William Tecumseh. *Memoirs.* New York: Library of America, 1990.

Sherwood, Elmer W. *A Soldier in World War I: The Diary of Elmer W. Sherwood.* Indianapolis: Indiana Historical Society Press, 2004.

Sibley, Frank P. *With the Yankee Division in France.* Boston: Little, Brown, 1919.

Silber, Nina. *The Romance of Reunion: Northerners and the South, 1865–1900.* Chapel Hill: University of North Carolina Press, 1993.

Silver, Jonathan M., Thomas W. McAllister, and Stuart C. Yudofsky, eds. *Textbook of Traumatic Brain Injury.* 2nd ed. Washington, DC: American Psychiatric Publishing, 2011.

Simpson, Andy, ed. *Hot Blood and Cold Steel: Life and Death in the Trenches of the First World War.* 2nd ed. Staplehurst, UK: Spellmount Publishers, 2003.

Siney, Marion C. *Allied Blockade of Germany 1914–1916.* Ann Arbor: University of Michigan Press, 1957.

Skillman, Willis Rowland. *The A.E.F.: Who They Were, What They Did, How They Did It.* Philadelphia: George W. Jacobs, 1920.

Sledge, E. B. *With the Old Breed: At Peleliu and Okinawa.* Annapolis, MD: Naval Institute Press, 1996.

Sloan, James J., Jr. *Wings of Honor: American Airmen in World War I.* Atglen, PA: Schiffer Publishing, 1994.

Slotkin, Richard. *Lost Battalions: The Great War and the Crisis of American Nationality*. New York: Henry Holt, 2005.

Smith, Leonard V. *Between Mutiny and Obedience: The Case of the French Fifth Infantry Division during World War I*. Princeton, NJ: Princeton University Press, 1994.

———. *The Embattled Self: French Soldiers' Testimony of the Great War*. Ithaca, NY: Cornell University Press, 2007.

Smith, Leonard V., Stéphane Audoin-Rouzeau, and Annette Becker. *France and the Great War, 1914–1918*. Cambridge: Cambridge University Press, 2003.

Smythe, Donald. *Guerrilla Warrior: The Early Life of John J. Pershing*. New York: Scribner, 1973.

———. *Pershing: General of the Armies*. Bloomington: Indiana University Press, 1986.

Snell, Mark A., ed. *Unknown Soldiers: The American Expeditionary Forces in Memory and Remembrance*. Kent, OH: Kent State University Press, 2008.

Solomon, Eric. "Stephen Crane's War Stories." *Texas Studies in Literature and Language* 3, 1 (Spring 1961): 67–80.

Spaatz, Carl. "Evolution of Air Power: Our Urgent Need for an Air Force Second to None." *Military Affairs* 11, 1 (Spring 1947): 2–16.

Sparks, George M. *The 327th under Fire: History of the 327th Infantry, 82nd Division in the Great World War*. Privately printed, 1920.

Spaulding, Oliver L., and John W. Wright. *The Second Division American Expeditionary Force in France 1917–1919*. New York: Hillman, 1937.

Spector, Ronald. "'You're Not Going to Send Soldiers over There Are You!' The American Search for an Alternative to the Western Front 1916–1917." *Military Affairs* 36, 1 (February 1972): 1–4.

Speed, Richard B. *Prisoners, Diplomats and the Great War: A Study in the Diplomacy of Captivity*. New York: Greenwood Press, 1990.

Stallings, Laurence. *The Doughboys: The Story of the AEF, 1917–1918*. New York: Harper and Row, 1963.

Stallman, R. W., and Lillian Gilkes, eds. *Stephen Crane: Letters*. New York: New York University Press, 1960.

Stearns, Gustav. *From Army Camps and Battlefields*. Minneapolis: Augsburg Publishing House, 1919.

Stephenson, Michael. *The Last Full Measure: How Soldiers Die in Battle*. New York: Crown Publishers, 2012.

Sterba, Christopher M. *Good Americans: Italian and Jewish Immigrants during the First World War*. New York: Oxford University Press, 2003.

———. "'Your Country Wants You': New Haven's Italian Machine Gun Company Enters World War I." *New England Quarterly* 74, 2 (June 2001): 179–209.

Stevenson, William Y. *From "Poilu" to Yank*. Boston: Houghton Mifflin, 1918.

Strachan, Hew. *The First World War*. New York: Viking, 2003.

———. *The First World War*, vol. 1, *To Arms*. Oxford: Oxford University Press, 2001.

———, ed. *The Oxford Illustrated History of the First World War*. Oxford: Oxford University Press, 1998.

Straubing, Harold Elk, ed. *The Last Magnificent War: Rare Journalistic and Eyewitness Accounts of World War I.* New York: Paragon House, 1989.

Strickland, Daniel W. *Connecticut Fights: The Story of the 102nd Regiment.* New Haven, CT: Quinnipiac Press, 1930.

Striner, Richard. *Woodrow Wilson and World War I: A Burden Too Great to Bear.* Lanham, MD: Rowman and Littlefield, 2014.

Summerfield, Derek. "Conflict and Health: War and Mental Health: A Brief Overview." *British Medical Journal* 321, 7255 (July 2000): 232–235.

———. "How Scientifically Valid Is the Knowledge Base of Global Mental Health?" *British Medical Journal* 336, 7651 (May 2008): 992–994.

———. "The Invention of Posttraumatic Stress Disorder and the Social Usefulness of a Psychiatric Category." *British Medical Journal* 322, 7278 (January 2001): 95–98.

———. "Post-traumatic Stress Disorder in Doctors Involved in the Omagh Bombing." *British Medical Journal* 320, 7244 (May 2000): 1276.

Swank, Roy L., and Walter E. Marchand. "Combat Neuroses: The Development of Combat Exhaustion." *Archives of Neurology and Psychiatry* 55 (1946): 236–247.

Sweeney, Daniel J., ed. *History of Buffalo and Erie County 1914–1919.* Buffalo, NY: Committee of One Hundred, 1919.

Sweeney, William A. *History of the American Negro in the Great World War: His Splendid Record in the Battle Zones of Europe.* New York: Negro Universities Press, 1969.

Tatu, Laurent, and Julien Bogousslavsky. *La folie au front: La grande bataille des névroses de guerre (1914–1918).* Paris: Imago, 2012.

Taylor, Emerson Gifford. *New England in France, 1917–1919: A History of the Twenty-Sixth Division U.S.A.* Boston: Houghton Mifflin, 1920.

Tennyson, Brian Douglas. *The Canadian Experience of the Great War: A Guide to Memoirs.* Plymouth, UK: Scarecrow Press, 2013.

Terraine, John. *To Win a War: 1918 the Year of Victory.* London: Cassell, 2000.

Thayer, John A. *Italy and the Great War: Politics and Culture, 1870–1915.* Madison: University of Wisconsin Press, 1964.

Thayer, Lucien H. *America's First Eagles: The Official History of the U.S. Air Service, A.E.F. 1917–1918.* Mesa, AZ: Champlin Fighter Museum Press, 1983.

Thomas, Gregory M. *Treating the Trauma of the Great War: Soldiers, Civilians, and Psychiatry in France, 1914–1940.* Baton Rouge: Louisiana State University Press, 2009.

Thomas, Lowell. *This Side of Hell, Dan Edwards, Adventurer.* New York: P. F. Collier and Son, 1932.

———. *Woodfill of the Regulars.* London: William Heinemann, 1930.

Thompson, Chris, and Phil Cowen, eds. *Violence: Basic and Clinical Science.* Oxford: Butterworth-Heinemann, 1993.

Thompson, Hugh S. *Trench Knives and Mustard Gas: With the 42nd Rainbow Division in France.* College Station: Texas A&M University Press, 2004.

Thompson, Mark. *The White War: Life and Death on the Italian Front 1914–1919.* New York: Basic Books, 2008.

Ticknor, Caroline, ed. *New England Aviators, 1914–1918.* 2 vols. Boston: Houghton Mifflin, 1919.

Todd, Frederick P. "The Knife and Club in Trench Warfare, 1914–1918." *Journal of the American Military History Foundation* 2, 3 (Autumn 1938): 139–153.

Todman, Dan. *The Great War: Myth and Memory*. London: Continuum, 2005.

Toland, John. *No Man's Land: 1918, the Last Year of the Great War*. Garden City, NY: Doubleday, 1980.

Toplin, Robert B. *History by Hollywood: The Use and Abuse of the American Past*. Urbana: University of Illinois Press, 1996.

Toulmin, H. A., Jr. *Air Service: American Expedition Force 1918*. New York: D. Van Nostrand, 1927.

Trask, David F. *The AEF and Coalition Warmaking, 1917–1918*. Lawrence: University Press of Kansas, 1993.

Traxel, David. *Crusader Nation: The United States in Peace and the Great War, 1898–1920*. New York: Knopf, 2006.

Triplet, William S. *A Youth in the Meuse-Argonne: A Memoir, 1917–1918*. Columbia: University of Missouri Press, 2000.

Trommler, Frank. "The *Lusitania* Effect: America's Mobilization against Germany in World War I." *German Studies Review* 32, 2 (May 2009): 241–266.

Trout, Steven. *On the Battlefield of Memory: The First World War and American Remembrance, 1919–1941*. Birmingham: University of Alabama Press, 2010.

Trudeau, Noah Andre. *Southern Storm: Sherman's March to the Sea*. New York: Harper, 2008.

Trumpener, Ulrich. "The Road to Ypres: The Beginnings of Gas Warfare in World War I." *Journal of Modern History* 47, 3 (September 1975): 460–480.

Tsao, Jack W., ed. *Traumatic Brain Injury: A Clinician's Guide to Diagnosis, Management, and Rehabilitation*. New York: Springer, 2012.

Tucker, Spencer C. *The Great War 1914–1918*. Bloomington: Indiana University Press, 1998.

Unger, Harlow Giles. *The Last Founding Father: James Monroe and a Nation's Call to Greatness*. Philadelphia: Da Capo Press, 2009.

Unger, Irwin, and Debi Unger. *The Guggenheims: A Family History*. New York: HarperCollins, 2005.

US Army. *Order of Battle of the United States Land Forces in the World War: American Expeditionary Forces*. 3 vols. Washington, DC: Center of Military History, 1988.

US Army. *United States Army in the World War 1917–1919*. 17 vols. Washington, DC: Center for Military History, 1988–1992.

US Bureau of the Census. *Fourteenth Census of the United States: State Compendium, Connecticut*. Washington, DC: Bureau of the Census, 1924.

Vance, Jonathan F. *Death so Noble: Memory, Meaning and the First World War*. Vancouver: University of British Columbia Press, 1997.

Vansoolen, Louwane, and the Fort Douglas Military Museum. *Fort Douglas*. Charleston, SC: Arcadia, 2009.

Viereck, George Sylvester. *As They Saw Us: Foch, Ludendorff and Other Leaders Write Our War History*. Garden City, NY: Doubleday, Doran, 1929.

Vincent, C. Paul. *The Politics of Hunger: The Allied Blockade of Germany, 1915–1919.* Athens: Ohio University Press, 1985.

Wainwright, Philip, ed. *History of the 101st Machine Gun Battalion.* Hartford, CT: 101st Machine Gun Battalion Association, 1922.

Wallenstein, Peter, and Bertram Wyatt-Brown, eds. *Virginia's Civil War.* Charlottesville: University of Virginia Press, 2005.

Ward, Larry Wayne. *The Motion Picture Goes to War: The U.S. Government Film Effort during World War I.* Ann Arbor, MI: UMI Research Press, 1985.

Warrum, Noble. *Utah in the World War: The Men behind the Guns and the Men and Women behind the Men behind the Guns.* Salt Lake City, UT: Arrow Press, 1924.

Warshauer, Matthew. *Connecticut in the American Civil War: Slaver, Sacrifice, and Survival.* Middletown, CT: Wesleyan University Press, 2011.

Washington, George. *Writings,* ed. John Rhodehamel. New York: Library of America, 1997.

Watson, Alexander. *Enduring the Great War: Combat, Morale and Collapse in the German and British Armies, 1914–1918.* Cambridge: Cambridge University Press, 2008.

Watson, Janet S. K. *Fighting Different Wars: Experience, Memory, and the First World War in Britain.* Cambridge: Cambridge University Press, 2004.

Weigley, Russell F. *The American Way of War: A History of United States Military Strategy and Policy.* Bloomington: Indiana University Press, 1977.

Welch, David. *Germany, Propaganda and Total War, 1914–1918: The Sins of Omission.* New Brunswick, NJ: Rutgers University Press, 2000.

Welsome, Eileen. *The General and the Jaguar: Pershing's Hunt for Pancho Villa: A True Story of Revolution and Revenge.* New York: Little, Brown, 2006.

Werstein, Irving. *The Lost Battalion: A Saga of American Courage in World War I.* New York: Norton, 1966.

Wertheim, Stanley. *The Crane Log: A Documentary Life of Stephen Crane, 1871–1900.* New York: G. K. Hall, 1994.

Westbrook, Stillman F. *Those Eighteen Months: October 9, 1917–April 8, 1919.* Hartford, CT: Case, Lockwood and Brainard, 1934.

Wilder, Amos N. *Armageddon Revisited: A World War I Journal.* New Haven, CT: Yale University Press, 1994.

Wiley, Bell Irvin. *The Life of Billy Yank: The Common Soldier of the Union.* 2nd ed. Baton Rouge: Louisiana State University Press, 2008.

———. *The Life of Johnny Reb: The Common Soldier of the Confederacy.* 2nd ed. Baton Rouge: Louisiana State University Press, 2008.

Wilgus, William J. *Transporting the AEF in Western Europe, 1917–1919.* New York: Columbia University Press, 1931.

Wilhelm II. *The Kaiser's Memoirs, Wilhelm II, Emperor of Germany, 1888–1918,* trans. Thomas R. Ybarra. New York: Harper, 1922.

Willett, Robert L. *Russian Sideshow: America's Undeclared War, 1918–1920.* Washington, DC: Brassey's, 2003.

Williams, Chad L. *Torchbearers of Democracy: African American Soldiers in the World War I Era.* Chapel Hill: University of North Carolina Press, 2010.

Williams, David. *Media, Memory, and the First World War*. Montreal: McGill-Queen's University Press, 2009.

Wilson, John P., and Catherine C. So-Kum Tang, eds. *Cross-Cultural Assessment of Psychological Trauma and PTSD*. New York: Springer, 2010.

Wilson, Woodrow. *War Messages*. 65th Congress, 1st Session. Senate Doc. No. 5, Serial No. 7264. Washington, DC, 1917.

Wingate, Jennifer. *Sculpting Doughboys: Memory, Gender, and Taste in America's World War I Memorials*. Farnham, UK: Ashgate, 2013.

Winter, Alison. *Memory: Fragments of a Modern History*. Chicago: University of Chicago Press, 2012.

Winter, Denis. *Death's Men: Soldiers of the Great War*. London: Penguin Books, 1979.

Winter, Jay. *Remembering War: The Great War between Memory and History in the Twentieth Century*. New Haven, CT: Yale University Press, 2006.

———. *Sites of Memory, Sites of Mourning: The Great War in European Cultural History*. Cambridge: Cambridge University Press, 1998.

———, ed. *The Legacy of the Great War: Ninety Years On*. Columbia: University of Missouri Press, 2009.

———. "Special Issue: Shell-shock." *Journal of Contemporary History* 35, 1 (January 2000): 1–127.

Winter, Jay, and Antoine Prost. *The Great War in History: Debates and Controversies, 1914 to the Present*. Cambridge: Cambridge University Press, 2005.

Winter, Jay, and Blaine Baggett. *The Great War and the Shaping of the 20th Century*. New York: Penguin Studio, 1996.

Winter, Jay, Geoffrey Parker, and Mary R. Habeck. *The Great War and the Twentieth Century*. New Haven, CT: Yale University Press, 2000.

Wise, Frederick M. *A Marine Tells It to You*. New York: J. I I. Sears, 1929.

Wise, Jennings C. *The Turn of the Tide: American Operations at Cantigny, Château Thierry, and the Second Battle of the Marne*. New York: Henry Holt, 1920.

Wood, Amy Louise. *Lynching and Spectacle: Witnessing Racial Violence in America, 1890–1940*. Chapel Hill: University of North Carolina Press, 2009.

Woodward, David R. *America and World War I: A Selected Annotated Bibliography of English-Language Sources*. New York: Routledge, 2007.

Woolley, Charles. *First to the Front: The Aerial Adventures of 1st Lt. Waldo Heinrichs and the 95th Aero Squadron, 1917–1918*. Atglen, PA: Schiffer Publishing, 1999.

———. *The Hat in the Ring Gang: The Combat History of the 94th Aero Squadron in World War I*. Atglen, PA: Schiffer Publishing, 2001.

Wright, Jack Morris. *A Poet of the Air: Letters of Jack Morris Wright First Lieutenant of the American Aviation in France April, 1917–January, 1918*. Boston: Houghton Mifflin, 1918.

Wright, William M. *Meuse-Argonne Diary: A Division Commander in World War I*. Columbia: University of Missouri Press, 2004.

Yockelson, Mitchell A. *Borrowed Soldiers: Americans under British Command, 1918*. Norman: University of Oklahoma Press, 2008.

York, Alvin C. *Sergeant York: His Own Life Story and War Diary*, ed. Tom Skeyhill. Garden City, NY: Doubleday, Doran, 1928.

Young, Allan. *The Harmony of Illusions: Inventing Posttraumatic Stress Disorder*. Princeton, NJ: Princeton University Press, 1995.

Zebecki, David T. *The German 1918 Offensives: A Case Study in the Operational Level of War*. London: Routledge, 2006.

———. *Steel Wind: Colonel Georg Brüchmuller and the Birth of Modern Artillery*. Westport, CT: Praeger, 1994.

Zeiger, Susan. *In Uncle Sam's Service: Women Workers with the American Expeditionary Force, 1917–1919*. Ithaca, NY: Cornell University Press, 1999.

Zieger, Robert H. *America's Great War: World War I and the American Experience*. Lanham, MD: Rowman and Littlefield, 2000.

Ziemann, Benjamin. *War Experiences in Rural Germany, 1914–1923*, trans. Alex Skinner. New York: Berg, 2007.

Zuckerman, Larry. *The Rape of Belgium: The Untold Story of World War I*. New York: New York University Press, 2004.

Index

Cosenzo, Joseph, 56
    overseas experiences of, 89–90
Costello, Frank, death of, 76
Costello, Mary, 76
Council of National Defense, 28, 177
County Councils of Defense, 182
Courage, 108, 110–115
Covington, John W., 37, 65, 144
biography of, 205
Cox, LeRoy H., on motivations, 112
Crane, Stephen, 33, 161, 162, 227n17, 232n2
    Civil War and, 17
    influence of, 19
    mental attitude and, 20
Crawford, Waverly L., 119
    biography of, 205
    enlistment of, 119
    on injustice in ranks, 167–169
Creel, George, 21, 22
Crisis (NAACP journal), 167
Crockett, George S., 81, 164
Cuddy, Finlan D., 11
Culver, Otis H., 165
Cummings, E. E., 42, 43
Curry, Harry E., 57, 70
    biography of, 205
    on patriotism, 157
    on war, 119

Daly, Daniel, 101
Daniel, Channing W., 39
    biography of, 205–206
    on combat, 112
    on military service, 90
Dano, sailing on, 79
D. Appleton & Company, 19, 161
Darmody, James, 250n65
Data collection, 182, 186
    method of/by state, 179 (table)
Davies, David E., 30
Davis, Arthur Kyle, 178, 182, 185, 187, 196
    questionnaires and, 181
Davis, Curtis R., 55
    biography of, 206

Davis, Jerry M., on Sherman quote, 11
Davis, Linda H., on Crane, 20
Davis, Westmoreland, 178, 187
Dawson, Coningsby, on novelists, 44
Day, Arlie I., 52, 63
    biography of, 206
Dean, Eric T., Jr., 55
Death, 105–106, 112, 132
De Forest, William, 17
Deilus, Robert, 170
    biography of, 206
Delaney, Joseph, 41
Deliverers, 98, 100–102, 104
Deloughery, John J., on war, 165
Deming, Lamar H., on killing, 109
Democracy, 23
    fighting for, 167, 168
Dennison, Franklin A., 156
Department of Historical Records, 178
Department of War Records, 178, 181
Der Weg züruck (Remarque), 232n6
Dettor, David C., 165–166
    biography of, 206
Devens, Charles, 66
*Diagnostic and Statistical Manual of Mental
    Disorders* (DSM), 146
Diaries, 93, 94, 108, 132
Dickerson, John N., 90
    biography of, 206
Dickman, J. T., 49
DiRubba, Antonio, 234n38
Distefano, Salvatore, 170
    biography of, 206
"Doggerel" (Duvall), text of, 164
Dorkendorff, Horton J., on military service, 90
Dos Passos, John, 34, 42, 43, 44
Dougan, Harold J., 23, 150
Doughboys, 12–15
    African American, 13, 57, 58, 118–119, 155–157, 167, 169, 171
    arrival of, 16
    behavior of, 137
    domestic, 51–54
    immigrant, 48–51

Renoir, Jean, 164
Reserve Officers Training Camp, 57
Resignation, 129–131
Resources, discovering, 179–181
Responsibility, 124–127, 138, 250n62
Return, restless, 172–175
Rhineland, occupation of, 134–139
Rice, Marcel W., 29
    on Sherman quote, 106
Rickenbacker, Eddie, 229n63
Rickey, Don, Jr., 8
RMS *Arabic,* sinking of, 78
RMS *Lusitania,* sinking of, 25, 27, 35, 78
RMS *Titanic,* 1, 2
Roberts, B. H., 74
Roberts, Needham, 118
Rochambeau, 36
Rockefeller, John D., Jr., 75
Roddy, Joe, on training, 62
Rodents, 108, 136
Roesch, Edward H., 57
Roesch, Etta, 57
Roesch, Louis, 57
Rogerson, Richard, 171
Romanticism, 16, 124, 130, 161–162, 163,
    176
Roosevelt, Franklin D., 82, 162
Roosevelt, Theodore, 22, 33, 47
    Kettle Hill and, 20, 105, 162
Roosevelt, Theodore, III, American Legion
    and, 140
Rosner, John A., on killing, 108–109
Ross, John M., 29, 89, 119, 157
Rough Riders, 20, 31
Rowe, Frederick W., on glory, 172–173
Roy, Dr., 74, 75
Royal Army Medical Corps, training with,
    96
Rubin, Richard, 8
Rubinousky, Adam P., wounding of, 149–150
Ryan, Joseph, 31, 142
    biography of, 216

Sacco, Nicola, 169
Sacrifice, 14, 15, 44, 113, 124, 158, 161, 165,
    167, 231n99, 252n4

Sage, Walter C., 55
Saint-Mihiel, 13, 53, 57, 102, 105, 109, 112,
    113, 114, 117, 129, 130
Salle d'Attente, 122
Salmon, Thomas, 147
Salovitz, Jacob, overseas experiences of, 89
Salvation Army, 75, 91–92
Sampson, Jacob M., 168
    biography of, 216
Sanford, Nora B., 73
    biography of, 216
Santa Teresa, sailing on, 164
Sassoon, Siegfried, 41
Saville, Evern E., combat experience of, 107,
    124, 128
Scars, physical/psychological, 147–148
Schadel, Joseph R., 56, 115
    biography of, 216–217
Schaefer, Christina K., 179, 257n8
Schramm, Karl, 137
Schultze, Carl J., 105
Schwabe, Sidney I., 147
Scowffield, Louis, 119
Sedition Act (1918), 21, 169
Sedlak, Mike, 164
    biography of, 217
Seeger, Alan, 44, 231n96
    poem by, 34–35
Seicheprey, 58, 92, 115, 128, 130
Selective Service Office, 48, 171
Selective Service System (SSS), 38, 47, 180,
    257n16
Sellers, James McBrayer, 79
Senegalese soldiers, 118, 166, 167
Senkbeil, Carl C., censorship and, 93
Seven Pines National Cemetery, 17
Shabazian, Vahow, 165
    biography of, 217
Sheehan, James P., 130, 153
Shell shock, 41, 123, 147, 148, 173, 174,
    249n57, 250n65
    meaning of, 249n58
    PTSD and, 146
Sherman, William Tecumseh, 17
    death of, 160–161
    legacy of, 256–257n91